T0240050

Vue. JS Framework

HcySun Yang

Vue. JS Framework

Design and Implementation

 Springer

人民邮电出版社

POSTS & TELECOM PRESS

HcySun Yang
Vue.js team
Beijing, China

ISBN 978-981-99-4946-5   ISBN 978-981-99-4947-2   (eBook)
https://doi.org/10.1007/978-981-99-4947-2

Jointly published with Posts & Telecom Press
The print edition is not for sale in China (Mainland). Customers from China (Mainland) please order the print book from: Posts & Telecom Press.
ISBN of the Co-Publisher's edition: 978-7-115-52483-6

This Springer imprint is published by the registered company Springer Nature Singapore Pte Ltd.
The registered company address is: 152 Beach Road, #21-01/04 Gateway East, Singapore 189721, Singapore

Foreword

Before the book was published, I had read HcySunYang's interpretation to the source code of Vue.js 3 and appreciated his commitment and devotion to technical details a lot. Later, SunYang submitted numerous patches for Vue.js 3, and fixed some very deep rendering update bugs, making significant contributions to Vue.js 3 and thus becoming an official team member of Vue.js. SunYang's understanding of Vue.js 3 source code comes from his experience in maintenance of the source code, which is the most difficult but most effective way to fully comprehend open-source projects. Therefore, the analysis of the technique features of Vue.js 3 in this book is very reliable, and it will be of invaluable help to users who need to have a solid grasp of Vue.js 3.

Sun Yang truly understands the high-level design concept of Vue.js, and he has his own sound reasoning on trade-offs of framework design. This is probably what makes this book distinctive than other books focusing solely on the source code analysis on the market; it explores the issues that frameworks need to pay attention to from a design perspective at high level, so as to help readers better learn why some specific implementations make their corresponding choices.

The front-end is a rapidly changing field. New technologies are constantly emerging, and Vue.js itself is consistently evolving. Therefore, we will continue to examine more optimized implementation details. Quite apart from specific implementations, this book serves as a valuable reference for modern front-end framework design.

Abstract This book, based on Vue.js 3, certain specifications, and the source code, explains the implementation of various functional modules in Vue.js step by step and illustrates framework design principles in detail with the help of many diagrams leading to intuitive comprehension. It consists of eighteen chapters, six parts, including overview of framework design, response system, renderers, componentization, compilers, and server-side rendering, etc. Reading this book, developers with hands-on experience in Vue.js2/3 will further their comprehension of implementation details of Vue.js framework, while front-end developers who are not experienced in Vue.js but interested in framework design can quickly master the design principles of Vue.js.

The potential audience of this book might be Vue.js users and front-end developers who are interested in Vue.js.

Vue.JS, New York, NY, USA   Evan You

Preface

Vue.js, one of the most popular front-end frameworks, has officially ushered in its version 3.0 release on September 18, 2020, characterizing in a variety of new features and many innovations in framework design and implementation, thanks to the experience obtained from designing Vue.js 2. To a certain extent, it can be said that Vue.js 3.0 pays off the technical debt owed in Vue.js 2.

From my perspective, Vue.js 3.0 is a very successful project. It inherits the ease of use of Vue.js 2. Further, compared with Vue.js 2, Vue.js 3.0 even manages to use less code for more functions.

Vue.js 3.0 splits and designs modules quite reasonably, with low coupling between modules, and many modules can be installed and used independently without relying on the complete Vue.js run time, such as the @vue/reactivity module.

Vue.js 3.0 has also spent a lot of effort on designing built-in components and modules. With the construction tools and tree-shaking mechanism, the built-in capabilities have been introduced on demand, thus minimizing the size of user bundles.

Vue.js 3.0 is very scalable. We can write custom renderers and even compiler plug-ins to customize template syntax. In addition, Vue.js 3.0 also endeavors to improve user experience.

The advantages of Vue.js 3.0 include but are not limited to the above. Since Vue. js 3.0 brings so many benefits, how do framework designers design and implement all these functions? In fact, it is of great significance to understand the core design ideas of Vue.js 3.0. Doing so will not only help us solve complex problems more calmly, but also guide us in architecture design in other fields.

What's more, the design of many functions in Vue.js 3.0 needs to follow specifications. For example, if you want to use a proxy to implement a complete response system, you must first pick up ECMAScript standard, while template parsers of Vue.js should be in accordance with the relevant WHATWG specifications. Thus, while learning core design ideas of Vue.js 3.0, we will also indirectly master the method of reading and understanding specifications, writing code accordingly then.

Target Audience

The target readers of this book include:

- developers who have hands-on experience with Vue.js 2/3 and want to further understand the design principles of Vue.js framework
- front-end developers who have not used Vue.js before but are interested in Vue.js framework design

The Content

The content of this book is not source code interpretation. Rather, it introduces how to realize each functional module in Vue.js, based on the author's understanding of Vue.js framework design, starting from what is simple to what is complex gradually.

This book will comply with specifications as much as possible to generate fully functional and rigorous Vue.js function modules. For example, by reading ECMAScript specification, a complete response system is implemented based on the proxy, and by WHATWG, a template parser similar to HTML-like syntax is accomplished, and hence a template compiler supporting plug-in architecture.

Besides, this book will also illustrate the following:

- core elements of framework design and trade-offs to be made in the frame design process
- three common Diff algorithms of virtual DOM
- realization of componentization and principles of Vue.js built-in components
- differences among server-side rendering, client-side rendering, isomorphic rendering, and principles of isomorphic rendering

The Structure

This book is divided into 6 parts, with a total of 18 chapters. The brief introduction to each chapter is as follows:

- Part I (Overview of Framework Design): consisting of three chapters.

  - Chapter 1 generally discusses differences between imperative and declarative paradigms, and their influence on framework design. It also presents the performance of virtual DOM. At the end, it introduces the relevant knowledge of run time and compile time and demonstrates Vue.js 3.0 is a runtime + compile-time framework.
  - Chapter 2 mainly explains what framework designers should consider when designing frameworks from the aspects of user development experience, volume control of framework code, working mechanism of tree-shaking, framework products, feature switches, error handling, TypeScript support, etc.
  - Chapter 3 illustrates the design idea of Vue.js 3.0 from a global perspective and presents how the various modules cooperate.

- Part II (Response System): consisting of three chapters.

  - Chapter 4 broadly describes the mechanism of implementing response system in Vue.js 3.0, beginning from side effect functions and finally making a perfect response system. This chapter also explains principles of implementing computational attributes and watch and discusses the problems encountered while implementing response system, as well as corresponding solutions.
  - Chapter 5 concentrates on ECMAScript standard, starting with the most fundamental working principles of Proxy, Reflect, JavaScript objects, and explores step-by-step ways to use Proxy for JavaScript objects.
  - Chapter 6 mainly talks about the concept of ref and comes up with the response scheme of the original value based on ref. How to use ref to solve the problem of response loss is also involved in this chapter.

- Part III (Renderers): consisting of five chapters.

  - Chapter 7 chiefly puts forward the relationship between renderers and response system, explains how the two work together for page update, introduces some basic terms and concepts in renderers, and presents the implementation and application of custom renderers.
  - Chapter 8 focuses on principles of doing renderer mount and update, including sub-node processing, property processing, and event processing. When mounting or updating a virtual node of a component type, the handling of the component lifetime function should also be taken into account.
  - Chapter 9 mostly introduces working principles of "simple Diff algorithms."
  - Chapter 10 is largely about working principles of "double-ended Diff algorithms."
  - Chapter 11 mainly discusses working principles of "Fast Diff algorithms."

- Part IV (Componentization): consisting of three chapters.

  - Chapter 12 illustrates implementation principles of components and introduces initialization of components' own state, self-update of components caused by changes in their own state, external state (props) of components, passive updates caused by changes in external state, and principles of implementing component events and slots.

- Chapter 13 mainly introduces the working mechanism and implementation principles of asynchronous components and functional components. Timeout and error handling, delayed display of loading components, load retry, etc. are discussed regarding async components.
- Chapter 14 generally explains implementation principles of the three built-in components of Vue.js, namely KeepAlive, Teleport, and Transition.

• Part V (Compilers): consisting of three chapters.

- Chapter 15 first introduces the workflow of Vue.js template compilers, then implementation principles of parsers and state machines, as well as the transformation and plug-in architecture of AST, and finally the specific implementation of producing rendering function code.
- Chapter 16 shows how to implement a parser that conforms to HTML parsing specifications of WHATWG, ranging from the text mode of the parser, the influence of the text mode on the parser, to how to use the recursive descent algorithm to construct the template AST. While parsing text content, how to decode character references according to the specifications is also explained.
- Chapter 17 mainly illustrates the related content of template compilation and optimization in Vue.js 3.0. Specifically, it includes the update mechanism of the block tree, the collection of dynamic nodes, static lifting, pre-stringing, processing functions of caching inline events, v-once, and other optimization mechanisms.

• Part VI (Server-Side Rendering): consisting of one chapter.

- Chapter 18 focuses on principles of Vue.js isomorphic rendering, discussing the advantages and disadvantages of schemes like CSR, SSR, and isomorphic rendering, talking about principles of server-side rendering and client-side activation of Vue.js, and finally summarizing the precautions for writing isomorphic code.

Source Code and Errata

When studying this book, you can test and learn all the code in it. You can also download all the source code from GitHub (HcySunYang).[1] I will do my best to ensure both the text and source code are correct. However, there are inevitably some errors in the book. If you find any errors, including but not limited to typos, code

---

[1] Or you can visit the home page of the book in Turing Community to download—Editor's Note.

fragments, incorrect descriptions, etc., please feel free to give me feedback. Please go to GitHub (HcySunYang) to view errata or submit errors for this book.[2]

Acknowledgment

I would like to express my gratitude to many people and things that directly or indirectly help me write this book. The following acknowledgments are only arranged randomly.

First and foremost, I want to thank Vue.js framework. There is no doubt that Vue. js has value to the world, and countless enterprises and individual developers have benefited from it. Doubtlessly, I would like to thank the creator of Vue.js, Evan You, and all other members of the Vue.js team. Excellent team operation has enabled Vue. js to continue to develop. I cannot have this book without Vue.js.

I would also like to thank Yubo for his recommendation and Wang Junhua's trust, bringing me the opportunity to complete such a book that I excel at. While I was writing the book, Wang Junhua's enthusiastic and meticulous work throughout the process has greatly enhanced my confidence in finishing the writing task. Once again, I would like to express my heartfelt thanks to Yubo and Wang Junhua.

I would also like to say thanks to a friend, my former colleague, Zhang Xiao. He put forward many valuable suggestions for this book and helped check the typos and expressions carefully.

Thanks to Luo Yonglin, another special friend of mine. Honestly, without him, I would not have even embarked on the cause of a programmer, let alone writing this book. Thanks bro.

Last but not least, I want to thank my wife. We got married recently. She was my girlfriend while I was writing the book. To finish the book and for some other reasons, I almost worked on this book full-time at home, earning little. Nevertheless, she never complained about it, and always gave me encouragement. I often joked, "How about you earn my daily bread?" By the time this book was published, she had become my wife. This book, in fact, was a gift to her. Million thanks to you.

Beijing, China   HcySun Yang

---

[2] You can also visit the home page of the book in Turing Community to view errata or submit errors—Editor's Note.

Contents

Part I
Overview of Framework Design

Chapter 1
Art of Trade-Offs

The art of trade-offs is everywhere in framework design.

Before we carry out a full exploration of implementation ideas and details of each module of Vue.js 3, it is worth discussing the view layer framework design first. Why? This is because when we design a framework, the various modules of it are not independent of each other but interrelated and mutually restrictive. Therefore, as a framework designer, one must have global control over the orientation and direction of the framework, so as to achieve the subsequent module design and splitting well. Likewise, when learning frameworks, we should also have a sound grasp of framework design from a global perspective, otherwise it is easy to be trapped by details without seeing the whole picture.

Further, from the perspective of paradigms, should our frameworks be designed to be imperative or declarative? What are the advantages and disadvantages of these two forms? Can we learn from both? Moreover, should our frameworks be purely runtime or compile-time, or runtime + compile-time? What are the differences between them? What are their limitations and advantages? The art of trade-offs is embodied in corresponding solutions.

1.1　Imperative and Declarative

In terms of paradigms, view layer frameworks are usually divided into imperative and declarative forms, each of which has its own strengths and weaknesses. As a framework designer, one should acquire sufficient knowledge of both paradigms to make the right choice, as well as to find ways to make the best of the two by combining their advantages.

Now let's look at the conception of imperative frameworks and declarative frameworks. jQuery, popular in its early years, is a typical imperative framework.

H. Yang, *Vue. JS Framework*, https://doi.org/10.1007/978-981-99-4947-2_1

One characteristic of imperative frameworks is being *process oriented*. For example, let's translate the following into the corresponding code:

```
01 - Get the div tag with id app
02 – Its textContent is hello world
03 - Bind click events to it
04 – Pop up prompt on click: ok
```

The code converted is:

```
01 $('#app') // get div
02 .text('hello world') // set textContent
03 .on('click', () => { alert('ok') }) // bind click events
```

The above is a code example of jQuery. Considering that some readers may not have used jQuery before, we will use native JavaScript to achieve the same function:

```
01 const div = document.querySelector('#app') // get div
02 div.innerText = 'hello world' // set textContent
03 div.addEventListener('click', () => { alert('ok') }) // bind click
events
```

Note the correspondence of each natural language description to a line of code. The code itself describes the process of doing things, which is in line with our logical intuition.

What is a declarative framework then? Unlike imperative frameworks, which focus on the process, declarative frameworks are *result oriented*. Let's take a look at how to implement the functions described in natural language above with Vue.js:

```
01 <div @click="() => alert('ok')">hello world</div>
```

This HTML-like template is how Vue.js realizes the functionalities above. As can be seen, what we are providing is a result; we do not care about how to achieve it. It's like we are telling Vue.js, "Hey, Vue.js! See, what I want is a div. The text content is hello world. It has an event binding. Please help me make it." As for the process of achieving this result, the Vue.js has completed it by itself. In other words, Vue.js has helped us encapsulate the process. Therefore, it indicates that the internal implementation of Vue.js must be imperative, while what is exposed to users is more declarative.

1.2   Trade-Offs Between Performance and Maintainability

Imperative and declarative forms have their own pros and cons, which could be reflected by the trade-offs between performance and maintainability regarding framework designing. Here we put forward the quick conclusion first: *The performance of declarative code is no better than that of imperative code.*

Let's look at the above example again. Suppose we want to modify the textContent of the div tag to hello vue3, then how can we obtain this result using imperative code? It is a piece of cake because we have already known exactly what to modify; therefore, we will simply call the relevant commands to operate:

```
01 div.textContent = 'hello vue3' // modify directly
```

Now consider whether there exist other approaches that outperform the above code. The answer is no. It may be noted that theoretically speaking, imperative code can achieve extreme performance optimization since we know for sure what has changed, so only certain necessary changes are required. But declarative code may not be able to do this job for it describes the result:

```
01 <!-- before: -->
02 <div @click="() => alert('ok')">hello world</div>
03 <!-- after: -->
04 <div @click="() => alert('ok')">hello vue3</div>
```

For the framework to achieve optimal update performance, it needs to find the differences before and after and only update the changes. But the code that finally fulfills this update is still:

```
01 div.textContent = 'hello vue3' // modify directly
```

If we define the performance cost of direct modification as A, and the cost of finding out differences as B, then there will be:

- Update performance cost of imperative code = A.
- Update performance cost of declarative code = B + A.

Note that declarative code has an extra performance cost to find out the difference than imperative code, so the most ideal situation is that when the performance consumption used to figure out the differentiation is 0, declarative code has the same performance, not surpassing, as imperative code. *After all, the framework itself is encapsulated with imperative code to achieve user-oriented declarative form.* This is consistent with the performance conclusion drawn above: *The performance of declarative code is no better than that of imperative code.*

Since imperative code is a better option at the performance level, why does Vue.js choose a declarative design solution? The reason lies in the fact that declarative code is more maintainable. From the code in the above example, we can also see that when using imperative code for development, we need to maintain the entire process of achieving the ultimate state, including manually creating, updating, and deleting DOM elements. By contrast, the declarative code shows the result we desire, which looks more obvious, and we do not take how to achieve that into account. Vue.js has done encapsulation for us already.

This illustrates the trade-offs between maintainability and performance that we have to make in framework design. While using declarative form to improve maintainability, there will be a certain loss of performance, and what framework designers have to do is: *Retain maintainability while minimizing performance loss.*

1.3 How Does the Virtual DOM Perform?

Due to the probability that some readers do not know what a virtual DOM is, we will not analyze it in depth here, but this will not stop you from understanding this section or reading the following chapters. It does not matter even if it does not make any sense to you; you will at least have an impression. You can come back to this section after the virtual DOM is fully explained. I believe you will have different feelings then.

As mentioned earlier, *the update performance cost of declarative code = the performance cost of finding differences + the performance cost of direct modification*. Thus, if we can minimize the performance cost of finding the difference, we will make the performance of declarative code infinitely close to that of imperative code. The so-called virtual DOM is to *minimize* the performance cost of finding differences.

So far, I believe you have known one fact; that is, the performance of the update technology using virtual DOM is theoretically impossible to be higher than that obtained by the native JavaScript operation DOM. Here we emphasize that it is *in theory* because this is very critical; why? It is because in most cases, *it is difficult for us to write absolutely optimized imperative code*, especially when the application scale is very large; even if you have optimized the code to a very large degree, it must have taken a lot of effort, and the return on investment then is actually not high.

So, the problem is where there is any method that does not require too much time and energy (writing declarative code), but can ensure the lower limit of the performance of an application, so that the performance of the application is not too bad, or a way to approximate the performance of imperative code could be found. This is definitely what the virtual DOM needs to solve.

However, the native JavaScript aforementioned indeed refers to DOM operations such as document.createElement but not innerHTML because the latter is rather special and needs to be discussed separately. In the past when using jQuery or directly using JavaScript to write page contents, making use of innerHTML for page operation was very common. In fact, we should think about this: What is the performance of manipulating pages using innerHTML compared with using virtual DOM? What is the difference between innerHTML and DOM operation methods like document.createElement?

Let's turn to the first question first. In order to compare the performance of innerHTML and virtual DOM, we need to understand the process of creating and updating pages. For innerHTML, in order to create pages, we need to construct an HTML string:

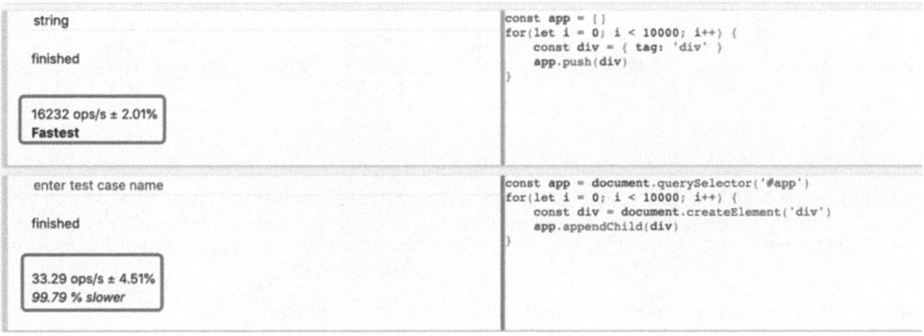

Fig. 1.1 The benchmark result

```
01 const html = `
02 <div><span>...</span></div>
03 `
```

The string is then assigned to the innerHTML property of the DOM element:

```
01 div.innerHTML = html
```

However, this sentence is far from being simple as it seems. In order to render the page, the string must first be parsed into a DOM tree, which is a DOM level computation. We know that the calculation performance involving DOM is far worse than that at the JavaScript level. A benchmark result is provided here for reference, as shown in Fig. 1.1.

In Fig. 1.1, what is at the top is the calculation at pure JavaScript level, which loops 10,000 times, creating a JavaScript object and adding it to the array at a time; the bottom part is the DOM operation, generating a DOM element at a time and adding it to the page. The benchmark result shows that the pure JavaScript level operations are much faster than the DOM operations, and they are not at the same order of magnitude. Based on this background, we can use a formula to express the performance of creating pages through innerHTML: *calculation of HTML string splicing + DOM calculation of innerHTML*.

Next, we will present the performance of the virtual DOM for creating pages. The virtual DOM page creation process is divided into two steps: the first step is to create a JavaScript object that represents the description of an actual DOM; the second step is to recursively traverse the virtual DOM tree and create the actual DOM. We can also express this in a formula: *calculation to create the JavaScript object + calculation to create the actual DOM*.

Figure 1.2 illustrates the difference in the performance of innerHTML and virtual DOM for creating a page.

As you can see, there is not much difference between pure JavaScript level calculation and DOM level calculation. Here we only pay attention to the difference on the order of magnitude from a macro perspective. If they are on the same order of

	Virtual DOM	innerHTML
Pure JavaScript Operations	• Create JavaScript Objects (VNode)	• Render HTML Strings
DOM Operations	• Newly Create All DOM Elements	• Newly Create All DOM Elements

Fig. 1.2 Performance of innerHTML and virtual DOM when creating pages

	Virtual DOM	innerHTML
Pure JavaScript Operations	• Create New JavaScript Objects + Diff	• Render HTML Strings
DOM Operations	• Necessary DOM Updates	• Destroy All Old DOMs • Newly Create All DOMs

Fig. 1.3 Performance of virtual DOM and innerHTML when updating pages

magnitude, then we think there is no difference. When creating a page, you always need to newly create all DOM elements.

Just now we have introduced the performance of creating a page. You might think that virtual DOM has no advantage over innerHTML, or it even performs worse if details are considered. Just hold on! Now we are going to analyze their performance when updating the page.

The process of updating a page with innerHTML is to *rebuild the HTML string*, and *then reset the innerHTML property of the DOM elements*, which means that even if we only change a word, we have to reset the innerHTML property. Resetting the innerHTML property is no less than *destroying all the old DOM elements and newly create all DOM elements*. Regarding to how the virtual DOM updates the page, the fact is it needs to recreate the JavaScript object (a virtual DOM tree), then compare the old and new virtual DOMs, find elements changed, and update them. Figure 1.3 show the comparison.

It can be found that when updating a page, the virtual DOM operation at the JavaScript level has an extra performance cost for Diff for creating the page. However, it is also a JavaScript level operation after all, so it will not produce difference of an order of magnitude. Then please look at the DOM operations, it is explicit that the virtual DOM will only update the necessary elements when updating the page, but innerHTML needs full data update. This is one advantage of the virtual DOM.

	Virtual DOM	innerHTML
Pure JavaScript Operations	• Create New JavaScript Objects + Diff	• Render HTML Strings
DOM Operations	• Necessary DOM Updates	• Destroy All Old DOMs • Newly Create All DOMs
Performance Factors	• Related to Data Variation	• Related to the Template Size

Fig. 1.4 Performance of virtual DOM and innerHTML when updating pages (with performance factors)

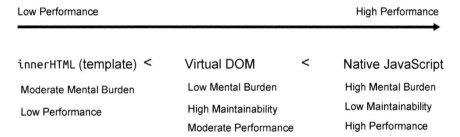

Low Performance   High Performance

innerHTML (template) <   Virtual DOM   <   Native JavaScript

Moderate Mental Burden	Low Mental Burden	High Mental Burden
Low Performance	High Maintainability	Low Maintainability
	Moderate Performance	High Performance

Fig. 1.5 Performance of innerHTML, virtual DOM, and native javascript when updating pages

We also could observe that when updating a page, the performance factors affecting the virtual DOM are different from those affecting innerHTML. For the virtual DOM, no matter how big the page is, only the changed content will be updated, while for innerHTML, the larger the page, the greater the performance consumption during updating. If you add performance factors, then the final performance of them for updating the page will be what Fig. 1.4 illustrates.

Based on this, we can roughly summarize the performance of innerHTML, virtual DOM, and native JavaScript (referring to methods such as createElement) for updating pages, as shown in Fig. 1.5.

There are several dimensions: mental burden, maintainability, and performance. The native DOM operation method has the greatest mental burden, because you have to manually create, delete, and modify a large number of DOM elements. However, its performance is the highest; but in order to make it perform best, we also have to bear a huge mental burden. In addition, the code written in this way is also of extremely poor maintainability. Yet for innerHTML, because part of our page writing process is achieved by splicing HTML strings, it is a bit similar to being declarative, but splicing strings always has certain mental burden, and we still have to use native JavaScript to deal with actions like event binding. If the innerHTML template is large, the performance of updating pages is the worst, especially when there are only a small number of updates. Finally, let's take a look at the virtual DOM. It is declarative, so the mental burden is small, and the maintainability is high. Although the performance of it is not as good as the extremely optimized native JavaScript, it is relatively good under the premise of decreasing the mental burden while ensuring maintainability.

At this point, it is necessary to think about the following question: Is there a way to describe UI declaratively and obtain the performance of native JavaScript? It seems to have your cake and eat it too. We will continue to discuss this in the next chapter.

1.4   Run Time and Compile Time

When designing a framework, we have three choices: pure run time, run time + compile time, or pure compile time. This requires you to make appropriate decisions based on the characteristics of the target framework and the expectations. In order to select correctly, you also need to know exactly what run time is and what compile time is, what their respective characteristics are, and how they affect frameworks. This section will explain these questions step by step.

Let's talk about a purely runtime framework. Suppose we have designed a framework that provides a render function. After users provide a data object of tree structure for the function, the render function will recursively render the data into DOM elements based on the object. We specify that the tree-shaped data object is as follows:

```
01   const obj = {
02     tag: 'div',
03     children: [
04       { tag: 'span', children: 'hello world' }
05     ]
06   }
```

Each object has two attributes: tag stands for the tag name, and children can be either an array (representing sub-nodes) or a piece of text (representing text sub-nodes). Now, let's implement the render function:

```
01   function Render(obj, root) {
02     const el = document.createElement(obj.tag)
03     if (typeof obj.children === 'string') {
04       const text = document.createTextNode(obj.children)
05       el.appendChild(text)
06     } else if (obj.children) {
07       // array, recursively call render, using el as the root
parameter
08       obj.children.forEach((child) => Render(child, el))
09     }
```

```
10
11    // add elements to root
12    root.appendChild(el)
13  }
```

With this function, users can use it like this:

```
01    const obj = {
02        tag: 'div',
03        children: [
04            { tag: 'span', children: 'hello world' }
05        ]
06    }
07    // render to under body
08    Render(obj, document.body)
```

Run the above code in the browser, and you can see what we expect.

It's time for us to think about how users use the render function. It can be noted that when users use it to render content, they directly provide a data object with a tree structure for the render function. There are no additional steps involved, and users do not need to have additional knowledge. But 1 day, your user may complain, "Writing tree-shaped data objects is too troublesome and not intuitive. Is there support for describing tree structured data objects in a similar way to HTML tags?" You then look at the current render function and reply, "Sorry, not yet supported." The framework we just wrote was indeed a purely runtime framework.

To meet the needs of users, you may be wondering whether you can introduce compilation methods to compile HTML tags into data objects of tree data structure. In this way, you will be able to continue to use the render function, won't you? The idea is shown in Fig. 1.6.

For this consideration, you write a program called compiler. Its function is to compile HTML strings into tree-structured data objects and deliver them to users. So how can users use it? In fact, this is also a problem we have to think about. The simplest way is to let users call the compiler function and render function, respectively:

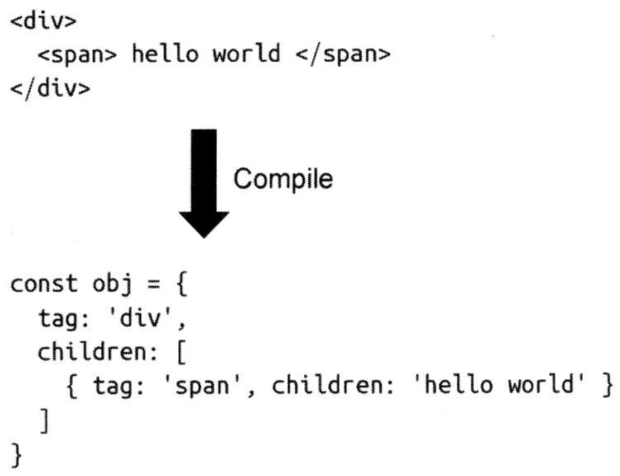

Fig. 1.6 Compile HTML tags into data objects of tree data structure

```
<div>
   <span> hello world </span>
</div>
```

⬇ Compile

```
const obj = {
   tag: 'div',
   children: [
      { tag: 'span', children: 'hello world' }
   ]
}
```

```
01    const html = `
02    <div>
03      <span>hello world</span>
04    </div>
05
06    // Call compiler to get tree-structured data objects by compiling
07    const obj = Compiler(html)
08    // Call render for rendering
09    Render(obj, document.body)
```

The above code works well, and then our framework becomes a runtime + compile-time framework. It supports both run time, where users can directly provide data objects without compilation, and compile time, where users can provide HTML strings, which we compile into data objects before hand over to the run time for processing. To be precise, the above code is actually compiled at run time, which means that the code starts to compile when it is running, and this will incur a certain performance overhead. Therefore, we can also execute the compiler program to compile the content provided by the user at the time of construction, so there is no need to compile during execution of the program. It is very performance friendly.

However, you must have become aware of another problem: Since the compiler can compile HTML strings into data objects, can it compile them directly into imperative code? Figure 1.7 illustrates the process of compiling HTML strings into imperative code.

In this way, we only need a compiler function, and no render is required. In fact, this has become a pure compile-time framework because we do not support any runtime content, and the user's code can only run after compiled through the compiler.

We have used simple examples to explain the run time, compile time, and run time + compile time at the framework design level. We have seen that a framework might be purely runtime, purely compile-time, or support both run time and compile time. So, what are their advantages and disadvantages? Is it best to support both runtime and compile-time frameworks? To find the answers, let's analyze these forms one by one.

Fig. 1.7 Compiling an HTML string into imperative code

```
<div>
  <span> hello world </span>
</div>
```

Compile

```
const div = document.createElement('div')
const span = document.createElement('span')
span.innerText = 'hello world'
div.appendChild(span)
document.body.appendChild(div)
```

What comes first is the purely runtime framework. Since it does not have a compilation process, we cannot analyze the content provided by the user, but if we add a compilation step, it may make a big difference. We can judge what content may change, and what will never change in the future by analyzing the content provided by the user, so that we can extract this information at the time of compiling and then pass it to the render function. After the render function gets this information, it can do further optimization. However, if the framework we designed is pure compile time, it can also analyze the content provided by the user. Since there is no need for any run time, but directly compiling into executable JavaScript code, the performance may be better. This approach, however, is detrimental to flexibility— that is, user-provided content must be compiled before it can be used. It is true that there are explorations in all the three directions within the field, of which Svelte is a pure compile-time framework, but its real performance may not reach what is expected in theory. Vue.js 3 still maintains the runtime + compile-time architecture and can be optimized as much as possible while maintaining flexibility. When the compilation optimization of Vue.js 3 is explained later, you will see that the performance of Vue.js 3 is not even inferior to the pure compile-time framework while retaining the run time.

1.5 Summary

In this chapter, we first introduced the difference between the imperative and declarative paradigms. The imperative forms pay more attention to the process, while the declarative ones focus more on the result. Imperative paradigms can be optimized in theory, but users have to bear a huge mental burden; declarative paradigms, on the other hand, can effectively reduce the mental burden of users, but there is certain sacrifice for performance, so that framework designers must find ways to minimize performance loss.

We then illustrated the performance of the virtual DOM and offered a formula: *the update performance cost of declarative code = the performance cost of finding differences + the performance cost of direct modification*. The significance of the virtual DOM is to minimize the performance consumption on finding the differences. We notice that the performance of using native JavaScript operation DOM (such as document.createElement), virtual DOM, and innerHTML for page operations has something to do with the size of the page and the size of the changed part. It is also different for creating a page and updating a page. Selecting which update strategy requires us to consider factors such as mental burden and maintainability. After some evaluation, we discover that virtual DOM is a good choice.

Finally, we explained the relevant knowledge of run time and compile time, illustrated the characteristics of purely runtime frameworks, purely compile-time frameworks, and frameworks supported by both, and concluded that Vue.js 3 was a compile-time + runtime framework. While maintaining flexibility, it is able to analyze content provided by users through compilation approaches to further improve update performance.

Chapter 2
Core Elements of Framework Design

The framework design is more complicated than imagined. Only completing the function development and ensuring it could be used is not enough. There is still a lot of learning acquired in that. For example, what bundles should our framework provide to users? What is the module format of the product? When users are not using the framework in the expected way, should appropriate warnings be printed to provide a better development experience and allow users to quickly locate problems? What is the difference between building a development version and building a production version? Hot Module Replacement (HMR) requires framework-level support, should we also consider it? In addition, when your framework provides multiple functions, and the user only needs a few of them, can the user choose to turn off other functions to reduce the packaging volume of the final resource? The above questions should be taken into account in the process of creating the framework.

As you study this chapter, you are required to have some experience with commonly used module packaging tools, especially rollup.js and webpack. It does not matter if you have only used or know one of them, because many of their concepts are actually similar. If you have not used any module packaging tools, then you need to understand it yourself, and it will be better to read this chapter after you have a preliminary understanding.

2.1 Improving User Experience in Development

One of the indicators to measure whether a framework is good enough is to see how its development experience is. Here we take Vue.js 3 as an example:

```
01    createApp(App).mount('#not-exist')
```

When we create a Vue.js application and try to mount it to a DOM node that does not exist, we get a warning message, as shown in Fig. 2.1.

H. Yang, *Vue. JS Framework*, https://doi.org/10.1007/978-981-99-4947-2_2

⚠ ▸ [Vue warn]: Failed to mount app: mount target selector "#not-exist" returned null.

Fig. 2.1 Warning message

▸ RefImpl {_rawValue: 0, _shallow: false, __v_isRef: true, _value: 0}

Fig. 2.2 Console output results

This message tells us that the mount failed and explains the reason for the failure: Vue.js cannot find the corresponding DOM element (returning null) according to the selector we provided. This information allows us to locate the problem clearly and quickly. Just imagine, if the Vue.js does nothing internally, then we are likely to get a JavaScript-level error message, such as UncaughtTypeError: Cannot read property 'xxx' of null. However, based on this information it is difficult to know what the problem is.

Hence, it is crucial to provide friendly warning messages during framework design and development. If this is not done well, you are likely to receive frequent complaints from users. Always providing friendly warning messages can not only help users quickly locate problems and save users' time, but also allow the framework to gain a good reputation and allow users to recognize the professionalism of the framework.

In Vue.js source code, we can often see the call of the warn function. For example, the information in Fig. 2.1 is printed by the following warning function call:

```
01      warn(
02              `Failed to mount app: mount target selector "${container}"
returned null.`
03          )
```

For the warn function, since it needs to provide as useful information as possible, it needs to collect information about the component stack where the error is currently occurring. If you look at the source code, it is a bit complicated, but it actually ends up calling the console.warn function.

In addition to providing the necessary warning information, there are many other aspects that can be used as entry points to further improve the user's development experience. For example, in Vue.js 3, when we print a ref. data in the console:

```
01 const count = ref(0)
02 console.log(count)
```

Open the console to view the output, and the result is shown in Fig. 2.2.

It can be found that the printed data is very unintuitive. Of course, we can choose to print count.value value directly, so that only 0 will be output, which is very intuitive. So is there a way to make the output information more friendly when

Fig. 2.3 Check the
"Console" → "Enable
custom formatters" option

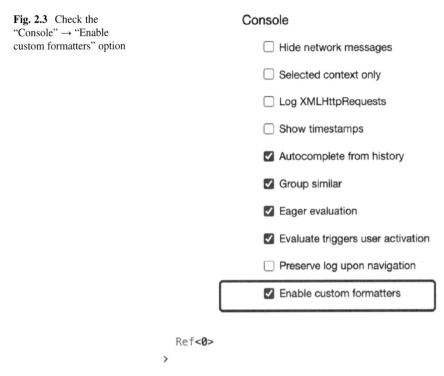

Fig. 2.4 caption and figure follow:

Fig. 2.4 Intuitive output content

printing count? Of course, the browser allows us to write custom formatters to customize the output form. In the source code of Vue.js 3, you can search for a function called initCustomFormatter, which is used to initialize custom formatters in the development environment. Taking Chrome as an example, we can open the DevTools settings and check the "Console" → "Enable custom formatters" option, as shown in Fig. 2.3.

Then refresh the browser and look at the console, you will find the output. The content then becomes very intuitive, as shown in Fig. 2.4.

2.2   Controlling the Volume of the Framework Code

The size of the framework is also one of the criteria for measuring the framework. In the case of implementing the same function, of course, the less code is used, the better, so the smaller the volume will be, and finally the less time the browser will load the resource. At this point, we can't help but think that providing more perfect warning information means we have to write more code. But isn't this contrary to controlling the size of the code? The answer is yes. So, we're going to figure out a way to fix this problem.

If we look at the source code of Vue.js 3, we will find that every call to the warn function will be accompanied by __DEV__ constant check, for example:

```
01    if  (__DEV__ && !res) {
02        warn(
03                  `Failed to mount app: mount target selector
"${container}" returned null.`
04          )
05      }
```

It can be seen that the premise of printing the warning message is: the constant __DEV__ must be true, and the __DEV__ constant here is the key to achieving the goal.

Vue.js uses rollup.js to build the project, and the __DEV__ constants here are actually predefined by rollup.js plugin configuration, which functions like the DefinePlugin plugin in webpack.

When Vue.js outputs resources, two versions will be output, one for the development environment, such as vue.global.js, and the other for the production environment, such as vue.global.prod.js, which can also be distinguished by the filename.

When Vue.js builds a resource for the development environment, the __DEV__ constant is set to true, and the above code that outputs a warning message is equivalent to

```
01    if  (true && !res) {
02        warn(
03                  `Failed to mount app: mount target selector
"${container}" returned null.`
04              )
05          }
```

As you can see, here we replace the __DEV__ constant with the literal true, so this code must exist in the development environment.

When Vue.js is employed to build resources for the production environment, the __DEV__ constant will be set to false, and this time the code above that outputs the warning message is equivalent to

```
01    if  (false && !res) {
02        warn(
03              `Failed to mount app: mount target selector "${container}"
returned null.`
04              )
05          }
```

As you can see, the __DEV__ constant is replaced with the literal false. At this time, we find that this branch code will never be executed, because the judgment condition is always false. This code that will never be executed is called dead code, and it will not appear in the final product; it will be removed when the resource is built, so this code will not exist in the vue.global.prod.js.

This way we can provide user-friendly warnings in the development environment without increasing the size of the production environment code.

2.3 Frameworks Need Good Tree-Shaking

As mentioned above, by setting predefined constant __DEV__ by the construction tool, the framework can be made not to contain code for printing warning messages in the production environment, so that the amount of code in the framework itself does not increase with the increase of warning messages. But from the user's point of view, this is still not enough. Let's explain this by taking Vue.js as an example. We know that Vue.js has many built-in components, such as the <Transition > component. If our project does not use this component at all, does its code need to be included in the final building resource of the project? The answer is "of course not"; then, how can we achieve this result? The protagonist of this section, Tree-Shaking, is what could be used to perform this task.

What is Tree-Shaking? In the front-end world, this concept is popularized because of rollup.js. Simply put, Tree-Shaking refers to eliminating code that will never be executed, that is, excluding dead code. Now both rollup.js and webpack support Tree-Shaking.

To implement Tree-Shaking, one condition must be met; that is, the module must be ESM (ES Module), because Tree-Shaking depends on the static structure of ESM. Let's use rollup.js as an example to see how Tree-Shaking works. Its directory structure is as follows:

```
01 ├── demo
02 │        └── package.json
03 │        └── input.js
04 │        └── utils.js
```

First install rollup.js:

```
01    yarn add rollup –D
02    # or npm install rollup -D
```

The following is what in the input.js and utils.js files:

```
01    // input.js
02    import { foo } from './utils.js'
03    foo()
04    // utils.js
05    export function foo(obj) {
```

```
06        obj && obj.foo
07      }
08   export function bar(obj) {
09        obj && obj.bar
10      }
```

The code is very simple, we define and export two functions in the utils.js file, the foo function and the bar function, respectively, and then import the foo function in the input.js and execute it. Note that we did not import the bar function.

Next, we execute the following command to build:

```
01 npx rollup input.js -f esm -o bundle.js
```

This command means, take the input.js file as the entry, output the ESM, and the output file is called bundle.js. After the command is executed successfully, we open the bundle.js to check its contents:

```
01   // bundle.js
02   function foo(obj) {
03        obj && obj.foo
04   }
05   foo();
```

As you can see, it does not contain the bar function, which means that Tree-Shaking works. Since we did not use the bar function, it was removed as dead code. But a closer study shows that the execution of the foo function is meaningless, because it just reads the value of the object, so its execution seems unnecessary. Since deleting this code will not affect our application, why rollup.js not remove this code as dead code as well?

This brings us to the second key point in Tree-Shaking—side effects. If a function call produces side effects, then it cannot be removed. What are side effects? Simply put, a side effect is that when a function is called, it will have an impact on the outside world, such as modifying a global variable. At this point you might say that the above code is obviously reading the value of the object, how can there be side effects? In fact, it is possible. Imagine if the obj object is a proxy object created through Proxy, then when we read the object properties, it will trigger the get trap of the proxy object, which may cause side effects in the get trap. For example, whether modifying a global variable in the get trap will have side effects in the end can only be known when the code is actually running. JavaScript itself is a dynamic language, so it is very difficult to statically analyze which code is dead code.

The above is just a simple example.

Because it is difficult to statically analyze JavaScript code, tools like rollup.js provide a mechanism that allows us to explicitly tell rollup.js, "Don't worry! This code has no side effects. You can remove it." How exactly? As shown in the following code, we modify the input.js file:

```
01     import {foo} from './utils'
02
03     /*#__PURE__*/ foo()
```

Note the comment code/*#__PURE__ */, its role is to tell rollup.js that the call to the foo function will not have side effects, so you can safely implement Tree-Shaking, during which time, when executing the build command again and then looking at the bundle.js file, you will find that its content is empty, which means that Tree-Shaking is in effect.

Based on this case, we will understand that the/* #__PURE__ */annotation needs to be used reasonably when we write the framework. If you search the source code of Vue.js 3, you will find that it uses this annotation a lot, such as in the following sentence:

```
01 export const isHTMLTag = /*#__PURE__*/ makeMap(HTML_TAGS)
```

Will this cause a lot of mental burden on writing code? Actually not, because the code that usually produces side effects is the top-level call to the function in the module. What is a top-level call? As shown in the following code:

```
01   foo () // Top-level call
02
03     function bar () {
04         foo() // In-function call
05     }
```

It can be seen that for top-level calls, side effects may occur; but for intra-function calls, as long as the function bar is not called, the call to the foo function will naturally not cause side effects. Therefore, in the source code of Vue.js 3, the/*#__PURE__ */annotation is always used on some top-level called functions. Of course, this annotation does not just apply to functions. It can be applied to any statement. This annotation is not only recognized by rollup.js but also by webpack and compression tools (such as terser).

2.4   What Kind of Bundle Should Frameworks Output

As mentioned above, Vue.js will output different packages for development environment and production environment, respectively. For example vue.global.js is for development environment, and it contains necessary warning information, whereas vue.global.prod.js is for production environment, and it does not contain warning information. In fact, Vue.js bundle will output other forms of products according to different usage scenarios in addition to environmental distinctions. In this section, we will discuss the purpose of these products and how to export them during the build phase.

Different types of products must have corresponding requirements background, so let's start with requirements. First of all, we hope that users can use the <script> tag to introduce the framework directly in the HTML page and use it:

```
01   <body>
02        <script src="/path/to/vue.js"></script>
03        <script>
04     const { createApp } = Vue
05     // ...
06        </script>
07   </body>
```

In order to achieve this requirement, we need to output a resource called IIFE format. The full name of IIFE is Immediately Invoked Function Expression, which is easy to express in JavaScript:

```
01     (function () {
02        // ...
03     }())
```

As shown in the above code, this is a function expression that executes immediately. In fact, vue.global.js file is a resource in the form of IIFE, and its code structure is as follows:

```
01   var Vue = (function (exports) {
02        // ...
03     exports.createApp = createApp;
04        // ...
05     return exports
06        }({}))
```

In this way, when we use the < script > tag to directly import the vue.global.js file, the global variable Vue is available. In rollup.js, we can output this form of resource by configuring format: 'iife':

```
01     // rollup.config.js
02     const config = {
03        input: 'input.js',
04        output: {
05          file: 'output.js',
06                format: 'iife' // Specify the module form
07        }
08        }
09
10          export default config
```

However, with the development of technology and browser support, mainstream browsers now have good support for native ESM, so users can not only reference

IIFE-formatted resources with the < script > tag, but also can directly import ESM-formatted resources. For example, Vue.js 3 will also output vue.esm-browser.js files. Users can directly import them with the < script type = "module" > tag:

```
01 <script type="module" src="/path/to/vue.esm-browser.js"></
script>
```

In order to output resources in ESM format, rollup.js output format needs to be configured as: format: 'esm'.

You may wonder why there is -browser in the vue.esm-browser.js file. In fact, for ESM format resources, Vue.js will also output a vue.esm-bundler.js file, where -browser becomes -bundler. Why do we do this? We know that no matter it is rollup.js or webpack, when looking for resources, if there is a module field in the package.json, the resource pointed to by the module field will be used first instead of the resource pointed to by the main field. We can open the packages/vue/package.json file in the Vue.js source code and take a look:

```
01    {
02        "main": "index.js",
03        "module": "dist/vue.runtime.esm-bundler.js",
04    }
```

Wherein, the module field points to the vue.runtime.esm-bundler.js file, which means that if the project is built using webpack, then the Vue.js resource you use is vue.runtime.esm-bundler.js; that is, the ESM resource with -bundler is for packaging tools such as rollup.js or webpack, while the ESM resource with -browser is used directly for < script type = "module" >. What is the difference between them? Do you still remember the __DEV__ constant mentioned above? When building an ESM resource for the < script > tag, the __DEV__ is set to true if it is for the development environment; if it is used in a production environment, the __DEV__ constant will be set to false and thus removed by Tree-Shaking. But when we build a resource in ESM format provided to the packaging tool, we cannot directly set the __DEV__ to true or false, but use (process.env.NODE _ENV! == 'production') to replace __DEV__ constant. The following source code is an example:

```
01    if  (__DEV__) {
02    warn (`useCssModule() is not supported in the global build.`)
03    }
```

In a resource with the word -bundler it will become

```
01    if  ((process.env.NODE_ENV !== 'production')) {
02     warn (`useCssModule() is not supported in the global build.`)
03    }
```

The advantage of this is that the user can decide the target environment of the build resource through the webpack configuration, but the end effect is the same. This code will only appear in the development environment.

The user can directly use the $<$ script $>$ tag to import resources. We also hope that users can refer to resources through the require statement in the Node.js. For instance:

```
01 const Vue = require('vue')
```

Why is there such a need? The answer is "server-side rendering." When doing server-side rendering, Vue.js code runs in a Node.js environment, not a browser environment. In a Node.js environment, the module format of the resource should be CommonJS, or cjs for short. In order to be able to output the resources of the cjs module, we can modify the rollup.config.js configuration format: 'cjs' to achieve corresponding results:

```
01    // rollup.config.js
02      const config = {
03            input: 'input.js',
04          output: {
05                  file:  'output.js',
06              format:  'cjs'   // specify the module form
07          }
08      }
09
10      export default config
```

2.5   Feature Switches

When designing the framework, the framework will provide users with many features (or functions). For example, we provide three features A, B, and C to users and also offer three corresponding feature switches a, b, and c. Users can set a, b, c to true or false to represent turning the corresponding feature on or off, which will bring many benefits.

- For features turned off by users, we can use the Tree-Shaking mechanism to keep them out of the final resource.
- This mechanism brings flexibility to the framework design, and new features can be added to the framework at will through feature switches without worrying about the resource volume becoming larger. At the same time, when the framework is upgraded, we can also support legacy APIs through feature switches, so that new users can choose not to use legacy APIs, thereby minimizing the final packaged resource volume.

So how do we implement the feature switch? In fact, it is very simple. The principle is the same as the __DEV__ constants mentioned above, which is essentially implemented by using rollup.js predefined constant plugins. Take a rollup.js configuration in the Vue.js 3 source code as an example:

```
01   {
02      __FEATURE_OPTIONS_API__ : isBundlerESMBuild ? `__VUE_OPTIONS_
API__` : true,
03   }
```

In the above code, __FEATURE_OPTIONS_API__ is similar to __DEV__. Searching the source code of Vue.js 3, you can find many judgment branches similar to the following code:

```
01 // support for 2.x options
02 if   (__FEATURE_OPTIONS_API__) {
03      currentInstance = instance
04      pauseTracking()
05      applyOptions(instance, Component)
06      resetTracking()
07      currentInstance = null
08 }
```

When Vue.js builds a resource, if the resource built is used by a packaging tool (that is, a resource with the word -bundler), then the above code is changed into the following in the resource:

```
01      // support for 2.x options
02      if   (__FEATURE_OPTIONS_API__) { Notice here
03         currentInstance = instance
04         pauseTracking()
05         applyOptions(instance, Component)
07      resetTracking()
08      currentInstance = null
09 }
```

Here, the __VUE_OPTIONS_API__ becomes a feature switch, and the user can control whether to include this code by setting the value of __VUE_OPTIONS_API__ predefined constant. Usually users can use webpack. DefinePlugin plugins to achieve this:

```
01      // webpack.DefinePlugin plugin setting
02      new webpack.DefinePlugin({
03         __VUE_OPTIONS_API__ : JSON.stringify(true) // turn on
features
04         })
```

Finally explain in detail what the __VUE_OPTIONS_API__ switch does. In Vue.
js 2, the component we wrote is called the Component Options API:

```
01    export default {
02        data() {}, // data option
03        computed: {}, // computed option
04        // other options
05    }
```

But in Vue.js 3, it is recommended to use the Composition API to write code, for
example:

```
01    export default {
02        setup() {
03            const count = ref(0)
04        const doubleCount = computed(() => count.value * 2) //
equivalent to computed option in Vue.js 2
05            }
06        }
```

But for compatibility with Vue.js 2, it is still possible to write code in Vue.js
3 using the options API. But if you know that you will not use the options API, you
can use the __VUE_OPTIONS_API__ switch to turn off this feature, so that this part
of the code of Vue.js will not be included in the final resource while packaging,
thereby reducing the resource size.

2.6 Error Handling

Error handling is a very important part of the framework development process. The
quality of the framework error handling mechanism directly determines the robustness of the user application and also determines the mental burden of handling errors
during user development.

In order to make everyone more intuitively feel the importance of error handling,
let's start with a small example. Suppose we develop a tool module with the
following code:

```
01    // utils.js
02    export default  {
03        foo(fn)  {
04            fn && fn()
05        }
06    }
```

This module exports an object where the foo attribute is a function that receives a callback function as an argument, which is executed when the foo function is called, when used on the user side:

```
01    import utils from 'utils.js'
02    utils. foo (() => {
03        // ...
04    })
```

Let's think about what if the callback function provided by the user makes an error during execution. There are two ways at this time. The first way is to let the user handle it by himself, which requires the user to execute try ... catch:

```
01    import utils from 'utils.js'
02    utils.foo (() => {
03        try {
04            // ...
05        } catch (e) {
06            // ...
07        }
08    })
```

But doing so will increase the burden on the user. Just imagine, if utils.js does not just provide a foo function, but provides dozens or hundreds of similar functions, then users need to add error handlers one by one when using them.

The second way is that we handle errors uniformly on behalf of the user, as shown in the following code:

```
01    // utils.js
02    export default   {
03        foo (fn)   {
04            try   {
05                fn && fn ()
06            } catch (e) {/* ... */}
07        },
08        bar (fn) {
09            try {
10                fn  &&  fn ()
11            } catch (e) {/* ... */}
12        },
13    }
```

Add a try ... catch code block to each function; in fact, we can further encapsulate the error handler as a function, assuming it is called callWithErrorHandling:

```
01    // utils.js
02    export default {
03        foo (fn) {
04            callWithErrorHandling (fn)
```

```
05              },
06              bar(fn) {
07                  callWithErrorHandling(fn)
08              },
09          }
10          function callWithErrorHandling(fn) {
11              try {
12                  fn && fn()
13              } catch (e) {
14                  console.log(e)
15              }
16          }
```

As you can see, the code has become much simpler. But simplicity is not the goal, the real benefit of this is that we can provide users with a unified error handling interface, as shown in the following code:

```
01      // utils.js
02      let handleError = null
03      export default {
04          foo (fn) {
05              callWithErrorHandling(fn)
06          },
07          // users can call this function to register a unified error
handling function
08          registerErrorHandler(fn) {
09              handleError = fn
10          }
11      }
12      function callWithErrorHandling(fn) {
13          try {
14              fn && fn()
15          } catch (e) {
16              // the error handler that passes the caught error to the
user
17              handleError(e)
18          }
19      }
```

We provide the registerErrorHandler function, which the user can use to register an error handler, and then pass the error to the user-registered error handler after catching the error inside the callWithErrorHandling function.

This way the code on the user side will be very concise and robust:

```
01      import utils from 'utils.js'
02      // Register an error handler
03      utils.registerErrorHandler((e) => {
04          console.log(e)
05      })
06      utils.foo (()   =>  {/*...*/})
07      utils.bar (()   =>  {/*...*/})
```

At this time, the ability of error handling is completely controlled by the user. The user can either choose to ignore the error or call the reporting program to report the error to the monitoring system.

In fact, this is the principle of Vue.js error handling, you can search the callWithErrorHandling function in the source code. In addition, in the Vue.js, we can also register the unified error handling function:

```
01      import App from 'App.vue'
02      const app = createApp(App)
03      app.config.errorHandler = () => {
04          // Error handler
05      }
```

2.7   Excellent TypeScript Support

TypeScript is an open-source programming language by Microsoft, referred to as TS. It is a superset of JavaScript and can provide type support for JavaScript. Now more and more developers and teams use TS in their projects. There are many benefits of using TS, such as code as doc, automatic prompts from the editor, avoidance of low-level bugs to a certain extent, and stronger code maintainability. Therefore, whether the support for TS types is perfect has also become an important indicator for evaluating a framework.

How to measure the level of TS type support of a framework? There is a common misunderstanding here. Many readers think that as long as they use TS to write a framework, it is equivalent to being friendly to TS type support. In fact, these are two completely different things. Considering that some readers may not have been exposed to TS, so there will be no in-depth discussion here, we will only give a simple example. The following is a function written in TS:

```
01      function foo(val: any) {
02          return val
03 }
```

This function is very simple, it takes the parameter val and the parameter can be of any type (any), the function directly takes the parameter as the return value, which means that the type of the return value is determined by the parameter. If the parameter is of type number, then the return value is also of type number. Then we try to use this function, as shown in Fig. 2.5.

When calling the foo function, we pass a parameter of type string 'str'. According to the previous analysis, the type of the obtained res should also be of type string. However, when we hover the mouse pointer over the res constant, we can see that its type is any, which is not the result we want. To achieve the ideal state, we only need to make simple modifications to the foo function:

```
function foo(val: any) {
  return val
}         const res: any

          'res' is declared but its value is never read. ts(6133)

|         Peek Problem (⌥F8)   Quick Fix... (⌘.)
const res = foo('str')
```

Fig. 2.5 The return value type is missing

```
function foo<T extends any>(val: T): T {
  return val
}         const res: "str"

          'res' is declared but its value is never read. ts(6133)

          Peek Problem (⌥F8)   Quick Fix... (⌘.)
const res = foo('str')
```

Fig. 2.6 Can deduce the return value type

```
01   function foo<T extends any>(val: T): T {
02           return val
03   }
```

You don't need to understand this code, let's look directly at the current performance, as shown in Fig. 2.6.

You can see that the type of res is the character literal 'str ' instead of any, which shows that our code is in effect.

Through this simple example, we realize that writing code with TS and being friendly to TS types are two different things. When writing large frameworks, it is not easy to achieve perfect TS type support. You can check the runtime-core/src/apiDefineComponent.ts file in the Vue.js source code. The code that will actually run in the browser in the whole file is actually only three lines, but all the code is close to 200 lines. In fact, these codes are serving type support. It can be seen that the framework needs to make considerable efforts to achieve perfect type support.

In addition to making great efforts to do type derivation to achieve better type support, it is also necessary to consider support for TSX, which will be discussed in detail in subsequent chapters.

2.8 Summary

This chapter first explained the content of development experience in framework design. Development experience is one of the important indicators to measure a framework. Providing friendly warning information is crucial, which helps developers quickly locate problems, because in most cases the "framework" knows better than the developer where the problem is, so throwing meaningful warning information at the framework level is very necessary.

But the more detailed the warning information provided, the larger the framework. Therefore, in order for the framework volume not to be affected by warning messages, we need to use the Tree-Shaking mechanism to cooperate with the ability of the build tool to predefine constants, such as predefined __DEV__ constants, so as to print warning messages only in the development environment, while in the production environment, these codes used to improve the development experience are not included, so as to achieve the controllability of the online code volume.

Tree-Shaking is a mechanism to exclude dead code. Various capabilities are built into the framework, such as Vue.js built-in components. For capabilities that users may not use, we can use the Tree-Shaking mechanism to minimize the size of the final packaged code. In addition, Tree-Shaking itself is based on ESM, and JavaScript is a dynamic language. It is difficult to perform Tree-Shaking by means of pure static analysis, so most tools can recognize/* #__PURE__ */comments. When writing framework code, we can use/* #__PURE__ */to assist build tools for Tree-Shaking.

Then we discussed the output products of the framework. Different types of products are to meet different needs. In order for users to directly reference and use through the < script > tag, we need to output resources in IIFE format, that is, function expressions that are called immediately. In order for users to be able to reference and use through <script type = "module">, we need to output resources in ESM format. It should be noted here that there are two types of resources in ESM format: esm-browser.js for browsers and esm-bundler.js for packaging tools. They differ in the handling of predefined constant __DEV__, which directly replaces the __DEV__ constant with the literal true or false, while the latter replaces the __DEV__ constant with the process.env.NODE_ENV! = = 'production' statement.

The framework provides a variety of capabilities or functions. Sometimes for flexibility and compatibility reasons, the framework provides two solutions for the same task. For example, the option object API and the combined API in the Vue.js can be used to complete the development of the page. Although the two are not mutual exclusion, but from the perspective of framework design, this is entirely based on compatibility considerations. Sometimes users clearly know that they will only use the combined API, not the option object API. At this time, the user can turn off the corresponding feature through the feature switch, so that during packaging, the code used to implement the shutdown function will be excluded by the Tree-Shaking mechanism.

The error handling of the framework directly determines the robustness of the user's application and also determines the mental burden of the user's handling errors when developing the application. The framework needs to provide users with a unified error handling interface, so that users can handle all framework exceptions by registering custom error handlers.

Finally, we point out a common cognitive misunderstanding that "writing a framework using TS and a framework that is friendly to TS type support are two completely different things." Sometimes it even takes more time and effort to make the framework provide more friendly type support than to implement the framework functionality itself.

Chapter 3
Design Patterns of Vue.js 3

In Chap. 1, we explained that framework design is the art of trade-offs, and there are trade-offs, such as the trade-off between performance and maintainability, runtime and compile time, etc. In Chap. 2, we discussed several core elements of framework design in detail. Some elements must be considered by framework designers, while others are considered from the perspective of professionalism and improving development experience. Framework design pays attention to the control of the overall perspective. No matter how big a project is, there is a core idea and it is developed around the core. In this chapter, we will understand the design idea, working mechanism, and important components of Vue.js 3 from a global perspective. We can treat these components as independent functional modules and see how they cooperate with each other. In subsequent chapters, we will dive into each functional module to understand how they work.

3.1 Describing UI Declaratively

Vue.js 3 is a declarative UI framework, which means that users describe the UI declaratively when developing pages with Vue.js 3. Think about it: if you were asked to design a declarative UI framework, how would you design it? In order to figure this out, we need to understand what is involved in writing front-end pages, as follows.

- DOM element: for example, div tag or a tag.
- Attributes: such as the href attribute of the a tag, and then general attributes such as id and class.
- Events: such as click, keydown, etc.
- Hierarchy of elements: The hierarchy of the DOM tree, with both sub-nodes and parent nodes.

© The Author(s), under exclusive license to Springer Nature Singapore Pte Ltd. 2023
H. Yang, *Vue. JS Framework*, https://doi.org/10.1007/978-981-99-4947-2_3

So, how do we describe the above declaratively? This is a question that frame-work designers need to think about. In fact, there are many solutions. Take Vue.js 3 as an example, the corresponding solution is as follows:

- Describe DOM elements in a manner consistent with HTML tags, such as when describing a div tag using <div></div>
- Describe attributes in a manner consistent with HTML tags, e.g., <div id="app"></div>
- Use: or v-bind to describe dynamically bound properties, e.g., <div : id="dynamicId"></div>
- Use @ or v-on to describe the event, such as the click event <div @click="handler"></div>
- Describe the hierarchy in a manner consistent with HTML tags, such as a div tag <div><span></span></div> with a span sub-node

It can be seen that in Vue.js, even events have corresponding descriptions. The user does not need to write any imperative code by hand, which is called declarative description of the UI.

In addition to the above use of templates to describe the UI declaratively, we can also use JavaScript objects to perform description, the code is as follows:

```
01    const title = {
02          // label name
03          tag: 'h1',
04          //tag properties
05          props: {
06                onClick: handler
07          },
08          //sub-node
09          children: [
10                { tag: 'span' }
11          ]
12    }
```

Corresponding to Vue.js template, it is actually:

```
01 <h1 @click="handler"><span></span></h1>
```

So, what is the difference between using templates and JavaScript objects to describe UI? The answer is: using JavaScript objects to describe UI is more flexible. For example, if we want to represent a title, according to the title level, we will use h1 ~ h6 tags, respectively. If we use JavaScript objects to describe it, we only need to use a variable to represent the h tag:

```
01    //h label level
02    let level = 3
03    const title = {
04    tag: `h${level}`, // h3 tag
05      }
```

It can be noticed that when the variable level value changes, the corresponding label name will also change between h1 and h6. But if you use a template to describe it, you have to be exhaustive:

```
01        <h1 v-if="level === 1"></h1>
02        <h2 v-else-if="level === 2"></h2>
03        <h3 v-else-if="level === 3"></h3>
04        <h4 v-else-if="level === 4"></h4>
05        <h5 v-else-if="level === 5"></h5>
06        <h6 v-else-if="level === 6"></h6>
```

This is far less flexible than JavaScript objects. The way of using JavaScript objects to describe UI is actually the so-called virtual DOM. Now everyone will understand that the virtual DOM is actually not so mysterious. It is just because of this flexibility of the virtual DOM that Vue.js 3 supports the use of virtual DOM to describe UI in addition to using templates. In fact, the handwritten rendering function in the Vue.js component uses the virtual DOM to describe the UI, as shown in the following code:

```
01     import { h } from 'vue'
02
03     export default {
04        render () {
05             return h ('h1', { onClick:  handler }) // virtual DOM
06          }
07     }
```

Some readers may say that this is an h function call, not a JavaScript object. In fact, the return value of the h function is an object, and its role is to make it easier for us to write virtual DOM. If you change the code of the h function call above to a JavaScript object, you need to write more:

```
01     export default  {
02          render ()  {
03             return {
04                tag: 'h1',
05                props: { onClick: handler }
06             }
07          }
08       }
```

If there is sub-node, then there is more content to write, so the h function is only a tool function to assist in the creation of virtual DOM. In addition, it is necessary to explain what is the rendering function of a component. The content to be rendered by a component is described by the rendering function, which is the render function in the above code. Vue.js will get the virtual DOM according to the return value of the component's render function, and then the content of the component can be rendered.

3.2   Getting to Know Renderers

Now that we have understood what a virtual DOM is. It actually uses JavaScript objects to describe the real DOM structure. So, how does the virtual DOM become the real DOM and render into the browser page? This needs the renderer we are going to introduce.

The role of the renderer is to render the virtual DOM into the real DOM, as shown in Fig. 3.1.

Renderer is a very important role. Vue.js components we usually write are dependent on the renderer to work, so later we will specifically explain the renderer. However, it is necessary to first pick up some knowledge about the renderer, in order to better understand the working principle of Vue.js.

Assumes that we have the following virtual DOM:

```
01    const vnode = {
02        tag: 'div',
03        props: {
04            onClick: () => alert('hello')
05        },
06        children: 'click me'
07    }
```

Here is a brief explanation for the above code first.

- Tag is used to describe the tag name, so tag: 'div' describes a < div > tag.
- Props is an object that describes the properties, events, etc. of the < div > tag. As you can see, we want to bind a click event to the div.
- Children is used to describe the sub-node of the tag. In the above code, children is a string value, meaning that the div tag has a text sub-node: < div > click me </ div >.

In fact, you can design the structure of the virtual DOM yourself; for example, you can use tagName instead of tag, because it is a JavaScript object itself and has no special meaning.

Next, we need to write a renderer that renders the above virtual DOM as a real DOM:

```
01    function renderer(vnode, container) {
02        //create DOM element with vnode.tag as tag name
03        const el = document.createElement(vnode.tag)
04        //traverse vnode.props and add attributes and events to DOM
```

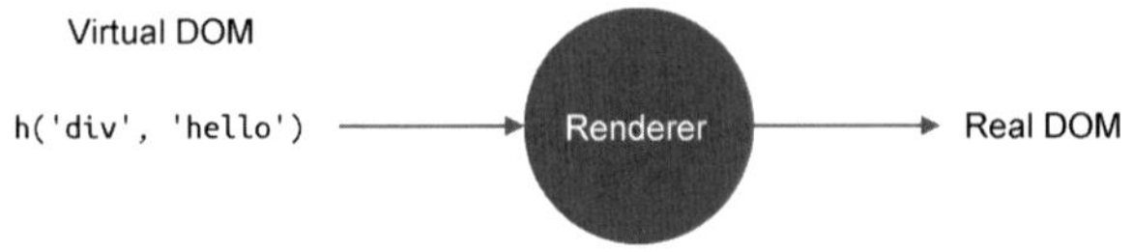

Fig. 3.1 The role of the renderer

Virtual DOM

h('div', 'hello') ⟶ Renderer ⟶ Real DOM

```
elements
05              for (const key in vnode.props) {
06                  if (/^on/.test(key)) {
07                      //if the key starts with on, it means it is an event
08                      el.addEventListener(
09                      key.substr(2).toLowerCase(), // event name onClick
---> click
10                          vnode.props[key] //event handler
11                      )
12                  }
13              }
14
15          //dealing with children
16          if  (typeof   vnode.children === 'string') {
17              // if children is a string, it is the text sub-node of the
element
18              el.appendChild(document.createTextNode(vnode.children))
19          } else if (Array.isArray(vnode.children)) {
20              //recursively call the renderer function to render the
sub-node,  using the current element el as the mount point
21              vnode.children.forEach(child => renderer(child, el))
22          }
23
24          //add element to mount point
25          container.appendChild(el)
26      }
```

The renderer function here receives the following two arguments.

- Vnode: Virtual DOM object.
- Container: A real DOM element that acts as a mount point to which the renderer will render the virtual DOM.

Next, we can call the renderer function:

```
01 renderer (vnode, document.body) //body as the mount point.
```

Running this code in the browser will render the text "click me." Clicking on the text will pop up alert ("hello").

Now let's go back and analyze the implementation idea of the renderer, which is generally divided into three steps.

- Create elements: Use vnode.tag as the tag name to create a DOM element.
- Add attributes and events to the element: Traverse the vnode.props object. If the key starts with the on character, it means that it is an event. Intercept the character on and then call the toLowerCase function to lowercase the event name, and finally get a legal event name, such as onClick becoming click, and eventually call the addEventListener binding event handler.
- Handling children: If children is an array, call renderer recursively to continue rendering. Note that at this time we want to use the element we just created as the mount point (parent node); if children are strings, use the createTextNode function to create a text node, and add it to the newly created element.

Now, does it feel that the renderer is not as mysterious as imagined? Don't forget that all we are doing now is creating nodes, and the essence of the renderer is in the stage of updating nodes. Suppose we make some small changes to vnode:

```
01    const vnode = {
02        tag: 'div',
03          props: {
04              onClick: () => alert('hello')
05          },
06            children: 'click again' // change from click me to click again
07        }
```

For the renderer, it needs to accurately find the change point of the vnode object and only update the changed content. As far as the above example is concerned, the renderer should only update the text content of the element, without going through the complete process of creating the element again. These processes will be explained later. But in any case, I hope everyone understands that the working principle of the renderer is actually very simple—some familiar DOM operation APIs are used to complete the rendering work.

3.3   Essence of Components

So far, we have had a preliminary understanding of the virtual DOM and renderer, and known that the virtual DOM is actually an ordinary JavaScript object used to describe the real DOM. The renderer will render this object as a real DOM element. So what are components? What is the relationship between components and virtual DOM? How does the renderer render components? Now, let's discuss these issues.

In fact, the virtual DOM can describe components in addition to the real DOM. For example, use {tag: 'div'} to describe the < div > tag, but the component is not a real DOM element, so how to use the virtual DOM to describe it? To understand this problem, you need to first figure out what the essence of the component is. In one sentence: a component is a package of a set of DOM elements, and this set of DOM elements is the content to be rendered by the component, so we can define a function to represent the component, and the return value of the function represents the content to be rendered by the component:

```
01    const MyComponent = function () {
02        return {
03            tag: 'div',
04            props: {
05                onClick: () => alert('hello')
06            },
07            children: 'click me'
```

```
08                    }
09              }
```

As you can see, the return value of the component is also the virtual DOM, which represents the content to be rendered by the component. Once we understand the nature of the component, we can define a virtual DOM to describe the component. Quite simply, we can let the tag attribute in the virtual DOM object store the component function:

```
01      const vnode = {
02            tag:  MyComponent
03      }
```

Just like tag: 'div' is used to describe the $<div>$ tag, tag: MyComponent is used to describe the component, but the tag attribute at this time is not the tag name, but the component function. In order to be able to render components, renderer support is required. Modify the renderer function mentioned earlier as follows:

```
01      function renderer(vnode, container) {
02            if  (typeof   vnode.tag === 'string') {
03                  //Explain that vnode describes the tag element
04                  mountElement(vnode, container)
05            } else if (typeof vnode.tag === 'function') {
06                  //Explain that vnode describes components
07                mountComponent(vnode, container)
08            }
09      }
```

If the type of vnode.tag is string, it means that it describes an ordinary label element, and the mountElement function is called to complete the rendering; if the type of vnode.tag is a function, it means that it describes a component, and the mountComponent function is called to complete the rendering. The mountElement function is the same as the content of the renderer function above:

```
01      function mountElement(vnode, container) {
02            //Create DOM element with vnode.tag as tag name
03            const el = document.createElement(vnode.tag)
04            //Traverse vnode.props and add attributes and events to DOM
elements
05            for (const key in vnode.props) {
06                  if  (/^on/.test(key)) {
07                        //If the key starts with string on, it means it is an
event
08                        el. addEventListener(
09                              key.substr(2).toLowerCase(), // event name
onClick --- > click
10                              vnode.props[key] //event handler
11                        )
12                  }
```

```
13        }
14
15        //Dealing with children
16        if   (typeof   vnode.children === 'string') {
17        //If children is a string, it means it is the text sub-node of
the element
18              el. appendChild(document.createTextNode(vnode.
children))
19        } else if (Array.isArray(vnode.children)) {
20            //Recursively call the renderer function to render the
sub-node, using the current element el as the mount point
21            vnode.children.forEach(child => renderer(child, el))
22        }
23
24        //Add element to mount point
25        container.appendChild(el)
26    }
```

Let's see how the mountComponent function is implemented:

```
01    function mountComponent(vnode, container) {
02          //Call the component function to get the content to be
rendered by the component (virtual DOM)
03          const subtree = vnode.tag()
04          //Recursively call renderer to render subtree
05          renderer(subtree, container)
06    }
```

As you can see, it is very simple. First call the vnode.tag function, we know that it is actually the component function itself, and its return value is the virtual DOM, that is, the content to be rendered by the component, which we call subtree here. Since subtree is also a virtual DOM, you can directly call the renderer function to complete the rendering.

Here I hope you can draw inferences from others. For example, does a component have to be a function? Of course not, we can use a JavaScript object to express the component, for example:

```
01    //MyComponent is an object
02    const MyComponent = {
03        render() {
04            return
05              tag: 'div',
06              props: {
07                    onClick:    () => alert('hello')
08              },
09              children: 'click me'
10            }
11        }
12    }
```

Here we use an object to represent the component. This object has a function called *render*, and its return value represents the content to be rendered by the component. In order to complete the rendering of the component, we need to modify the renderer *renderer* and the mountComponent function.

First, modify the judgment conditions of the renderer:

```
01      function renderer(vnode, container) {
02          if (typeof  vnode.tag === 'string') {
03              mountElement(vnode, container)
04          } else if (typeof vnode.tag === 'object ') { // If it is an
object, it means that vnode describes a component
05              mountComponent(vnode, container)
06          }
07      }
```

Now we use objects instead of functions to express components, so change typeof vnode.tag === 'function' to typeof vnode.tag === 'object'.

Next, modify the mountComponent function:

```
01    function mountComponent(vnode, container) {
02        //vnode.tag is a component object, call its render function to
get the content to be rendered by the component (virtual DOM)
03        const subtree = vnode.tag.render()
04        //Recursively call renderer to render subtree
05        renderer(subtree, container)
06    }
```

In the above code, vnode.tag is the object that expresses the component, and the render function of the object is called to get the content to be rendered by the component, which is the virtual DOM.

It can be found that we can meet the needs of expressing components with objects with only minor modifications. Then you can continue to use your imagination to see if you can create other ways of expressing components. In fact, stateful components in Vue.js are expressed using object structures.

3.4   Working Principle of Templates

Whether it is handwriting the virtual DOM (rendering function) or using templates, it is a declarative way to describe the UI, and Vue.js supports both ways of describing the UI. Above we explained how the virtual DOM is rendered into the real DOM, so how does the template work? This brings us to another important part of the Vue.js framework: The Compiler.

A compiler, like a renderer, is just a program, but their job content is different. The role of the compiler is actually to compile the template into a rendering function, such as the following template:

```
01      <div @click="handler">
02            click me
03      </div>
```

To the compiler, a template is just a plain string, which parses the string and generates a render function that does the same thing:

```
01      render() {
02            return  h('div', { onClick: handler }, 'click me')
03      }
```

Take the familiar .vue file as an example, a .vue file is a component, as follows:

```
01      <template>
02          <div   @click="handler">
03              click me
04          </div>
05      </template>
06
07      <script>
08      export default {
09            data() {/* ... */},
10            methods: {
11                  handler:   ()  =>  {/*  ...  */}
12            }
13      }
14      </script>
```

The content in the <template> tag is the template content. The compiler will compile the template content into a render function and add it to the component object of the < script > tag block, so the final code to run in the browser is as follows:

```
01      export default  {
02          data()  {/*  ...  */},
03          methods: {
04                handler :  ()  =>  {/*  ...  */}
05          },
06          render() {
07                return h('div', {  onClick:  handler },  'click me')
08          }
09      }
```

Therefore, whether using a template or a direct handwritten rendering function, for a component, the content it wants to render is ultimately generated through the rendering function, and then the renderer renders the virtual DOM returned by the rendering function as the real DOM, which is the working principle of the template, also the process of Vue.js rendering the page.

The compiler is a big topic, we will focus on explaining later. Here we only need to be clear about the role and role of the compiler.

3.5   Vue.js Is an Organic Whole Composed of Various Modules

As mentioned above, the implementation of the component depends on the renderer; the compilation of the template depends on the compiler, and the code generated after compilation is determined according to the design of the renderer and the virtual DOM, so the various modules of the Vue.js are related to each other and restrict each other, forming an organic whole together. Therefore, when we learn the principles of Vue.js, we should combine the various modules to see, in order to understand what is going on.

Here we take the compiler and renderer, two very critical modules, as an example to see how they work together and achieve performance improvements.

Suppose we have the following template:

```
01 <div id="foo" :class="cls"></div>
```

From the above introduction, we know that the compiler will compile this code into a render function:

```
01      render()   {
02          //In order to make the effect more intuitive, the h function
is not used here, but the virtual DOM object is directly used
03          //The following code is equivalent to:
04          // return h('div', { id: 'foo', class: cls })
05          return {
06              tag: 'div',
07              props: {
08                  id:   'foo',
09                  class:   cls
10              }
11          }
12      }
```

As you can see, in this code, cls is a variable, and it may change. We know that one of the roles of the renderer is to find and only update the changed content, so when the value of the variable cls changes, the renderer will find the change point on its own. For the renderer, this "finding" process takes some effort. So from the compiler's point of view, can it know what will change? If the compiler has the ability to analyze dynamic content, extract this information at the compilation stage, and then directly hand it over to the renderer, wouldn't the renderer need to spend a lot of effort to find the change point? This is a good idea and can be implemented.

Vue.js template is characteristic, take the above template as an example, we can see at a glance that id = "foo" will never change, and: class = "cls" is a v-bind binding, which is subject to change. So the compiler can identify which are static properties and which are dynamic properties and can attach this information when generating code:

```
01     render()  {
02         return  {
03             tag: 'div',
04             props: {
05                 id: 'foo',
06                 class: cls
07             },
08             patchFlags: 1//Suppose the number 1 means the class is
dynamic
09             }
10         }
```

As shown in the code above, there is an additional patchFlags attribute in the virtual DOM object generated. We assume that the number 1 represents "class is dynamic," so that when the renderer sees this flag, it knows: "Oh, it turns out that only the class attribute will change." For the renderer, it is equivalent to eliminating the workload of finding the change point, and the performance is naturally improved.

Through this example, we learned that there is information exchange between the compiler and the renderer, and they cooperate with each other to further improve performance. The medium of communication between them is the virtual DOM object. Later in the study, we will see that a virtual DOM object will contain a variety of data fields, each field representing a certain meaning.

3.6   Summary

In this chapter, we first introduced the concept of declarative description of UI. We know that Vue.js is a declarative framework. The advantage of declarative is that it directly describes the result, and the user does not need to pay attention to the process. Vue.js uses templates to describe UI, but it also supports the use of virtual DOM to describe UI. Virtual DOM is more flexible than template, but template is more intuitive than virtual DOM.

Then we explained the implementation of the most basic renderer. The role of the renderer is to render virtual DOM objects into real DOM elements. It works by recursively traversing the virtual DOM object and calling the native DOM API to complete the creation of the real DOM. The essence of the renderer lies in the subsequent updates. It will find the change point through the Diff algorithm, and only update the content that needs to be updated. Later we will explain the relevant knowledge of the renderer.

Next, we discussed the essence of components. A component is actually an encapsulation of a set of virtual DOM elements. It can be a function that returns a virtual DOM or an object, but there must be a function under this object to produce the virtual DOM that the component wants to render. When the renderer renders the component, it will first obtain the content to be rendered by the component, that is, execute the rendering function of the component and get its return value, which we call subtree, and finally call the renderer recursively to render the subtree.

Vue.js templates will be compiled into rendering functions by a program called a compiler. Later, we will focus on the knowledge of the compiler. Finally, the compiler and the renderer are the core components of the Vue.js. They together form an organic whole, and different modules cooperate with each other to further improve the performance of the framework.

Part II
Response System

Chapter 4
The Role and Implementation of Response System

Though the response system was not mentioned in the previous article, it is also an important part of the Vue.js, so we will spend a lot of time introducing it now. In this chapter, we will first discuss what reactive data and side effect functions are, and then try to implement a relatively complete response system. In the process, we will encounter various problems, such as how to avoid infinite recursion? Why are nested side effect functions needed? What are the effects between two side effect functions? There are also many other details to consider. Next, we will discuss in detail what is related to reactive data. We know that Vue.js 3 uses Proxy to implement reactive data, which involves knowledge at the language specification level. This part includes how to implement proxies for data objects according to language specifications, and some important details. Now, we will start from understanding reactive data and side effect functions, and get to know the design and implementation of responsive systems step by step.

4.1 Responsive Data and Side Effect Functions

Side effect functions are functions that produce side effects, as shown in the following code:

```
01    function effect () {
02        document.body.innerText = 'hello vue3'
03    }
```

When the effect function executes, it sets the text content of the *body*, but any function other than the effect function can read or set the text content of the *body*. That is to say, the execution of the effect function will directly or indirectly affect the execution of other functions. Basing on this fact, we say that the effect function has a

© The Author(s), under exclusive license to Springer Nature Singapore Pte Ltd. 2023
H. Yang, *Vue. JS Framework*, https://doi.org/10.1007/978-981-99-4947-2_4

side effect. Side effects can easily occur. For example, a function modifies a global variable, which is actually a side effect, as shown in the following code:

```
01    //Global Variables
02    let val = 1
03
04    function effect () {
05         val = 2 // Modify the global variable, resulting in side
effects
06    }
```

After explaining what a side effect function is, let's talk about what reactive data is. Suppose you read the properties of an object in a side effect function:

```
01    const obj  =  { text:  'hello world'  }
02      function effect () {
03      //  The execution of the effect function will read obj.text
04          document.body.innerText = obj.text
05      }
```

As shown in the code above, the side effect function will set the innerText property of the *body* element with a value of obj.text. When the value of the obj.text changes, we hope that the side effect function effect will re-execute:

```
01 obj.text = 'hello vue3'  // Modify the value of obj. text, and hope
that the side effect function will be re-executed
```

This code modifies the value obj.text field. We hope that when the value changes, the side effect function will be automatically re-executed. If this goal can be achieved, then *obj* is reactive data. But obviously, from the above code, we can't do this yet, because *obj* is a normal object, and when we modify its value, there will be no other reaction other than the value itself changing. In the next section, we will discuss how to make data reactive.

4.2   Basic Implementation of Responsive Data

Now think about how can *obj* become reactive data? By observing, we can find two clues:

- When the side effect function effect is executed, it will trigger the read operation of the field obj.text
- When the value of the obj.text is modified, the setting operation of the field obj. text is triggered

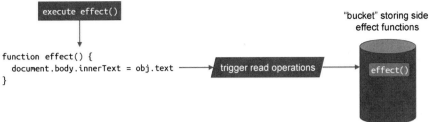

```
function effect() {
    document.body.innerText = obj.text
}
```

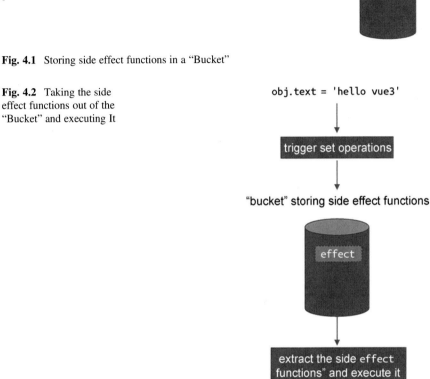

Fig. 4.1 Storing side effect functions in a "Bucket"

Fig. 4.2 Taking the side effect functions out of the "Bucket" and executing It

If we can intercept the read and set operations of an object, things become easier, and when reading fields obj.text, we can store the side effect function effect in a "bucket," as shown in Fig. 4.1.

Next, when the obj.text is set, remove the side effect function from the "bucket" and execute it, as shown in Fig. 4.2.

Now the crux of the matter becomes how do we intercept the reading and setting of an object's properties. Before ES2015, this task could only be done through Object.defineProperty functions, which is the way Vue.js 2 used. In ES2015 +, we can use the proxy object Proxy to achieve this, which is also the way Vue.js 3 used.

Now, we are going to use Proxy to carry out the above task according to the idea mentioned above:

```
01      //  bucket to store side effect functions
02      const bucket = new Set ()
03
04      //  original data source
05      const data = { text:   'hello world'  }
06      //  proxy to original data source
07      const obj = new Proxy (data,   {
08              // intercept read operations
09              get (target, key) {
10              //add the side effect function effect to the bucket where
the side effect function is stored
11                      bucket.add (effect)
12                      //return property value
13                      return target [key]
14              } ,
15              // intercept setup operation
16              set (target, key, newVal) {
17                      // set property value
18                      target [key] = newVal
19                      // take the side effect function out of the bucket and
execute it
20                      bucket.forEach (fn = > fn ())
21                      // return true to indicate that the setting operation was
successful
22                      return true
23              }
24      })
```

First, we created a *bucket* for storing side effect functions, which is of type Set.
Then define the original data source data; obj is the proxy object of the original data
source; and we set the *get* and *set* interceptor functions, respectively, to intercept
read and set operations. When reading the property, add the side effect function to
the bucket, that is, bucket.add (effect), and then return the property value; when
setting the property value, first update the original data source, and then take the side
effect function out of the bucket and execute it again, so that the reactive data is
implemented. You can test it with the following code:

```
01      //  side effect functions
02      function effect ()   {
03          document. body. innerText   =   obj.text
04      }
05      //  execute side effect function to trigger read
06      effect ()
07      //  modify responsive data after 1 second
08      setTimeout (() => {
09              obj.text = 'hello vue3'
10          }, 1000)
```

Running the above code in a browser will get the desired result.

However, there are still many defects in the current implementation. For example, we directly obtain side effect functions by name (effect), which is very inflexible in hardcoding. The name of the side effect function can be taken arbitrarily. We can name the side effect function myEffect, or even an anonymous function, so we need to find a way to remove this hardcoding mechanism. The next section will explain this in detail. Here you only need to get a general picture of implementation and working principles of reactive data.

4.3   Designing a Perfect Response System

In the previous section, we saw how to implement reactive data. But in fact, in the process, we have implemented a micro-responsive system. The reason why we say "micro" is because it is not perfect. In this section, we will try to construct a more complete response system.

From the example in the previous section, it is not difficult to see that the workflow of a response system is as follows:

- Collect side effect functions into "buckets" when a read operation occurs
- When a setup operation occurs, remove the side effect function from the "bucket" and execute it

It looks simple, but there are quite a few details to deal with. For example, in the implementation in the previous section, we hardcoding the name of the side effect function (effect), so that once the name of the side effect function is not called *effect*, then this code will not work correctly. What we want is that even if the side effect function is an anonymous function, it can be properly collected into the "bucket." In order to achieve this, we need to provide a mechanism for registering side effect functions, as shown in the following code:

```
01      //Use a global variable to store the registered side effect
function
02      let activeEffect
03      //The effect function is used to register side effect functions
04      function effect (fn) {
05      //When calling effect to register a side effect function, assign
the side effect function fn to activeEffect
06        activeEffect = fn
07        //Execute side effect function
08        fn ()
09      }
```

First, a global variable activeEffect is defined, the initial value is undefined, and its function is to store the registered side effect function. Then the *effect* function is redefined, it becomes a function used to register side effect functions, and the effect function takes a parameter fn, which is the side effect function to be registered. We can use the effect function as follows:

```
01     effect (
02         //An anonymous side effect function
03         ( )   =>  {
04             document. body. innerText   =   obj. text
05         }
06     )
```

As you can see, we use an anonymous side effect function as the parameter of the *effect* function. When the *effect* function executes, the anonymous side effect function fn is first assigned to the global variable activeEffect. Then execute the registered anonymous side effect function fn, which will trigger the read operation of the reactive data obj.text, which in turn triggers the *get* interception function of the proxy object Proxy:

```
01       const obj = new Proxy (data, {
02         get (target, key) {
03             //collect side effect functions stored in activeEffect
into "bucket"
04             if  (activeEffect ) { // newly added
05                 bucket. add (activeEffect)   //  newly added
06             }  //  newly added
07             return target [key]
08         },
09         set (target, key, newVal) {
10             target [key]   =   newVal
11             bucket . forEach (fn = > fn ())
12             return true
13         }
14     })
```

As shown in the code above, since the side effect function has been stored in the activeEffect, the activeEffect should be collected in the "bucket" inside the *get* interceptor function, so that the response system does not depend on the name of the side effect function.

But if we test this system a little more, for example, when setting a non-existing property on the reactive data obj:

```
01     effect (
02         //Anonymous side effect function
03         ()   =>  {
04             console.log ('effect run')   //  will print twice
05             document. body. innerText   =   obj.text
06         }
07     )
08
09     setTimeout (()   =>   {
```

```
10          //The value of the notExist property is not read in the side
effect function
11              obj. notExist = 'hello vue3'
12      }, 1000)
```

As can be seen, the anonymous side effect function internally reads the value of the field obj.text, so a response connection is established between the anonymous side effect function and the field obj.text. Next, we start a timer and add a new notExist property to the object obj 1 s later. We know that the value of the obj. notExist property is not read in the anonymous side effect function, so in theory, the field obj.notExist does not establish a response connection with the side effect; hence the execution of the statement in the timer should not trigger the re-execution of the anonymous side effect function. But if we execute the above code, we will find that after the timer expires, the anonymous side effect function is re-executed, which is incorrect. To solve this problem, we need to redesign the data structure of the "bucket."

In the example in the previous section, we used a Set data structure as the "bucket" for storing side effect functions. The root cause of this problem is that we *did not establish an explicit connection between the side effect function and the target field being operated on*. For example, when reading a property, no matter which property is read, it is actually the same, and the side effect function will be collected into the "bucket"; when setting a property, no matter which property is set, the side effect function in the "bucket" will also be taken out and executed. There is no clear connection between the side effect function and the field being operated on. The solution is very simple: just need to establish a connection between the side effect function and the field being operated on, which requires us to redesign the data structure of the "bucket," instead of simply using a Set type of data as the "bucket."

So what kind of data structure should be designed? Before answering this question, we need to carefully observe the following code:

```
01      effect (function effectFn ( )   {
02          document. body. innerText  =  obj.text
03      })
```

There are three roles in this code:

- The proxy object obj being manipulated (read)
- The field name text to be manipulated (read)
- The side effect function effectFn registered with the effect function

If *target* is used to represent the original object represented by a proxy object, *key* is used to represent the field name to be operated on, and effectFn is used to represent the registered side effect function, then the following relationship can be established for these three roles:

```
01      target
02            └── key
03                  └── effectFn
```

This is a tree structure. The following are a few examples to illustrate it.

If two side effect functions read the property value of the same object at the same time:

```
01      effect (function effectFn1 ( )   {
02          obj.text
03      })
04      effect (function effectFn2 ( )   {
05          obj.text
06      })
```

Then the relationship is as follows:

```
01      target
02            └── text
03                    └── effectFn1
04                    └── effectFn2
```

If two different properties of the same object are read in a side effect function:

```
01      effect (function effectFn ( )   {
02        obj.text1
03        obj.text2
04      })
```

Then the relationship is as follows:

```
01      target
02          └── text 1
03                  └── effectFn
04          └── text 2
05                  └── effectFn
```

If you read different properties of two different objects in different side effect functions:

```
01      effect(function effectFn1( )   {
02          obj1.text1
03      })
04      effect(function effectFn2( )   {
05          obj2.text2
06      })
```

Then the relationship is as follows:

```
01        target1
02            └── text1
03                    └── effectFn1
04        target2
05            └── text2
06                    └── effectFn2
```

In short, this is actually a tree data structure. Once this connection is established, the problem mentioned above can be solved. Taking the above example as an example, if we set the value of obj2.text 2, it will only cause the effectFn2 function to be re-executed, not the effectFn1 function.

Next, we try to implement this new "bucket" in code. First, we need to use WeakMap instead of Set as the data structure of the bucket:

```
01    // bucket to store side effect functions
02    const bucket  =  new WeakMap ( )
```

Then modify the get/set interceptor code:

```
01        const  obj  =  new Proxy (data, {
02            // intercept read operation
03            get (target, key) {
04                // no activeEffect, return directly
05                if  (! activeEffect) return target [key]
06            // get depsMap from "bucket" according to target; it is
also a Map type: key -- > effects
07                let depsMap = bucket.get (target)
08                // if depsMap does not exist, create a new Map and
associate it with target
09                if  (! depsMap)  {
10                    bucket.set (target, (depsMap = new Map ()))
11                }
12            // get deps from depsMap according to key; it is a Set
type,
13                // stores all side effects associated with the
current key: effects
14                let deps = depsMap.get (key)
15                // if deps does not exist, also create a new Set and
associate it with key
16                if  (! deps)  {
17                    depsMap.set (key, (deps = new Set ()))
18                }
19            // finally add the currently active side effect function
to the "bucket"
20                deps. add ( activeEffect )
21
22                // return property value
23                return target [key]
24            } ,
25            // intercept setup operation
26            set (target, key, newVal)  {
```

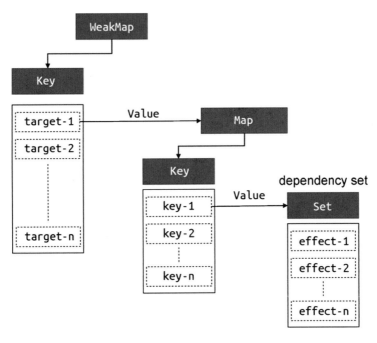

Fig. 4.3 The relationship between weakmap, map, and set

```
27                      //  set property value
28                      target [key] = newVal
29                  //get depsMap from bucket according to target; it is key
-- > effects
30                      const depsMap = bucket.get (target)
31                       if  (! depsMap) return
32                  //get all side effects function effects according to key
33                      const effects = depsMap.get (key)
34                      //execute side effect function
35                      effects & & effects.forEach (fn = > fn ())
36              }
37      })
```

From this code, we can see the way to build the data structure, we use WeakMap, Map, and Set, respectively:

- WeakMap consists of target—> Map;
- Map consists of key—> Set.

Here the key of WeakMap is the original object target, the value of WeakMap is a Map instance, the key of Map is the key of the original object target, and the value of Map is a Set composed of side effect functions. Their relationship is shown in Fig. 4.3.

For the convenience of description, we call the set of side effects functions stored in the Set data structure in Fig. 4.3 as the dependency set of *key*.

Having understood the relationship between them, we need to explain why we use WeakMap here, which actually involves the difference between WeakMap and Map. We will use a piece of code to explain:

```
01    const  map  =  new  Map ( );
02    const  weakmap = new  WeakMap ( );
03
04    (function ( ) {
05            const  foo = {foo: 1};
06            const  bar = {bar: 2};
07
08            map.set (foo, 1);
09            weakmap.set (bar, 2);
10    }) ( )
```

First, we define the map and weakmap constants, corresponding to instances of Map and WeakMap, respectively. Then we define an immediately executing function expression (IIFE). Inside the function expression, we define two objects: *foo* and *bar*, which are used as the keys of map and weakmap, respectively. After the function expression is executed, it is still referenced as the key of the map to the object *foo*, so the garbage collector will not remove it from memory, we can still print object *foo* out by map.keys. However, for object *bar*, since WeakMap's key is a weak reference, it does not affect the work of the garbage collector, so once the expression is executed, the garbage collector will remove the object bar from memory, and we cannot get the key value of weakmap, and the object bar cannot be obtained through weakmap.

Simply put, WeakMap is a weak reference to the key and does not affect the work of the garbage collector. According to this feature, once the key 4.3 is collected by the garbage collector, the corresponding keys and values cannot be accessed. So WeakMap is often used to store information that is only valuable when the object referenced by the key exists (not collected). For example, in the above scenario, if the target object has no reference, it means that the user side no longer needs it. At this time, the garbage collector will complete the collection task. But if you use Map instead of WeakMap, then even if the code on the user side has no reference to the target, the target will not be collected, which may eventually lead to memory overflow.

Finally, we do some encapsulation of the code above. In the current implementation, when reading the property value, we directly write this part of the logic to collect the side effect functions into the "bucket" in the get interceptor function, but a better approach is to encapsulate this part of the logic separately into a *track* function. The name of the function is *track* to express the meaning of tracking. Similarly, we can encapsulate the logic that triggers the re-execution of the side effect function into the trigger function:

```
01          const obj = new Proxy (data, {
02              //  intercept read operation
03              get (target, key)  {
04                  //  add the side effect function activeEffect to the
bucket where the side effect functions are stored
05                      track (target, key)
06                          //return property value
07                          return target [key]
08                  } ,
09              //  intercept setup operation
10              set (target,  key,  newVal)  {
11                  //  set property value
12                  target [key] = newVal
13                  //  take the side effect function out of the bucket and
execute it
14                      trigger (target,   key)
15                  }
16          })
17
18              //  call the track function inside the get interception
function to track changes
19              function track (target, key) {
20                  //  no activeEffect, return directly
21                  if   (! activeEffect) return
22                  let depsMap = bucket.get (target)
23                    if   (! depsMap) {
24                      bucket . set (target,   ( depsMap  =  new Map ()))
25                    }
26                  let deps = depsMap.get (key)
27                  if  (! deps) {
28                      depsMap.set (key, (deps = new Set ()))
29                    }
30                  deps . add (activeEffect)
31              }
32              //  call the trigger function inside the set interception
function to trigger the change
33              function trigger (target, key) {
34                  const depsMap = bucket.get (target)
35                  if  ( ! depsMap) return
36                  const effects = depsMap.get (key)
37                  effects & & effects.forEach (fn = > fn ())
38              }
```

As shown in the above code, wrapping the logic into the track and trigger functions, respectively, gives us great flexibility.

4.4 Branch Switching and Cleanup

First, we need to define the branch switch explicitly, as shown in the following code:

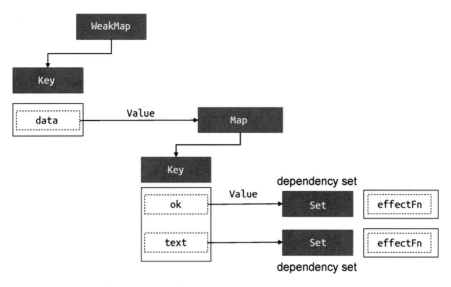

Fig. 4.4 Connection between side effect functions and reactive

```
01        const data = { ok:    true,    text:    'hello world'  }
02        const obj   =   new Proxy(data,   {  /*  ...  */  })
03
04        effect ( function effectFn ( )   {
05           document. body. innerText  =  obj.ok ?  obj. text  :  'not'
06        } )
```

There is a ternary expression inside the effectFn function that executes different branches of code depending on the value obj.ok field. When the value obj.ok field changes, the branch of code execution will change accordingly, which is called a branch switch.

Branch switching may have legacy side effects. Take the above code as an example, the initial value of the field obj.ok is true, and the value obj.text the field will be read at this time, so when the effectFn function executes, the read operation of the two properties of the field obj.ok and the field obj.text will be triggered. At this time, the connection between the side effect function effectFn and the reactive data is as follows:

```
01        data
02              └── ok
03                     └── effectFn
04              └── text
05                     └── effectFn
```

Figure 4.4 gives a more detailed description.

It can be seen that the side effect function effectFn is collected by the dependency sets corresponding to the field data.ok and field data.text, respectively. When the

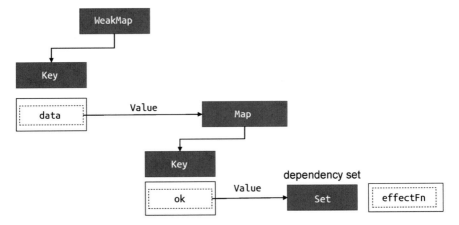

Fig. 4.5 The ideal connection between side effect functions and reactive data

value of the field obj.ok is modified to false and the side effect function is triggered to be re-executed, since the field obj.text will not be read at this time, it will only trigger the read operation of the field obj.ok, so ideally the side effect function effectFn should not be collected by dependency set corresponding to the field obj.text, as shown in Fig. 4.5.

But according to the previous implementation, we cannot do this yet. That is, when we change the value obj.ok field to false and trigger the side effect function to re-execute, the entire dependency remains as described in Fig. 4.4, and the legacy side effect function is generated.

Legacy side effect functions can cause unnecessary updates, as in the following code:

```
01    const data  =  { ok: true, text: 'hello world' }
02    const obj  =  new Proxy(data, { /* ... */ })
03
04    effect( function effectFn() {
05        document.body.innerText = obj.ok ? obj.text : 'not'
06    })
```

The initial value of obj.ok is true when we change it to false:

```
01 obj.ok = false
```

This triggers an update, that is, the side effect function is re-executed. But since obj.ok value is false at this point, the value obj.text the field is no longer read. In other words, no matter how the value obj.text the field changes, the value of the document.body.innerText is always the string "not." So the best result is that no matter how obj.text value changes, there is no need to re-execute the side effect function. But this is not the case, if we try to modify obj.text value again:

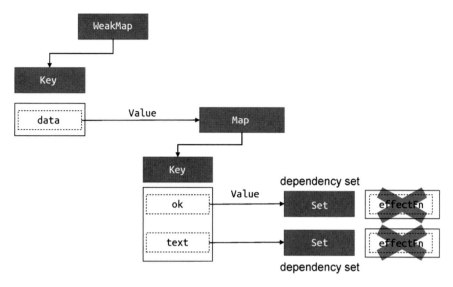

Fig. 4.6 Disconnecting the side effect function from the reactive data

```
01   obj.text = 'hello vue3'
```

This still causes the side effect function to re-execute, even if document.body. innerText value does not need to change.

The solution to this problem is simple: each time a side effect function executes, we can first remove it from all dependent sets associated with it, as shown in Fig. 4.6.

When the side effect function is executed, the connection is re-established, but the legacy side effect function will not be included in the new connection, as described in Fig. 4.5. So, if we can remove the side effect function from the associated set of dependencies before each execution, then the problem is solved.

To remove a side effect function from all dependent sets associated with it, we need to know exactly which dependent sets contain it, so we need to redesign the side effect function, as shown in the following code. Inside effect we define a new effectFn function and add effectFn.deps property to it, which is an array to store all dependent sets containing the current side effect function:

```
01      // use a global variable to store the registered side effect
function
02      let activeEffect
03      function effect (fn) {
04          const effectFn = () => {
05              // when effectFn executes, set it to the currently
active side effect function
06              activeEffect = effectFn
07              fn ()
08          }
09      // activeEffect.deps is used to store all dependencies
associated with this side effect function
```

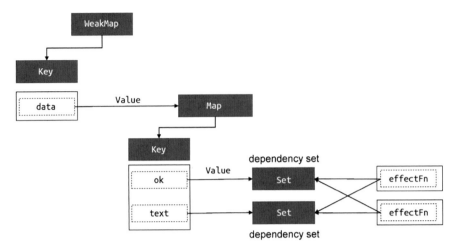

Fig. 4.7 Collection of dependency sets

```
10        effectFn.deps = []
11        //  execute side effect function
12        effectFn ()
13    }
```

So how is the collection of dependencies in effectFn.deps array collected? In fact, in the track function:

```
01        function track (target, key) {
02            //  no activeEffect, return directly
03            if  ( ! activeEffect) return
04            let  depsMap = bucket.get (target)
05            if  ( ! depsMap)  {
06                bucket.set (target, (depsMap  =  new Map ()))
07            }
08            let  deps = depsMap.get (key)
09            if  ( ! deps)  {
10                depsMap.set (key, (deps =  new  Set ()))
11            }
12            //  add the currently active side effect function to the
dependency set deps
13            deps.add (activeEffect)
14            //  deps is a collection of dependencies associated with
the current side effect function
15            //  add it to activeEffect.deps array
16            activeEffect . deps.push (deps)  //  new
17        }
```

As shown in the above code, in the track function we add the currently executed side effect function activeEffect to the dependency set deps, which means that *deps* is a dependency set related to the current side effect function, so we also add it to the activeEffect.*deps* array. This completes the collection of dependency sets. Figure 4.7 depicts the relationship established in this step.

With this connection, we can use the effectFn.Deps to get all associated dependency sets each time the side effect function is executed, and then removes side effects from the dependency sets:

```
01      //  use a global variable to store the registered side effect
function
02      let activeEffect
03      function effect (fn) {
04          const effectFn = () => {
05          //  call the cleanup function to complete the cleanup work
06              cleanup (effectFn)   //  new
07              activeEffect = effectFn
08              fn ( )
09          }
10      effectFn.deps = []
11      effectFn ()
12      }
```

The following is the implementation of the cleanup function:

```
01      function cleanup (effectFn) {
02          //  traverse effectFn.deps array
03          for   ( let i = 0; i < effectFn.deps.length; i++) {
04              //  deps is a collection of dependencies
05              const deps = effectFn.deps [i]
06              //  remove effectFn from the dependency collection
07              deps. delete (effectFn) From
08          }
09          //  finally effectFn.deps array needs to be reset
10          effectFn.deps.length = 0
11      }
```

The cleanup function takes a side effect function as a parameter, iterates over the effectFn.deps array of side effect functions, each item of which is a dependency set, then removes the side effect function from the dependency set, and finally resets effectFn.deps array.

Till now, our response system can avoid the legacy of side effect functions. But if you try to run the code, you will find that the current implementation will cause infinite loop execution. The problem is in the trigger function:

```
01      function trigger (target, key) {
02          const depsMap = bucket.get (target)
03          if   ( ! depsMap) return
04          const effects  =  depsMap.get (key)
05          effects  &&  effects . forEach (fn => fn ( ) )   //  the
problem lies in this code
06      }
```

Inside the trigger function, we traverse the *effects* collection, which is a *Set* collection that stores side effect functions. When the side effect function executes, it will call *cleanup* to clear it, which is actually to remove the currently executed side effect function from the effects collection, but the execution of the side effect function will cause it to be re-collected into the collection, and the traversal of the effects collection is still in progress. This behavior can be expressed in the following short code:

```
01      const set = new Set ([1])
02
03      set.forEach (item = > {
04          set.delete (1)
05          set.add (1)
06          console.log ('Traversing')
07      })
```

In the above code, we created a collection *set* with an element number 1 in it, and then we called forEach to iterate over the collection. During the traversal process, first call delete (1) to delete the number 1, then call add (1) to add the number 1 back, and finally print "traversing." If we execute this code in a browser, we will find that it will execute indefinitely.

This is clearly stated in the language specification: when calling forEach to traverse the Set collection, if a value has already been accessed, but the value is deleted and re-added to the collection, then the value will be re-accessed if the forEach traversal does not end at this time. Therefore, the above code will execute indefinitely. The solution is simple, we can construct another *Set* set and traverse it:

```
01      const  set  =  new  Set ([1])
02
03      const  newSet  =  new  Set (set)
04      newSet.forEach (item = > {
05          set.delete (1)
06          set.add (1)
07          console.log ('traversing')
08      })
```

This way there will be no infinite execution. Going back to the trigger function, we need the same means to avoid infinite execution:

```
01      function trigger (target, key) {
02      const depsMap = bucket.get (target)
03        if  ( ! depsMap) return
04        const effects = depsMap.get (key)
05
06        const effectsToRun  =  new Set (effects)   //  new
07        effectsToRun.forEach (effectFn = > effectFn ())   //  new
08        //  effects && effects. forEach (effectFn => effectFn ())
```

```
//  delete
  09            }
```

As shown in the above code, instead of directly iterating over the effects collection, we newly construct the effectsToRun collection and iterate over it, thus avoiding infinite execution.

Tips
The ECMA specification for Set.prototype.forEach can be found in ECMAScript 2020 Language Specification.

4.5   Nested Effects and Effect Stacks

Effects can be nested, for example:

```
01    effect (function effectFn1 ( )  {
02        effect (function effectFn2 ( )  {  /*  ...  */  })
03         /* ...  */
04    })
```

In the above code, effectFn1 is nested inside effectFn2, and the execution of effectFn1 will lead to the execution of effectFn2. So, in what scenarios will nested effects appear? For instance, in fact the rendering function of Vue.js is executed in an *effect*:

```
01  //  Foo components
02  const Foo = {
03       render () {
04           Return  /*  ...  */
05       }
06  }
```

Execute the rendering function of the Foo component in an effect:

```
01    effect (()  =>  {
02        Foo. render ()
03    })
```

When components are nested, for example, when the Foo component renders the Bar component:

```
01    //  Bar component
02    const Bar = {
03        render () {/*... */},
04  }
05  //  the Foo component renders the Bar component
```

```
06   const Foo = {
07          render () {
08                  return < Bar /> // jsx syntax
09          } ,
10   }
```

At this point effect nesting occurs, which is equivalent to

```
01      effect (()   =>  {
02         Foo.render ()
03         //  nesting
04         effect (() => {
05             Bar.render ()
06          })
07      })
```

This example illustrates why effects are designed to be nested. Next, we need to figure out what happens if effect does not support nesting. In fact, according to the previous introduction and implementation, the response system we implemented does not support effect nesting. You can test it with the following code:

```
01   //  original data source
02   const data  =  { foo:  true,  bar :  true}
03   //  Proxy object
04   const obj  =  new Proxy (data,  {  /*  ...  */  })
05
06   //  Global Variables
07    let temp1, temp2
08
09   //  effectFn1 nested effectFn2
10   effect (function effectFn1 ( )  {
11       console . log ( 'effectFn1 execute' )
12
13       effect (function effectFn2 ( )  {
14           console.log ('effectFn2 execute')
15           //  read obj.bar properties in effectFn2
16           temp2  =  obj . bar
17        })
18        //  read obj.foo properties in effectFn1
19        temp1  =  obj.foo
20   })
21
```

In the above code, effectFn1 is nested inside effectFn2. Obviously, the execution of effectFn1 will lead to the execution of effectFn2. Note that we read the field obj. bar in effectFn2, read the field obj.foo in effectFn1, and effectFn2 executes before the read operation on the field obj.foo. Ideally, we want the connection between side effect functions and object properties to be as follows:

```
01      Data
02           └── foo
03               └── effectFn1
04           └─ bar
05             └── effectFn2
06
```

In this case, we want to trigger effectFn1 execution when modifying the obj.foo. Since effectFn2 is nested in effectFn1, effectFn2 execution is triggered indirectly, while when modifying the obj.bar, only effectFn2 execution is triggered. But the result is not like this. We try to modify the value of the obj.foo and find that the output is

```
01      'effectFn1 execute'
02      'effectFn2 execute'
03      'effectFn2 execute'
```

Printed three times in total. The first two times were the printing results of the initial execution of the side effect functions effectFn1 and effectFn2. This step is normal, and the problem lies in the printing of the third line. We modified the value obj.foo the field and found that effectFn1 was not re-executed, but made effectFn2 re-executed, which obviously did not meet expectations.

Where is the problem? In fact, it lies in the *effect* function and activeEffect we implemented. Observe the following code:

```
01      //  use a global variable to store the currently active effect
function
02      let activeEffect
03      function effect (fn) {
04          const effectFn = () => {
05              cleanup (effectFn)
06          // when calling effect to register a side effect function,
assign the side effect function to activeEffect
07              activeEffect  =  effectFn
08              fn ()
09          }
10      //activeEffect.deps to store all dependencies associated with
this side effect function
11      effectFn.deps = []
12      //   execute side effect function
13      effectFn ()
14 }
```

We use the global variable activeEffect to store the side effect functions registered through the effect function, which means that there can only be one side effect function stored by activeEffect at the same time. When side effect functions are nested, the execution of the inner side effect function will overwrite the value of the activeEffect and never return to the original value. At this time, if there is reactive data for dependency collection, even if the reactive data is read in the outer side effect function, the side effect functions they collect will also be inner side effect functions, which is the problem.

In order to solve this problem, we need a side effect function stack effectStack. When the side effect function is executed, the current side effect function is pushed onto the stack. After the side effect function is executed, it will be popped from the stack, and the activeEffect will always point to the side effect function at the top of the stack. In this way, a reactive data will only collect side effect functions that directly read their values, without affecting each other, as shown in the following code:

```
01    // use a global variable to store the currently active effect
function
02    let activeEffect
03    //  effect stack
04    const effectStack = [] // newly added
05
06    function effect (fn) {
07        const effectFn = () => {
08            cleanup (effectFn)
09            //  when calling effect to register a side effect
function, assign the side effect function to activeEffect
10            activeEffect  =  effectFn
11            //  push the current side effect function onto the stack
before calling it
12            effectStack . push (effectFn)   //  newly added
13            fn ()
14            //  after the current side effect function is executed,
pop the current side effect function off the stack and restore the
activeEffect to the previous value
15            effectStack.pop () // newly added
16            activeEffect = effectStack [effectStack.length - 1] //
newly added
17        }
18    // activeEffect.deps to store all dependencies associated with
this side effect function
19    effectFn . deps  =  [ ]
20    //  execute side effect functions
21    effectFn ()
22 }
```

We define the effectStack array and use it to simulate the stack. The activeEffect does not change, and it still points to the currently executing side effect function. The difference is that the currently executed side effect function will be pushed to the top of the stack, so that when the side effect function is nested, the outer side effect function is stored at the bottom of the stack, and the inner side effect function is stored at the top of the stack, as shown in Fig. 4.8.

Fig. 4.8 Side effect function stack

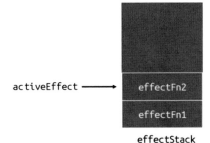

Fig. 4.9 Side effect functions pop up from the stack

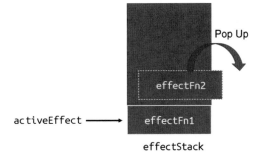

When the inner side effect function effectFn2 is executed, it will be popped off the stack, and the side effect function effectFn1 will be set to activeEffect, as shown in Fig. 4.9.

This way, reactive data will only collect side effect functions that directly read their values as dependencies, thus avoiding confusion.

4.6 Avoiding Infinite Recursive Loops

As mentioned earlier, there are many details to consider when we implement a perfect response system. And the infinite recursive loop to be introduced in this section is one of them. Let's take an example:

```
01    const data  =  {foo: 1}
02    const obj  =  new Proxy (data, {/*... */})
03
04    effect ( ()  =>  obj . foo ++)
```

As you can see, there is an auto-increment operation obj.foo ++ in the side effect function registered with effect, which will cause a stack overflow:

```
01 Uncaught RangeError: Maximum call stack size exceeded.
```

Why is this happening? Next we will try to figure out this problem and provide a solution.

In fact, we can separate the obj.foo ++ auto-increment operation, which is equivalent to

```
01    effect (( ) => {
02        //  statement
03        obj . foo  =  obj . foo  +  1
04    })
```

In this statement, both the value of the obj.foo is read and the value of the obj.foo is set, which is the root cause of the problem. We can try to reason about the execution flow of the code: first read the obj.foo value, which will trigger the track operation, collect the current side effect function into the "bucket," then add 1 to it and then assign it to the obj.foo. At this time, the trigger operation will be triggered, that is, the side effect function in the "bucket" is taken out and executed. But the problem is that the side effect function is executing, and the next execution is about to start before the execution is completed. This results in an infinite recursive call to itself, resulting in a stack overflow.

The solution is not difficult. By analyzing this problem, we can find that the read and set operations are performed in the same side effect function. At this time, whether it is the side effect function collected while tracking, or the side effect function to trigger execution when triggering, it is an activeEffect. Based on this, we can add a guard condition when the trigger action occurs: if the side effect function triggered by the trigger is the same as the side effect function currently being executed, the execution will not be triggered, as shown in the following code:

```
01    function trigger (target, key) {
02        const depsMap = bucket.get (target)
03        if   (! depsMap) return
04        const effects  =  depsMap . get (key)
05
06        const effectsToRun  =  new Set ()
07        effects  &&  effects. forEach (effectFn  =>  {
08            // if the side effect function triggered by trigger is
the same as the side effect function currently being executed, the
execution will not be triggered
09            if  ( effectFn  ! == activeEffect ) {   // newly added
10                effectsToRun . add (effectFn)
11            }
12        })
13        effectsToRun . forEach (effectFn  =>  effectFn ())
14        // effects && effects . forEach (effectFn  =>  effectFn ())
15    }
```

This way we can avoid infinite recursive calls and thus stack overflow.

4.7 Scheduling Execution

Schedulability is a very important feature of a response system. First of all, we need to clarify what schedulability is. The so-called schedulability refers to the ability to determine the timing, frequency, and method of side effect function execution when the trigger action triggers the re-execution of the side effect function.

First, let's take a look at how to decide how the side effect function is executed. Take the following code as an example:

```
01    const data  =  { foo:  1 }
02    const obj  =  new Proxy (data, {/*... */})
03
04    effect (( ) => {
05         console.log (obj.foo)
06    })
07
08    obj . foo ++
09
10    console.log ( 'finished' )
```

In the side effect function, we first print the obj.foo value using the console.log statement, then perform an auto-increment operation on the obj.foo, and finally use the console.log statement to print "finished." The output of this code is as follows:

```
01    1
02    2
03    ' finished '
```

Now suppose the requirements change and the output order needs to be adjusted to

```
01    1
02    ' finished '
03    2
```

According to the printed results, we can easily think of countermeasures; that is, the positions of the statement obj.foo ++ and the statement console.log ("finished") can be swapped. So, is there any way to achieve the requirements without adjusting the code? At this time, the response system needs to support scheduling.

We can design an option parameter options for the effect function to allow the user to specify the scheduler:

```
01    effect(
02         ( )   =>  {
03              console . log(obj . foo)
04         },
05         // options
```

```
06        {
07              //   the scheduler is a function 08 scheduler
08              scheduler(fn) {
09                  // ...
10              }
11        }
12     )
```

As shown in the code above, the user can pass the second parameter options when calling the effect function to register the side effect function. It is an object that allows specifying the scheduler scheduling function, and inside the effect function we need to mount the options option to the corresponding side effect function:

```
01      function effect (fn, options = {}) {
02          const effectFn = () => {
03              cleanup (effectFn)
04              //   when calling effect to register a side effect
function, assign the side effect function to activeEffect
05              activeEffect = effectFn
06              //   push the current side effect function to the stack
before calling the side effect function
07              effectStack.push (effectFn)
08              fn ( )
09              //   after the current side effect function is executed,
pop the current side effect function off the stack and restore the
activeEffect to the previous value
10              effectStack . pop ()
11              activeEffect = effectStack [effectStack.length - 1]
12          }
13          //   mount options on effectFn
14          effectFn . options  =  options   //  new
15          //   activeEffect.deps to store all dependencies
associated with this side effect function
16          effectFn . deps  =  [ ]
17          //   execute side effect functions
18          effectFn ( )
19      }
```

With the scheduler function, when we trigger the side effect function to re-execute in the trigger function, we can directly call the scheduler function passed by the user, thereby giving control to the user:

```
01      function trigger (target, key) {
02          const depsMap = bucket.get (target)
03          if   ( ! depsMap)   return
04          const effects = depsMap.get (key)
05
06          const effectsToRun = new Set ()
07          effects  &&  effects . forEach (effectFn   =>   {
08              if   (effectFn  ! ==   activeEffect)   {
09                  effectsToRun . add (effectFn)
```

```
10                }
11        })
12        effectsToRun.forEach (effectFn  =>  {
13              //  if a side effect function has a scheduler, call the
scheduler and pass the side effect function as an argument
14                if  (effectFn . options.scheduler) {    //  newly added
15                  effectFn.options.scheduler (effectFn)   // newly added
16        }  else  {
17              //  otherwise execute the side effect function directly
(previous default behavior)
18                effectFn ()   //  newly added
19            }
20        })
21    }
```

As shown in the above code, when the trigger action triggers the execution of the side effect function, we first judge whether there is a scheduler for the side effect function. If there is, we will directly call the scheduler function, and pass the current side effect function as a parameter, which is up to the user himself to control how to execute; otherwise keep the previous behavior, that is, execute the side effect function directly.

With this infrastructure, we can implement the previous requirements, as shown in the following code:

```
01    const data  =  { foo:  1 }
02    const obj  =  new Proxy (data,  {  /* ...  */  })
03
04    effect (
05        ()  =>  {
06              console . log (obj . foo)
07        },
08        //  options
09        {
10              //  the scheduler is a function
11              scheduler (fn)  {
12                  //  put the side effect function into the macro task
queue for execution
13                    setTimeout (fn)
14                }
15          }
16    )
17
18    effect (( ) => {
19          console.log (lbj.foo)
20    })
21
22    obj.foo ++
23
24    console . log ( 'finished' )
```

We use setTimeout to start a macro task to execute the side effect function fn, so that the desired print order can be achieved:

```
01   1
02   'finished'
03   2
```

In addition to controlling the execution order of side effect functions, it is also particularly important to control the number of times it is executed through the scheduler. Consider the following example:

```
01   const data  =  { foo:  1 }
02   const obj  =  new Proxy(data,  {  /*  ...  */  })
03
04   effect(()  =>  {
05       console.log(obj.foo)
06   })
07
08   obj.foo++
09   obj.foo++
```

First print the value of the obj.foo in the side effect function, and then perform two consecutive auto-increment operations on it. Without specifying a scheduler, its output is as follows:

```
01   1
02   2
03   3
```

As can be seen from the output, the value obj.foo field must increment from 1 to 3, and 2 is just its transitional state. If we only care about the final result and not the process, then performing three print operations is redundant, and the expected print result is as follows:

```
01 1
02 3
```

It does not contain transition states, which we can easily implement based on the scheduler:

```
01   //   define a task queue
02   const jobQueue  =  new Set ()
03   // use Promise.resolve () to create a promise instance, which we
use to add a task to the microtask queue
04   const p = Promise.resolve ()
05
06   //   a flag indicates whether the queue is being refreshed
07   let isFlushing  =  false
```

```
08    function flushJob () {
09          //  if the queue is flushing, do nothing
10          if (isFlushing) return
11          //  set to true to indicate that it is refreshing
12          isFlushing = true
13          //  refresh the jobQueue queue in the microtask queue
14          p.then (() => {
15              jobQueue.forEach (job = > job ())
16          }) . finally (() => {
17              //  reset isFlushing after it is over
18              isFlushing = false
19          })
20    }
21
22
23    effect (() => {
24        console . log (obj . foo)
25    } , {
26      scheduler (fn) {
27          //  add the side effect function to the jobQueue queue every
time it is scheduled
28            jobQueue.add (fn)
29            //  call flushJob to refresh the queue
30            flushJob ()
31        }
32    })
33
34    obj.foo ++
35    obj.foo ++
```

Observe the above code. First, we define a task queue jobQueue, which is a Set data structure, the purpose is to take advantage of the automatic deduplicate capability of the Set data structure. Then we look at the implementation of the scheduler. Each time the schedule is executed, the current side effect function is added to the jobQueue queue, and then the flushJob function is called to refresh the queue. Then we turn our attention to the flushJob function, which uses the isFlushing flag to determine whether it needs to be executed. It only needs to be executed when it is false. Once the flushJob function starts executing, the isFlushing flag will be set to true, which means that no matter how many times the flushJob function is called, it will only be executed once in a cycle. It should be noted that in flushJob, a function is added to the microtask queue by p.then, and the traversal execution of jobQueue is completed in the microtask queue.

The effect of the whole code is that performing two auto-increment operations on the obj.foo in a row will execute the scheduler's scheduling function twice synchronously and continuously, which means that the same side effect function will be added twice by the jobQueue.add (fn) statement, but due to the ability of the structure Set data to deduplicate, in the end there will only be one item in the jobQueue, that is, the current side effect function. Similarly, flushJob will execute twice synchronously and continuously, but due to the existence of the isFlushing flag, the flushJob function will actually only be executed once in an event loop, that is, once in the microtask queue. When the microtask queue starts executing, it will traverse the jobQueue and execute the side effect functions stored in it. Since there is only one side effect function in the jobQueue queue at this time, it will only be executed once, and when it executes, the value obj.foo field is already 3, so we achieve the desired output:

```
01    1
02    3
```

As you may have noticed, this function is somewhat similar to modifying reactive data several times in a row in a Vue.js but only triggering an update. In fact, Vue.js implements a more complete scheduler internally. The idea is the same as that described above.

4.8   Computation Attributes Computed and Lazy

The previous article introduced the effect function, which is used to register side effect functions, and it also allows to specify some option parameters options, such as specifying the scheduler to control the execution timing and method of side effect functions; it also explained the use of tracking and collecting, the track function, and the trigger function used to trigger the re-execution of the side effect function. In fact, combining these contents, we can implement a very important and very distinctive capability in the Vue.js—computing properties.

Before going into the discussion of computing properties, we need to talk about the effect of lazy execution, that is, lazy effect. What does this mean? For example, the effect function we now implement will immediately execute the side effect function passed to it. For example:

```
01    effect (
02        //  this function will be executed immediately
03        ( )  => {
04            console . log (obj . foo)
05        }
06    )
```

But in some scenarios, we do not want it to execute immediately, but we want it to execute when needed, such as when computing properties. At this time, we can achieve the purpose by adding the lazy property to options, as shown in the following code:

```
01    effect (
02         //  the lazy option is specified; this function will not be
executed immediately
03           ()   =>  {
04               console . log (obj . foo)
05         },
06         //  options
07         {
08             lazy :   true
09         }
10    )
```

The lazy option, like the scheduler described earlier, is specified through the
options option object. With it, we can modify the implementation logic of the effect
function, and when the options.lazy is true, the side effect function is not executed
immediately:

```
01    function effect (fn,   options  =  { })  {
02         const effectFn  =  ()  =>  {
03             cleanup (effectFn)
04             activeEffect = effectFn
05             effectStack.push (effectFn)
06             fn ( )
07             effectStack . pop ( )
08           activeEffect = effectStack [effectStack . length - 1 ]
09         }
10        effectFn.options  =  options
11        effectFn.deps  =  [ ]
12        //  execute only when not lazy
13        if  ( ! options.lazy )  {    //  newly added
14            //  execute side effect functions
15            effectFn ()
16        }
17        //  return the side effect function as the return value
18        return effectFn   //  newly added
19    }
```

Through this judgment, we have achieved the function of making the side effect
function not execute immediately. But the question is when the side effect function
should be executed. As you can see from the above code, we use the side effect
function effectFn as the return value of the effect function, which means that when
the effect function is called, the corresponding side effect function can be obtained
through its return value, so that we can manually execute the side effect function:

```
01    const effectFn = effect (( )  =>  {
02         console . log (obj.foo)
03    },   { lazy:  true })
04
05    //  manually execute side effect functions
06    effectFn ()
```

It does not make much sense if we can only execute side effects manually. But if we think of the function passed to effect as a getter, then this getter function can return any value, for example:

```
01    const effectFn  =   effect (
02         //  getter returns the sum of obj.foo and obj.bar
03         ()   =>   obj.foo + obj.bar,
04         {  lazy :   true }
05    )
```

In this way, when we manually execute the side effect function, we can get its return value:

```
01    const effectFn  =   effect (
02         //  getter returns the sum of obj.foo and obj.bar
03         ()   =>   obj.foo + obj.bar,
04         {  lazy :   true   }
05    )
06    //value is the return value of getter
07    const value  =   effectFn ( )
```

In order to achieve this goal, we need to make some changes to the effect function, as shown in the following code:

```
01    function effect (fn, options = {}) {
02        const effectFn = () => {
03             cleanup (effectFn)
04             activeEffect = effectFn
05              effectStack.push (effectFn)
06             //  store the execution result of fn in res
07          const res = fn ()   // new
08          effectStack.pop ()
09          activeEffect = effectStack [effectStack.length - 1]
10          //   return res as effectFn
11           return res//new
12    }
13    effectFn.options = options
14    effectFn.deps  =   [ ]
15    if  ( ! options.lazy)   {
16      effectFn ()
17    }
18
19      return effectFn
20    }
```

As you can see from the newly added code, the parameter fn passed to the effect function is the real side effect function, and effectFn is our wrapped side effect function. In order to get the execution result of the real side effect function fn through effectFn, we need to save it in the res variable and use it as the return value of the effectFn function.

Now that we have been able to implement the lazy side effect function, and can get the execution result of the side effect function, we can implement the calculation property next, as follows:

```
01    function computed (getter) {
02          //   use getter as a side effect function to create a lazy
effect
03          const effectFn = effect (getter, {
04              lazy: true
05          })
06
07          const obj = {
08              //   execute effectFn when reading value
09              get value ( )   {
10                  return effectFn ()
11              }
12          }
13
14          return obj
15    }
```

First we define a computed function that takes a getter function as a parameter, and we use the getter function as a side effect function to create a lazy effect. The execution of the computed function returns an object whose value property is an accessor property, and only when the value of value is read will effectFn be executed and its result returned as the return value.

We can use the computed function to create a computed property:

```
01    const data = { foo:   1, bar :   2 }
02    const obj = new Proxy (data,   { /* ...   */  })
03
04    const sumRes = computed (() => obj.foo + obj.bar)
05
06    console . log (sumRes.value)   // 3
```

You can see that it works correctly. But now the calculation property we implement is only lazy calculation, that is, it will only evaluate and get the value when you actually read the value of the sumRes.value. But it is not possible to cache the value. In other words, accessing sumRes multiple times will cause effectFn to be evaluated multiple times, even if the values of obj.foo and obj.bar themselves do not change:

```
01    console . log (sumRes . value)   // 3
02    console . log (sumRes . value)   // 3
03    console . log (sumRes . value)   // 3
```

The above code accesses the value of the sumRes.value multiple times, and each time it accesses, it will call effectFn to recalculate.

In order to solve this problem, we need to add the function of caching the value when implementing the computed function, as shown in the following code:

```
01    function computed (getter) {
02          //   value is used to cache the value of the last calculation
03          let value
04          //   dirty flag, used to identify whether the value needs to be
recalculated; true means "dirty" and calculation is needed
05          let dirty = true
06
07          const effectFn = effect (getter, {
08                lazy: true
09    })
10
11    const obj = {
12          get value () {
13                //  calculate the value only if it is "dirty" and cache the
resulting value into value
14                      if   ( dirty )   {
15                            value = effectFn ()
16                            //  set dirty to false; the next visit directly uses
the value cached into value
17                            dirty  =  false
18                      }
19                      return value
20                }
21          }
22
23          return obj
24    }
```

We added two new variables value and dirty, where value was used to cache the value of the last calculation, and dirty was an identifier that represents whether it needed to be recalculated. When we access the value through the sumRes.value, effectFn will only be called to recalculate the value when dirty is true, otherwise the value cached in value last time will be used directly. This way, no matter how many times we access the sumRes.value, the real calculation will only be performed on the first visit, and subsequent visits will directly read the cached value value.

I think you must have found the problem: if we modify the value of obj.foo or obj. bar at this time, and then access the sumRes.value, we will find that the assessed value has not changed:

```
01    const data = { foo :   1, bar :   2 }
02    const obj = new Proxy (data,   { /* ...   */ })
03
04    const sumRes   =   computed ( ( )   =>   obj . foo   +   obj . bar )
05
06    console . log (sumRes . value)   //   3
```

```
07     console . log (sumRes . value)    //  3
08
09     //  modify obj.foo
10     obj . foo ++
11
12     //  visit again and still get 3, but the expected result should be 4
13     console.log (sumRes.value)    //  3
```

This is because the variable dirty is set to false when the value of the sumRes. value is accessed for the first time, which means that no calculation is required. Even if we modify the value of obj.foo, as long as the value of dirty is false, it will not be recalculated, so we get the wrong value.

The solution is simple. When the value of obj.foo or obj.bar changes, just reset the dirty value to true. So what should be done? At this time, the scheduler option introduced in the previous section is used, as shown in the following code:

```
01     function computed (getter) {
02           let value
03           let dirty  =  true
04
05           const effectFn = effect (getter, {
06                 lazy :  true,
07                 //  add scheduler; reset dirty to true in scheduler
08                 scheduler () {
09                       dirty  =  true
10                 }
11           })
12
13           const obj  =  {
14                 get value ( ) {
15                       if  ( dirty )  {
16                             value  =  effectFn ( )
17                             dirty  =  false
18                       }
19                       return value
20                 }
21           }
22
23           return obj
24     }
```

We added the scheduler function to effect, which executed when the reactive data relied on in the getter function changed, so that we reset dirty to true inside the scheduler function. Therefore the next time we access the sumRes.value, we will re-call effectFn to evaluate the value, so that we can get the expected result.

Now, the computed property we designed is perfect, but there is a flaw, which is reflected when we read the value of the computed property in another effect:

```
01    const sumRes  =  computed ( ( )  => obj . foo  +  obj . bar )
02
03    effect ( ( )  => {
04        //  read in the side effect function sumRes.value
05        Console . log ( sumRes . value )
06    })
07
08    //  modify the value of obj.foo
09    obj . foo ++
```

As shown in the code above, sumRes is a computed property and reads sumRes. value value in side effect function of another *effect*. If the value of the obj.foo is modified at this time, we expect the side effect function to re-execute, just as when we read the computed property value in the Vue.js template, the re-rendering will be triggered once the computed property changes. But if you try to run the above code, you will find that modifying the value of the obj.foo does not trigger the rendering of the side effect function, so we say this is a bug.

Analyzing the cause of the problem, we found that this is essentially a typical effect nesting. A computed property has its own effect inside, and it is lazily executed, only executed when the value of the computed property is actually read. For the getter function of the computed property, the reactive data accessed in it will only collect the effect inside the computed as a dependency. When the computed property is used for another effect, effect nesting occurs, and the outer effect will not be collected by the reactive data in the inner effect.

The solution is not difficult. When reading the value of a computed property, we can manually call the track function to track it; when the reactive data on which the computed property depends changes, we can manually call the trigger function to trigger the response:

```
01    function computed (getter) {
02        let value
03        let dirty = true
04
05        const effectFn = effect (getter, {
06                lazy :  true,
07              scheduler () {
08                  if  ( !dirty )  {
09                      dirty = true
10                      //  manually call the trigger function to trigger
the response when the reactive data dependent on the calculation
attribute changes
11                      trigger ( obj ,  'value' )
12                  }
13              }
14    })
15
16    const obj  =  {
17        get value ()  {
18              if  ( dirty )  {
```

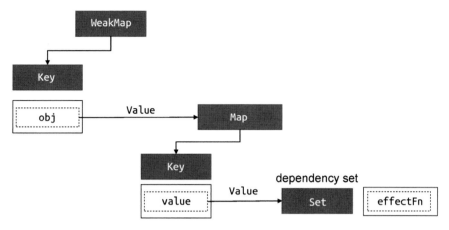

Fig. 4.10 Response connections for computed properties

```
19                      value  =  effectFn ( )
20                       dirty  =  false
21              }
22          // when reading value, manually call the track function to
trace
23              track (obj ,  'value' )
24              return value
25          }
26      }
27
28      return obj
29  }
```

As shown in the above code, when reading the value of a computed property, we manually call the track function, take the object obj returned by the computed property as the target, and pass it to the track function as the first parameter. When calculating the sound on which the property depends, the response data changes, the scheduler function will be executed, and the trigger function can be manually called in the scheduler function to trigger the response. At this time, for the following code:

```
01    effect ( function effectFn ( )  {
02        console . log (sumRes . value)
03    } )
```

it will make the following connection:

```
01    computed (obj)
02         └── value
03               └── effectFn
```

Figure 4.10 gives a more detailed description:

4.9   Implementation Principles of Watch

For the so-called watch, its essence is to observe a responsive data, notify and execute the corresponding callback when the data changes. For example:

```
01    watch (obj , () => {
02            console.log ('Data has changed')
03    })
04
05    //  modifying the value of the response data will cause the
callback function to execute
06    obj.foo ++
```

Suppose obj is a response data, use the watch function to observe it, and pass a callback function. When the value of the reactive data is modified, the callback function will be triggered to execute.

In fact, the implementation of *watch* essentially utilizes *effect* and options.scheduler options, such as the following code:

```
01    effect ( ( )   =>   {
02        console.log (obj.foo)
03    } ,  {
04       scheduler ()  {
05          //  when the value of the obj . foo changes, the scheduler
scheduling function will be executed
06          }
07    })
```

Accessing reactive data in a side effect function obj.foo, through the previous introduction, we know that this will establish a connection between the side effect function and the reactive data. When the reactive data changes, the side effect function will be triggered to re-execute. But there is an exception, that is, if there is a scheduler option in the side effect function, when the reactive data changes, it will trigger the scheduler function execution of the *scheduler* instead of directly triggering the side effect function execution. From this point of view, in fact, the scheduler scheduling function is equivalent to a callback function, and the implementation of *watch* takes advantage of this feature. Here is the simplest implementation of the watch function:

```
01    //  the watch function takes two arguments - source is the
reactive data and cb is the callback function
02    function watch (source, cb) {
03        effect (
04           //  trigger read operation to establish contact
05           ( ) => source.foo,
06           {
07              scheduler () {
08                 //  when the data changes, call the callback
function cb
```

```
09                            cb ( )
10                   }
11              }
12          )
13      }
```

We can use the *watch* function as follows:

```
01      const data  =  { foo :  1 }
02      const obj  =  new Proxy (data,  { /*  ...  */ } )
03
04      watch (obj ,  ( )  =>  {
05              console . log ( 'data has changed' )
06      })
07
08      obj . foo ++
```

The above code works fine, but we noticed that in the implementation of the *watch* function, the read operation of the source.foo is hardcoding. In other words, only obj.foo changes can be observed now. To make the watch function generic, we need to encapsulate a generic read operation:

```
01      function watch (source, cb) {
02          effect (
03              //  call traverse to read recursively
04              ( )  =>  traverse (source),
05              {
06                  scheduler ( ) {
07                      //  when the data changes, call the callback
function cb
08                      cb ( )
09                  }
10              }
11          )
12      }
13
14      function traverse (value, seen = new Set ( )) {
15          //  if the data to be read is the original value, or has
already been read, then do nothing
16          if ( typeof value ! == 'object' | | value === null | | seen.has
(value)) return
17          //  add data to seen, which means that it has been read
iteratively, avoiding endless loops caused by circular references
18          seen.add (value)
19          //  other structures such as arrays are not considered for the
time being
20          //  assuming value is an object, use for...in to read each value of
the object and recursively call traverse for processing
21          for (const k in value) {
22              traverse (value [k],  seen)
23          }
```

```
24
25      return value
26    }
```

As shown in the above code, the traverse function is called in the effect inside the watch to perform a recursive read operation instead of hardcoding, so that any property on an object can be read, and when any property changes, it can trigger callback function execution.

In addition to observing reactive data, the watch function can also receive a *getter* function:

```
01    watch (
02            //  getter function
03            ( )  =>  obj . foo,
04            //   callback function
05            ( )  =>  {
06                console . log ( 'the value of obj . foo has changed' )
07            }
08    )
```

As shown in the above code, the first parameter passed to the watch function is no longer a reactive data, but a *getter* function. Inside the *getter* function, the user can specify which reactive data the watch depends on, and only when these data change will the callback function be triggered to execute. The following code implements this function:

```
01    function watch (source, cb) {
02            //   define getter
03            let getter
04         //  if source is a function, it means that the user is passing
a getter, so assign source directly to the getter
05            If  ( typeof source === 'function') {
06                getter = source
07            } else  {
08            //  otherwise call traverse to read recursively according
to the original implementation
09                getter = () => traverse (source)
10            }
11
12        effect (
13            //  execute getter
14            ( )  =>  getter ( ) ,
15            {
16                scheduler ( ) {
17                    cb ( )
18                }
19            }
20        )
21    }
```

First determine the type of source. If it is a function type, it means that the user directly passed the *getter* function, and then the user's *getter* function is directly used; if it is not a function type, then keep the previous practice, that is, call the traverse function to read recursively. This implements the function of custom *getter* function and makes the *watch* function more powerful.

As you may have noticed, the current implementation still lacks a very important ability, that is, the old and new values cannot be obtained in the callback function. Usually when we use the *watch* function in the Vue.js, we can get the values before and after the change in the callback function:

```
01   watch (
02       ( )  =>  obj.foo,
03       ( newValue,  oldValue )  =>  {
04            console . log ( newValue,  oldValue )  //  2,1
05       }
06   )
07
08   obj.foo ++
```

So how to get the new value and the old value? This requires taking full advantage of the lazy option of the effect function, as shown in the following code:

```
01      function watch (source, cb) {
02           let getter
03           if   ( typeof source  ===  'function') {
04               getter  =  source
05           } else  {
06               getter  =  ( )  =>  traverse ( source )
07           }
08           //   define old and new values
09           let oldValue, newValue
10               //   when using effect to register a side effect function,
enable the lazy option and store the return value in effectFn for
subsequent manual calls
11           const effectFn = effect (
12               ( )  =>  getter (),
13               {
14                   lazy:  true ,
15                   scheduler ( )  {
16                       //  re-execute the side effect function in the
scheduler and get the new value
17                       newValue  =  effectFn ( )
18                       //  take the old value and the new value as arguments
to the callback function
19                       cb (newValue, oldValue)
20                       //  update the old value, otherwise you will get the
wrong old value next time
21                       oldValue  =  newValue
22                   }
23               }
```

```
24         )
25         //  manually call the side effect function; the value obtained
is the old value
26            oldValue = effectFn ()
27         }
```

In this code, the core change is to use the *lazy* option to create a lazy execution effect. Note the bottom part of the above code. The return value we get by manually calling the effectFn function is the old value, i.e., the value obtained by the first execution. When a change occurs and triggers the scheduler to execute, the effectFn function is called again with the new value, so we get the old and new values, and then pass them as parameters to the callback function cb. The last very important thing is not to forget to update the old value with the new value: oldValue = newValue, or you will get the wrong old value the next time the change occurs.

4.10   Immediate Watch and Callback Execution Timing

In the previous section, we introduced the basic implementation of watch. In the process, we realized that the essence of *watch* was actually a secondary encapsulation of effect. In this section, we continue to discuss two features about watch: one is an immediate callback function, and the other is the execution timing of the callback function.

First look at the callback function that executes immediately. By default, a watch callback will only execute when the reactive data changes:

```
01    //  the callback function is only executed when the reactive data
obj changes subsequently
02       watch (obj ,  ( )  =>  {
03             console . log  ( 'changed' )
04       })
```

In Vue.js, you can specify whether the callback needs to be executed immediately through the option parameter immediate:

```
01    watch (obj ,    ()  =>  {
02             console.log ('changed')
03       } ,   {
04         //  the callback function will be executed immediately when
the watch is created
05           immediate: true
06       } )
```

When the immediate option exists and is true, the callback function will be executed immediately when the watch is created. If you think about it carefully, you will find that the immediate execution of the callback function is essentially no different from the subsequent execution, so we can encapsulate the scheduler function as a general function, which is executed during initialization and change, respectively, as shown in the following code:

```
01    function watch (source,  cb,  options  =  { })  {
02         let getter
03         if  ( typeof  source  ===  'function' )  {
04              getter  =  source
05         } else  {
06              getter  = ( )  =>  traverse (source
07         }
08
09         let oldValue, newValue
10
11         //  extract the scheduler scheduling function as an
independent job function
12         const  job  =  ( )  =>  {
13              newValue  =  effectFn ( )
14              cb (newValue,  oldValue)
15              oldValue  =  newValue
16         }
17
18         const effectFn = effect (
19              //  execute getter
20              ( )  =>  getter ( ),
21              {
22                   lazy:  true,
23                   //  use the job function as the scheduler function
24                      scheduler :  job
25              }
26         )
27
28         if  (options. immediate) {
29              //  execute the job immediately when immediate is true,
triggering callback execution
30              job ( )
31         } else  {
32              oldValue  =  effectFn ( )
33         }
34    }
```

This implements the immediate execution function of the callback function. Since the callback function is executed immediately, there is no so-called old value when the callback is executed for the first time, so the oldValue value of the callback function is undefined at this time, which is also expected.

In addition to specifying that the callback function is executed immediately, you can also specify the execution timing of the callback function through other option parameters, such as using the flush option in Vue.js 3 to specify:

```
01    watch (obj , ( )   =>  {
02           console . log ( 'changed' )
03        } ,  {
04        //  the callback function will be executed immediately when
the watch is created
05        flush:   'pre' // can also be specified as 'post ' | ' sync' (
06        } )
```

Flush essentially specifies the timing of the execution of the scheduler function. The previous part has explained how to execute the scheduler function in the microtask queue, which is the same function as flush. When the value of flush is "post," it means that the scheduler function needs to put the side effect function in a microtask queue and wait for the DOM update to finish before executing it. We can use the following code to simulate:

```
01    function watch ( source,   cb,   options  =  { }) {
02        let getter
03        if   ( typeof source   ===   ' function ' )   {
04            getter = source
05        } else   {
06            getter  = ( )   =>  traverse (source)
07        }
08
09        let oldValue, newValue
10
11        const job  = ( )   =>  {
12            newValue  =  effectFn ()
13            cb (newValue,   oldValue)
14            oldValue  =  newValue
15        }
16
17        const effectFn = effect (
18            //  execute getter
19            ( )  =>  getter ( ),
20            {
21                lazy :   true ,
22                scheduler :   ( )   =>  {
23                    //  determine whether flush is 'post 'in the
scheduling function; if so, put it in the microtask queue for execution
24                    if   (options . flush === ' post ' )   {
25                        const p = Promise.resolve ()
26                        p. then ( job )
27                    } else   {
28                        job ( )
29                    }
30                }
31            }
32        )
33
34        if   ( options . immediate )   {
35            job ( )
36        } else {
```

```
37                  oldValue  =  effectFn ()
38         }
39    }
```

As shown in the above code, we have modified the implementation of the scheduler function of scheduler to detect whether the value of the options.flush is *post* in the scheduler function, and if so, put the job function in the microtask queue to achieve asynchronous delayed execution; otherwise Execute the job function directly, which is essentially equivalent to the implementation mechanism of "sync," which is synchronous execution. For the case where the value of options. flush is "pre," we have no way to simulate it for the time being, because this involves the update timing of the component, where the original semantics of "pre" and "post" refer to before and after the component is updated, but this does not affect our understanding of how to control the update timing of callback functions.

4.11 Side Effects of Expiration

Race problems are often mentioned in multi-process or multi-threaded programming, and front-end engineers may rarely discuss it, but you may have encountered scenarios similar to race problems in your daily work. For example:

```
01    let finalData
02
03    watch ( obj,  async  ()  => {
04         //  send and wait for network requests
05         const  res  =  await fetch ( '/path/to/request' )
06         //  assign the request result to data
07         finalData = res
08    })
```

In this code, we use *watch* to observe the changes of the *obj* object. Every time the *obj* object changes, a network request will be sent, such as requesting interface data. After the data request is successful, the result will be assigned to the finalData variable.

Looking at the above code, at first glance it seems that there is no problem. But if you think about it carefully, you will find that this code will have a race problem. Suppose we modify a field value of the *obj* object for the first time, which will cause the callback function to execute and send the first request A. Over time, before the result of request A is returned, we make a second modification to a field value of the *obj* object, which causes a second request B to be sent. At this time, both request A and request B are in progress, so which request will return the result first? We are not sure. If request B returns a result before request A, it will cause the final finalData to store the result of request A, as shown in Fig. 4.11.

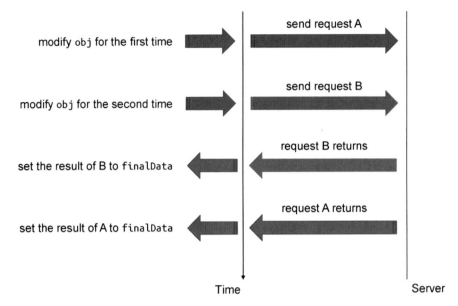

Fig. 4.11   The result of request A overrides the result of request B

However, since request B is sent later, we consider the data returned by request B to be the "latest," while request A should be regarded as "expired," so we want the value stored in the variable finalData to be the value returned by request B rather than that returned by request A. In fact, we can summarize this problem further. Request A is the side effect of the first execution of the side effect function, and request B is the side effect of the second execution of the side effect function. Since request B occurs later, the result of request B should be considered "up-to-date," while request A has "expired," and its result should be considered invalid. In this way, erroneous results caused by race problems can be avoided.

At the end of the day, what we need is a way to expire the side effects. To make the problem clearer, let's take the *watch* function in the Vue.js to restore the scene to see how Vue.js can help developers solve this problem, and then try to implement this function.

In Vue.js, the callback function of the watch function receives the third parameter onInvalidate, which is a function, similar to the event listener. We can use the onInvalidate function to register a callback, which will execute when the current side effect function expires:

```
01    watch (obj, async (newValue, oldValue, onInvalidate ) => {
02         // define a flag to represent whether the current side effect
function has expired. The default is false, which means that it has not
expired.
03              let expired = false
04              // call onInvalidate () to register an expired callback
05              onInvalidate ( ( )   =>   {
```

```
06                    //  set expired to true when expired.
07                    expired = true
08                })
09
10                //  send a network request
11                const res = await fetch ('/path/to/request')
12
13                //  subsequent operations will only be performed if the
execution of the side effect function has not expired.
14                    if   ( ! expired )   {
15                        finalData  =   res
16                    }
17        } )
```

As shown in the above code, before sending the request, we define the expired flag variable to identify whether the execution of the current side effect function has expired; then call the onInvalidate function to register an expired callback, and when the execution of the side effect function expires, the expired flag variable will be set to true; finally, the request result is only used when there is no expiration, which can effectively avoid the above problems.

So how does Vue.js do it? In other words, what is the principle of onInvalidate? In fact, it is very simple. After each change is detected inside watch, before the side effect function is re-executed, the expired callback that we registered through the onInvalidate function will be called first, and that's it, as shown in the following code:

```
01      function watch (source,  cb,  options  =  { }) {
02          let getter
03          if   ( typeof source  ===  ' function ' )   {
04              getter = source
05          } else  {
06              getter  =  ()  =>  traverse (source)
07          }
08
09          let oldValue, newValue
10
11              //  cleanup is used to store expired callbacks for user
registration
12              let cleanup
13              //  define the onInvalidate function
14      function onInvalidate ( fn )   {
15              //  store expired callbacks in cleanup
16              cleanup  =  fn
17      }
18
19      const job  =  ()  =>  {
20          newValue = effectFn ()
21          //  call the expired callback before calling the callback
function cb
22          if   ( cleanup )   {
23              cleanup ()
```

```
24              }
25              //  use onInvalidate as the third parameter of the callback
function for the user to use
26              cb (newValue,  oldValue,  onInvalidate)
27              oldValue  =  newValue
28       }
29
30       const effectFn = effect (
31              //  execute getter
32              ( )  =>  getter ( ),
33              {
34                   lazy :   true ,
35                   scheduler :   ( )  =>  {
36                        if  (options.flush  ===  ' post ' )   {
37                             const p = Promise . resolve ()
38                             p . then ( job )
39                        } else  {
40                             jobs ( )
41                        }
42                   }
43              }
44       )
45
46       if  (options . immediate )   {
47            jobs ( )
48       } else  {
49            oldValue = effectFn ()
50       }
51    }
```

In this code, we first define the cleanup variable, which is used to store the expired callbacks registered by the user through the onInvalidate function. You can see that the implementation of the onInvalidate function is very simple—just assign the expired callback to the cleanup variable. The key point here is in the *job* function. Before executing the callback function cb each time, check whether there is an expired callback, and if so, execute the expired callback function cleanup. Finally, we pass the onInvalidate function as the third parameter of the callback function to cb for the user to use.

Let's go further with an example:

```
01    watch (obj, async (newValue, oldValue, onInvalidate ) => {
02           let expired  =  false
03           onInvalidate ( ( )  =>  {
04                expired = true
05           } )
06
07           const res = await fetch ('/path/to/request')
08
09            if  ( ! expired )   {
10                 finalData = res
11            }
12       } )
```

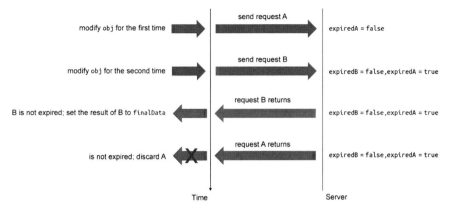

Fig. 4.12 Request expiration

```
13
14              //  first Modification
15              obj.foo ++
16              setTimeout ( ( )   => {
17                      //  second modification after 200ms
18                      obj . foo ++
19        },  200 )
```

As shown in the above code, we modified the value of the obj.foo twice; the first modification was executed immediately, which caused the watch's callback function to execute. Since we called onInvalidate inside the callback function, an expired callback is registered, and request A is sent. Suppose request A takes 1000 ms to return a result, and we modify the obj.foo value a second time at 200 ms, which in turn causes watch's callback function to execute. At this time, it should be noted that in our implementation, before executing the callback function each time, we must first check whether the expired callback exists. If it exists, the expired callback will be executed first. Since we have already registered an expired callback when the watch callback function is executed for the first time, before the watch callback function is executed for the second time, the previously registered expired callback will be executed first, which will make the value of the variable *expired* of the closure in the side effect function during the first execution becomes true; that is, the execution of the side effect function has expired. So, when the result of request A is returned, its result will be discarded, thus avoiding the impact of expired side effects, as shown in Fig. 4.12.

4.12   Summary

In this chapter, we first introduced the concept of side effect functions and reactive data, and the relationship between them. The most basic implementation of a reactive data relies on the interception of "read" and "set" operations to establish a connection between side effect functions and reactive data. When a "read" operation occurs, we store the currently executed side effect function in the "bucket"; when a "set" operation occurs, the side effect function is taken out of the "bucket" and executed. This is the fundamental implementation principle of the response system.

Next, we implemented a relatively complete response system. Using WeakMap with *Map* to build a new "bucket" structure, which can establish a more precise connection between reactive data and side effect functions. At the same time, we also introduced the difference between the two data structures, WeakMap and Map. WeakMap is weakly referenced and does not affect the work of the garbage collector. When user code has no reference to an object, WeakMap does not prevent the garbage collector from reclaiming the object.

We also discussed the issue of redundant side effects caused by branch switching, which could cause unnecessary updates to side effect functions. In order to solve this problem, we need to clear the response link established last time before each side effect function is re-executed, and when the side effect function is re-executed, a new response link will be established again. There is no redundant side effect problem in the new response link; thus, the problem is solved. But in the process, we also encountered a new problem of traversing the Set data structure causing an infinite loop. The reason for this problem can be known from the ECMA specification, that is, "When calling forEach to traverse the Set collection, if a value has already been accessed but removed and re-added to the collection, and if the forEach traversal does not end at this time, then the value will be re-accessed." The solution is to create a new Set data structure to traverse.

Then, we discussed the problem of nested side effect functions. In real scenarios, nested side effect functions occur in scenarios where components are nested, that is, the relationship between parent and child components. At this time, in order to avoid confusion in the response connection established between the reactive data and the side effect function, we need to use the side effect function stack to store different side effect functions. When a side effect function is executed, it is popped off the stack. When reading reactive data, the read reactive data will only establish a response connection with the side effect function at the top of the current stack, thus solving the problem. Then, we encountered the problem that the side effect function called itself infinitely recursively, causing stack overflow. The root cause of the problem is that the read and set operations on reactive data occur within the same side effect function. The solution is simple. If the *trigger* triggers the execution of the same side effect function as the currently executing side effect function, the execution is not triggered.

Subsequently, we discussed the schedulability of the response system. The so-called schedulability refers to the ability to determine the timing, number, and method of side effect function execution when the trigger action triggers the re-execution of the side effect function. In order to achieve scheduling capability, we have added a second option parameter to the effect function, which can specify the caller through the scheduler option, so that users can complete the scheduling of tasks through the scheduler. We also explained how to implement task deduplicate through the scheduler, that is, to cache tasks through a microtask queue to achieve deduplicate.

Then, we explained the computed property, which was computed. The computed property is actually a lazy side effect function, and we make the side effect function lazy through the lazy option. Side effects marked as lazy can be executed manually. Using this feature, we designed the computed property. When reading the value of the computed property, we only need to manually execute the side effect function. When the responsive data on which the computed property depends changes, the dirty flag will be set to true through the scheduler, which means "dirty." In this way, the next time we read the value of the computed property, we will recalculate the true value.

After that, we discussed the implementation principle of watch. It essentially takes advantage of the schedulability when side effect functions are re-executed. A *watch* itself creates an effect, and when the reactive data that this *effect* depends on changes, it executes the effect's scheduler function, the *scheduler*. The scheduler here can be understood as a "callback," so we only need to execute the callback function registered by the user through the *watch* function in the scheduler. In addition, we also explained the watch that executes the callback immediately, which is achieved by adding a new *immediate* option. We also discussed how to control the execution timing of the callback function. The flush option is used to specify the specific execution timing of the callback function, essentially, the caller and asynchronous microtask queue.

Finally, we discussed the expired side effect function, which can cause race problems. To solve this problem, Vue.js designed a third parameter for callback function of *watch*, onInvalidate. It is a function that registers expired callbacks. Whenever *watch*'s callback function executes, the expired callback registered by the user through onInvalidate is preferentially executed. In this way, the user has the opportunity to mark the last side effect as "expired" in the expired callback, thus solving the race problem.

Chapter 5
Responsive Schemes for Non-original Values

In the previous chapter, we focused on the concept and implementation of responsive systems and briefly introduced the basic principles of reactive data. In this chapter, we will focus on reactive data itself and delve into what needs to be considered to implement reactive data, and what are the difficulties. In fact, implementing reactive data is much more difficult than expected, not simply intercepting *get/set* operations as described in the previous chapter. For example, how do we intercept *for ... in* loops? How does the track function track intercepted *for ... in* loops? There are many similar questions. In addition, we should also consider how to proxy arrays. Vue.js 3 also supports collection types, such as Map, Set, WeakMap, and WeakSet, etc., so how should we proxy collection types? In fact, to achieve perfect reactive data, we need to go deep into the language specification. While revealing the answer, this chapter will also analyze the reasons from the level of language specifications, so that you can have a deeper understanding of reactive data.

In addition, this chapter will refer to the ECMA-262 specification. Unless otherwise specified, it refers to the 2021 version of the specification.

5.1 Understanding Proxy and Reflect

Since the reactive data of Vue.js 3 is implemented based on Proxy, it is necessary for us to understand Proxy and its associated Reflect. What is a proxy? Simply put, a proxy object can be created using Proxy. It can implement proxies to other objects. The key word here is other objects; that is to say, Proxy can only proxy objects, not non-object values, such as string, Boolean, etc. So, what does proxy refer to? The so-called proxy refers to the proxy of the basic semantics of an object. It allows us to intercept and redefine basic operations on an object. There are many keywords in this sentence, and we will explain them one by one.

© The Author(s), under exclusive license to Springer Nature Singapore Pte Ltd. 2023　　101
H. Yang, *Vue. JS Framework*, https://doi.org/10.1007/978-981-99-4947-2_5

What is basic semantics? Given an object obj, you can perform some operations on it, such as reading property values, setting property values:

```
01   obj . foo //   read the value of the attribute foo
02   obj . foo ++  //   read and set the value of the property foo
```

Operations like reading and setting property values are basic semantic operations, that is, basic operations. Since it is a basic operation, it can be intercepted using Proxy:

```
01   const p  =   new Proxy (obj ,  {
02       //  intercept read attribute operation
03       get ()  { /* ...  */ },
04       //  intercept setting property operation
05       set ()  { /* ...  */ }
06   })
```

As shown in the code above, the Proxy constructor takes two parameters. The first parameter is the object being proxied, and the second parameter is also an object, which is a set of traps. The get function is used to intercept read operations, and the set function is used to intercept set operations.

In the JavaScript world, everything is an object. For example, a function is also an object, so calling a function is also a basic operation on an object:

```
01   const fn  =   (name )  =>  {
02     Console . log ( ' I am:  ' ,  name)
03   }
04
05   //  calling a function is a basic operation on an object
06   fn ( )
```

Therefore, we can use Proxy to intercept the call operation of functions. Here we use *apply* to intercept the call of functions:

```
01   const  p2  =   new Proxy (fn ,  {
02       //  use apply to intercept function calls
03       apply (target,  thisArg,  argArray)  {
04           target . call ( thisArg ,  ... argArray)
05       }
06   } )
07
08   p2 ( ' hcy ' )  //  output :  'I am :  hcy'
```

The above two examples illustrate what a basic operation is. Proxy can only intercept basic operations on an object. So, what are non-basic operations? In fact, calling the method under the object is a typical non-basic operation. We call it a compound operation:

```
01    obj.fn ()
```

In fact, calling a method under an object consists of two basic semantics. The first basic semantics is get, that is, the obj.fn attribute is obtained through the get operation. The second basic semantics is function calling, that is, getting the obj.fn value through *get* and then calling it, which is the *apply* we mentioned above. It is important to understand the basic semantics that Proxy can only proxy objects. Later, when we explain how to implement proxies for arrays or data types such as Map and Set, we will take advantage of this feature of Proxy. Now that we understand Proxy, let's talk about Reflect. Reflect is a global object with many methods under it, such as

```
01    Reflect . get ( )
02    Reflect . set ( )
03    Reflect . apply ( )
04    // ...
```

You may have noticed that the methods under Reflect have the same name as Proxy's interceptor methods, but this is no accident. Any method that can be found in Proxy's interceptor can find functions of the same name in Reflect, so what are the functions of these functions? In fact, their role is not mysterious at all. Take Reflect. get function, its function is to provide the default behavior for accessing an object property. For example, the following two operations are equivalent:

```
01    const obj  =  {  foo :   1 }
02
03    //  direct read
04    console.log(obj.foo) // 1
05    //  read with Reflect . get
06    console.log (Reflect.get (obj, 'foo ')) // 1
```

Some readers may wonder: since the operation is equivalent, what is the meaning of its existence? In fact Reflect.get can also receive a third parameter, which specifies the receiver *receiver*, which you can understand as *this* in the function call process, for example:

```
01    const  obj  =  {
02        get foo () {
03            return this.foo
04        }
05    }
06    console . log (Reflect . get (obj,  'foo' ,  { foo: 2 }))   //
outputs 2 instead of 1
```

In this code, we specify the third parameter receiver as an object {foo: 2}, and the value read is the value of the foo property of the receiver object. In fact, the method Reflect. * has many other meanings, but we only care about and discuss this here, as it is closely related to the implementation of reactive data. To illustrate, review the code implementing reactive data in the previous section:

```
01    const obj  =  { foo:  1 }
02
03    const  p  =  new Proxy (obj ,  {
04        get ( target,  key )  {
05            track (target,  key)
06        // note that we are not using Reflect.get to complete the read
here
07            return target [key]
08        } ,
09        set (target, key, newVal) {
10            // there is also no Reflect.set to complete the setup here
11            target [key] = newVal
12            trigger (target, key)
13        }
14    } )
```

This is the most basic code used to implement reactive data in the previous chapter. In the *get* and *set* interception functions, we directly use the original object target to complete the reading and setting operations of the properties, where the original object target is the obj object in the above code.

So, what's wrong with this code? We use *effect* to expose the problem. First, let's modify the *obj* object and add the *bar* property to it:

```
01    const obj  =  {
02        foo:  1 ,
03        get bar ()   {
04            return this . foo
05        }
06    }
```

As you can see, the bar property is an accessor property that returns the value of the *this.foo* property. Next, we access the bar property through the proxy object *p* in the effect side effect function:

```
01    effect (() => {
02        console.log (p.bar) //1
03    } )
```

Let's analyze what happens in this process. When the effect-registered side effect function executes, it reads the *p.bar* property. It finds that *p.bar* is an accessor property, so it executes the getter function. Since the value of the foo property is read through *this.foo* in the *getter* function, we think that the side effect function will also establish a connection with the property *foo*. When we modify the value of the p. foo, we should be able to trigger a response, causing the side effect function to re-execute. However, this is not the case, when we try to modify p.foo value:

```
01   p.foo ++
```

The side effect function is not re-executed. What is the problem? In fact, the problem lies in the accessor function getter of the bar property:

```
01   const obj  =  {
02      foo :   1 ,
03      get bar () {
04          // who is this pointing to here?
05          return this . foo
06      }
07   }
```

When we use *this.foo* to read the value of the foo property, who is this pointing to here? Let's review the whole process. First, we access the p.bar through the proxy object p, which triggers the execution of the proxy object's *get* interceptor function:

```
01   const p = new Proxy (obj ,  {
02      get (target, key)  {
03          track (target, key)
04          // note that we are not using Reflect.get to complete the
read here
05          return target [key]
06      } ,
07      // omit some code
08   })
```

In the *get* interception function, the property value is returned by *target [key]*, where target is the original object obj, and key is the string 'bar', so target [key] is equivalent to obj.bar. Therefore, when we use p.bar to access the bar property, the *this* in its *getter* function actually points to the original object obj, which means that we are actually accessing obj.foo in the end. Obviously, accessing one of its properties through the original object in a side effect function does not establish a response connection, which is equivalent to:

```
01   effect (()  => {
02      // obj is the original data source, not the proxy object; such
access cannot establish a response connection
03      obj.foo
04   } )
```

Since this does not establish a response connection, there is a problem that the response cannot be triggered. So how should this problem be solved? At this point Reflect.get function comes in handy. First give the code to solve the problem:

```
01    const p  =  new Proxy (obj, {
02         //  intercept read operation; receive the third parameter
receiver
03         get (target,  key,  receiver)  {
04               track (target, key)
05                 //  use Reflect . get to return the read property value
06               return Reflect . get (target,  key,  receiver)
07            },
08            //  omit some code
09    } )
```

As shown in the code above, the *get* interceptor function of the proxy object receives the third parameter receiver, which represents who is reading the property, for example:

```
01   p.bar//proxy object p is reading the bar property
```

When we use the proxy object p to access the bar property, then receiver is p, which you can simply understand as this in the function call. Then the crucial step happens: we use Reflect.get (target, key, receiver) instead of the previous target [key]. The key point here is the third parameter receiver. We already know that it is the proxy object p, so *this* in the *getter* function of the accessor property bar points to the proxy object p:

```
01    const obj  =  {
02       foo :  1 ,
03       get bar ( )  {
04            //  now this here is the proxy object p
05          return this . foo
06       }
07    }
```

As you can see, this has changed from the original object obj to the proxy object p. Obviously, this will establish a response connection between the side effect function and the reactive data, so as to achieve the effect of dependency collection. If you perform an auto-increment operation on the p.foo at this time, you will find that you can trigger the re-execution of the side effect function.

It is for the above reasons that the Reflect. * method will be used uniformly in the following explanation.

5.2 How JavaScript Objects and Proxy Work

We often hear the saying "Everything in JavaScript is an object." So, what exactly is an object? This question requires us to consult the ECMAScript specification to get an answer. In fact, according to the ECMAScript specification, there are two kinds of objects in JavaScript, one of which is called ordinary object, and the other is called exotic object. These two types of objects contain all objects in the JavaScript world, and any object that is not a regular object is a heterogeneous object. So, what exactly is a regular object and what is a heterogeneous object? This requires us to first understand the internal methods and internal slots of the object.

We know that in JavaScript, functions are actually objects. Suppose an object obj is given, how do we distinguish whether it is a normal object or a function? In fact, in JavaScript, the actual semantics of an object are specified by the object's internal methods. The so-called internal methods refer to the methods called inside the engine when we operate on an object, and these methods are invisible to JavaScript users. For example, when we access object properties:

```
01    obj.foo
```

The internal method [[Get]] is called inside the engine to read the property value. Please note that [[xxx]] is used in the ECMAScript specification to represent internal methods or internal slots.

If an object needs to be called as a function, then the object must deploy the internal method [[Call]]. Now we can answer the previous question: how do we distinguish whether an object is a normal object or a function? Under what circumstances can an object be called as a function? The answer is to distinguish objects by internal methods and internal slots. For example, function objects deploy internal methods [[Call]], while ordinary objects do not.

What does it mean that internal methods are polymorphic? This is similar to the concept of polymorphism in object oriented. That is, different types of objects may deploy the same internal methods but have different logic. For example, both plain objects and Proxy objects deploy the [[Get]] internal method, but their logic is different. The logic of the [[Get]] internal method deployed by plain objects is defined by Section 10.1.8 in the ECMA specification, while the logic of the [[Get]] internal method deployed by the Proxy object is defined by Section 10.5.8 in the ECMA specification.

Knowing the internal methods, you can explain what a regular object is, and what a heterogeneous object is. Objects that meet the following three requirements are regular objects:

- For the internal methods listed in Table 5.1, they must be implemented using the definitions given in Section 10.1.x of the ECMA specification
- For the internal method [[Call]], it must be implemented using the definition given in Section 10.2.1 of the ECMA specification
- For the internal method [[Construct]], it must be implemented using the definitions given in section 10.2.2 of the ECMA specification

And all objects that do not meet these three requirements are heterogeneous objects. For example, since the internal method [[Get]] of the Proxy object is not implemented using the definitions given in Section 10.1.8 of the ECMA specification, the Proxy is a heterogeneous object.

Table 5.1 Necessary internal methods for objects

Internal methods	Signatures	Description
`[[GetPrototypeOf]]`	`( ) → Object ∣ Null`	Identify the object that provides inherited properties for this object; null means no inherited properties
`[[SetPrototypeOf]]`	`(Object ∣ Null) → Boolean`	Associate this object with another object that provides inherited properties. Pass null to indicate no inherited properties; return true to indicate that the operation completed successfully; return false to indicate that the operation failed
`[[IsExtensible]]`	`( ) → Boolean`	Find out whether additional properties are allowed to be added to this object
`[[PreventExtensions]]`	`( ) → Boolean`	Control whether new properties can be added to this object. Return true if the operation succeeded; false if the operation failed
`[[GetOwnProperty]]`	`(propertyKey) → Undefined ∣ Property Descriptor`	Return the descriptor of the attribute of the object itself, whose key is propertyKey, or undefined if no such property exists
`[[DefineOwnProperty]]`	`(propertyKey, PropertyDescriptor) → Boolean`	Create or change your own property whose key is propertyKey to have the state described by the PropertyDescriptor. Return true if the property has been successfully created or updated; false if the property cannot be created or updated
`[[HasProperty]]`	`(propertyKey) → Boolean`	Return a Boolean value indicating whether the object already has its own or inherited property with key propertyKey
`[[Get]]`	`(propertyKey, Receiver) → any`	Return the value of the property whose key is propertyKey from this object. If you must run ECMAScript code to retrieve the property value, use Receiver as the this value when running the code
`[[Set]]`	`(propertyKey, value, Receiver) → Boolean`	Set the key value with the value propertyKey to value. If you must run ECMAScript code to set the property value,

(continued)

Table 5.1   (continued)

Internal methods	Signatures	Description
		use Receiver as this value when running the code. Return true if the property value is successfully set, false if it cannot be set
[[Delete]]	(propertyKey) → Boolean	Deletes the property whose key is propertyKey from this object. Return false if the property has not been removed and still exists; return true if the property has been removed or does not exist
[[OwnPropertyKeys]]	( ) → List of propertyKey	Return a list whose elements are the property keys of the object itself

Table 5.2   Additional necessary internal methods

Internal methods	Signatures	Description
[[Call]]	(any, a List of any) → any	Associates the running code with the this object. Triggered by a function call. The arguments to this inner method are a this value and a list of arguments
[[Construct]]	(a List of any, Object) → Object	Create an object. Triggered by the new operator or super call. The first argument to this inner method is a List whose elements are arguments to the constructor call or super call, and the second argument is the object to which the new operator was originally applied. The object that implements this inner method is called the constructor

As can be seen from Table 5.1, including [[Get]], an object must deploy 11 necessary internal methods. In addition to the internal methods listed in Table 5.1, there are two additional necessary internal methods : [[Call]] and [[Construct]], as shown in Table 5.2.

Now that we have a deeper understanding of objects in JavaScript. Next, let's look at the Proxy object in detail. Since a Proxy is also an object, it itself deploys the necessary internal methods described above. When we access property values through a proxy object:

```
01  const p = new Proxy (obj, { /* ... */ } )
02  p.foo
```

In effect, the engine calls the internal method [[Get]] deployed on object p. At this point, there is not much difference between proxy objects and ordinary objects. Their difference lies in the implementation of the internal method [[Get]], which reflects the polymorphism of internal methods, i.e., different objects deploy the same internal method, but their behavior may be different. The specific difference is that if the corresponding interception function is not specified when we create the proxy object, for example, the get () interception function is not specified, then when we access the property value through the proxy object, the internal method [[Get]] of the proxy object will call the internal method [[Get]] of the original object to obtain the property value, which is actually the nature of proxy transparency.

Now I believe you have understood that the interceptor function specified when the proxy object is created is actually used to customize the internal methods and behaviors of the proxy object itself, rather than to specify the internal methods and behaviors of the proxied object. Table 5.1 lists all the internal methods deployed by the Proxy object and the names of the interceptors used to customize the internal methods and behaviors.

Of course, the internal methods [[Call]] and [[Construct]] are deployed only when the proxied objects are functions and constructors (Table 5.2).

As can be seen from Table 5.1, when we want to intercept the delete property operation, we can use the deleteProperty interception function to achieve:

```
01    const obj = { foo :  1 }
02    const p = new Proxy ( obj ,    {
03        deleteProperty(target, key) {
04            return Reflect . deleteProperty ( target ,   key )
05        }
06    })
07
08    console . log ( p . foo )    //  1
09    delete p.foo
10    console . log ( p . foo)    //  undefined
```

It should be emphasized here that deleteProperty implements the internal methods and behaviors of the proxy object p, so in order to delete the property value on the proxied object, we need to use Reflect.deleteProperty (target, key) to do it.

5.3   How to Proxy Objects

Starting with this section, we will start implementing reactive data. Earlier we used the get interception function to intercept read operations on properties. But in response systems, "read" is a very broad concept. For example, using the in operator to check whether an object has a given key is also a "read" operation, as shown in the following code:

```
01    effect (( )  =>  {
02       ' foo ' in obj
03    } )
```

This is also essentially a "read" operation. The response system should intercept all reads so that the response can be triggered correctly when the data changes. All possible reads to a normal object are listed below.

- Access properties: obj.foo.
- Determine whether the given key exists on the object or prototype: key in obj.
- Use a *for ... in* loop to iterate over objects: for (const key in obj) {}.

Next, we will discuss how to intercept these reads step by step. The first is the reading of properties, such as obj.foo, which we know can be achieved with the *get* interception function:

```
01    const obj = { foo:  1 }
02
03    const p  =  new Proxy (obj ,  {
04       get ( target ,  key ,  receiver )  {
05          //  make contact
06          track (target, key)
07          //  return property value
08          return Reflect . get ( target ,  key ,  receiver )
09       },
10    } )
```

For the *in* operator, how should we intercept it? We can first look at Table 5.3 and try to find the interception function corresponding to the in operator, but there is no content related to the *in* operator in Table 5.3. How can we deal with this situation? At this time, we need to review the relevant specifications on the in operator. In

Table 5.3 All internal methods for proxy object deployment

Internal methods	Processor functions
[[GetPrototypeOf]]	getPrototypeOf
[[SetPrototypeOf]]	setPrototypeOf
[[IsExtensible]]	isExtensible
[[PreventExtensions]]	preventExtensions
[[GetOwnProperty]]	getOwnPropertyDescriptor
[[DefineOwnProperty]]	defineProperty
[[HasProperty]]	has
[[Get]]	get
[[Set]]	set
[[Delete]]	deleteProperty
[[OwnPropertyKeys]]	ownKeys
[[Call]]	apply
[[Construct]]	construct

Fig. 5.1 Runtime logic of
the in operator

1. Let *lref* be the result of evaluating *RelationalExpression*.
2. Let *lval* be ? GetValue(*lref*).
3. Let *rref* be the result of evaluating *ShiftExpression*.
4. Let *rval* be ? GetValue(*rref*).
5. If Type(*rval*) is not Object, throw a **TypeError** exception.
6. Return ? HasProperty(*rval*, ? ToPropertyKey(*lval*)).

Fig. 5.2 The logic of the
has property abstract
method

1. Assert: Type(O) is Object.
2. Assert: IsPropertyKey(P) is **true**.
3. Return ? O.[[HasProperty]](P).

Section 13.10.1 of the ECMA-262 specification, the runtime logic of the in operator
is clearly defined, as shown in Fig. 5.1.

Figure 5.1 describes the content as follows.

```
1. Let the value of lref be the execution result of RelationalExpression.
2. Let the value of lval be? GetValue (lref).
3. Let the value of rref be the result of ShiftExpression execution.
4. Let the value of rval be? GetValue (rref).
5. Throw a TypeError exception if Type (rval) is not an object.
6. Return? HasProperty (rval,? ToPropertyKey (lval)).
```

The key point is in step. It can be found that the result of the operation of the *in*
operator is obtained by calling an abstract method called HasProperty. About the
HasProperty abstract method, you can find in Section 7.3.11 of the ECMA-262
specification. Its operation is as shown in Fig. 5.2.

Figure 5.2 describes the content as follows.

In step 3, you can see that the return value of the HasProperty abstract method is
obtained by calling the object's internal method [[HasProperty]]. The
[[HasProperty]] internal method, however, can be found in Table 5.3, and its
corresponding interceptor function is named *has*, so we can implement the proxy
for the *in* operator through the *has* interceptor function:

```
01    const obj  =  {  foo :  1 }
02    const p  =  new Proxy (obj, {
03      has ( target ,  key )  {
04            track (target, key)
05            return Reflect . has ( target ,  key )
06      }
07    } )
```

This way, when we manipulate reactive data with the in operator in a side effect
function, we can establish dependencies:

14.7.5.6 ForIn/OfHeadEvaluation (*uninitializedBoundNames, expr, iterationKind* **)**

The abstract operation ForIn/OfHeadEvaluation takes arguments *uninitializedBoundNames, expr,* and *iterationKind* (either enumerate, iterate, or async-iterate). It performs the following steps when called:

1. Let *oldEnv* be the running execution context's LexicalEnvironment.
2. If *uninitializedBoundNames* is not an empty List, then
   a. Assert: *uninitializedBoundNames* has no duplicate entries.
   b. Let *newEnv* be NewDeclarativeEnvironment(*oldEnv*).
   c. For each String *name* of *uninitializedBoundNames*, do
      i. Perform ! *newEnv*.CreateMutableBinding(*name*, **false**).
   d. Set the running execution context's LexicalEnvironment to *newEnv*.
3. Let *exprRef* be the result of evaluating *expr*.
4. Set the running execution context's LexicalEnvironment to *oldEnv*.

5. Let *exprValue* be ? GetValue(*exprRef*).
6. If *iterationKind* is enumerate, then
   a. If *exprValue* is **undefined** or **null**, then
      i. Return Completion { [[Type]]: **break**, [[Value]]: empty, [[Target]]: empty }.
   b. Let *obj* be ! ToObject(*exprValue*).
   c. Let *iterator* be ? EnumerateObjectProperties(*obj*).
   d. Let *nextMethod* be ! GetV(*iterator*, **"next"**).
   e. Return the Record { [[Iterator]]: *iterator*, [[NextMethod]]: *nextMethod*, [[Done]]: **false** }.
7. Else,
   a. Assert: *iterationKind* is iterate or async-iterate.
   b. If *iterationKind* is async-iterate, let *iteratorHint* be async.
   c. Else, let *iteratorHint* be sync.
   d. Return ? GetIterator(*exprValue*, *iteratorHint*).

Fig. 5.3 Execution rules of for . . . in header

```
01    effect(() => {
02       'foo' in p   // will create dependencies
03    })
```

Let's look at how to intercept *for . . . in* loops. Likewise, all the methods we can intercept are in Table 5.3, which lists all the basic semantic methods of an object; that is, every operation is actually implemented by these basic semantic methods and their combinations, and the *for . . . in* loop is no exception. In order to figure out which basic semantic methods the *for . . . in* loop depends on, you also need to look at the specification.

Since this part of the specification has a lot of content, only the key parts are intercepted here. Execution rules for the *for . . . in* header are defined in the 14.7.5.6 section of the specification, as shown in Fig. 5.3.

The content described in step 6 in Fig. 5.3 is as follows.

```
6. If iterationKind is enumerate, then
a. If exprValue is undefined or null, then.
       i. Return Completion { [[Type]]: break, [[Value]]: empty,
[[Target]]: empty}.
b. Let obj be! ToObject(exprValue).
c. Let iterator be? EnumerateObjectProperties(obj).
```

d. Let *nextMethod* be! GetV(*iterator*, "next").
e. Return the *Record* {[[Iterator]]: *iterator*, [[NextMethod]]:
nextMethod, [[Done]]: false}.

Take a closer look at sub-step c of step 6:

Let the value of iterator be? EnumerateObjectProperties(obj).

The key point here is EnumerateObjectProperties(obj). Here EnumerateObjectProperties is an abstract method that returns an iterator object, and section 14.7.5.9 of the specification gives example implementations that satisfy this abstraction, as shown in the following code:

```
01   function* EnumerateObjectProperties ( obj )  {
02     const visited = new Set ();
03     for  ( const key of Reflect.ownKeys ( obj ) )  {
04         if ( typeof key  ===  " symbol " )   continue;
05         const desc = Reflect.getOwnPropertyDescriptor(obj, key);
06         if  ( desc )  {
07             visited . add ( key ) ;
08             if (desc . enumerable)  yield  key;
09         }
10     }
11     const proto = Reflect.getPrototypeOf(obj);
12     if  ( proto  ===  null )   return;
13     for  ( const protoKey of EnumerateObjectProperties ( proto ) )  {
14         if  (!  visited . has ( protoKey ) ) yield protoKey;
15     }
16   }
```

As you can see, this method is a *generator* function that takes a parameter *obj*. In fact, *obj* is the object traversed by the *for ... in* loop. The key point is to use Reflect.ownKeys(obj) to obtain keys that only belong to the object itself. With this clue, it is already obvious how to intercept the answer of the *for ... in* loop. We can use the ownKeys interception function to intercept Reflect.ownKeys operations:

```
01   const obj  =  {  foo :  1 }
02   const ITERATE_KEY  =  Symbol ()
03
04    const p  =  new Proxy ( obj ,  {
05      ownKeys ( target )  {
06          // associate side effect functions with ITERATE_KEY
07          track ( target ,   ITERATE_KEY )
08          return Reflect . ownKeys ( target )
09      }
10   } )
```

As shown in the code above, intercepting ownKeys operations can indirectly intercept *for ... in* loops. But I believe everyone has noticed that when we use the track function for tracking, we use ITERATE_KEY as the tracking key. Why do we do this? This is because ownKeys intercepting function is different from get/set intercepting function. In *set/get*, we can get the *key* of the specific operation, but in ownKeys, we can only get the target object *target*. This is also intuitive, because when reading and writing property values, we can always know exactly which property is currently being operated on, so we only need to establish a connection between the property and the side effect function. And ownKeys is used to obtain all its own key values of an object. This operation is obviously not bound to any specific key, so we can only construct a unique *key* as an identifier, that is, ITERATE_KEY.

Since the tracking is ITERATE_KEY, it should also be triggered when the response is triggered:

```
01    trigger ( target , ITERATE_KEY )
```

But under what circumstances does an operation on the data need to trigger the re-execution of the side effect function associated with the ITERATE_KEY? To figure this out, we use a piece of code to illustrate. Suppose there is a *for ... in* loop inside the side effect function:

```
01    const obj = { foo: 1 }
02    const p = new Proxy(obj, { /* ...   */ } )
03
04    effect ( ( )   =>  {
05       //  for...in loop
06      for   ( const key in p )   {
07          console . log ( key )   // foo
08       }
09    } )
```

After the side effect function executes, it will establish a response connection with the ITERATE_KEY. Next, we try to add a new property bar to the object *p*:

```
01 p.bar = 2
```

Since object *p* originally only had the foo property, the *for ... in* loop will only execute once. Now that a new property bar has been added to it, the *for ... in* loop will change from executing once to executing twice. That is, when adding a new property to an object, it will have an impact on the *for ... in* loop, so the side effect function associated with the ITERATE_KEY needs to be triggered to re-execute. But the current implementation cannot do this yet. When we add a new property bar to object *p*, it does not trigger the side effect function to be re-executed. Why? Let's take a look at the current implementation of the set interceptor function:

```
01    const p = new Proxy (obj, {
02       //  intercept setup operation
03      set ( target ,   key ,   newVal ,   receiver )   {
04          //  set property value
05          const res = Reflect.set (target, key, newVal, receiver)
06          //  take the side effect function out of the bucket and
```

```
execute it
    07              trigger ( target ,   key )
    08
    09              return res
    10      },
    11      //  omit other interception functions
    12  } )
```

When a new bar property is added to object *p*, the execution of the set interceptor function will be triggered. At this time, the key received by the *set* interceptor function is the string "bar," so the final call to the trigger function only triggers the re-execution of the side effect function associated with "bar." But from the previous introduction, we know that the *for* ... *in* loop is to establish a connection between the side effect function and the ITERATE_KEY, which has nothing to do with "bar," so when we try to perform the p.bar = 2 operation, it does not trigger the response correctly.

Once we figure out what the problem is, the solution follows. When adding properties, we can also take out the side effects functions associated with the ITERATE_KEY and execute them:

```
    01   function trigger ( target ,   key )    {
    02     const depsMap   =   bucket . get ( target )
    03     if   ( !depsMap ) return
    04       //  get the side effect function associated with the key
    05       const effects   =   depsMap . get ( key )
    06       //  get the side effect function associated with the
ITERATE_KEY
    07       const iterateEffects = depsMap . get ( ITERATE_KEY )
    08
    09       const effectsToRun   =   new Set ( )
    10       //   add the side effect function associated with key to
effectsToRun
    11       effects  &&  effects . forEach ( effectFn   =>   {
    12         if   ( effectFn!   ==   activeEffect )   {
    13           effectsToRun . add ( effectFn )
    14         }
    15       } )
    16       //  add side effect functions associated with ITERATE_KEY to
effectsToRun as well
    17       iterateEffects  &&  iterateEffects.forEach(effectFn => {
    18         if   ( effectFn!   ==   activeEffect)   {
    19           effectsToRun . add ( effectFn )
    20         }
    21       } )
    22
    23       effectsToRun . forEach ( effectFn   =>   {
    24         if   ( effectFn . options . scheduler )   {
    25           effectFn . options . scheduler ( effectFn )
    26         } else  {
    27           effectFn ()
    28         }
```

```
29        } )
30    }
```

As shown in the above code, when the trigger function is executed, in addition to those side effects that are directly associated with the key of the specific operation, those side effects associated with the ITERATE_KEY should also be taken out and executed.

But I believe that you have found that there is no problem with adding new properties, but if you only modify the value of existing properties instead of adding new properties, then the problem will come. Please see the following code:

```
01    const obj = { foo: 1 }
02    const p   =   new Proxy ( obj ,   { /* ... */ } )
03
04    effect ( ( )   =>   {
05      //   for...in loop
06        for   ( const key in p )   {
07          console. log ( key )   // foo
08        }
09    } )
```

We change the value of p.foo:

```
01 p.foo = 2
```

Unlike adding new properties, modifying properties does not affect the *for ... in* loop. Because no matter how you modify the value of a property, it will only loop once for the *for ... in* loop. So in this case, we do not need to trigger the side effect function to re-execute; otherwise, it will cause unnecessary performance overhead. However, whether it is adding a new property or modifying an existing property value, its basic semantics are [[Set]], and we all achieve interception through the set interception function, as shown in the following code:

```
01    const p   =   new Proxy ( obj ,   {
02        //   intercept setup operation
03        set ( target ,   key ,   newVal ,   receiver)   {
04            //   set property value
05            const res = Reflect . set ( target ,   key ,   newVal ,
receiver)
06            //   take the side effect function out of the bucket and
execute it
07            trigger ( target ,   key )
08
09            return res
10        },
11        //   omit other interception functions
12    } )
```

So in order to solve the above problem, when the setting property operation occurs, we need to be able to distinguish the type of operation in the set interceptor function, whether to add a new property or set an existing property:

```
01    const p  =  new Proxy ( obj ,   {
02        //  intercept setup operation
03        set ( target ,   key ,   newVal ,   receiver )   {
04            //  if the property does not exist, it means that a new
property is being added; otherwise, an existing property is set
05              const type = Object.prototype.hasOwnProperty.call
(target, key)? 'SET': 'ADD'
06
07              //  set property value
08              const res = Reflect.set (target, key, newVal, receiver)
09
10          //  pass type as the third argument to the trigger function
11              trigger (target, key, type)
12
13              return res
14        },
15        //  omit other interception functions
16    } )
```

As shown in the above code, we preferentially use the Object.prototype. hasOwnProperty to check whether the attribute of the current operation already exists on the target object. If it exists, it means that the current operation type is "SET"; that is, the attribute value is modified; otherwise, the current operation type is considered to be "ADD," i.e., adding a new property. Finally, we pass the type result *type* as the third parameter to the trigger function.

Within the *trigger* function, the current operation type can be distinguished by the type *type*, and only when the operation *type* is "ADD," the side effect function associated with the ITERATE_KEY will be triggered to re-execute, thus avoiding unnecessary performance loss:

```
01    function trigger ( target ,   key ,   type )   {
02      const depsMap  =  bucket . get ( target )
03      if  ( !depsMap ) return
04      const effects  =  depsMap . get ( key )
05
06      const effectsToRun  =  new Set ( )
07      effects && effects . forEach ( effectFn  =>  {
08          if  ( effectFn!  ==  activeEffect )  {
09            effectsToRun. add ( effectFn )
10          }
11      } )
12
13      console. log ( type,  key )
14      //  trigger the side effect function associated with the
ITERATE_KEY to re-execute only if the operation type is 'ADD '
15          if  ( type  ===  ' ADD ' )   {
```

```
16              const iterateEffects  =  depsMap . get ( ITERATE_KEY )
17              iterateEffects && iterateEffects . forEach (effectFn  =>
{
18                  if  (effectFn !  ==  activeEffect )     {
19                      effectsToRun. add ( effectFn )
20                  }
21              })
22          }
23
24      effectsToRun . forEach ( effectFn  =>  {
25          if  ( effectFn . options . scheduler )   {
26              effectFn . options . scheduler ( effectFn )
27          } else  {
28          effectFn ( )
29          }
30      } )
31   }
```

Usually, we encapsulate the operation type as an enumeration value, for example:

```
01   const TriggerType = {
02      SET: 'SET',
03      ADD: 'ADD'
04   }
```

This is very helpful for both the maintenance of the later code and the clarity of the code. But we will not discuss these minutiae here.

Regarding the proxy for the object, there is one last job left to do, which is to remove the proxy for the property operation:

```
01 delete p.foo
```

How to proxy the delete operator? Please look at the specification. The behavior of the *delete* operator is clearly defined in the 13.5.1.2 section of the specification, as shown in Fig. 5.4.

The contents of the fifth step described in Fig. 5.4 are as follows.

```
5. If IsPropertyReference (ref) is true, then
a. Assert:! IsPrivateReference (ref) is false.
b. If IsSuperReference (ref) is also true, throw a ReferenceError
exception.
c. Let baseObj be! ToObject (ref, [[Base]]).
d. Let deleteStatus be? baseObj. [[Delete]] (ref. [[ReferencedName]]).
e. If the value of deleteStatus is false, and the value of ref. [[Strict]]
is true, throw a TypeError exception.
f. Return deleteStatus.
```

13.5.1.2 Runtime Semantics: Evaluation

UnaryExpression : **delete** *UnaryExpression*

1. Let *ref* be the result of evaluating *UnaryExpression*.
2. ReturnIfAbrupt(*ref*).
3. If *ref* is not a Reference Record, return **true**.
4. If IsUnresolvableReference(*ref*) is **true**, then
   a. Assert: *ref*.[[Strict]] is **false**.
   b. Return **true**.
5. If IsPropertyReference(*ref*) is **true**, then

   a. Assert: ! IsPrivateReference(*ref*) is **false**.
   b. If IsSuperReference(*ref*) is **true**, throw a **ReferenceError** exception.
   c. Let *baseObj* be ! ToObject(*ref*.[[Base]]).
   d. Let *deleteStatus* be ? *baseObj*.[[Delete]](*ref*.[[ReferencedName]]).
   e. If *deleteStatus* is **false** and *ref*.[[Strict]] is **true**, throw a **TypeError** exception.
   f. Return *deleteStatus*.
6. Else,
   a. Let *base* be *ref*.[[Base]].
   b. Assert: *base* is an Environment Record.
   c. Return ? *base*.DeleteBinding(*ref*.[[ReferencedName]]).

Fig. 5.4 Behavior of the delete operator

As can be seen from the d substep in step 5, the behavior of the *delete* operator depends on the [[Delete]] internal method. Then look at Table 5.3. As you can see, this internal method can be intercepted using deleteProperty:

```
01   const p  =  new Proxy (obj ,  {
02      deleteProperty  ( target , key )   {
03         // check if the property being manipulated is the object's
own property
04         const hadKey =  Object. Prototype. hasOwnProperty. call (
target ,  key )
05         // use Reflect. deleteProperty to complete the deletion of
attributes
06         const res  =  Reflect.deleteProperty ( target ,  key )
07
08            if  (res & & hadKey) {
09            // update will only be triggered if the deleted property
is an object's own property and was successfully deleted
10               trigger (target, key, 'DELETE')
11            }
12
13            return res
```

```
14        }
15    } )
```

As shown in the above code, first check whether the deleted property belongs to the object itself, and then call the Reflect.deleteProperty function to complete the deletion of the property. Only when the results of these two steps meet the conditions, call the trigger function to trigger the side effect function to re-execute. It should be noted that when calling the trigger function, we pass the new operation type "DELETE." Since the delete operation will make the object have fewer keys, it will affect the number of times the *for ... in* loop, so when the operation type is "DELETE," we should also trigger those side effects associated with the ITERATE_KEY to re-execute:

```
01    function trigger ( target,   key,   type )   {
02        const depsMap   =   bucket. get ( target )
03        if   ( !depsMap) return
04        const effects   =   depsMap. get ( key )
05
06        const effectsToRun   =   new Set ( )
07        effects && effects. forEach (effectFn   =>   {
08            if   ( effectFn !   == activeEffect )   {
09                effectsToRun. add ( effectFn )
10            }
11        })
12
13        //   when the operation type is ADD or DELETE, the side effect
function associated with the ITERATE_KEY needs to be triggered to
re-execute
14        if   ( type   ===   'ADD'   ||   type === 'DELETE' )   {
15            const iterateEffects = depsMap.get (ITERATE_KEY)
16        iterateEffects  &&  iterateEffects. forEach (effectFn  =>  {
17                if   (effectFn!   == activeEffect )   {
18                    effectsToRun. add ( effectFn )
19                }
20            } )
21        }
22
23        effectsToRun . forEach ( effectFn   =>   {
24            if   (effectFn. options. scheduler)   {
25                effectFn. options. scheduler (effectFn)
26            } else {
27                effectFn ( )
28            }
29        })
30    }
```

In this code, we added the type === 'DELETE' judgment so that the deletion of the attribute action triggers the re-execution of the side effect function associated with the ITERATE_KEY.

5.4 Reasonable Response Trigger

In the previous section, we detailed how to proxy objects from a canonical point of view. In the process, a lot of boundary conditions are handled. For example, we need to know exactly whether the type of the operation is '"DD" or "SET," or some other type of operation, so that the response can be triggered correctly. But there is still a lot of work to be done to trigger responses reasonably.

First, let's look at the first problem to face; that is, when the value does not change, there should be no need to trigger a response:

```
01    const obj  =  { foo:  1 }
02    const p  =  new Proxy (obj,  { /* ...  */ } )
03
04    effect ( ( )  =>  {
05        console. Log ( p. foo )
06    })
07
08    //  set the value of p.foo, but the value does not change
09    p.foo = 1
```

As shown in the code above, the initial value of the p.foo is 1. When setting a new value for p.foo, if the value does not change, there is no need to trigger a response. In order to meet the requirements, we need to modify the code of the set interceptor function. Before calling the trigger function to trigger the response, we need to check whether the value has really changed:

```
01    const p  =  new Proxy (obj, {
02      set ( target ,  key ,  newVal ,  receiver )  {
03          //  get the old value first
04          const oldVal = target [key]
05
06          const type = Object.prototype.hasOwnProperty.call
(target, key) ?  'SET'  :  'ADD'
07          const res = Reflect. set (target,  key,  newVal,  receiver)
08          //  compare the new value with the old value; only trigger
the response when it is in09complete
09              if  ( oldVal!  ==  newVal )  {
10                  trigger ( target,  key,  type )
11              }
12
13              return res
14      },
15    })
```

As shown in the code above, we first get the old value oldVal in the *set* interceptor function, then compare the new value with the old value, and only trigger a response if they are not equal. Now, if we test the example at the beginning of this section again, we will find that resetting the same value no longer triggers a response.

However, just doing congruent comparisons is flawed, which is reflected in the handling of NaNs. We know that a congruent comparison of NaN to NaN always yields false:

```
01 NaN === NaN // false
02 NaN! == NaN // true
```

In other words, if the initial value of the p.foo is NaN, and then NaN is set as a new value for it, then the flaw of just doing congruent comparisons is exposed:

```
01    const obj  =  { foo:  NaN }
02    const p  =  new Proxy ( obj,  { /*  ...  */ } )
03
04    effect ( ( )  => {
05        console. log ( p. foo )
06        } )
07
08 //  still trigger a response because NaN!  == NaN is true
09 p.foo  =  NaN
```

This will still trigger the response and cause unnecessary updates. To fix this, we need to add one more condition, i.e., in the case of incomplete new and old values, ensure that they are not NaN:

```
01    const p  =  new Proxy(obj, {
02      set ( target ,  key ,  newVal ,  receiver )  {
03          //  get the old value first
04          const oldVal  =  target [ key ]
05
06              const type = Object.prototype.hasOwnProperty.call
(target, key) ?  'SET' : 'ADD'
07              const res = Reflect.set (target, key, newVal, receiver)
08          //  compare the new value with the old value and only trigger
a response if they are not all equal and not both NaN
09              if  (oldVal  !== newVal && (oldVal  === oldVal ||
newVal  === newVal ) )  {
10                  trigger (target, key, type)
11              }
12
13              return res
14      },
15    } )
```

This solves the NaN problem.

But to trigger a response reasonably, it's not enough to just deal with NaN questions. Next, we discuss a situation where properties are inherited from a prototype. For the convenience of the following explanation, we need to encapsulate a reactive function that takes an object as a parameter and returns the reactive data created for it:

```
01    function reactive (obj)  {
02      return new Proxy (obj,  {
03            //  omit the interception function explained above
04      })
05    }
```

As you can see, the *reactive* function just encapsulates the proxy. Next, we create an example based on *reactive*:

```
01    const obj = { }
02    const proto = { bar: 1 }
03    const child = reactive (obj)
04    const parent = reactive (proto)
05      //  use parent as the prototype of child
06      Object.setPrototypeOf (child, parent)
07
08      effect ( ( )   =>  {
09          console.log (child.bar)  //  1
10      })
11      //  modify the value of child.bar
12      child.bar  =  2 //  will cause the side effect function to
re-execute twice
```

Observing the above code, you will find that we define the empty object *obj* and the object *proto*, create the corresponding reactive data *child* and *parent* for them respectively, and use the Object.setPrototypeOf method to set the *parent* as the prototype of the *child*. Next, we access the value of the child.bar in the side effect function. As you can see from the code, the *child* itself does not have a *bar* attribute, so when accessing the child.bar, the value is inherited from the prototype. But anyway, since *child* is reactive data, there is a connection between it and the side effect function, so when we execute child.bar = 2, we expect the side effect function to execute again. But if you try to run the above code, you will find that the side effect function not only executes, but also executes twice, which causes unnecessary updates.

In order to figure out the cause of the problem, we need to analyze the whole process step by step. When reading the value of the child.bar in the side effect function, the *get* interceptor function of the *child* proxy object will be triggered. We know that Reflect.get (target, key, receiver) is used in the interceptor function to get the final result. Corresponding to the above example, this sentence is equivalent to:

```
Reflect.get (obj, 'bar', receiver)
```

This actually implements the default behavior of accessing property values through obj.bar. That is to say, the engine internally obtains the final result by calling the [[Get]] internal method deployed by the *obj* object, so it is necessary for us to review the 10.1.8.1 section of the specification to understand the execution flow of the [[Get]] internal method, as shown in Fig. 5.5.

Fig. 5.5 Execution flow of
the [[Get]] internal method

1. Assert: IsPropertyKey(P) is **true**.
2. Let *desc* be ? O.[[GetOwnProperty]](P).
3. If *desc* is **undefined**, then
   a. Let *parent* be ? O.[[GetPrototypeOf]]().
   b. If *parent* is **null**, return **undefined**.
   c. Return ? *parent*.[[Get]](P, *Receiver*).
4. If IsDataDescriptor(*desc*) is **true**, return *desc*.[[Value]].
5. Assert: IsAccessorDescriptor(*desc*) is **true**.
6. Let *getter* be *desc*.[[Get]].
7. If *getter* is **undefined**, return **undefined**.
8. Return ? Call(*getter*, *Receiver*).

Step 3 in Fig. 5.5 is described below.

```
3. If desc is undefined, then
a. Let the value of parent be? O.[[GetPrototypeOf]]().
b. If parent is null, return undefined.
c. Return? parent.[[Get]] (P, Receiver).
```

In step 3, we can learn very critical information: if the object itself does not have the property, then the prototype of the object will be obtained, and the [[Get]] method of the prototype will be called to get the final result. Corresponding to the above example, when reading the value of the child.bar attribute, since the object *obj* of the *child* proxy does not have a *bar* attribute itself, it will obtain the prototype of the object *obj*, that is, the *parent* object, so the final result is actually the parent.bar value. But let's not forget that *parent* itself is also reactive data, so when accessing the value of parent.bar in the side effect function, it will cause the side effect function to be collected, which will also establish a response connection. So, we can conclude that both child.bar and parent.bar have a response connection with the side effect function.

But this still does not explain why when setting the value of child.bar, the side effect function execution is triggered twice in a row, so next we need to look at the specific execution flow when the setting operation occurs. We know that when executing child.bar = 2, the *set* interceptor function of the *child* proxy object is called. Similarly, in the *set* interception function, we use Reflect.set (target, key, newVal, receiver) to complete the default setting behavior, i.e., the engine will call the [[Set]] internal method deployed by the *obj* object. According to the 10.1.9.2 section of the specification, we can know the execution flow of the [[Set]] internal method, which is shown in Fig. 5.6.

The contents described in step 2 in Fig. 5.6 are as follows.

```
2. If ownDesc is undefined, then
a. Let the value of parent be O.[[GetPrototypeOf]]().
b. If parent is not null, then.
       i. Return? parent.[[Set]] (P, V, Receiver);
c. Else.
```

1. Assert: IsPropertyKey(P) is **true**
2. If *own Desc* is **undefined**, then
   a. Let *parent* be? *O*.[[GetPrototypeOf]]().
   b. If *parent* is not **null**, then
       i. Return? *parent*.[[Set]](*P, V, Receiver*).
   c. Else,
       i. Set *own Desc* to the PropertyDescriptor {[[Value]]: **undefined**, [[Writable]]: **true**, [[Enumerable]]: **true**, [[Configurable]]: **true** }.
3. If IsDataDescriptor(*own Desc*) is **true**, then
   a. If *own Desc*.[[Writable]] is **false**, return **false**.
   b. If Type(*Receiver*) is not Object, return **false**.
   c. Let *existing Descriptor* be? *Receiver*.[[GetOwnProperty]](*P*).
   d. If *existing Descriptor* is not **undefined**, then
       i. If IsAccessorDescriptor(existingDescriptor) is **true**, return **false**.
       ii. If *existingDescriptor*.[[Writable]] is **false**, return **false**.
       iii. Let *valueDesc* be the PropertyDescriptor { [[Value]]: *V*).
       iv. Return? *Receiver*.[[DefineOwnProperty]](*P, value Desc*).
   e. Else,
       i. Assert: *Receiver* does not currently have a property *P*.
       ii. Return? CreateDataProperty(*Receiver, P, V*).
4. Assert: IsAccessorDescriptor(*ownDesc*) **is true**.
5. Let *setter* be *ownDesc*.[[Set]].
6. If *setter* is **undefined**, return **false**.
7. Perform? Call(*setter, Receiver,* « *V*»).
8. Return **true**.

Fig. 5.6 Execution flow of [[Set]] internal method

i. Set *ownDesc* to {[[Value]]: undefined, [[Writable]]: true, [[Enumerable]]: true, [[Configurable]]: true}.

As can be seen from step 2, if the set property does not exist on the object, its prototype will be obtained, and the [[Set]] method of the prototype will be called, which is the [[Set]] internal method of *parent*. Since *parent* is a proxy object, this is equivalent to executing its *set* interceptor function. In other words, although we are operating on the child.bar, this will also cause the *set* interceptor function of the *parent* proxy object to be executed. Earlier we analyzed that when reading the value of the child.bar, the side effect function would not only be collected by the child.bar, but also by the parent.bar. Hence, when the *set* of the *parent* proxy object intercepts the execution of the function, it will trigger the re-execution of the side effect function, which is why modifying the value of the child.bar will cause the side effect function to be re-executed twice.

Next, we need to think about the solution. The idea is very simple: since it is executed twice, cannot it just block one of them? We can block the re-execution of the side effect function triggered by parent.bar. How do we block it? We know that the two updates are caused by the *set* interceptor being fired twice, so as long as we can distinguish the two updates within the set interceptor, we can finish the task. When we set child.bar value, the *set* interceptor function of the child proxy object is executed:

```
01    //  set interception function of child
02      set (target,  key,  value,  receiver)  {
03          //  target is the original object obj
```

```
04              //receiver is the proxy object child
05    }
```

At this time, the *target* is the original object *obj*, and the receiver is the proxy object *child*. We found that the receiver is actually the proxy object of the *target*.

However, since there is no bar attribute on *obj*, the prototype parent of *obj* will be obtained, and the *set* interceptor function of the *parent* proxy object will be executed:

```
01    //  set interception function of parent
02    set  (target,  key,  value,  receiver) {
03              //  target is the original object proto
04              //receiver is still the proxy object child
05    }
```

We find that when the *set* interception function of the *parent* proxy object is executed, the *target* is the original object *proto*, and the *receiver* is still the proxy object *child*, not the proxy object of the *target*. Through this feature, we can see the difference between *target* and *receiver*. Since we initially set the value of child.bar, in any case, the receiver is a child, while the target is variable. According to this difference, it is easy to think of a solution—just need to determine whether the receiver is a proxy object of target. The update is triggered only when the *receiver* is a proxy object of *target*, so that the update caused by the prototype can be blocked.

So the next question becomes how to determine whether the *receiver* is a proxy object for *target*, which requires us to add an ability to the *get* interceptor function, as shown in the following code:

```
01    function  reactive ( obj )  {
02      return new Proxy (obj  {
03          get (target,  key,  receiver)  {
04              // the proxy object can access the original data source
through the raw attribute
05                  if  ( key === 'raw' )  {
06                      return target
07                  }
08
09                  track ( target, key )
10                  return Reflect. get ( target,  key,  receiver )
11              }
12          // omit other interception functions
13      })
14    }
```

We added a piece of code that implements the function that the proxy object can read the original data source through the raw property, for example:

```
01    child. raw   ===   obj // true
02    parent. raw   ===   proto // true
```

With this, we can determine whether the *receiver* is a proxy object of *target* in the *set* interception function:

```
01    function reactive ( obj )   {
02       return new Proxy ( obj   {
03              set (target,  key,  newVal,  receiver )  {
04                   const oldVal = target [key]
05                 const type = Object.prototype.hasOwnProperty. call
(target,  key)  ?  ' SET '  :  ' ADD '
06                 const res = Reflect.set (target, key, newVal, receiver)
07
08                 // target  ===  receiver.raw indicates that the
receiver is the proxy object of target
09                  if  (target  ===  receiver.raw) {
10                       if  (oldVal  !==  newVal  &&  (oldVal  ===
oldVal  ||  newVal  ===  newVal ) )   {
11                            trigger (target,  key,  type )
12                        }
13                   }
14
15                 return res
16             }
17          //  omit other interception functions
18       })
19    }
```

As shown in the above code, we added a new judgment condition that triggers the update only when the *receiver* is a proxy object of the *target*, so that the update caused by the prototype can be blocked, thereby avoiding unnecessary update operations.

5.5   Shallow Response VS Deep Response

In this section, we will introduce the difference between reactive and shallowReactive, i.e., the difference between deep response and shallow response. In fact, the *reactive* we currently implement is shallow responsive. Take the following code as an example:

```
01    const obj = reactive ({ foo: { bar: 1 } })
02
03    effect ( ( )  =>  {
04       console. log ( obj. foo. bar )
05    })
06    //  modifying the value of obj.foo.bar does not trigger a
```

response
```
07    obj.foo.bar = 2
```

First, create an *obj* proxy object whose *foo* property value is also an object, i.e., {bar: 1}. Next, access the value of the obj.foo.bar inside the side effect function. But we found that subsequent modifications to the obj.foo.bar could not trigger the re-execution of the side effect function, why? Take a look at the current implementation:

```
01    function reactive(obj) {
02        return new Proxy(obj {
03            get ( target,  key,  receiver )  {
04                if  (key  ===  ' raw ' )  {
05                    return target
06                }
07
08                track(target, key)
09                // when reading the property value, the result is
returned directly
10                return Reflect.get(target, key, receiver)
11            }
12            //  omit other interception functions
13        })
14    }
```

As can be seen from the above code, when we read the obj.foo.bar, we must first read the value of the obj.foo. Here we directly use the Reflect.get function to return obj.foo result. Since the result obj.foo obtained by Reflect.get is an ordinary object, that is, {bar: 1}, it is not a reactive object, so when accessing obj.foo.bar in the side effect function, the response connection cannot be established. To solve this problem, we need to wrap the result returned by the Reflect.get:

```
01    function reactive (obj)  {
02        return new Proxy(obj  {
03            get (target, key, receiver)  {
04                if  (key === 'raw')  {
05                    return target
07                }
08
09                track (target, key)
10                // get the original value result
11                const res = Reflect. get ( target,  key,  receiver )
12                if  (typeof res === 'object' && res !== null)  {
13                    // call reactive to wrap the result in reactive data
and return
14                    return reactive ( res )
15                }
16                // return res
17                return res
18            }
```

```
19          //   omit other interception functions
20          })
21     }
```

As shown in the code above, when reading the property value, we first detect whether the value is an object, and if it is an object, we recursively call the reactive function to wrap it into responsive data and return it. In this way, when the *foo* property value is read using the obj.foo, the result will be a responsive data, so when the bar property value is read through the obj.foo.bar, a response connection will naturally be established. In this way, when the value of the obj.foo.bar is modified, the side effect function can be triggered to re-execute.

However, we do not always want deep responses, which gives rise to shallowReactive, or shallow responses. The so-called shallow response means that only the first-level properties of the object are responsive, for example:

```
01   const obj  =  shallowReactive ({ foo:  { bar: 1 }  })
02
03   effect ( ( )  =>  {
04        console. log ( obj . foo. bar )
05     })
06     //  obj .foo is responsive and can trigger the side effect
function to re-execute
07      obj. foo  =  { bar :  2 }
08     //  obj . foo. bar is not responsive, and cannot trigger side
effect function re-execution
09      obj.foo.bar = 3
```

In this example, we use the shallowReactive function to create a shallow responsive proxy object *obj*. It can be found that only the first-level properties of the object are responsive, and the second-level and deeper properties are not. It is not difficult to implement this function, as shown in the following code:

```
01    //  encapsulate the createReactive function and receive a
parameter isShallow, which represents whether it is a shallow response.
The default is false, that is, a non-shallow response
02    function createReactive (obj, isShallow = false) {
03       return new Proxy (obj, {
04            //  intercept read operation
05            get ( target,  key,  receiver )   {
06                 if    ( key  ===  ' raw ')   {
07                     return target
08                 }
09
10                 const res = Reflect .get (target, key, receiver)
11
12                 track (target, key)
13
14                 //  if it is a shallow response, the original value
will be returned directly
```

```
15                         if   ( isShallow )    {
16                             return res
17                         }
18
19                         if   ( typeof res   ===   ' object '   &&   res   !==
null )   {
20                             return reactive (res)
21                         }
22
23                         return res
24                     }
25              //   omit other interception functions
26          })
27      }
```

In the above code, we encapsulated the work of object creation into a new function createReactive. In addition to receiving the original object obj, this function also receives the parameter isShallow, which is a Boolean value representing whether to create a shallow response object. By default, the value of isShallow is false, which means creating a deep response object. It should be noted here that when the read property operation occurs, if it is found to be a shallow response in the *get* interception function, it can directly return the original data source. With the createReactive function, we can use it to easily implement the *reactive* and *shallowReactive* functions:

```
01   function reactive (obj) {
02          return createReactive (obj)
03   }
04   function shallowReactive ( obj )    {
05          return createReactive ( obj,    true)
06   }
```

5.6   Read-Only and Shallow Read-Only

We want some data to be read-only, and when the user tries to modify the read-only data, they will receive a warning message. This implements data protection, for example, the props object received by the component should be read-only data. This is where we use the *readonly* function discussed next, which can make a data read-only:

```
01   const obj = readonly ({foo: 1})
02   //   try to modify the data, you will get a warning
03   obj. foo   =   2
```

Read-only is essentially a proxy for data objects, and we can also use the createReactive function to achieve this. As shown in the following code, we add a third parameter isReadonly to the createReactive function:

```
01  // add the third parameter isReadonly, which means whether it is
read-only; the default is false, that is, not read-only
02  function createReactive (obj, isShallow = false, isReadonly
= false) {
03      return new Proxy (obj, {
04          // intercept setup operation
05          set (target, key, newVal, receiver) {
06              // if it is read-only, print a warning message and
return
07              if (isReadonly) {
08                  console.warn ('attribute ${key} is read-only')
09                  return true
10              }
11              const oldVal = target [key]
12              const type = Object.prototype.hasOwnProperty.call
(target, key)? 'SET': 'ADD'
13              const res = Reflect.set (target, key, newVal, receiver)
14              if (target === receiver.raw) {
15                  if (oldVal ! == newVal && (oldVal ===
oldVal || newVal === newVal ) ) {
16                      trigger (target, key, type)
17                  }
18              }
19
20              return res
21          },
22          deleteProperty (target, key) {
23              // if read-only, print a warning message and return
24              if (isReadonly) {
25                  console.warn ('attribute ${key} is read-only')
26                  return true
27              }
28              const hadKey = Object.prototype. hasOwnProperty.
call (target, key)
29              const res = Reflect. deleteProperty (target, key)
30
31              if (res && hadKey) {
32                  trigger (target,  key,  ' DELETE ' )
33              }
34
35              return res
36          }
37          // omit other interception functions
38      })
39  }
```

In this code, when using createReactive to create a proxy object, you can specify whether to create a read-only proxy object through the third parameter. At the same time, we also modified the implementation of the set interceptor function and the deleteProperty interceptor function, because for an object, read-only means that neither the property value of the object can be set nor the property of the object can be deleted. In these two intercepting functions, we have added a judgment on whether it is read-only. Once the data is read-only, when these operations occur, a warning message will be printed to remind the user that this is an illegal operation.

Of course, if a piece of data is read-only, that means it cannot be modified in any way. Therefore, there is no need to establish a response link for read-only data. For this reason, when reading the value of a read-only property in a side effect function, there is no need to call the track function to trace the response:

```
01    const obj = readonly ({foo: 1})
02        effect (() => {
03            obj.foo//The value can be read, but there is no need to
establish a response connection between the side effect function and the
data
04        })
```

In order to implement this function, we need to modify the implementation of the get interceptor function:

```
01    function createReactive (obj,  isShallow  =  false,
isReadonly  =  false) {
02        return new Proxy (obj, {
03            //  intercept read operation
04            get (target,  key,  receiver)  {
05                if  (key  ===  'raw')  {
06                    return target
07                }
08            //  only need to establish response contact when it is not
read-only
09                if  (!isReadonly)  {
10                    track (target,  key)
11                }
12
13                const res  =  Reflect . get (target,  key,  receiver)
14
15                if  (isShallow)  {
16                    return res
17                }
18
19            if  (typeof res  ===  'object'  &&  res !  ==  null) {
20                    return reactive (res)
21                }
22
23                return res
24            }
25            //  omit other interception functions
26        })
27    }
```

As shown in the above code, the value of the isReadonly variable is detected in the *get* interceptor function to determine whether it is read-only. Only in the case of non-read-only, the track function will be called to establish a response connection. Based on this, we can implement the readonly function:

```
01   function readonly ( obj )   {
02      return createReactive ( obj,   false,   true/*   read only */)
03   }
```

However, the readonly function implemented above should be called shallowReadonly because it is not deep read-only:

```
01   const obj   =   readonly ({ foo:  { bar :  1 }  } )
02   obj.foo.bar  =   2 //   can still be modified
```

So in order to achieve deep read-only, we should also recursively call readonly inside the get interceptor function to wrap the data into a read-only proxy object and return it as a return value:

```
01   function createReactive(obj, isShallow = false, isReadonly =
false) {
02        return new Proxy(obj, {
03           // intercept read operation
04           get ( target,  key,  receiver )   {
05              if   ( key  ===  ' raw ')   {
06                 return target
07              }
08              if   ( !isReadonly )   {
09                 track ( target,  key )
10              }
11
12              const res = Reflect. get ( target,  key,  receiver )
13
14              if    ( isShallow )   {
15                 return res
16              }
17
18              if    ( typeof res   ===   'object '  &&  res  !==
null )   {
19                 // if the data is read-only, call readonly to wrap
the value
20                 return isReadonly ?  readonly(res)  :  reactive (
res )
21              }
22
23              return res
24           }
25        // omit other interception functions
```

```
26          } )
27      }
```

As shown in the above code, we determine whether the property value is read-only before returning it. If it is read-only, we call the readonly function to wrap the value and return the wrapped read-only object.

For shallowReadonly, we actually only need to modify the second parameter of createReactive:

```
01    function readonly(obj) {
02          return createReactive ( obj,   false,   true )
03    }
04
05    function shallowReadonly (obj)   {
06      return createReactive (obj,   true   /* shallow */,   true)
07    }
```

As shown in the code above, when calling the createReactive function inside the shallowReadonly function to create a proxy object, set the second parameter isShallow to true, so that a shallow read-only proxy object can be created.

5.7 Proxy Arrays

Starting with this section, we will explain how to proxy arrays. In fact, in JavaScript, an array is just a special object, so to better implement the proxy of arrays, it is necessary to understand what is special about arrays compared to ordinary objects.

In Sect. 5.2, we went into depth about objects in JavaScript. We know that there are two kinds of objects in JavaScript: regular objects and heterogeneous objects. We also discussed the differences between the two. The array we are going to introduce in this section is a heterogeneous object, because the [[DefineOwnProperty]] internal methods of array objects are different from regular objects. In other words, the logic of all internal methods of an array object except for the internal method [[DefineOwnProperty]] is the same as that of a regular object. Therefore, when implementing proxies to arrays, most of the code used to proxy ordinary objects can continue to be used, as follows:

```
01    const arr   =   reactive ( [ 'foo' ] )
02
03    effect ( ( )   =>   {
04          console. log ( arr [ 0 ] )   //   'foo'
05    } )
06
07    arr [ 0 ]   =   'bar'   //   can trigger a response
```

The above code works as expected. In fact, when we read or set the value of an array element through the index, the proxy object's *get/set* interceptor function also executes, so we can make the read and set operations of the array index reactive without any extra work.

But operations on arrays are still different from operations on ordinary objects, and the following summarizes all "read" operations on array elements or properties.

- Access array element values by index: arr [0].
- The length of the access array: arr.length.
- Use the *for ... in* loop to iterate over an array as an object.
- Use *for ... of* to iterate over an array.
- Prototype methods for arrays, such as concat/join/every/some/find/findIndex/ includes, etc., and other prototype methods that do not change the original array.

As you can see, the read operations on arrays are much richer than ordinary objects. Let's take a look at the set operations on array elements or properties.

- Modify array element values by index: arr [1] = 3.
- Change the length of the array: arr.length = 0.
- The stack method of the array: push/pop/shift/unshift.
- Modify the prototype methods of the original array: splice/fill/sort, etc.

In addition to the basic operation of modifying the value of an array element through an array index, the array itself has many prototype methods that modify the original array. Calling these methods is also an operation on an array. Some methods have the operation semantics of "read" and some methods have the operation semantics of "set." Therefore, when these operations occur, the response connection or trigger response should also be properly established.

Judging from the operations on arrays listed above, it seems that proxying arrays is much more difficult than proxying ordinary objects. But this is not the case, this is because the array itself is also an object, but it is a heterogeneous object, and it is not much different from regular objects. Therefore, most of the code used to proxy regular objects also works for arrays. Next, we are going to explain reading or setting the element values of the array by index.

5.7.1   Index and Length of Arrays

Taking the example at the beginning of this section, when accessing the value of an element by the index of the array, it is already possible to establish a response connection:

```
01   const arr  =  reactive ( [ 'foo' ] )
02
03   effect ( ( )  =>   {
04       console.log(arr[0]) // 'foo'
```

10.4.2.1 [[DefineOwnProperty]] (P, $Desc$)

The [[DefineOwnProperty]] internal method of an Array exotic object A takes arguments P (a property key) and $Desc$ (a Property Descriptor). It performs the following steps when called:

1. Assert: IsPropertyKey(P) is **true**.
2. If P is **"length"**, then
   a. Return ? ArraySetLength(A, $Desc$).
3. Else if P is an array index, then
   a. Let *oldLenDesc* be OrdinaryGetOwnProperty(A, **"length"**).
   b. Assert: ! IsDataDescriptor(*oldLenDesc*) is **true**.
   c. Assert: *oldLenDesc*.[[Configurable]] is **false**.
   d. Let *oldLen* be *oldLenDesc*.[[Value]].
   e. Assert: *oldLen* is a **non-negative** integral Number.
   f. Let *index* be ! ToUint32(P).
   g. If *index* ≥ *oldLen* and *oldLenDesc*.[[Writable]] is **false**, return **false**.
   h. Let *succeeded* be ! OrdinaryDefineOwnProperty(A, P, $Desc$).
   i. If *succeeded* is **false**, return **false**.
   j. If *index* ≥ *oldLen*, then
      i. Set *oldLenDesc*.[[Value]] to *index* + 1_{F}.
      ii. Let *succeeded* be OrdinaryDefineOwnProperty(A, **"length"**, *oldLenDesc*).
      iii. Assert: *succeeded* is **true**.
   k. Return **true**.
4. Return OrdinaryDefineOwnProperty(A, P, $Desc$).

Fig. 5.7 Execution flow of [[Define own property]] internal method

```
05      } )
06
07      arr [ 0 ]  =  'bar'  //  can trigger a response
```

But there is still a fundamental difference between setting the value of an element of an array by index and setting the property value of an object, because the internal method [[DefineOwnProperty]] deployed by an array object is different from a regular object. In fact, when we set the value of an array element by index, the internal method [[Set]] deployed by the array object is executed, which is the same as setting the property value of a regular object. According to the specification, the internal method [[Set]] actually depends on [[DefineOwnProperty]], and the difference is reflected here. The logic for the internal method [[DefineOwnProperty]] deployed by an array object is defined in the 10.4.2.1 section of the specification, as shown in Fig. 5.7.

The contents of the j sub-step of step 3 in Fig. 5.7 are described as follows.

```
j. If index > = oldLen, then
     I. Set oldLenDesc. [[Value]] to index + 1.
     II. Let the value of succeeded be OrdinaryDefineOwnProperty (A,
'length', oldLenDesc).
     III. Assert: Succeeded is true.
```

As you can see, the specification clearly states that if the set index value is greater than the current length of the array, then the length property of the array should be updated. So, when setting an element value by index, the property value of length may be implicitly modified. Therefore, when triggering a response, the side effect function associated with the length property should also be triggered to re-execute, as shown in the following code:

```
01   const arr  =  reactive ( [ 'foo' ] )  //  the original length of
the array is 1
02
03   effect ( ( )  =>  {
04        console. log ( arr. length )  //  1
05 } )
06 //  setting the value of index 1 will cause the length of the array
to become 2
07 arr [ 1 ]  =  ' bar '
```

In this code, the original length of the array is 1, and the length property is accessed in the side effect function. Then set the element value of the array index to 1, which will cause the length of the array to become 2, so the side effect function should be triggered to re-execute. But the current implementation cannot do this yet. In order to achieve the goal, we need to modify the set interceptor function, as shown in the following code:

```
01   function createReactive ( obj,  isShallow  =  false ,
isReadonly  =  false )  {
02          return new Proxy (obj, {
03              // intercept setup operation
04              set ( target,  key,  newVal,  receiver )  {
05                  if  (isReadonly) {
06                      console. warn ( ' attribute  ${key}  is read-
only')
07                          return true
08                  }
09                  const oldVal  =  target [ key ]
10                  // if the property does not exist, it means that you
are adding a new property, otherwise you are setting an existing property
11                  const type  =  Array. isArray (target)
12                  // if the proxy target is an array, check whether
the set index value is less than the length of the array,
13                          // if yes, it is regarded as a SET operation,
otherwise it is an ADD operation
14                      ?  Number (key) < target. length?  'SET' : 'ADD'
15                      :  Object. prototype. hasOwnProperty. call
(target, key) ?  ' SET '  :  ' ADD '
16
17              const res = Reflect. set (target, key, newVal, receiver)
18              if  ( target  ===  receiver. raw )  {
19              if  (oldVal  !==  newVal  && (oldVal  ===  oldVal  ||
newVal  ===  newVal ) )  {
20                      trigger ( target,  key,  type )
```

```
21                    }
22                 }
23
24            return res
25          }
26          // omit other interception functions
27    }
```

When we judge the operation type, we have added a judgment on the array type. If the target object of the proxy is an array, then the judgment of the operation type will be different. That is, if the set index value is less than the length of the array, it is regarded as a SET operation, because it does not change the length of the array; if the set index value is greater than the current length of the array, it is regarded as an ADD operation, because this will implicitly change the *length* property value of the array. With this information, we can correctly trigger the re-execution of the side effect function associated with the *length* property of the array object in the trigger function:

```
01    function trigger ( target,  key,  type )  {
02        const depsMap  =  bucket.get(target)
03        if  ( !depsMap )  return
04        // part of the content is omitted
05
06        // when the operation type is ADD and the target object is an
array, the side effects associated with the length property should be
fetched and executed
07        if  (type  ===  'ADD'  && Array.isArray(target))  {
08            // extract the side effect function associated with
length
09            const lengthEffects = depsMap.get('length')
10            // add these side effect functions to effectsToRun, to
be executed
11        lengthEffects && lengthEffects.forEach ( effectFn => {
12                if  ( effectFn !== activeEffect )     {
13                    effectsToRun. add ( effectFn )
14                }
15            })
16        }
17
18        effectsToRun. forEach (effectFn   =>   {
19            if   (effectFn. options.scheduler) {
20                effectFn. options.scheduler(effectFn)
21            } else  {
22                effectFn ( )
23            }
24        } )
25    }
```

But thinking about it in reverse: in fact, modifying the length property of the array will also implicitly affect the array elements, for example:

```
01    const arr  =  reactive ( [ ' foo ' ] )
02
03    effect ( ( )  =>  {
04          //  access the 0th element of the array
05          console. log ( arr [ 0 ] )   //   foo
06    })
07    //  changing the length of the array to 0 causes the 0th element
to be removed, so the response should be triggered
08    arr. length  =  0
```

As shown in the code above, the 0th element of the array is accessed in the side effect function, and then the length attribute of the array is changed to 0. We know that this will implicitly affect the array elements, that is, all elements are deleted, so the side effect function should be triggered to re-execute. However, not all modifications to the *length* attribute will affect existing elements in the array. Taking the above example, if we set the *length* attribute to 100, this will not affect the 0th element, so there is no need to trigger the side effect function to re-execute. This makes us realize that when modifying the *length* attribute value, only those elements whose index value is greater than or equal to the new *length* attribute value need to trigger the response. But in any case, the current implementation cannot do this; in order to achieve the goal, we need to modify the set interceptor function. When calling the *trigger* function to trigger the response, the new property value should be passed:

```
01    function createReactive (obj,  isShallow  =  false,
isReadonly  =  false)  {
02        return new Proxy (obj,  {
03            //  intercept setup operation
04            set ( target,  key,  newVal,  receiver )  {
05                if   ( isReadonly )   {
06                console.warn ( ' attribute ${key}  is read-only ' )
07                    return true
08                }
09            const oldVal  =  target [ key]
10
11            const type  =  Array.  isArray (target)
12                ?  Number (key) < target.length?  'SET' : 'ADD'
13                :  Object.prototype.hasOwnProperty. call (
target,  key ) ?  'SET' : 'ADD'
14
15            const res  =  Reflect. set ( target,  key,  newVal,
receiver )
16                if   (target  ===  receiver. raw)  {
17                if  (oldVal  !== newVal  &&  (oldVal  ===  oldVal
||  newVal  ===  newVal ) )  {
18                    // add the fourth parameter, i.e., the new value
that triggers the response
19                        trigger (target, key, type, newVal)
20                }
21            }
```

```
22
23                          return res
24                  },
25          })
26    }
```

Next, we also need to modify the *trigger* function:

```
01     //  add a fourth parameter to the trigger function,  newVal,
which is the new value
02     function trigger (target,  key,  type,  newVal)  {
03          const depsMap  =  bucket. get ( target )
04          if   ( !depsMap ) return
05          //  omit other codes
06
07              //  if the target of the operation is an array, and the
length property of the array is modified
08              if  (Array. isArray(target) && key === 'length') {
09          //  for elements whose index is greater than or equal to
the new length value,
10              //  all associated side effects need to be removed and
added to effectsToRun to be executed
11              depsMap. forEach ( ( effects,  key )  =>  {
12                  if  ( key  >=  newVal )  {
13                      effects. forEach ( effectFn  =>  {
14                      if  (effectFn !==  activeEffect )  {
15                          effectsToRun. add ( effectFn )
16                      }
17                  })
18              }
19          })
20    }
21
22     effectsToRun. forEach (effectFn => {
23          if   (effectFn. options.scheduler )   {
24            effectFn. options.scheduler ( effectFn )
25          } else  {
26            effectFn ( )
27          }
28      })
29    }
```

As shown in the code above, a fourth parameter is added to the trigger function, which is the new value when the response is triggered. In this case, the new value refers to the new length attribute value, which represents the new array length. Next, we determine whether the target of the operation is an array. If so, we need to find all elements whose index value is greater than or equal to the new length value, and then take out and execute the side effect functions associated with them.

5.7.2 Traversal of Arrays

Since arrays are also objects, it means that you can also iterate over them using a *for*
... *in* loop:

```
01   const arr  =  reactive ( [ ' foo ' ] )
02
03    effect ( ( )  =>  {
04          for  ( const key in arr )  {
05                console . log ( key )  //  0
06          }
07    } )
```

It is important to point out here that we should try to avoid using *for* ... *in* loops to
traverse arrays. But since it is syntactically feasible, of course it also needs to be
considered. As we mentioned earlier, the difference between array objects and
regular objects is only reflected in the internal method [[DefineOwnProperty]]; that
is to say, using a *for* ... *in* loop to traverse an array is no different from traversing a
regular object, so you can also use ownKeys to intercept. Here is the ownKeys
interception function we implemented earlier:

```
01   function createReactive (obj,  isShallow  =  false,
isReadonly  =  false )  {
02          return new Proxy (obj,  {
03                //  omit other interception functions
04                ownKeys ( target )  {
05                      track ( target,  ITERATE_KEY )
06                      return Reflect . ownKeys (target)
07                }
08          })
09    }
```

This code is taken from the previous paragraph. At the beginning, in order to track
the *for* ... *in* operation on ordinary objects, we artificially created the
ITERATE_KEY as the tracking key. But this is considered for proxying ordinary
objects. For an ordinary object, only when adding or deleting property values will
affect the result of the *for* ... *in* loop. So, when the add or delete property operation
occurs, we need to take out the side effect function associated with the
ITERATE_KEY and re-execute it. However, the situation is different for arrays.
Let's see which operations affect the *for* ... *in* loop traversing the array.

- Add a new element: arr [100] = 'bar'.
- Change the length of the array: arr.length = 0.

In fact, whether adding new elements to the array or directly modifying the length
of the array, it is essentially because of modifying the length property of the array.
Once the length property of the array is modified, the result of the *for* ... *in* loop
traversing the array will change, so in this case we should trigger a response.

Naturally, we can determine whether the target is an array in the ownKeys interception function. If so, length could be used as the key to establish the response connection:

```
01   function createReactive(obj,  isShallow  =  false,
isReadonly  =  false )   {
02          return new Proxy ( obj,   {
03              // omit other interception functions
04              ownKeys ( target )   {
05                 // if the target of the operation is an array, use
the length property as the key and establish a response connection
06                    track ( target,  Array.isArray  (target) ?   '
length '  :  ITERATE_KEY )
07                       return Reflect.ownKeys (target)
08                 }
09          })
10      }
```

This way, whether adding new elements to the array or directly modifying the length property, the response can be triggered correctly:

```
01   const arr = reactive (['foo'])
02
03   effect (( )   =>   {
04          for   ( const key in arr )   {
05              console.log (key)
06          }
07   })
08
09   arr [1] =   ' bar '  //  can trigger the re-execution of side
effect functions
10      arr.length = 0  // can trigger the side effect function to
re-execute
```

After explaining the use of *for* ... *in* to traverse arrays, let's take a look at the use of *for* ... *of* to traverse arrays. Unlike *for* ... *in*, *for* ... *of* is used to traverse iterable objects, so we need to figure out what an iterable object is first. ES2015 defines an iteration protocol for JavaScript, which is not a new syntax, but a protocol. Specifically, whether an object can be iterated depends on whether the object or the prototype of the object implements the @@iterator method. The @@[name] flag here is used in the ECMAScript specification to refer to the built-in symbols value of JavaScript, for example, @@iterator refers to the value Symbol.iterator. An object can iterate if it implements Symbol.iterator methods, for example:

```
01   const obj  =  {
02       Val :  0,
03        [ Symbol.iterator ] ( )   {
04              return   {
05                  next ( )  {
```

```
06                              return  {
07                                    value:   obj. val ++,
08                              done:   obj. val  > 10 ?  true   :        false
09                                    }
10                            }
11                        }
12                    }
13      }
```

The object has realized Symbol.iterator, and for...of can be used to traverse it:

```
01    for   ( const value of obj )   {
02        console. log ( value )    //  0, 1, 2, 3, 4, 5, 6, 7, 8, 9
03      }
```

The array has built-in implementation of Symbol.iterator method. We can do an experiment:

```
01    const arr  =   [1, 2, 3, 4, 5]
02      //  get and call the built-in iterator method of the array
03    const itr  =   arr [ Symbol. Iterator ] ( )
04
05    console. log (itr. next ( ) )    //  {value:  1, done:  false}
06    console. log (itr. next ( ) )    //  {value:  2, done:  false}
07    console. log (itr. next ( ) )    //  {value:  3, done:  false}
08    console. log (itr. next ( ) )    //  {value:  4, done:  false}
09    console. log (itr. next ( ) )    //  {value:  5, done:  false}
10    console. log (itr. next ( ) )    //  {value:  undefined, done:
true}
```

As you can see, we can get the built-in iterator method of the array by using Symbol.iterator as the key. Then manually execute the next function of the iterator, which can also get the desired result. This is also why arrays can use by default *for . . . of* traversal:

```
01 const arr = [1, 2, 3, 4, 5]
02
03 for   ( const val of arr )   {
04        console.log(val)   // 1, 2, 3, 4, 5
05      }
```

In fact, in order to intercept *for . . . of* traversal operations on arrays, the key point is to find the basic semantics of the *for . . . of* operation dependencies. The execution flow of array iterators is defined in the 23.1.5.1 section of the specification, as shown in Fig. 5.8.

The contents of the b sub-step of step 3 in Fig. 5.8 are described below.

```
b. Repeat the following steps.
      i. If the array has a [[TypedArrayName]] internal slot, then.
```

23.1.5.1 CreateArrayIterator (*array, kind*)

The abstract operation CreateArrayIterator takes arguments *array* and *kind*. This operation is used to create iterator objects for Array methods that return such iterators. It performs the following steps when called:

1. Assert: Type(*array*) is Object.
2. Assert: *kind* is key+value, key, or value.
3. Let *closure* be a new Abstract Closure with no parameters that captures *kind* and *array* and performs the following steps when called:
   a. Let *index* be 0.
   b. Repeat,
      i. If *array* has a [[TypedArrayName]] internal slot, then
         1. If IsDetachedBuffer(*array*.[[ViewedArrayBuffer]]) is **true**, throw a **TypeError** exception.
         2. Let *len* be *array*.[[ArrayLength]].
      ii. Else
         1. Let *len* be ? LengthOfArrayLike(*array*).
      iii. If *index* ≥ *len*, return **undefined**.
      iv. If *kind* is key, perform? Yield(F(*index*)).
      v. Else,
         1. Let *elementKey* be! ToString(F(*index*)).
         2. Let *elementValue* be? Get(*array*, *element Key*).
         3. If *kind* is value, perform? Yield(*element Value*).
         4. Else,
            a. Assert: *kind* is key+value.
            b. Perform? Yield(! CreateArrayFromList(«F(*index*), *element Value* »)).
      vi. Set *index* to *index* + 1.
4. Return! CreateIteratorFromClosure(*closure*, "**% ArrayIteratorPrototype%**", % ArrayIteratorPrototype%).

Fig. 5.8 Execution flow of array iterator

> 1. If IsDetachedBuffer (*array*. [[ViewedArrayBuffer]]) is true, throw a TypeError exception.
> 2. Let the value of *len* be *array*. [[ArrayLength]].
> ii. Otherwise.
> 1. Let the value of *len* be LengthOfArrayLike (*array*).
> iii. Returns undefined if *index* > = *len*.
> iv. If *kind* is key, perform? Yield (IF(*index*)).
> v. Otherwise.
> 1. Let the value of *elementKey* be! ToString (IF(*index*)).
> 2. Let the value of *elementValue* be? Get (*array*, *elementKey*).
> 3. If *kind* is value, perform? Yield (*elementValue*).
> 4. Else.
> a. Assert: *kind* is key + value.
> b. Perform? Yield (! CreateArrayFromList (« IF (*index*), *elementValue* »)).
> vi. Set *index* to *index* + 1.

As you can see, the execution of the array iterator will read the length property of the array. If the iteration is an array element value, it will also read the index of the array. In fact, we can give a simulation implementation of an array iterator:

```
01   const arr = [1, 2, 3, 4, 5]
02
03   arr[Symbol.iterator] = function()  {
04     const target  =  this
05     const len = target.length
06     let index = 0
07
08     return  {
```

```
09              next ( )   {
10                  return {
11                  value:  index  <  len ?  target [index]   :   undefined,
12                      done:  index++   >= len
13                      }
14                  }
15          }
16 }
```

As shown in the code above, we override the array's built-in iterator method with a custom implementation, but it still works fine.

This example shows that when iterating over an array, a reactive *for ... of* iteration can be achieved by simply establishing a response connection between the side effect function and the length and index of the array:

```
01 const arr = reactive ( [1, 2, 3, 4, 5] )
02
03 effect ( ( ) => {
04      for   (const val of arr)   {
05          console. log (val)
06      }
07 } )
08
09 arr [1]  =   'bar'   //  can trigger a response
10 arr. length = 0   //  can trigger a response
```

As you can see, you do not need to add any code to make it work correctly. This is because the side effect function will naturally re-execute whenever the length and element values of the array change.

It has to be mentioned here that the return value of *values* method of the array is actually the array's built-in iterator. We can verify this:

```
01 console.log (Array.prototype.values === Array.prototype
[Symbol.iterator ] ) // true
```

In other words, we can get the array's iterator method to work correctly without adding any code:

```
01 const arr = reactive ( [1, 2, 3, 4, 5] )
02
03   effect ( ( )   = > {
04          for (const val of arr. values ( )) {
05              console.log (val)
06          }
07 } )
08
09 arr [1]  =   'bar'   // can trigger a response
10 arr. length  =  0   // can trigger a response
```

Finally, it should be pointed out that whether you use a *for* ... *of* loop, or call methods such as *values*, they will read the Symbol.iterator property of the array. This property is a *symbol* value. In order to avoid unexpected errors and performance considerations, we should not establish a response link between side effect functions and *symbol* values such as Symbol.iterator, so we need to modify the *get* interceptor function, as shown in the following code:

```
01  function createReactive(obj, isShallow = false,  isReadonly =
false)  {
02        return new Proxy(obj,  {
03              // intercept read operation
04              get (target, key, receiver)  {
05                    console.log('get: ', key)
06                    if   (key === 'raw') {
07                        return target
08                    }
09
10                    // add judgment; if the type of key is symbol, no
tracking will be performed
11                    if  ( !isReadonly && typeof key  !==  'symbol' )  {
12                        track(target, key)
13                    }
14
15                const res = Reflect. get (target, key, receiver)
16
17                if  (isShallow)  {
18                    return res
19                }
20
21                if  ( typeof res  ===  'object' && res !== null) {
22                    return isReadonly?  readonly(res) : reactive(res)
23                }
24
25                return res
26            },
27      })
28 }
```

Before calling the track function to trace, you need to add a judgment condition; that is, only trace when the type of key is not symbol, which avoids the above problem.

5.7.3   *Array Search Method*

From the introduction in the previous section, we realized that the methods of arrays actually depend on the basic semantics of objects. So in most cases, we do not need to do special handling to make these methods work as expected, for example:

Fig. 5.9 Execution flow of
the method includes

When the `includes` method is called, the following steps are taken:

1. Let O be ? ToObject(**this value**).
2. Let len be ? LengthOfArrayLike(O).
3. If len is 0, return **false**.
4. Let n be ? ToIntegerOrInfinity(*fromIndex*).
5. Assert: If *fromIndex* is **undefined**, then n is 0.
6. If n is $+\infty$, return **false**.
7. Else if n is $-\infty$, set n to 0.
8. If $n \geq 0$, then
    a. Let k be n.
9. Else,
    a. Let k be $len + n$.
    b. If $k < 0$, set k to 0.
10. Repeat, while $k < len$,
    a. Let *elementK* be the result of ? Get(O, ! ToString(F(k))).
    b. If SameValueZero(*searchElement*, *elementK*) is **true**, return **true**.
    c. Set k to $k + 1$.
11. Return **false**.

```
01 const arr   =   reactive ( [1, 2] )
02
03 effect (( )   =>   {
04     console. log (arr. includes (1) )   //   initial Printing true
05 })
06
07 arr[0]  =   3 // the side effect function executes again and prints
false
```

This is because the *includes* method internally accesses the *length* property of the array and the index of the array in order to find the given value, so when we modify an index pointing to the element value can trigger a response.

However the *includes* method does not always work as expected, for example:

```
01 const obj   =   { }
02 const arr   =   reactive ( [obj] )
03
04 console.log (arr.includes (arr [ 0 ]))   // false
```

As shown in the code above, we first define an object *obj* as the first element of the array, then call the reactive function to create a responsive object for it, and then try to call the includes method to look up the array to see if it contains the first element. Obviously, this operation should return *true*, but if you try to run this code, it will return *false*.

Why is this happening? This requires us to consult the language specification to see how the execution flow of the includes method looks. The 23.1.3.13 section of the specification shows the execution flow of the includes method, as shown in Fig. 5.9.

Figure 5.9 shows the execution flow of the *includes* method of the array, and we focus on steps 1 and 10. Among them, the first step 1 is described below.

```
1. Let the value of O be? ToObject (this value).
Step 10 is described below.
10. Repeat, while loop (condition k < len),
     a. Let the value of elementK be the result of? Get (O, ! ToString
(IF (k))).
     b. Return true if SameValueZero (searchElement, elementK) is true.
     c. Set k to k + 1.
```

Here we pay attention to step 1—let the value of O be? ToObject (this value). Then, who is this here? In the arr.includes (arr [0]) statement, *arr* is the proxy object, so *this* when the *includes* function executes points to the proxy object, that is, *arr*. Then we look at step 10.a. We can see that the *includes* method will read the value of the array element through the index, but here O is the proxy object *arr*. We know that when accessing an element value through a proxy object, if the value is still proxyable, the resulting value is the new proxy object rather than the original object. The following code inside the *get* interceptor function proves this:

```
01 if ( typeof res  ===  'object' && res  !== null) {
02      // if the value can be proxied, return the proxy object
03      return isReadonly?  readonly(res) :  reactive(res)
04 }
```

Knowing this, let's go back to this code: arr.includes (arr [0]). Among them, arr [0] gets a proxy object, and inside the includes method, it will also access the array elements through *arr*, so as to get a proxy object. The problem is that these two proxy objects are different. This is because a new proxy object is created every time the *reactive* function is called:

```
01 function reactive(obj) {
02     // every time reactive is called, a new proxy object is created
03         return createReactive (obj)
04 }
```

Even if the argument obj is the same, a new proxy object is created each time the reactive function is called. The solution to this problem is as follows:

```
01 // define a Map instance that stores the mapping of the original
object to the proxy object
02 const reactiveMap = new Map()
03
04 function reactive(obj)  {
05      // the priority is to find the previously created proxy object
through the original object obj; if found, return the existing proxy
object directly
06         const existionProxy  =  reactiveMap. get (obj)
07         if  ( existionProxy ) return existionProxy
08
09          // otherwise, create a new proxy object
10          const proxy = createReactive (obj)
```

```
11              // store in Map to avoid duplicate creation
12              reactiveMap. set ( obj, proxy )
13
14              return proxy
15 }
```

In the above code, we define reactiveMap, which is used to store the mapping of
the original object to the proxy object. Before each call to the reactive function to
create a proxy object, it is preferable to check whether the corresponding proxy
object already exists. If so, the existing proxy object is directly returned, which
avoids the problem of creating proxy objects for the same original object multiple
times. Next, we run the example at the beginning of this section again:

```
01 const obj  =  { }
02 const arr = reactive ( [ obj ] )
03
04 console. log (arr. includes (arr [0]))     //  true
```

It can be found that the behavior at this time has been in line with expectations.
However, it is not too early to be happy, let's look at the following code:

```
01 const obj = { }
02   const arr = reactive ( [ obj ] )
03
04 console. log (arr.includes (obj))   //  false
```

In the above code, we directly pass the original object as a parameter to the
includes method, which is very intuitive behavior. From the user's point of view, I
have used *obj* as the first element of the array, why is it not in the array? In fact, the
reason is very simple. It is because the *this* inside *includes* points to the proxy object
arr, and the value obtained when obtaining the array element is also the proxy
object, so it could not be found using the original object *obj*, so it returns false. To
find it, we need to rewrite the *includes* method of the array and implement custom
behavior to solve this problem. First, let's see how to rewrite the *includes* method, as
shown in the following code:

```
01 const arrayInstrumentations   =   {
02        includes: function ( )   {/* . . . */}
03 }
04
05 function createReactive ( obj, isShallow  =  false,  isReadonly
= false)  {
06        return new Proxy ( obj,  {
07             // intercept read operations
08             get ( target,  key,  receiver )  {
09                console. log ( 'get:  ',  key)
10                  if  ( key  ===  'raw' )  {
11                    return target
```

```
12                    }
13              // if the target object of the operation is an array and the
key exists on arrayInstrumentations,
14              // then return the value defined on arrayInstrumentations
15              if  (Array.isArray(target) && arrayInstrumentations.
hasOwnProperty(key))  {
16                    return Reflect.get(arrayInstrumentations, key,
receiver)
17                  }
18
19                  if   ( !isReadonly && typeof key !== 'symbol' )   {
20                      track (target, key )
21                  }
22
23                  const res = Reflect. get ( target, key, receiver )
24
25                  if   (isShallow)   {
26                      return res
27                  }
28
29              if  (typeof res  ===  'object' &&  res  !== null )  {
30              return isReadonly?  readonly ( res )  :  reactive( res )
31                  }
32
33                  return res
34              },
35    })
36 }
```

In the above code, we modified the get interceptor function to override the includes method of the array. How did we do it? We know that arr.includes can be understood as reading the includes property of the proxy object *arr*, which will trigger the *get* interceptor function, which checks whether the target is an array, and if it is an array and the read key value exists on arrayInstrumentations, it returns the corresponding value defined on the arrayInstrumentations object. That is, when the arr.includes is executed, the includes function defined on the arrayInstrumentations is actually executed, thus implementing the override.

Next, we can customize the *includes* function:

```
01 const originMethod  =  Array.prototype.includes
02  const arrayInstrumentations  =  {
03      includes:  function ( ... args )   {
04              // this is the proxy object; first look in the proxy object
and store the result in res
05              let res = originMethod.apply ( this,  args )
06
07              if  (res === false) {
08              // res is false, indicating that it was not found. Get
the original array through this.raw, and then go to it to find and update
the res value
09                  res = originMethod.apply ( this. raw, args )
```

```
10             }
11             // return the final result
12             return res
13     }
14 }
```

As shown in the above code, the *this* in the *includes* method points to the proxy object. Let's start with the proxy object. This actually implements the default behavior of arr.include (obj). If you cannot find it, get the original array through this.raw, then go to find it, and finally return the result, which solves the above problem. Run the following test code:

```
01 const obj = { }
02 const arr = reactive ([obj])
03
04 console. log (arr. includes (obj))   //   true
```

As you can see, the code now behaves as expected.

In addition to the *includes* method, the array methods that need to do similar processing are indexOf and lastIndexOf, because they are both methods that return search results based on the given value. The complete code is as follows:

```
01 const arrayInstrumentations  =  { }
02
03 ;['includes', 'indexOf', 'lastIndexOf']. forEach (method => {
04     const originMethod  =  Array. prototype[method]
05     arrayInstrumentations[method]  =  function(... args)  {
06         // this is the proxy object; first look in the proxy object and
store the result in res
07         let res = originMethod. apply (this, args)
08
09         if   (res  ===  false  ||  res  ===  -1)  {
10             // res is false, indicating that it was not found. Get the
original array through this. raw, then go to it to find it, and update the
res value
11             res  =  originMethod. apply (this. raw, args)
12         }
13         // return the final result
14         return res
15     }
16 })
```

5.7.4   Prototype Method for Implicitly Modifying Array Length

In this section, we will explain how to deal with methods that implicitly modify the length of the array, mainly referring to the stack methods of the array, such as push/

When the **push** method is called with zero or more arguments, the following steps are taken:

1. Let O be ? ToObject(**this** value).
2. Let len be ? LengthOfArrayLike(O).
3. Let $argCount$ be the number of elements in *items*.
4. If $len + argCount > 2^{53} - 1$, throw a **TypeError** exception.
5. For each element E of *items*, do
    a. Perform ? Set(O, ! ToString($\mathbb{F}(len)$)), E, **true**).
    b. Set len to $len + 1$.
6. Perform ? Set(O, **"length"**, $\mathbb{F}(len)$, **true**).
7. Return $\mathbb{F}(len)$.

The **"length"** property of the **push** method is $1_{\mathbb{F}}$.

Fig. 5.10 Execution flow of the array push method

pop/shift/unshift. In addition, the *splice* method also implicitly modifies the length of the array. We can refer to the specification to confirm this. Taking the push method as an example, the 23.1.3.20 section of the specification defines the execution flow of the push method, as shown in Fig. 5.10.

The contents described in Fig. 5.10 are as follows.

When the *push* method is called with 0 or more arguments, the following steps are performed.

```
1. Let the value of O be? ToObject (this value).
2. Let the value of len be? LengthOfArrayLike (O).
3. Let the value of argCount be the number of elements of items.
4. If len + argCount > 2^53-1, a TypeError exception is thrown.
5. For each element E in items:
   a. Perform? Set (O,! ToString (IF (len)), E, true);
   b. Set len to len + 1.
6. Perform? Set (O, 'length', IF (len), true).
7. Return IF (len).
```

As can be seen from steps 2 and 6, when calling the *push* method of the array to add an element to the array, the *length* attribute value of the array will be read and the length attribute value of the array will be set. This causes two independent side effects functions to affect each other. Take the following code as an example:

```
01 const arr = reactive ([])
02   // The first side effect function
03   effect (() => {
04       arr.push(1)
05 })
06
07 // the second side effect function
08 effect (() => {
```

```
09        arr.push(1)
10  })
```

If you try to run the above code in a browser, you will get a stack overflow error (Maximum call stack size Exceeded).

Why is this happening? Let's analyze the execution process of the above code in detail.

- The first side effect function is executed. Inside this function, calling the arr.push method adds an element to the array. We know that calling the *push* method of the array will indirectly read the *length* property of the array. So, when the first side effect function is executed, it will establish a response connection with the *length* property.
- Next, the second side effect function executes. Again, it will also establish a response connection with the *length* property. But do not forget that calling arr. push method will not only indirectly read the *length* property of the array, but also indirectly set the value of the length property.
- The call to the arr.push method in the second function sets the *length* property value of the array. Therefore, the response system tries to take out and execute all the side effects associated with the *length* property, including the first side effect function. The problem lies here. It can be found that the second side effect function has not been executed yet, and the first side effect function must be executed again.
- The first side effect function is executed again. Again, this indirectly sets the *length* property of the array. Therefore, the response system tries to extract and execute all side effect functions associated with the *length* property, including the second side effect function.
- This cycle goes back and forth, eventually causing the call stack to overflow.

The reason for the problem is that the call to the *push* method indirectly reads the length property. So, as long as we "mask" the reading of the length property to avoid establishing a response connection between it and the side effect function, the problem is solved. This idea is correct, because the *push* method of the array is semantically a modification operation, not a read operation, so avoiding the response connection will not have other side effects. With the solution, we try to implement it, which requires rewriting the push method of the array, as shown in the following code:

```
01 // A flag variable indicating whether to trace. The default value is
true, which allows tracing
02 let shouldTrack = true
03 // Override the push method of the array
04 ; ['push'] . forEach (method => {
05 // Get the original push method
06 const originMethod = Array.prototype [method]
07 // Rewrite
08 arrayInstrumentations [method] = function(...args) {
```

```
09 // Disable tracking before calling the original method
10 shouldTrack = false
11 // Default behavior of push method
12 let res = originMethod.apply(this, args)
13 // After calling the original method, restore the original
behavior, that is, allow tracing
14 shouldTrack = true
15 return res
16 }
17 })
```

In this code, we define a marker variable shouldTrack, which is a Boolean value that represents whether tracking is allowed. Next, we rewrite the push method of the array to take advantage of the arrayInstrumentations object introduced earlier. The rewritten push method retains the default behavior, but before executing the default behavior, the value of the marker variable shouldTrack is set to false, that is, tracking is prohibited. When the default behavior of the push method is executed, the value of the marker variable shouldTrack is restored to true, which means that tracking is allowed. Finally, we also need to modify the track function, as shown in the following code:

```
01 function track(target, key) {
02 // When tracking is disabled, return directly
03 if (!activeEffect || !shouldTrack) return
04 // Omit some code
05 }
```

As you can see, when the value of the marker variable shouldTrack is false, that is, when tracking is prohibited, the track function will return directly. In this way, when the *push* method indirectly reads the value of the *length* attribute, since tracking is prohibited at this time, no response connection will be established between the *length* attribute and the side effect function. This implements the solution given above. Let's try running the following test code again:

```
01 const arr = reactive([])
02 //The first side effect function
03 effect(() => {
04 arr.push(1)
05 })
06
07 //The second side effect function
08 effect(() => {
09 arr.push(1)
10 }) You will find that it works correctly and does not cause the call
stack to overflow.
```

In addition to the push method, the pop, shift, unshift, and splice methods all require similar processing. The complete code is as follows:

```
01 let shouldTrack = true
02 //Override the push, pop, shift, unshift and splice methods of
arrays
03 ; ['push', 'pop', 'shift', 'unshift', 'splice'] .forEach (method
= > {
04 const originMethod = Array.prototype [method]
05 arrayInstrumentations [method] = function (... args) {
06 shouldTrack = false
07 let res = originMethod.apply (this, args)
08 shouldTrack = true
09 return res
10 }
11 })
```

5.8 Proxies Set and Map

Starting with this section, we will introduce reactive schemes for collection type data. Collection types include Map/Set and WeakMap/WeakSet. Proxying collection type data using Proxy is different from proxying ordinary objects because the manipulation of collection type data is very different from ordinary objects. The prototype properties and methods of the Set and Map data types are summarized below.

The prototype properties and methods of the Set type are as follows.

- Size: Return the number of elements in the collection.
- Add (value): Add the given value to the collection.
- Clear (): Clear the collection.
- Delete (value): Delete the given value from the collection.
- Has (value): Determine whether the given value exists in the collection.
- Keys (): Return an iterator object. Can be used in *for ... of* loops; the iterator object produces the value of the element in the collection.
- Values (): for Set collection typesFor example, keys () is equivalent to values ().
- Entries (): Return an iterator object. The iteration produces an array value for each element in the collection [Value, value].
- forEach (callback [, thisArg]): The forEach function iterates over all elements in the collection and calls the callback function for each element. The forEach function receives an optional second parameter, thisArg, which specifies the this value when the callback function executes.

The prototype properties and methods of the Map type are as follows.

- Size: Return the number of key-value pairs in the Map data.
- Clear (): Clear the Map.
- Delete (key): Delete the key-value pair of the specified key.
- Has (key): Determine whether there is a key-value pair for the specified key in the Map.

- Get (key): Read the value corresponding to the specified key.
- Set (key, value): Set a new key-value pair for the Map.
- Keys (): Return an iterator object. The key value of the key-value pair is generated during the iteration.
- Values (): Return an iterator object. The value of the key-value pair is generated during iteration.
- Entries (): Return an iterator object. The iteration produces an array of values consisting of [key, value].
- forEach (callback [, thisArg]): The forEach function iterates over all key-value pairs of the Map data, and for each key-value pair calls the callback function. The forEach function receives an optional second argument, thisArg, which specifies the value of this when the callback function executes.

Looking at the above list, you can see that the operation methods of the two data types, Map and Set, are similar. The biggest difference between them is that the Set type uses the add (value) method to add elements, while the Map type uses the set (key, value) method to set key-value pairs, and the Map type can use the get (key) method to read the corresponding values. Since the two are so similar, does that mean we can proxy them in the same way? That's right, next, we will dive into how to implement proxies for Set and Map type data.

5.8.1   How to Proxy Set and Map

As mentioned earlier, Set and Map types of data have specific properties and methods to manipulate themselves. This is different from normal objects, as shown in the following code:

```
01 // read and set operations for common objects
02 const obj   =   { foo: 1 }
03 obj.foo//Read properties
04 obj.foo = 2//Set properties
05
06 // manipulate Map data with get/set method
07 const map = new Map ()
08 map.set ('key', 1)//Set data
09 map.get ('key')//read data
```

It is precisely because of these differences that we cannot proxy Set and Map data like normal objects. But the overall idea remains the same, that is, when a read operation occurs, the track function should be called to establish a response connection; when a set operation occurs, the trigger function should be called to trigger the response, for example:

24.2.3.9 get Set.prototype.size

Set.prototype.size is an accessor property whose set accessor function is **undefined**. Its get accessor function performs the following steps:

1. Let *S* be the **this** value.
2. Perform ? RequireInternalSlot(*S*, [[SetData]]).
3. Let *entries* be the List that is *S*.[[SetData]].
4. Let *count* be 0.
5. For each element *e* of *entries*, do
    a. If *e* is not **empty**, set *count* to *count* + 1.
6. Return F(*count*).

Fig. 5.11 Definition of Set. prototype. Size attributes

```
01 const proxy  =  reactive (new Map (['key', 1]])
02
03 effect (() => {
04    console.log (proxy.get ('key ')) // read the value of key as key
05 })
06
07 proxy.set ('key', 2) // modify the key to the value of key; it
should trigger a response
```

Of course, the effect this code shows is what we want to achieve in the end. But before we do it, it is necessary to understand the precautions about using Proxy to proxy Set or Map type data. Let's first look at a piece of code, as follows:

```
01 const s  =  new Set ([1, 2, 3])
02 const p  =  new Proxy (s, {})
03
04 console.log (p.size) // TypeError: Method get Set.prototype.size
called on incompatible receiver
```

In this code, we first define a data *s* of type Set, and then create a proxy object *p* for it. Since the target object of the proxy is of type Set, we can get the number of elements by reading its p.size property. But unfortunately, we get an error. The gist of the error message is "get Set.prototype.size method was called on an incompatible receiver." From this we can probably guess that the *size* property should be an accessor property, so it is called as a method. This can be confirmed by consulting the specification, as shown in Fig. 5.11.

The contents described in Fig. 5.11 are as follows.

Set.prototype.size is an accessor property whose set accessor function is undefined and whose get accessor function performs the following steps.

```
1. Let the value of S be this.
2. Perform? RequireInternalSlot (S, [[SetData]]).
3. Let the value of entries be List, which is S. [[SetData]].
4. Let the value of count be 0.
5. For each element e in entries, execute:
```

```
      a. If e is not empty, set count to count + 1.
6. Return IF (count).
```

From this, Set.prototype.size is an accessor property. The key points here are in steps 1 and 2. According to the description of step 1: let the value of *S* be *this*. Who is *this* here? Since we access the size property through the proxy object p, *this* is the proxy object p. Then in step 2, call the abstract method RequireInternalSlot (S, [[SetData]]) to check whether *S* has an internal slot [[SetData]]. Obviously, the proxy object *S* does not have an internal slot [[SetData]], so it will throw an error, which is the error obtained in the previous example.

To fix this, we need to fix the this pointer when the getter function of the accessor property executes, as shown in the following code:

```
01 const s = new Set ([1, 2, 3])
02 const p = new Proxy (s, {
03 get (target, key, receiver) {
04 if (key === 'size') {
05 // If the size attribute is read
06 // Fix the problem by specifying the third parameter receiver as
the original object target
07 return Reflect.get (target, key, target)
08 }
09 // Default behavior for reading other properties
10 return Reflect.get (target, key, receiver)
11 }
12 })
13
14 console.log (s.size) // 3
```

In the above code, we added the get interceptor function when creating the proxy object. Then check whether the read property name is size. If so, specify the third parameter as the original Set object when calling the Reflect.get function, so that when the getter function of the accessor property size is executed, its *this* points to the original Set object instead of the proxy object. The program runs correctly due to the [[SetData]] internal slot on the original Set object.

Next, we try to delete the data from the Set, as shown in the following code:

```
01 const s = new Set ([1, 2, 3])
02 const p = new Proxy (s, {
03 get (target, key, receiver) {
04 if (key === 'size') {
05 return Reflect.get (target, key, target)
06 }
07 // Default behavior for reading other properties
08 return Reflect.get (target, key, receiver)
09 }
10 }
11 )
12
```

```
13 // Call the delete method to delete the element with a value of 1
14 // TypeError: Method Set.prototype.delete called on incompatible
receiver [object Object]
15 p.delete(1)
```

As you can see, calling the p.delete method will get an error, which is very similar to the error that occurs when accessing p.size properties explained earlier. To understand the cause of the problem, we need to analyze in detail what happens when the p.delete (1) method is called.

In fact, accessing p.size is different from accessing p.delete. This is because *size* is a property, an accessor property, and *delete* is a method. When accessing the p.size, the getter function of the accessor property will be executed immediately. At this time, we can change the pointer of this of the getter function by modifying the receiver. When accessing the p.delete, the *delete* method is not executed, and the statement that actually makes it execute is the p.delete (1) function call. Therefore, no matter how you modify the receiver, the this when the delete method is executed will point to the proxy object p, not the original Set object. It is not difficult to fix this problem; just bind the delete method to the original data source object, as shown in the following code:

```
01 const s = new Set([1, 2, 3])
02 const p = new Proxy(s, {
03 get(target, key, receiver) {
04 if (key === 'size') {
05 return Reflect.get(target, key, target)
06 }
07 // Return after binding the method to the original data source
object target
08 return target[key].bind(target)
09 }
10 }
11 )
12
13 // Call the delete method to delete the element with a value of 1;
execute it correctly
14 p.delete(1)
```

In the above code, we use target [key].bind (target) instead of Reflect.get (target, key, receiver). As you can see, we use the bind function to bind the method used to manipulate the data to the original data source object target. In this way, when the p. delete (1) statement executes, the *this* of the *delete* function always points to the original data source object instead of the proxy object, so the code can be executed correctly.

Finally, for the convenience of subsequent explanations and the extensibility of the code, we also encapsulate new Proxy into the createReactive function introduced earlier:

```
01 const reactiveMap = new Map ()
02 // The reactive function is unchanged from before
03 function reactive (obj) {
04
05 const existionProxy = reactiveMap.get (obj)
06 if (existionProxy) return existionProxy
07 const proxy = createReactive (obj)
08
09 reactiveMap.set (obj, proxy)
10
11 return proxy
12 }
13 // Encapsulate the logic for proxying Set/Map type data in
createReactive
14 function createReactive (obj, isShallow = false, isReadonly =
false) {
15 return new Proxy (obj, {
16 get (target, key, receiver) {
17 if (key === 'size') {
18 return Reflect.get (target, key, target)
19 }
20
21 return target [key] .bind (target)
22 }
23 })
24 }
```

This way, we can easily create proxy data:

```
01 const p = reactive (new Set ([1, 2, 3]))
02 console.log (p.size) //3
```

5.8.2   Establishing Responsive Linkages

After understanding the precautions when creating proxies for Set and Map type data, we can start implementing a responsive scheme for Set type data. In fact, the idea is not complicated. Take the following code as an example:

```
01 const p = reactive (new Set ([1, 2, 3]))
02
03 effect (() => {
04 // Access the size property inside the side effect function
05 console.log (p.size)
06 })
07 // Adding an element with a value of 1 should trigger a response
08 p.add (1)
```

This code shows how reactive Set type data works. First, the p.size property is accessed inside the side effect function; then, the p.add function is called to add data to the collection. Since this behavior indirectly changes the size property value of the collection, we expect the side effect function to be re-executed. To achieve this, we need to call the *track* function for dependency tracing when accessing the size property, and then call the *trigger* function when the *add* method executes to trigger the response. The following code shows how to do dependency tracing:

```
01 function createReactive(obj, isShallow = false, isReadonly =
false) {
02 return new Proxy(obj, {
03 get(target, key, receiver) {
04 if (key === 'size') {
05 // Call the track function to establish a response contact
06 track(target, ITERATE_KEY)
07 return Reflect.get(target, key, target)
08 }
09
10 return target[key].bind(target)
11 }
12 })
13 }
```

As you can see, when reading the *size* attribute, you only need to call the *track* function to establish a response link. It should be noted here that the response link needs to be established between the ITERATE_KEY and the side effect function, because any add and delete operations will affect the *size* attribute. Next, let's see how to trigger the response. How should the response be triggered when the *add* method is called to add a new element to the collection? Obviously, this requires us to implement a custom *add* method, as shown in the following code:

```
01 // Define an object and define the custom add method under this object
02 const mutableInstrumentations = {
03 add(key) {/* ... */}
04 }
05
06 function createReactive(obj, isShallow = false, isReadonly =
false) {
07 return new Proxy(obj, {
08 get(target, key, receiver) {
09 // If the raw attribute is read, return the original data source
object target
10 if (key === 'raw') return target
11 if (key === 'size') {
12 track(target, ITERATE_KEY)
13 return Reflect.get(target, key, target)
14 }
15 // return the method defined under the mutableInstrumentations
object
16 return mutableInstrumentations[key]
```

```
17 }
18 })
19 }
```

First, define an object mutableInstrumentations, and we will define all custom implemented methods under this object, such as mutableInstrumentations.add methods. Then, return the method defined in the mutableInstrumentations object inside the *get* interceptor function. In this way, when the method is obtained through p.add, what we get is our custom mutableInstrumentations.add method. With a custom implemented method, we can call the trigger function in it to trigger the response:

```
01 // Define an object and define the custom add method under this object
02 const mutableInstrumentations = {
03 add(key) {
04 // this still points to the proxy object; get the original data
source object through the raw attribute
05 const target = this.raw
06 // Execute the add method to add the specific value through the
original data source object,
07 // Note that .bind is no longer needed here, because it is called and
executed directly through target
08 const res = target.add(key)
09 // Call the trigger function to trigger the response, and specify
the operation type as ADD
10 trigger(target, key, 'ADD')
11 // Return the result of the operation
12 return res
13 }
14 }
```

As shown in the code above, the *this* in the custom add function still points to the proxy object, so you need to get the original data source object through the this.raw. Once you have the original data source object, you can call the target.add method through it, so you no longer need the .bind binding. After the add operation is complete, call the trigger function to trigger the response. It is important to note that we specified the action type as ADD. Remember the implementation of the trigger function? Let's review it, as shown in the following code snippet:

```
01 function trigger(target, key, type, newVal) {
02 const depsMap = bucket.get(target)
03 if (!depsMap) return
04 const effects = depsMap.get(key)
05
06 // Omit irrelevant content
07
08 // When the operation type is ADD, the side effect function
associated with the ITERATE_KEY is fetched and executed
09 if (type === 'ADD' || type === 'DELETE') {
```

```
10 const iterateEffects = depsMap.get(ITERATE_KEY)
11 iterateEffects && iterateEffects.forEach(effectFn => {
12 if (effectFn !== activeEffect) {
13 effectsToRun.add(effectFn)
14 }
15 })
16 }
17
18 effectsToRun.forEach(effectFn => {
19 if (effectFn.options.scheduler) {
20 effectFn.options.scheduler(effectFn)
21 } else {
22 effectFn()
23 }
24 })
25 }
```

When the operation type is ADD or DELETE, the side effect function associated with the ITERATE_KEY is fetched and executed, which triggers the execution of the side effect function collected by accessing the size attribute.

Of course, if the element added by calling the add method already exists in the Set collection, there is no need to trigger a response, which is more performance-friendly. Therefore, we can optimize the code as follows:

```
01 const mutableInstrumentations = {
02 add(key) {
03 const target = this.raw
04 // First determine whether the value already exists
05 const hadKey = target.has(key)
06 // Only trigger a response if the value does not exist
07 const res = target.add(key)
08 if (!hadKey) {
09 trigger(target, key, 'ADD')
10 }
11 return res
12 }
13 }
```

In the above code, we first call the target.has method to determine whether the value already exists, and we only need to trigger a response if the value does not exist.

On this basis, we can easily implement the delete method along similar lines:

```
01 const mutableInstrumentations = {
02 delete(key) {
03 const target = this.raw
04 const hadKey = target.has(key)
05 const res = target.delete(key)
06 // The response is triggered when the element to be deleted does
exist
```

```
07 if (hadKey) {
08 trigger(target, key, 'DELETE')
09 }
10 return res
11 }
12 }
```

As shown in the code above, the difference from the add method is that the delete method only needs to trigger a response if the element to be deleted actually exists in the collection, which is exactly the opposite of the add method.

5.8.3   Avoiding Contaminating the Original Data Source

In this section, we use the set and get methods of Map type data to explain what "avoid polluting the original data source" and why.

The Map data type has two methods, *get* and *set*. When calling the get method to read the data, you need to call the track function to track the dependency to establish a response connection; when calling the set method to set the data, you need to call the trigger method to trigger the response. As shown in the following code:

```
01 const p = reactive(new Map([['key', 1]]))
02
03 effect(() => {
04 console.log(p.get('key'))
05 })
06
07 p.set('key', 2) // trigger response
```

In fact, it is not difficult to implement the functions shown in the above code, because we already have experience in implementing methods such as add and delete. The following is the specific implementation of the *get* method:

```
01 const mutableInstrumentations = {
02 get(key) {
03 // Get the original object
04 const target = this.raw
05 // Determine if the read key exists
06 const had = target.has(key)
07 // Track dependencies and establish response contacts
08 track(target, key)
09 // Return the result if it exists. It should be noted here that if
the obtained result res is still proxyable data,
10 // Return reactive data wrapped with reactive
11 if (had) {
12 const res = target.get(key)
13 return typeof res === 'object'?  reactive(res) : res
14 }
```

```
15 }
16 }
```

As shown in the code and comments above, the overall idea is very clear. One thing to note here is that in the case of a non-shallow response, if the obtained data can still be proxied, then call reactive (res) to convert the data into reactive data and return it. In shallow response mode, this step is not required. Since the previous article explained how to implement a shallow response, I will not discuss it in detail here.

Next, let's discuss the implementation of the set method. Simply put, when the set method is called, the *trigger* method needs to be called to trigger the response. It's just that when the response is triggered, it is necessary to distinguish whether the type of operation is SET or ADD, as shown in the following code:

```
01 const mutableInstrumentations = {
02 set(key, value) {
03 const target = this.raw
04 const had = target.has(key)
05 // Get the old value
06 const oldValue = target.get(key)
07 // Set a new value
08 target.set(key, value)
09 // If it does not exist, it means that it is an ADD-type operation,
which means that the new
10 if (!had) {
11 trigger(target, key, 'ADD')
12 } else if (oldValue !== value || (oldValue === oldValue && value
=== value)) {
13 // If it does not exist and the value has changed, it is an operation
of type SET, which means modification
14 trigger(target, key, 'SET')
15 }
16 }
17 }
```

The key point of this code is that we need to determine whether the set key exists in order to distinguish between different operation types. We know that for SET-type and ADD-type operations, the side effect functions they ultimately trigger are different. Because ADD-type operations affect the size property of the data, any side effect functions that depend on the size property need to be re-executed when ADD-type operations occur.

The implementation of the *set* function given above works fine, but it still has the problem that the *set* method pollutes the original data source. What does this mean? Take a look at the code below:

```
01 // Original Map object m
02 const m = new Map()
03 // p1 is the proxy object of m
```

```
04 const p1 = reactive(m)
05 // p2 is another proxy object
06 const p2 = reactive(new Map())
07 // Set a key-value pair for p1; the value is the proxy object p2
08 p1.set('p2', p2)
09
10 effect(() => {
11 // Note that here we access p2 via original data source m
12 console.log(m.get('p2').size)
13 })
14 // Note that here we set a key-value pair foo -- > 1 for p2 via
original data source m
15 m.get('p2').set('foo', 1)
```

In this code, we first create a primitive Map object m. p1 is the proxy object of object m. Then create another proxy object p2 and set it as a value to p1, which is p1. set ('p2', p2). Next the problem arises. In the side effect function, we read the data value through the original data source m, and then set the data value through the original data source m. At this time, we found that the side effect function was re-executed. This is actually not the behavior we expect, because the original data source should not have the capability of reactive data, otherwise it means that the user can manipulate both the original data source and the reactive data, so the code is messed up.

So, what is causing the problem? It's actually very simple. Observe the *set* method we implemented earlier:

```
01 const mutableInstrumentations = {
02 set(key, value) {
03 const target = this.raw
04 const had = target.has(key)
05 const oldValue = target.get(key)
06 // We set the value intact to the original data source
07 target.set(key, value)
08 if (!had) {
09 trigger(target, key, 'ADD')
10 } else if (oldValue !== value || (oldValue === oldValue && value
=== value)) {
11 trigger(target, key, 'SET')
12 }
13 }
14 }
```

In the *set* method, we set the *value* to the original data source target as it is. If *value* is reactive data, it means that it is also reactive data set to the original object. We call the behavior of setting reactive data to the original data source data pollution.

It is not difficult to solve data pollution, just check the value before calling the target.set function to set the value: as long as it is found that the value to be set is

reactive data, then get the original data source through the raw property, and then set
the original data source to the target, as shown in the following code:

```
01 const mutableInstrumentations = {
02 set (key, value) {
03 const target = this.raw
04 const had = target.has (key)
05
06 const oldValue = target.get (key)
07 // Get the original data source. Since the value itself may already
be the original data source, the value.raw does not exist at this time,
then use value directly 08 const rawValue = value.raw || value
09 target.set (key, rawValue)
10
11 if (!had) {
12 trigger (target, key, 'ADD')
13 } else if (oldValue !== value || (oldValue === oldValue && value
=== value)) {
14 trigger (target, key, 'SET')
15 }
16 }
17 }
```

The current implementation will no longer cause data pollution. However, a
closer look at the above code will reveal new problems. We have been using the
raw attribute to access the original data source is flawed, because it may conflict with
the user-defined raw attribute, so in a rigorous implementation, we need to use a
unique identifier as the key to access the original data source, such as using the
Symbol type instead.

In this section, we explained the problem of avoiding polluting the original data
source through the set method of Map type data. In fact, in addition to the set method
to avoid polluting the original data source, the add method of Set type, the write
value operation of ordinary objects, and the method of adding elements to the array
need to do similar processing.

5.8.4   *Handling forEach*

The forEach method of the collection type is similar to the forEach method of the
array. Let's first see how it works:

```
01 const m = new Map ([
02 [{ key: 1 }, { value: 1 }]
03 ])
04
05 effect (() => {
06 m.forEach (function (value, key, m) {
07 console.log (value) // { value: 1 }
```

```
08 console.log(key) // { key: 1 }
09 })
10 })
```

Taking Map as an example, the forEach method receives a callback function as a parameter, which will be called on each key-value pair of the Map. The callback function receives three parameters, namely the value, the key, and the original Map object. As shown in the code above, we can use the forEach method to iterate over each set of key-value pairs in the Map data.

The traversal operation is only related to the number of key-value pairs, so any operation that modifies the number of key-value pairs of the Map object should trigger the re-execution of side effects functions, such as delete and add methods, etc. So when the forEach function is called, we should let the side effect function establish the response relationship with the ITERATE_KEY, as shown in the following code:

```
01 const mutableInstrumentations = {
02 forEach(callback) {
03 // Get the original data source object
04 const target = this.raw
05 // Contact ITERATE_KEY 06 track (target, ITERATE_KEY)
06 track(target, ITERATE_KEY)
07 // Call the forEach method through the original data source object
and pass the callback
08 target.forEach(callback)
09 }
10 }
```

In this way, we can track the forEach operation, which can be tested using the following code:

```
01 const p = reactive(new Map([
02 [{ key: 1 }, { value: 1 }]
03 ]))
04
05 effect(() => {
06 p.forEach(function (value, key) {
07 console.log(value) // { value: 1 }
08 console.log(key) // { key: 1 }
09 })
10 })
11
12 // can trigger a response
13 p.set({ key: 2 }, { value: 2 })
```

It can be found that this code works as expected. However, the forEach function given above still has flaws. We call the native forEach method through the original data source object in the custom implementation of the forEach method, that is.

```
01//Call the forEach method through the original data source object
and pass the callback
02 target.forEach (callback)
```

This means that the arguments passed to the callback function will be non-responsive data. This causes the following code to not work as expected:

```
01 const key = { key: 1 }
02 const value = new Set ([1, 2, 3])
03 const p = reactive (new Map ([
04 [key, value]
05 ]))
06
07 effect (() => {
08 p.forEach (function (value, key) {
09 console.log (value.size) // 3
10 })
11 })
12
13 p.get (key).delete (1)
```

In the above code, the reactive data p has a key-value pair, where the key is a normal object {key: 1} and the value is the original data source new Set ([1,2,3]) of type Set. Next, we use the forEach method to iterate over p in the side effect function and access the value.size in the callback function. Finally, we tried to delete the element with a value of 1 in the Set type data, but found that it failed to trigger the side effect function to re-execute. The reason for the problem is mentioned above. When accessing the size property through value.size, the value here is the original data source object, that is, the new Set ([1,2,3]), not the reactive data object, so it is impossible to establish a response connection. But this is not intuitive, because reactive itself is a deep response, and the parameters received by the callback function of the forEach method should also be reactive data. To solve this problem, we need to make some changes to the existing implementation, as shown in the following code:

```
01 const mutableInstrumentations = {
02 forEach (callback) {
03 // The wrap function is used to convert proxyable values to
reactive data
04 const wrap = (val) => typeof val === 'object'?  reactive (val) :
val
05 const target = this.raw
06 track (target, ITERATE_KEY)
07 // Call the original forEach method through target to traverse
08 target.forEach ((v, k) => {
09 // Manually call callback, wrap value and key with wrap function
and then pass it to callback, thus realizing deep response
10 callback (wrap (v), wrap (k), this)
11 })
```

```
12 }
13 }
```

In fact, the idea is very simple. Since the parameters of the callback function are not reactive, convert it to reactive. So, in the above code, we have made another layer of wrapping for the parameters of the callback function, that is, wrapping the parameters passed to the callback function into reactive ones. At this point, if you try to run the example given above again, you will find that it works as expected.

Finally, for the sake of rigor, we need to make some additions. Because the forEach function receives a second parameter in addition to the callback as an argument, which can be used to specify the *this* value when the callback function executes. A more complete implementation looks like this:

```
01 const mutableInstrumentations = {
02 // Receive the second parameter
03 forEach(callback, thisArg) {
04 const wrap = (val) => typeof val === 'object'?  reactive(val) :
val
05 const target = this.raw
06 track(target, ITERATE_KEY)
07
08 target.forEach((v, k) => {
09 // Call callback via .call and pass thisArg
10 callback.call(thisArg, wrap(v), wrap(k), this)
11 })
12 }
13 }
```

So far, our work is still not done. Now we know that whether we use a *for ... in* loop to traverse an object or a forEach loop to traverse a collection, their response connection is established between the ITERATE_KEY and the side effect function. However, there is a fundamental difference between using *for ... in* to traverse an object and using forEach to traverse a collection. Specifically, when using a *for ... in* loop to traverse an object, it only cares about the object's keys, not the object's values, as shown in the following code:

```
01 effect(() => {
02 for (const key in obj) {
03 console.log(key)
04 }
05 })
```

The side effect function needs to be re-executed only when the key of the object is added or deleted. So, we determine whether the operation type is ADD or DELETE in the trigger function, and then know whether the side effect function associated with the ITERATE_KEY needs to be triggered to re-execute. For SET-type operations, because it does not change the number of keys of an object, there is no need to trigger the side effect function to re-execute when a SET-type operation occurs.

But this rule does not apply to forEach traversal of Map type, as shown in the following code:

```
01 const p = reactive(new Map([
02 ['key', 1]
03 ]))
04
05 effect(() => {
06 p.forEach(function (value, key) {
07 // forEach loop not only cares about the key of the collection, but
also the value of the collection
08 console.log(value) // 1
09 })
10 })
11
12 p.set('key', 2) // should trigger a response even if the action
type is SET
```

When using forEach to iterate over data of type Map, it cares about both keys and values. This means that when calling p.set ("key," 2) modifies the value, the side effect function should also be triggered to re-execute, even if its operation type is SET. Therefore, we should modify the code of the trigger function to make up for this flaw:

```
01 function trigger(target, key, type, newVal) {
02 console.log('trigger', key)
03 const depsMap = bucket.get(target)
04 if (!depsMap) return
05 const effects = depsMap.get(key)
06
07 const effectsToRun = new Set()
08 effects && effects.forEach(effectFn => {
09 if (effectFn !== activeEffect) {
10 effectsToRun.add(effectFn)
11 }
12 })
13
14 if (
15 type === 'ADD' ||
16 type === 'DELETE' ||
17 // If the operation type is SET and the target object is data of type
Map,
18 // should also trigger the re-execution of those side effects
associated with the ITERATE_KEY
19 (
20 type === 'SET' &&
21 Object.prototype.toString.call(target) === '[object Map]'
22 )
23 ) {
24 const iterateEffects = depsMap.get(ITERATE_KEY)
25 iterateEffects && iterateEffects.forEach(effectFn => {
```

```
26 if (effectFn !== activeEffect) {
27 effectsToRun.add(effectFn)
28 }
29 })
30 }
31
32 // omit some content
33
34 effectsToRun.forEach(effectFn => {
35 if (effectFn.options.scheduler) {
36 effectFn.options.scheduler(effectFn)
37 } else {
38 effectFn()
39 }
40 })
41 }
```

As shown in the code above, we added a condition: if the target object of the operation is of type Map, the operation of type SET should also trigger the re-execution of those side effects associated with the ITERATE_KEY.

5.8.5   Iterator Methods

Next, we will talk about iterator methods for collection types; in fact, we explained how to intercept *for ... of* loop traversal arrays earlier when iterators were introduced. The collection type has three iterator methods:

- entries
- keys
- values

Calling these methods yields corresponding iterators, and loops can be iterated over using *for ... of*, for example:

```
01 const m = new Map([
02 ['key1', 'value1'],
03 ['key2', 'value2']
04 ])
05
06 for (const [key, value] of m.entries()) {
07 console.log(key, value)
08 }
09 // output:
10 // key1 value1
11 // key2 value2
```

Also, since the Map or Set types themselves deploy Symbol.iterator methods, they can iterate with *for ... of*:

```
01 for (const [key, value] of m) {
02 console.log(key, value)
03 }
04 // output:
05 // key1 value1
06 // key2 value2
```

Of course, we can also call the iterator function to get the iterator object, and manually call the next method of the iterator object to get the corresponding value:

```
01 const itr = m [Symbol.iterator] ()
02 console.log (itr.next ()) // { value: ['key1', 'value1'], done:
false}
03 console.log (itr.next ()) // { value: ['key2', 'value2'], done:
false}
04 console.log (itr.next ()) // { value: undefined, done: true}
```

In fact, m [Symbol.iterator] is equivalent to m.entries:

```
01 console.log (m [Symbol.iterator ] === m.entries) //true
```

This is why in the above example *for . . .of* loop iterates over m.entries and m to get the same result.

Now that we understand this, we can try to implement proxies to iterator methods. But before that, let's do some experimentation and see what happens, as shown in the following code:

```
01 const p = reactive (new Map ( [
02 ['key1', 'value1'],
03 ['key2', 'value2']
04 ]))
05
06 effect (() => {
07 // TypeError: p is not iterable
08 for (const [key, value] of p) {
09 console.log(key, value)
10 }
11 })
12
13 p.set ('key3', 'value3')
```

In this code, we first create a proxy object p, then try to iterate over it using a *for . . . of* loop but get an error: "p is not iterable." We know that whether an object can iterate depends on whether the object implements the iteration protocol, and if an object implements Symbol.iterator methods correctly, then it is iterable. Obviously, proxy object p does not implement Symbol.iterator methods, so we get the above error.

But in reality, when we iterate over a proxy object using a *for … of* loop, we internally try to read the p [Symbol.iterator] property from the proxy object p, which triggers the get interceptor function, so we can still put the implementation of Symbol.iterator method into mutableInstrumentations, as shown in the following code:

```
01 const mutableInstrumentations = {
02 [Symbol.iterator] () {
03 // Get the original data source object target
04 const target = this.raw
05 // Get the original iterator method
06 const itr = target [Symbol.iterator] ()
07 // return it
08 return itr
09 }
10 }
```

The implementation is very simple: just return the original iterator object, so that you can use the *for … of* loop to iterate over the proxy object p, but things cannot be that simple. When we explained the forEach method in Sect. 5.8.4, we mentioned that the parameters passed to the callback are wrapped reactive data, such as

```
01 p.forEach ((value, key ) => {
02 //value and key are proxy objects if they can be proxied,
i.e. reactive data
03 })
```

Similarly, when using a for … of loop to iterate over a collection, if the value produced by the iteration can also be proxied, it should also be wrapped as reactive data, for example:

```
01 for (const [key, value] of p) {
02 //Expect key and value to be reactive data
03 }
```

Therefore, we need to modify the code:

```
01 const mutableInstrumentations = {
02 [Symbol.iterator] () {
03 // Get the original data source object target
04 const target = this.raw
05 // Get the original iterator method
06 const itr = target [Symbol.iterator] ()
07
08 const wrap = (val) => typeof val === 'object' && val !== null?
reactive (val) : val
09
10 // Return a custom iterator
11 return {
```

```
12 next () {
13 // Call the next method of the original iterator to get value and
done
14 const { value, done } = itr.next ()
15 return {
16 // Wrap value if it is not undefined
17 value: value?  [wrap(value [0]), wrap(value [1])] : value,
18 done
19 }
20 }
21 }
22 }
23 }
```

As shown in the above code, in order to implement the wrapping of key and value, we need to customize the iterator of the implementation, in which the original iterator is called to get the value *value* and *done* which represents whether the end is done. If the value *value* is not undefined, wrap it, and finally return the wrapped proxy object, so that when iterating with a *for . . . of* loop, the resulting value will be reactive data.

Finally, in order to track the iterative operation of *for . . . of* on the data, we also need to call the track function to let the side effect function connect with the ITERATE_KEY:

```
01 const mutableInstrumentations = {
02 [Symbol.iterator] () {
03 const target = this.raw
04 const itr = target [Symbol.iterator] ()
05
06 const wrap = (val) => typeof val === 'object' && val !== null?
reactive(val) : val
07
08 // Call the track function to establish a response contact
09 track(target, ITERATE_KEY)
10
11 return {
12 next () {
13 const { value, done } = itr.next ()
14 return {
15 value: value?  [wrap(value [0]), wrap(value [1])] : value,
16 done
17 }
18 }
19 }
20 }
21 }
```

Since the iteration operation is related to the number of elements in the collection, whenever the size of the collection changes, the iteration operation should be triggered to re-execute. Therefore, when we call the track function, we let the

ITERATE_KEY connect with the side effect function. After completing this step, the reactive data function of the collection is relatively complete. We can test it with the following code:

```
01 const p = reactive(new Map([
02 ['key1', 'value1'],
03 ['key2', 'value2']
04 ]))
05
06 effect(() => {
07 for (const [key, value] of p) {
08 console.log(key, value)
09 }
10 })
11
12 p.set('key3', 'value3') // can trigger a response
```

As we said earlier, since p.entries is equivalent to p [Symbol.iterator], we can use the same code to intercept the p.entries function, as shown in the following code:

```
01 const mutableInstrumentations = {
02 // Common iterationMethod method
03 [Symbol.iterator] : iterationMethod,
04 entries: iterationMethod
05 }
06 // Extracted as an independent function for easy reuse
07 function iterationMethod() {
08 const target = this.raw
09 const itr = target[Symbol.iterator]()
10
11 const wrap = (val) => typeof val === 'object'?  reactive(val) :
val
12
13 track(target, ITERATE_KEY)
14
15 return {
16 next() {
17 const { value, done } = itr.next()
18 return {
19 value: value?  [wrap(value[0]), wrap(value[1])] : value,
20 done
21 }
22 }
23 }
24 }
```

But when you try to run the code to iterate with *for ... of*, you get an error:

```
01//TypeError: p.entries is not a function or its return value is not
iterable
02 for (const [key, value] of p.entries()) {
```

```
03 console.log (key, value)
04 }
```

The gist of the error is that the return value of the p.entries is not an iterable object. Obviously, the return value of the p.entries function is an object with a *next* method but no Symbol.iterator method, so it is indeed not an iterable object. This is where things often go wrong. Don not confuse the iterable protocol with the iterator protocol. The iterable protocol refers to an object implementing Symbol.iterator methods, while the iterator protocol refers to an object implementing the *next* method. But an object can implement both the iterable protocol and the iterator protocol, for example:

```
01 const obj = {
02 //Iterator protocol
03 next () {
04 //...
05 }
06 //Iterable protocol
7 [Symbol.iterator ] () {
08 return this
09 }
10 }
```

So the solution to the problem came naturally:

```
01 //Extracted as an independent function for easy reuse
02 function iterationMethod () {
03 const target = this.raw
04 const itr = target [Symbol.iterator] ()
05
06 const wrap = (val) = > typeof val === 'object'? reactive (val) : val
07
08 track (target, ITERATE_KEY)
09
10 return {
11 next () {
12 const { value, done } = itr.next ()
13 return {
14 value: value?  [wrap(value[0]), wrap(value[1])] : value,
15 done
16 }
17 }
18 // Implement an iterable protocol
19 [Symbol.iterator] () {
20 return this
21 }
22 }
23 }
```

Everything is working normally now.

5.8.6 Values and Keys Methods

The implementation of the values method is similar to the entries method, except that
when using *for ... of* to iterate over values; only the value of the Map data is
obtained, not the key-value pair:

```
01 for (const value of p.values ()) {
02 console.log (value)
03 }
```

The implementation of the values method is as follows:

```
01 const mutableInstrumentations = {
02 // Common iterationMethod method
03 [Symbol.iterator] : iterationMethod,
04 entries: iterationMethod,
05 values: valuesIterationMethod
06 }
07
08 function valuesIterationMethod () {
09 // Get the original data source object target
10 const target = this.raw
11 // Get the original iterator method by target.values
12 const itr = target.values ()
13
14 const wrap = (val) => typeof val === 'object'?  reactive (val) :
val
15
16 track (target, ITERATE_KEY)
17
18 // return it
19 return {
20 next () {
21 const { value, done } = itr.next ()
22 return {
23 // value is a value, not a key-value pair, so just wrap value
24 value: wrap (value) ,
25 done
26 }
27 },
28 [Symbol.iterator] () {
29 return this
30 }
31 }
32 }
```

Among them, valuesIterationMethod and iterationMethod have two differences:

• iterationMethod gets the iterator object through target [Symbol.iterator], while
valuesIterationMethod gets the iterator object through target.values;

- IterationMethod handles key-value pairs, i.e., [wrap (value [0]), wrap (value [1])], while valuesIterationMethod only handles values, i.e., wrap (value).

Since most of their logic is the same, we can encapsulate them into a reusable function. But for ease of understanding, they are still designed to be implemented as two separate functions here.

The *keys* method is very similar to the *values* method, except that the former handles keys rather than values. Therefore, we only need to modify one line of code in the valuesIterationMethod method to implement a proxy for the *keys* method. Replace the following code.

```
01 const itr = target.values ()
```

with: 01 const itr = target.keys ().

This does serve the purpose, but if we try to run the following test case, we will find a flaw:

```
01 const p = reactive (new Map ([
02 ['key1', 'value1'],
03 ['key2', 'value2']
04 ]))
05
06 effect (() => {
07 for (const value of p.keys ()) {
08 console.log (value) // key1 key2
09 }
10 })
11
12 p.set ('key2', 'value3') // This is a SET operation that modifies the
value of key2
```

In the above code, we use a *for . . . of* loop to iterate over the p.keys, then call p.set ("key2," "value3") to modify the value of the key to key2. During this process, all keys of type Map data remain unchanged, still key1 and key2, so ideally side effects should not be executed. But if you try to run the above example, you will find that the side effect function is still re-executed.

This is because we have special treatment for data of type Map. As mentioned earlier, even if the operation type is SET, it will trigger the re-execution of those side effects associated with the ITERATE_KEY. The code of the trigger function can prove this:

```
01 function trigger (target, key, type, newVal) {
02 // Omit other code
03
04 if (
05 type === 'ADD' ||
06 type === 'DELETE' ||
07 // Even SET-type operations trigger the re-execution of side
```

effect functions associated with ITERATE_KEY

```
08 (
09 type === 'SET' &&
10 Object.prototype.toString.call(target) === '[object Map]'
11 )
12 ) {
13 const iterateEffects = depsMap.get(ITERATE_KEY)
14 iterateEffects && iterateEffects.forEach(effectFn => {
15 if (effectFn !== activeEffect) {
16 effectsToRun.add(effectFn)
17 }
18 })
19 }
20
21 // Omit other code
22 }
```

This is necessary for methods such as values or entries, but not for keys methods, which only care about changes in keys of type Map data, not changes in values.

The solution is simple, as shown in the following code:

```
01 const MAP_KEY_ITERATE_KEY = Symbol()
02
03 function keysIterationMethod() {
04 // Get the original data source object target
05 const target = this.raw
06 // Get the original iterator method
07 const itr = target.keys()
08
09 const wrap = (val) => typeof val === 'object'?  reactive(val) :
val
10
11 // Call the track function to track the dependency and establish a
response connection between the side effect function and the
MAP_KEY_ITERATE_KEY
12 track(target, MAP_KEY_ITERATE_KEY)
13
14 // return it
15 return {
16 next() {
17 const { value, done } = itr.next()
18 return {
19 value: wrap(value),
20 done
21 }
22 },
23 [Symbol.iterator]() {
24 return this
25 }
26 }
27 }
```

In the above code, when calling the track function to track dependencies, we use MAP_KEY_ITERATE_KEY   instead   of   ITERATE_KEY. MAP_KEY_ITERATE_KEY is a new Symbol type similar to ITERATE_KEY, used as an abstract key. This achieves the separation of dependency collection, that is, methods such as values and entries still depend on ITERATE_KEY, while keys methods depend on MAP_KEY_ITERATE_KEY. When an operation of type SET only triggers the re-execution of side effects associated with ITERATE_KEY, it is natural to ignore those side effects associated with MAP_KEY_ITERATE_KEY. But when ADD and DELETE type operations occur, in addition to triggering the re-execution of the side effect function associated with the ITERATE_KEY, it is also necessary to trigger the re-execution of the side effect function associated with the MAP_KEY_ITERATE_KEY, so we need to modify the *trigger*. The code for the function looks like this:

```
01 function trigger(target, key, type, newVal) {
02 // Omit other code
03
04 if (
05 // Operation type is ADD or DELETE
06 (type === 'ADD' || type === 'DELETE') &&
07 // and is data of type Map
08 Object.prototype.toString.call(target) === '[object Map]'
09 ) {
10 // Take out those side effects associated with the
MAP_KEY_ITERATE_KEY and execute
11 const iterateEffects = depsMap.get(MAP_KEY_ITERATE_KEY)
12 iterateEffects && iterateEffects.forEach(effectFn => {
13 if (effectFn !== activeEffect) {
14 effectsToRun.add(effectFn)
15 }
16 })
17 }
18
19 // Omit other codes
20 }
```

In this way, unnecessary updates can be avoided:

```
01 const p = reactive(new Map([
02 ['key1', 'value1'],
03 ['key2', 'value2']
04 ]))
05
06 effect(() => {
07 for (const value of p.keys()) {
08 console.log(value)
09 }
10 })
11
12 p.set('key2', 'value3') // will not trigger a response
13 p.set('key3', 'value3') // will trigger a response
```

5.9 Summary

In this chapter, we first introduced Proxy and Reflect. The reactive data of Vue.js 3 is implemented based on Proxy, which can create a proxy object for other objects. The so-called proxy refers to the proxy of the basic semantics of an object. It allows us to intercept and redefine the basic operation on an object. In the process of implementing the proxy, we encountered the problem of this pointing to the accessor property, which needs to be solved by using the Reflect. * method and specifying the correct receiver.

Then we discussed the concept of objects in JavaScript in detail, and how proxies work. In the ECMAScript specification, there are two kinds of objects in JavaScript, one of which is called regular objects and the other is called heterogeneous objects. Objects that meet the following three requirements are regular objects:

- For the internal methods given in Table 5.1, they must be implemented using the definitions given in Section 10.1.x of the specification
- For the internal method [[Call]], it must be implemented using the definition given in section 10.2.1 of the specification
- For the internal method [[Construct]], the definition implementation given in section 10.2.2 of the specification must be used

All objects that do not meet these three requirements are heterogeneous objects. Whether an object is a function or other object is determined by the internal methods and internal slots deployed on the object.

Next, we discussed proxies for Objects. The essence of proxy objects is to look up the specification and find ways to intercept basic operations. There are some operations that are not basic operations, but compound operations, which requires us to look up the specification to understand which basic operations they all depend on, so as to indirectly handle compound operations through the interception method of basic operations. We also analyzed the impact of adding, modifying, and deleting properties on *for ... in* operations in detail. Both adding and deleting properties affect the number of executions of the *for ... in* loop, so when these operations occur, they need to trigger the side effect function associated with the ITERATE_KEY to re-executed. Modifying the property value does not affect the number of executions of the *for ... in* loop, so there is no need to deal with it. We also discussed how to reasonably trigger the re-execution of side effect functions, including the handling of NaN, and the re-execution of side effect functions caused by accessing properties on the prototype chain twice. For NaN, our main concern is that NaN === NaN always equals false. For the prototype chain attribute problem, we need to consult the reason for the specification positioning problem. It can be seen that if you want to implement a relatively complete response system based on Proxy, it is inevitable to understand the ECMAScript specification.

Then, we discussed deep and shallow responses, as well as deep read-only and shallow read-only. The deep and shallow here refer to the hierarchy of objects, and the shallow response (or read-only) represents only the first-level property of an object, that is, only the first-level property value of the object is responsive (or read-only). Deep response (or read-only) is the exact opposite. In order to implement a deep response (or read-only), we need to wrap the value in a layer before returning the property value, wrap it as responsive (or read-only) data before returning it.

After that, we discussed about proxying arrays. An array is a heterogeneous object because the internal method [[DefineOwnProperty]] deployed by an array object is different from a regular object. Setting new elements to an array by indexing may implicitly change the value of the array length attribute. Correspondingly, modifying the value of the array length attribute may also indirectly affect existing elements in the array. So extra care is required when triggering responses. We also discussed how to intercept *for . . . in* and *for . . . of* traversing arrays. Using a for . . . in loop to traverse an array is not much different from traversing a normal object, the only thing to note is that when tracking *for . . . in* operations, the length of the array should be used as the tracking key. *For . . . of* works based on an iteration protocol, and arrays have Symbol.iterator built-in methods. According to the 23.1.5.1 section of the specification, when the array iterator is executed, it will read the length property of the array or the index of the array. Therefore, we can implement reactive support for *for . . . of* iterations without doing other processing.

We also discussed array lookup methods. Such as includes, indexOf, and lastIndexOf, etc. For the lookup of array elements, it should be noted that the user may use either the proxy object to search, or the original object to search. In order to support these two forms, we need to rewrite the array lookup method. The principle is very simple, when the user uses these methods to find an element, we can first go to the proxy object to find it, and if we cannot find it, then go to the original array to find it.

We also introduced prototype methods that implicitly modify the length of the array, namely push, pop, shift, unshift, and splice methods. Calling these methods indirectly reads and sets the length property of the array, so executing the above methods on the same array within different side effect functions will cause multiple side effect functions to be called in a loop, eventually causing the call stack to overflow. To solve this problem, we use a flag variable shouldTrack to represent whether tracing is allowed, and then override the above methods, the purpose is that when these methods indirectly read the value of the length property, we will first set the value of shouldTrack to false; that is, tracking is prohibited. This disconnects the response link between the length property and the side effect function, thereby avoiding call stack overflow caused by circular calls.

Finally, we discussed reactive schemes for collection type data. Collection types refer to Set, Map, WeakSet, and WeakMap. We discussed some considerations for using Proxy to create proxy objects for collection types. Collection types are different from ordinary objects in that they have specific data manipulation methods. Pay special attention when using Proxy to proxy data of collection type. For example, the size property of collection type is an accessor property. When accessing the size property through a proxy object, since the proxy object itself does not deploy [[SetData]] such an internal slot, an error will occur. In addition, when executing the operation methods of the collection type through the proxy object, we should pay attention to the *this* pointing when these methods are executed. We need to bind the correct this value for these methods through the.bind function within the get interceptor function. We also discussed the implementation of reactive data of the collection type. We need to implement the custom capability by "overriding" the collection method. When the add method of the Set collection executes, we need to call the trigger function to trigger the response. We also discussed the issue of "data pollution." Data pollution refers to accidentally adding reactive data to the original data source, which causes the user to perform reactive related operations through the original data source, which is not what we expect. To avoid this kind of problem, we access the corresponding original data source object through the raw property of the reactive data object, and subsequent operations can use the original data source object. We also discussed traversal about collection types, the forEach method. The forEach method of a collection is similar to the *for ... in* traversal of an object. The biggest difference is that when using *for ... in* to traverse an object, we only care about whether the object's key changes, not the value; but when using forEach to traverse a collection, we care about both key changes and value changes.

Chapter 6
Responsive Schemes for Raw Values

In Chap. 5, we discussed reactive schemes for non-primitive values. In this chapter, we will discuss reactive schemes for primitive values. Primitive values are values of types such as Boolean, Number, BigInt, String, Symbol, undefined, and null. In JavaScript, primitive values are passed by value, not by reference. This means that if a function receives a primitive value as a parameter, then there is no reference relationship between the formal parameters. They are two completely independent values, and changes to the formal parameter will not affect the argument. In addition, Proxy in JavaScript cannot provide a proxy for the original value, so if you want to turn the original value into responsive data, you must wrap it in a layer, which is the ref we will introduce next.

6.1 Introducing the Concept of Ref

Since the proxy target of Proxy must be a non-primitive value, we have no means to intercept the operation on the original value, for example:

```
01 let str = 'vue'
02 //Unable to intercept the modification of the value
03 str = 'vue3'
```

For this problem, the only way we can think of is to use a non-primitive value to "wrap" the original value, for example, use an object to wrap the original value:

```
01 const wrapper = {
02 value: 'vue'
03 }
04 //You can use the proxy wrapper to indirectly intercept the original
value
05 const name = reactive (wrapper)
```

© The Author(s), under exclusive license to Springer Nature Singapore Pte Ltd. 2023
H. Yang, *Vue. JS Framework*, https://doi.org/10.1007/978-981-99-4947-2_6

```
06 name.value//vue
07//Modifying the value can trigger the response
08 = 'vue3'
```

But doing so will cause two problems:

- The user has to create a wrapper object incidentally in order to create a responsive original value
- The wrapper object is user-defined, which means non-standard. The user can name it at will, such as, wrapper.value, wrapper.val are fine.

To solve these two problems, we can encapsulate a function to encapsulate the creation of the wrapper object into this function:

```
01//encapsulate a ref function
02 function ref (val) {
03//create the wrapper object inside the ref function
04 const wrapper = {
05 value: val
06}
07//turn the wrapper object into responsive data
08 return reactive (wrapper)
09}
```

As shown in the above code, the work of creating the wrapper object is encapsulated inside the ref function, and then the reactive function is used to wrap the object into reactive data and return it. This solves the above two problems. Run the following test code:

```
01//Create the reactive data of the original value
02 const refVal = ref (1)
03
04 effect (() => {
05//Read the original value through the value property inside the side
effect function
06 console.log(refVal.value)
07})
08//Modifying the value triggers the side effect function to
re-execute
09 refVal.value = 2
```

The above code works as expected. Is everything perfect now? No, the first problem we face next is how to distinguish whether refVal is a wrapped object of primitive values or a reactive data of non-primitive values, as shown in the following code:

```
01 const refVal1 = ref (1)
02 const refVal2 = reactive ({value: 1})
```

Think about it: what is the difference between refVal1 and refVal2 in this code? From our implementation, they do not make any difference. However, it is necessary to distinguish whether a data is a ref or not, because this involves the automatic deref ability explained below.

It is very simple to distinguish whether a data is a ref or not, how to do it?

```
01 function ref (val) {
02 const wrapper = {
03 value: val
04 }
05 // Use Object.defineProperty to define a non-enumerable property
__v_isRef on the wrapper object with the value true
06 Object.defineProperty (wrapper, '__v_isRef', {
07 value: true
08 })
09
10 return reactive (wrapper)
11 }
```

We use Object.defineProperty to define a non-enumerable and unwritable property __v_isRef for wrapper, and its value is true, which means that the object is a ref, not a normal object. This way, we can judge whether a data is a ref by checking the __v_isRef property.

6.2   Response Loss Problems

Ref can also be used to solve the response loss problem in addition to reactive solutions that can be used for primitive values. First, let's see what the response loss problem is. When writing Vue.js components, we usually expose the data to the template, for example:

```
01 export default {
02 setup () {
03 // reactive data
04 const obj = reactive ({ foo: 1, bar: 2 })
05
06 // expose the data to the template
07 return {
08 ...obj
09 }
10 }
11 }
```

Then, we can access the exposed data from the setup in the template:

```
01 < template >
02 < p > {{foo }} / {{ bar}} </p >
03 </template >
```

However, this will result in a missing response. When we change the value of the reactive data, it will not trigger the re-rendering:

```
01 export default {
02 setup () {
03 //reactive data
04 const obj = reactive ({foo: 1, bar: 2})
05
06 //1s after modifying the value of the reactive data, it will not
trigger the re-rendering
07 setTime out (() => {
08 obj.foo = 100
09 }, 1000)
10
11 return {
12 ...obj
13 }
14 }
15 }
```

What causes the response to be lost? This is caused by the expansion operator (...). In fact, the following code:

```
01 return {
02 ... obj
03 }
```

It is equivalent to:

```
01 return {
02 foo: 1,
03 bar: 2
04 }
```

It can be found that this is actually returning a normal object, which does not have any reactive capabilities. Exposing a normal object to use in the template will not establish a reactive connection between the render function and the reactive data. So, when we try to modify the value of the obj.foo in a timer, it will not trigger a re-rendering. We can describe the response loss problem in another way:

```
01 //obj is reactive data
02 const obj = reactive ({foo: 1, bar: 2})
03
04 //expand the reactive data to a new object newObj
05 const newObj = {
06 ... obj
```

```
07 }
08
09 effect (() => {
10 //read the foo property value from the new object newObj inside the
side effect function
11 console.log (newObj.foo)
12 })
13
14 //Obviously, modifying the   at this point does not trigger a
response
15  obj.foo = 100
```

As shown in the code above, first create a reactive data object obj, and then use the expand operator to get a new object newObj, which is a normal object and not responsive. The key point here is that the side effect function is accessing the normal object newObj, which has no responsiveness, so when we try to modify the value of the obj.foo, it will not trigger the side effect function to re-execute.

How to solve this problem? In other words, is there a way to help us achieve: in the side effect function, even if the property value is accessed through the normal object newObj, it can establish a response relationship? In fact, it is possible. The code is as follows:

```
01 // obj is responsive data
02 const obj = reactive ({ foo: 1, bar: 2 })
03
04 // newObj object has properties with the same name as obj object, and
each property value is an object,
05 // The object has an accessor property value; when reading the value
of value, it actually reads the corresponding property value under obj
object
06 const newObj = {
07 foo: {
08 get value () {
09 return obj.foo
10 }
11 },
12 bar: {
13 get value () {
14 return obj.bar
15 }
16 }
17 }
18
19 effect (() => {
20 // Read the foo property value via the new object newObj in the side
effect function
21 console.log (newObj.foo.value)
22 })
23
24 // This triggers the response
25 obj.foo = 100
```

In the above code, we modified the implementation of the newObj object. As you can see, in the current newObj object, there is the same name as the obj object property, and the value of each property is an object, for example, the value of the foo property is as follows:

```
01 {
02 get value () {
03 return obj.foo
04 }
05 }
```

The object has an accessor property value. When reading the value of value, the final read is the property value of the same name under the response data *obj*. That is to say, when we read newObj.foo in the side effect function, it is equivalent to reading the value of the obj.foo indirectly. In this way, the reactive data can naturally establish a response relationship with the side effect function. Therefore, when we try to modify the value of the obj.foo, we can trigger the side effect function to re-execute.

Looking at the newObj object, we can see that its structure is similar:

```
01 const newObj = {
02 foo: {
03 get value () {
04 return obj.foo
05 }
06 },
07 bar: {
08 get value () {
09 return obj.bar
10 }
11 }
12 }
```

The structure of the two properties *foo* and *bar* is very similar, which inspires us to abstract this structure and encapsulate it into a function, as shown in the following code:

```
01 function toRef (obj, key) {
02 const wrapper = {
03 get value () {
04 return obj[key]
05 }
06 }
07
08 return wrapper
09 }
```

toRef function takes two arguments: the first argument obj is a reactive data, and the second argument is a key of the obj object. The function returns a wrapper object similar to the ref structure. With the toRef function, we can re-implement the newObj object:

```
01 const newObj = {
02 foo: toRef(obj, 'foo'),
03 bar: toRef(obj, 'bar')
04 }
```

As you can see, the code becomes very concise. But if the reactive data obj has many keys, we still have to spend a lot of effort to do this layer of conversion. To do this, we can wrap the toRefs function to do the conversion in batches:

```
01 function toRefs(obj) {
02 const ret = {}
03 // loop through objects using for... in
04 for (const key in obj) {
05 // call toRef one by one to complete the conversion
06 ret[key] = toRef(obj, key)
07 }
08 return ret
09 }
```

Now, we only need one operation to complete the conversion of an object:

```
01 const newObj = {... toRefs (obj) }
```

It can be tested with the following code:

```
01 const obj = reactive({ foo: 1, bar: 2 })
02
03 const newObj = { ...toRefs(obj) }
04 console.log(newObj.foo.value) // 1
05 console.log(newObj.bar.value) // 2
```

Now, the problem of missing responses is completely solved. The idea to solve the problem is to convert the reactive data into data similar to the ref structure. But for the sake of conceptual consistency, we will treat the result obtained by toRef or toRefs conversion as real ref data, for which we need to add a piece of code to the toRef function:

```
01 function toRef(obj, key) {
02 const wrapper = {
03 get value() {
04 return obj[key]
05 }
06 }
```

```
07 // Define __v_isRef property
08 Object.defineProperty(wrapper, '__v_isRef', {
09 value: true
10 })
11
12 return wrapper
13 }
```

You can see that we use the Object.defineProperty function to define __v_isRef properties for the wrapper object. In this way, the return value of the toRef function is the real ref. Through the above explanation, we can notice that the role of ref is not only to implement the reactive solution of the original value. It is also used to solve the problem of missing response.

However, the toRef function implemented above has a defect, that is, the ref created by the toRef function is read-only, as shown in the following code:

```
01 const obj = reactive({ foo: 1, bar: 2 })
02 const refFoo = toRef(obj, 'foo')
03
04 refFoo.value = 100 //invalid
```

This is because the value property of the wrapper object returned by toRef is only getter, no setter. For completeness, we should add setter function to it, so the final implementation is as follows:

```
01 function toRef(obj, key) {
02 const wrapper = {
03 get value() {
04 return obj[key]
05 },
06 // allow setting value
07 set value(val) {
08 obj[key] = val
09 }
10 }
11
12 Object.defineProperty(wrapper, '__v_isRef', {
13 value: true
14 })
15
16 return wrapper
17 }
```

As you can see, when you set the value of the value property, you end up setting the value of the property of the same name for the reactive data, which triggers the response correctly.

6.3   Automatic Ref Removal

toRefs function does solve the problem of lost response, but it also brings new problems. Since toRefs converts the value of the first layer attribute of the reactive data to ref, the value must be accessed through the value attribute, as shown in the following code:

```
01 const obj = reactive({ foo: 1, bar: 2 })
02 obj.foo // 1
03 obj.bar // 2
04
05 const newObj = { ...toRefs(obj) }
06 // Value must be used to access the value
07 newObj.foo.value // 1
08 newObj.bar.value // 2
```

This actually increases the user's mental burden, because usually the user accesses the data in the template, for example:

```
01 < p > {{foo }} / {{ bar}} </p >
```

The user definitely does not want to write the following code:

```
01 < p > {{foo.value }} / {{ bar.value}} </p >
```

Therefore, we need the ability to automatically deref the so-called automatic deref refers to the access behavior of the attribute; that is, if the read attribute is a ref, the value of the value attribute corresponding to the ref is directly returned, for example:

```
01 newObj.foo // 1
```

You can see that even if the newObj.foo is a ref, there is no need to access its value through newObj.foo.value. To achieve this function, you need to use Proxy to create a proxy object for newObj and achieve the final goal through the proxy. Now you have used the ref identifier described above, that is, the __v_isRef attribute, as shown in the following code:

```
01 function proxyRefs(target) {
02 return new Proxy(target, {
03 get(target, key, receiver) {
04 const value = Reflect.get(target, key, receiver)
05 // automatic removal of ref implementation: if the value read of is
ref, return its value property value
06 return value.__v_isRef ? value.value : value
07 }
08 })
09 }
```

```
10
11 // Call the proxyRefs function to create a proxy
12 const newObj = proxyRefs({ ...toRefs(obj) })
```

In the code above, we define the proxyRefs function, which takes an object as an argument and returns a proxy object for that object. The role of the proxy object is to intercept the get operation. When the read property is a ref, the value property value of the ref is directly returned, which implements the automatic removal of ref:

```
01 console.log (newObj.foo)//1
02 console.log (newObj.bar)//2
```

In fact, when we write a Vue.js component, the data returned by the setup function in the component will be passed to the proxyRefs function for processing:

```
01 const MyComponent = {
02 setup () {
03 const count = ref(0)
04
05 // The returned object will be passed to proxyRefs
06 return { count }
07 }
08 }
```

This is why we can access the value of a ref directly in the template without accessing it through the value attribute:

```
01 < p > {{count}} </p >
```

Since reading the value of the attribute has the ability to automatically deref. Correspondingly, setting the value of the attribute should have the ability to automatically set the value for ref., for example:

```
01 newObj.foo = 100//should take effect
```

To achieve this function is very simple. Just need to add the corresponding set interception function:

```
01 function proxyRefs (target) {
02 return new Proxy (target, {
03 get (target, key, receiver) {
04 const value = Reflect.get (target, key, receiver)
05 return value.__v_isRef ? value.value : value
06 },
07 set (target, key, newValue, receiver) {
08 // Read the real value via target
09 const value = target [key]
10 // If the value is Ref, set its corresponding value property value
11 if (value.__v_isRef) {
```

```
12 value.value = newValue
13 return true
14 }
15 return Reflect.set(target, key, newValue, receiver)
16 }
17 })
18 }
```

As shown in the code above, we add a set interceptor function to the proxy object returned by the proxyRefs function. If the property of set is a ref., then indirectly set the value of the value property of the ref.

In fact, auto-deref not only exists in the above scenarios. In Vue.js, the reactive function also has the ability to automatically deref, as shown in the following code:

```
01 const count = ref(0)
02 const obj = reactive({count})
03
04 obj.count//0
```

As you can see, obj.count should be a ref., but due to the existence of auto-deref ability, we can read the value of ref. without using the value attribute. The purpose of this design is to reduce the mental burden of users, because in most cases, users do not know whether a value is a ref. or not. With the ability to automatically deref, users will no longer need to care about what is and is not a ref. when using reactive data in templates.

6.4 Summary

In this chapter, we first introduced the concept of ref. A ref is essentially a "wrapping object." Because JavaScript's Proxy cannot provide a proxy for the original value, we need to use a layer of objects as wrappers to indirectly implement the response of the original value. Since the "wrapped object" is essentially no different from the normal object, in order to distinguish the ref from the normal reactive object, we also define a property with a value of true for the "wrapped object," that is, __v_isRef, and use it as the identifier of the ref.

Ref can be used to solve the problem of missing responses in addition to the reactive scheme that can be used for the original value. To solve this problem, we implement toRef and toRefs functions. They essentially wrap reactive data, or "access proxy."

Finally, we explained the ability to automatically deref. To reduce the user's mental burden, we automatically deref the reactive data exposed to the template. In this way, users do not need to care whether a value is ref or not when using reactive data in the template.

Part III
Renderers

Chapter 7
Renderer Design

In Chap. 3, we first discussed the virtual DOM and how renderers work and tried to write a miniature renderer. Starting from this chapter, we will discuss the implementation details of renderers in detail. In the process, you will realize that renderers are a very important part of the Vue.js. In Vue.js, many functions rely on renderers to implement, such as Transition components, Teleport components, Suspense components, as well as template refs and custom directives.

In addition, the renderer is also the core of the framework performance, and the implementation of the renderer directly affects the performance of the framework. Vue.js 3 renderer not only includes the traditional Diff algorithm, but also creates a shortcut update method, which can make full use of the information provided by the compiler and greatly improve the update performance.

The code volume of the renderer is very large, and it requires a reasonable architecture design to ensure maintainability, but its implementation idea is not complicated. Next, we will start by discussing how the renderer integrates with the response system and gradually implement a complete renderer.

7.1 Integration of Renderers and Response System

As the name suggests, renderer is used to perform rendering tasks. On the browser platform, it is used to render real DOM elements. The renderer can not only render real DOM elements, but it is also the key to the framework's cross-platform capabilities. Therefore, when designing the renderer, be sure to consider the customizable capabilities.

In this section, we will limit the renderer to the DOM platform for the time being. Since the renderer is used to render real DOM elements, then strictly speaking, the following function is a qualified renderer:

```
01 function renderer (domString, container) {
02      container.innerHTML = domString
03 }
```

We can use it as follows:

```
renderer ('<h1>Hello</h1>', document. getElementById ('app'))
```

If there is a DOM element with id *app* in the page, then the above code will insert $< h1 >$ hello $</h1 >$ into the DOM element. Of course, we can render not only static strings, but also dynamically stitched HTML content, as follows:

```
01 let count = 1
02 renderer ('<h1>Hello</h1>', document.getElementById ('app'))
```

In this way, the final rendered content will be $< h1 > 1 </h1 >$. Note the variable count in the above code. If it is a reactive data, what will happen? This brings us to side effect functions and reactive data. Using a responsive system, we can automate the entire rendering process:

```
01 const count = ref (1)
02
03  effect (() => {
04      renderer ( `<h1>${count.value}</h1>`, document.
getElementById ('app'))
05  })
06
07 count.value++
```

In this code, we first define a reactive data count, which is a ref., and then call the renderer function inside the side effect function to perform the rendering. After the side effect function finishes executing, it will establish a response connection with the reactive data. When we modify the value of the count.value, the side effect function will be re-executed, completing the re-rendering. So, after the above code is run, the final content rendered to the page is $< h1 > 2 </h1 >$.

This is the relationship between the response system and the renderer. We use the ability of the response system to automatically call the renderer to complete the rendering and update of the page. This process has nothing to do with the specific implementation of the renderer. In the implementation of the renderer given above, only the innerHTML content of the element is set.

From the beginning of this chapter, we will use the responsive API provided by the @vue/reactivity package to explain. The implementation principle of @vue/reactivity has been explained in the second part. @Vue/reactivity provides the IIFE module format, so we can refer to the page directly through the $< $ script $> $ tag to use:

```
01 <script src="https://unpkg.com/@vue/reactivity@3.0.5/dist/
reactivity.global.js"></script>
```

The global API it exposes is named VueReactivity, so the complete code for the above is as follows:

```
01   const{ effect, ref } = VueReactivity
02
03   functionrenderer(domString, container) {
04       container.innerHTML = domString
05 }
06
07   const count = ref(1)
08
09   effect(() => {
10       renderer(`<h1>${count.value}</h1>`, document.
getElementById('app'))
11   })
12
13   count.value++
```

As you can see, we got the two APIs effect and ref. through VueReactivity.

7.2   Fundamentals of Renderers

Understanding the basic concepts involved in renderers is beneficial to understand the following content. Therefore, in this section, we will introduce the terms and meanings of renderer and illustrate them with code examples.

We usually use the English renderer to express "renderer." Please do not confuse renderer with render—the former stands for renderer, and the latter is a verb, which means "render." The role of the renderer is to render the virtual DOM as a real element on a specific platform. On the browser platform, the renderer will render the virtual DOM as a real DOM element.

Virtual DOM is usually expressed in English virtual DOM, sometimes abbreviated as vdom. Virtual DOM has the same structure as real DOM and is a tree structure composed of nodes. Therefore, we often hear the expression "virtual node," sometimes abbreviated as vnode. Virtual DOM is a tree structure. Any vnode node in this tree can be a subtree, so vnode and vdom can sometimes be used interchangeably. To avoid confusion, we will use vnodes in this book.

The process of rendering virtual DOM nodes into real DOM nodes by the renderer is called mounting, which is usually expressed in English word *mount*. For example, the mounted hook in the Vue.js component will be triggered when the mounting is complete. This means that the real DOM elements can be accessed from the mounted hook. Understanding these terms helps us better understand the API design of the framework.

So, where does the renderer mount the real DOM? In fact, the renderer does not know where to mount the real DOM. Therefore, the renderer usually needs to receive a mount point as a parameter to specify the specific mount position. The "mount point" here is actually a DOM element. The renderer will use the DOM element as a container element and render the content into it. We usually use English word *container* to express container.

The concepts of renderer, virtual DOM (or virtual node), mount, and container are explained above. For ease of understanding, here is an example:

```
01   function createRenderer () {
02       function render (vnode, container) {
03           // . . .
04       }
05
06       return render
07   }
```

As shown in the code above, the createRenderer function is used to create a renderer. Calling the createRenderer function will get a render function, which will take the container as the mount point, render the vnode as the real DOM and add it to the mount point.

You may be wondering why you need the createRenderer function? Why not just define render directly? In fact, as mentioned above, renderer is different from rendering. Renderer is a broader concept, it includes rendering. The renderer can be used not only to render, but also to activate existing DOM elements. This process usually occurs in the case of isomorphic rendering, as shown in the following code:

```
01 function createRenderer () {
02       function render (vnode, container) {
03           // . . .
04       }
05
06       function hydrate (vnode, container) {
07           // . . .
08       }
09
10       return {
11           render,
12           hydrate
13       }
14 }
```

As you can see, when calling the createRenderer function to create a renderer, the renderer contains not only the render function, but also the hydrate function. About the hydrate function, it will be explained in detail when introducing server-side rendering. This example shows that the renderer's content is very extensive, and the render function used to render vnode as the real DOM is only part of it. In fact, in

Vue.js 3, even the createApp function that creates the application is part of the renderer.

With the renderer, we can use it to perform rendering tasks, as shown in the following code:

```
01 const renderer = createRenderer ()
02 // first rendering
03 renderer.render(vnode, document.querySelector('#app'))
```

In the above code, we first call the createRenderer function to create a renderer, and then call the renderer.render function of the renderer to perform rendering. When the renderer.render function is called for the first time, only a new DOM element needs to be created, and this process only involves mounting.

When the renderer.render function is called multiple times on the same container for rendering, the renderer must perform an update action in addition to the mount action. For example:

```
01 const renderer = createRenderer ()
02 // first rendering
03 renderer.render(oldVNode, document.querySelector('#app'))
04 // second rendering
05 renderer.render(newVNode, document.querySelector('#app'))
```

As shown in the above code, since the oldVNode has been rendered into the container at the first render, when the renderer.render function is called again and trying to render newVNode, it cannot simply perform the mount action. In this case, the renderer compares the newVNode with the last rendered oldVNode, trying to find and update the change point. This process is called "patching" (or updating), which is usually expressed in English as patch. But in fact, the mount action itself can also be regarded as a kind of special patch, which is special in that the old vnode does not exist. So, we do not have to tear the concepts of "mounting" and "patching" too much. The code example is as follows:

```
01 function createRenderer() {
02         function render(vnode, container) {
03             if  (vnode) {
04                 // the new vnode exists; pass it to the patch function
together with the old vnode to patch
05                 patch(container._vnode, vnode, container)
06             } else  {
07                 if  (container._vnode) {
08                     // the old vnode exists, and the new vnode does not
exist, indicating that it is an unmount operation
09                     // just clear the DOM in the container
10                     container.innerHTML = ''
11                 }
12             }
13             // store the vnode in container._vnode, that is, the old
```

```
vnode in subsequent rendering
  14                  container._vnode = vnode
  15              }
  16
  17              return {
  18                  render
  19              }
  20      }
```

The above code gives the basic implementation of the render function. We can analyze its execution flow with the following code to better understand the implementation idea of the render function. Suppose we call renderer.render function three times in a row to execute rendering:

```
01  const renderer = createRenderer()
02
03  // first rendering
04  renderer.render(vnode1, document.querySelector('#app'))
05  // second rendering
06   renderer.render(vnode2, document.querySelector('#app'))
07  // third rendering
08  renderer.render(null, document.querySelector('#app'))
```

- Upon the first rendering, the renderer will render vnode1 as the real DOM. After rendering, vnode1 will be stored in the container._vnode property of the container element, which will be used as the old vnode in subsequent renderings.
- On the second rendering, the old vnode exists, and the renderer will treat vnode2 as the new vnode and pass the old and new vnodes together to the patch function for patching.
- On the third rendering, the value of the new vnode is null, that is, nothing is rendered. But at this time, the container is rendering what vnode2 describes, so the renderer needs to empty the container. As you can see from the above code, we use container.innerHTML = "to empty the container. It should be noted that this is problematic to empty the container, but here we temporarily use it for the purpose.

In addition, in the code given above, we notice the signature of the patch function, as follows:

```
01 patch (container._vnode, vnode, container)
```

We did not give the specific implementation of the patch, but from the above code, we can still spy on some details of the patch function. In fact, the patch function is the core entry point of the whole renderer. It carries the most important rendering logic. We will spend a lot of time explaining it in detail, but it is still necessary to do some preliminary explanation here. The patch function takes at least three parameters:

```
01 function patch (n1, n2, container) {
02 //...
03 }
```

- The first parameter n1: old vnode.
- The second parameter n2: new vnode.
- The third parameter container: container.

On the first render, the container._vnode attribute of the container element does not exist, that is, undefined. This means that the first parameter n1 passed to the patch function on first render is also undefined. At this time, the patch function will perform the mount action; it will ignore n1 and directly render the content described by n2 into the container. From this point, it can be seen that the patch function can be used not only to complete the patch, but also to perform the mount.

7.3   Custom Renderers

As we have always emphasized, the renderer can not only render the virtual DOM as the real DOM on the browser platform. By designing the renderer as a configurable "general purpose" renderer, it can be rendered to any target platform. In this section, we will write a renderer with the browser as the rendering target platform. In this process, we will see what content can be abstracted, and then abstract away the browser-specific API, so that the core of the renderer is not dependent on the browser. Based on this, we can implement the cross-platform capability of the renderer by providing configurable interfaces for those extracted APIs.

We start by rendering a normal $< h1 >$ tag. A $< h1 >$ tag can be described using the following vnode object:

```
01 const vnode = {
02 type: 'h1',
03 children: 'hello'
04 }
```

Observe the above vnode object. We use the *type* attribute to describe the type of a vnode. Different types of *type* attribute values can describe multiple types of vnodes. When the *type* attribute is a string *type* value, it can be considered to describe a normal label, and the string value of the type attribute is used as the name of the label. For such a vnode, we can render it using the render function, as shown in the following code:

```
01 const vnode = {
02 type: 'h1',
03 children: 'hello'
04 }
05 // create a renderer
06 const renderer = createRenderer()
07 // call the render function to render the vnode
08 renderer.render(vnode, document.querySelector('#app'))
```

To do the rendering, we need to add the patch function:

```
01 function createRenderer() {
02 function patch(n1, n2, container) {
03 // Write the rendering logic here
04 }
05
06 function render(vnode, container) {
07 if (vnode) {
08 patch(container._vnode, vnode, container)
09 } else {
10 if (container._vnode) {
11 container.innerHTML = ''
12 }
13 }
14 container._vnode = vnode
15 }
16
17 return {
18 render
19 }
20 }
```

As shown in the above code, we also write the patch function inside the createRenderer function. In the following explanation, if there is no special declaration, the functions we write are defined inside the createRenderer function.

The code of the patch function is as follows:

```
01 function patch(n1, n2, container) {
02 // If n1 does not exist, it means mounting, then call the
mountElement function to complete the mounting
03 if (!n1) {
04 mountElement(n2, container)
05 } else {
06 // n1 exists, meaning patched, omitting
07 }
08 }
```

In the above code, the first parameter n1 represents the old vnode. The second parameter n2 represents the new vnode. If n1 does not exist, it means old vnode does not exist. Under such circumstance, do the mounting, then call the mountElement function to complete the mounting as the following:

```
01 function mountElement(vnode, container) {
02 // Create DOM element
03 const el = document.createElement(vnode.type)
04 // Handle sub-node; if sub-node is a string, the representative
element has text node
05 if (typeof vnode.children === 'string') {
06 // So you only need to set the element's textContent property
07 el.textContent = vnode.children
08 }
09 // Add Element to Container
10 container.appendChild(el)
11}
```

The above code is not unfamiliar to us for Chap. 3 has initially explained the renderer related content. First, call the document.createElement function to create a new DOM element with the value of the as the tag name. Then process vnode. children. If its value is of type string, it means that the element has text sub-node. In this case, you only need to set the textContent of the element. Finally, call the appendChild function to add the newly created DOM element to the container element. In this way, we have completed the mounting of a vnode.

The work of mounting a normal tag element is completed. Next, we analyze the problem with this code. Our goal is to design a general-purpose renderer that does not depend on the browser platform, but obviously, the mountElement function calls a lot of browser-dependent APIs, such as document.createElement, el.textContent, and appendChild. If you want to design a general-purpose renderer, the first step is to extract these browser-specific APIs. How do we do it? We can use these DOM APIs as configuration items, which can be used as parameters of the createRenderer function, as shown in the following code:

```
01 // Passing in the configuration item when creating the renderer
02 const renderer = createRenderer({
03 // used to create the element
04 createElement(tag) {
05 return document.createElement(tag)
06 },
07 // used to set the element's text node
08 setElementText(el, text) {
09 el.textContent = text
10 },
11 // used to specify the element under the parent given
12 insert(el, parent, anchor = null) {
13 parent.insertBefore(el, anchor)
14 }
15 })
```

As you can see, we encapsulate the API for manipulating the DOM as an object and pass it to the createRenderer function. In this way, you can get the API to manipulate the DOM through configuration items in functions such as mountElement:

```
01 function createRenderer(options) {
02
03 // Get the API to manipulate the DOM through options
04 const {
05 createElement,
06 insert,
07 setElementText
08 } = options
09
10 // Functions defined in this scope can access those APIs
11 function mountElement(vnode, container) {
12 // ...
13 }
14
15 function patch(n1, n2, container) {
16 // ...
17 }
18
19 function render(vnode, container) {
20 // ...
21 }
22
23 return {
24 render
25 }
26 }
```

Next, we can reimplement the mountElement function using the API obtained from the configuration item:

```
01 function mountElement(vnode, container) {
02 // call the createElement function to create the element
03 const el = createElement(vnode.type)
04 if (typeof vnode.children === 'string') {
05 // Call setElementText to set the text node of the element
06 setElementText(el, vnode.children)
07 }
08 // Call the insert function to insert the element into the container
09 insert(el, container)
10 }
```

As shown in the code above, the refactored mountElement function does not change in function. The difference is that it no longer directly depends on the browser's specific API. This means that as long as you pass in a different configuration item, you can complete the rendering work in a non-browser environment. To demonstrate this, we can implement a custom renderer that prints out the renderer workflow, as shown in the following code:

```
01 const renderer = createRenderer({
02 createElement(tag) {
03 console.log(`create the element ${tag}`)
04 return { tag }
05 },
06 setElementText(el, text) {
07 console.log(`set the text content of ${JSON.stringify(el)} :
${text}`)
08 el.textContent = text
09 },
10 insert(el, parent, anchor = null) {
11 console.log(`add ${JSON.stringify(el)} under ${JSON.stringify
(parent)}`)
12 parent.children = el
13 }
14 })
```

Observe that the code above passes in different configuration items when calling the createRenderer function to create the renderer. In createElement, instead of calling the browser API, we just return an object {tag} as a created "DOM element." Similarly, in setElementText and *insert* functions, we do not call the browser, the related API, but customize some logic and print information to the console. Thus, we have implemented a custom renderer, which can be checked with the following code:

```
01 const vnode = {
02 type: 'h1',
03 children: 'hello'
04 }
05 // emulate the mount point with an object
06 const container = {type: 'root'}
07 renderer2.render(vnode, container)
```

It should be noted that since the custom renderer implemented above does not rely on browser-specific APIs, so this code can be run not only in the browser, but also in the Node.js.

Now we have a deeper understanding of the custom renderer. Custom renderers are not "black magic," they just make the core code no longer rely on platform-specific APIs by abstracting means, and then achieve cross-platform through the ability to support personalized configuration.

7.4   Summary

In this chapter, we first introduced the relationship between renderers and responsive systems. Using the capabilities of responsive systems, we can automatically complete page updates (or re-rendering) when responsive data changes. At the same time, we note that this has nothing to do with the specific implementation of renderers. We implemented a minimalist renderer that can only use the innerHTML attribute to set the content of a given HTML string into a container.

Next, we discussed basic terms and concepts related to renderers. The role of renderers is to render virtual DOM as real elements on a specific platform. We use English word *renderer* to express renderers. Virtual DOM is usually expressed in English virtual DOM, sometimes abbreviated as vdom or vnode. The renderer will perform mount and patch operations. For new elements, the renderer will mount it into the container; for the case where both old and new vnodes exist, the renderer will perform patch operations, that is, compare the old and new vnodes and only update the changed content.

Finally, we discussed the implementation of custom renderers. On the browser platform, the renderer can use the DOM API to complete the creation, modification, and deletion of DOM elements. In order to make the renderer not directly depend on browser platform-specific APIs, we abstract these operations for creating, modifying, and deleting elements into configurable objects. Users can specify custom configuration objects when calling the createRenderer function to create the renderer, thereby implementing custom behavior. We also implement a custom renderer that prints the renderer operation flow, which can run not only in the browser, but also in the Node.js.

Chapter 8
Mount and Update

In Chap. 7, we mainly introduced the basic concepts and overall architecture of the renderer. In this chapter, we will explain the core function of the renderer: mounting and updating.

8.1 Mounting Properties of Sub-Nodes and Elements

Chapter 7 mentioned that when the value of the vnode.children was of type string, it would be set to the text content of the element. In addition to the text sub-nodes, one element can also contain sub-nodes of other elements, and sub-nodes can be many. To describe the sub-node of an element, we need to define vnode.children as an array:

```
01 const vnode  =  {
02    type: 'div',
03    children: [
04        {
05            type: 'p',
06            children: 'hello'
07        }
08    ]
09 }
```

The above code describes "a div tag has a sub-node, and the sub-node is a p tag." As you can see, vnode.children is an array, and each of its elements is an independent virtual node object. This forms a tree structure, that is, a virtual DOM tree.

In order to complete the sub-node rendering, we need to modify the mountElement function, as shown in the following code:

© The Author(s), under exclusive license to Springer Nature Singapore Pte Ltd. 2023   213
H. Yang, *Vue. JS Framework*, https://doi.org/10.1007/978-981-99-4947-2_8

```
01 function mountElement(vnode, container) {
02      const el = createElement(vnode.type)
03      if  (typeof vnode.children === 'string') {
04        setElementText(el, vnode.children)
05      } else if(Array.isArray(vnode.children)) {
06        // if children is an array, traverse each child node and
call the patch function to mount them
07        vnode.children.forEach(child => {
08            patch(null, child, el)
09        })
10      }
11      insert(el, container)
12 }
```

In the above code, we added a new judgment branch. Use the Array.isArray function to determine whether the vnode.children is an array; if it is an array, loop through it, and call the patch function to mount virtual nodes in the array. When mounting child nodes, you need to pay attention to the following two points.

- The first argument passed to the patch function is null. Because it is the mount phase, there is no old vnode, so we only need to pass null. In this way, when the patch function executes, the mountElement function will be called recursively to complete and mount.
- The third parameter passed to the patch function is the mount point. Since the child element we are mounting is the child node of the div tag, we need to use the div element just created as the mount point to ensure that these sub-nodes are mounted to the correct position.

After mounting the sub-node, let's take a look at how to use vnode to describe the attributes of a tag and how to render these attributes. We know that HTML tags have many attributes, some of which are general, such as id, class, etc., and some attributes are unique to specific elements, such as the action attribute of the form element. In fact, rendering an element's attributes is more complicated than expected, but we still adhere to the principle of simplicity. Let's first look at the most basic attribute handling.

To describe the attributes of an element, we need to define a new vnode.props field for the virtual DOM, as shown in the following code:

```
01 constvnode = {
02     type: 'div',
03      // describe the attributes of an element using props
04     props: {
05         id:  'foo'
06      },
07     children:  [
08        {
09           type: 'p',
10            children: 'hello'
11        }
```

```
12        ]
13  }
```

Is an object whose key represents the attribute name of the element and whose value represents the value of the corresponding attribute. In this way, we can render these properties to the corresponding elements by traversing the props object, as shown in the following code:

```
01   function mountElement (vnode, container) {
02       const el = createElement (vnode.type)
03       // omit the handling of children
04
05       // only if vnode.props exists, it will be processed
06       if   (vnode.props) {
07           // traverse vnode.props
08           for   (const key in vnode.props) {
09           //   call setAttribute to set attributes to elements
10             el. setAttribute (key, vnode.props [key] )
11           }
12       }
13
14       insert (el, container)
15  }
```

In this code, we first check if the vnode.props field exists; iterate over it if it does, and call the setAttribute function to set the attribute on the element. In fact, in addition to using the setAttribute function to set the attribute for the element, it can also be set directly through the DOM object:

```
01  function mountElement (vnode, container) {
02       const el = createElement (vnode.type)
03       // omit the handling of children
04
05       if   (vnode.props) {
06         for   (const key in vnode.props) {
07               // directly set
08               el [key]   =   vnode. Props [key]
09         }
10       }
11
12       insert (el, container)
13   }
```

In this code, instead of using the setAttribute function, we set the attribute directly on the DOM object, i.e., el [key] = vnode.props [key]. In fact, both using the setAttribute function and directly manipulating DOM objects have flaws. As mentioned earlier, setting attributes on elements is more complicated than expected. However, before discussing the specific flaws, it is necessary to clarify two important concepts: HTML attributes and DOM properties.

8.2   HTML Attributes and DOM Properties

It is important to understand the differences and associations between HTML attributes and DOM properties, which can help us design the structure of virtual nodes reasonably, and is the key to correctly setting attributes for elements.

Let's start with the most basic HTML. The following HTML code is given:

```
01   < input id = "my-input" type = "text" value = "foo"/>
```

HTML attributes refer to the attributes defined on the HTML tag; in this case id = "my-input," type = "text," and value = "foo." When the browser parses this HTML code, it will create a DOM element object that matches it. We can read the DOM object through JavaScript code:

```
01   const el = document.querySelector ( '#my-input' )
```

This DOM object will contain many properties, as shown in Fig. 8.1.

These attributes are called DOM properties. Many HTML attributes have DOM properties with the same name on DOM objects, such as id = "my-input" for el.id, type = "text" for el.type, value = "foo" for el.value, etc. However, the names of DOM properties and HTML attributes are not always the same, for example:

Fig. 8.1 The attributes under the DOM objects

```
$0.accept
 ""  accept                                          HTMLInputElement
     align
     alt
     autocomplete
     checkValidity
     checked
     constructor
     defaultChecked
     defaultValue
     dirName
     disabled
     files
     form
     formAction
     formEnctype
     formMethod
     formNoValidate
     formTarget
     height
     incremental
```

```
< div class = "foo" > </div >
```

class = "foo" for DOM properties is el.className. In addition, not all HTML attributes have corresponding DOM properties, for example:

```
< div aria-valuenow = "75" > </div >
```

HTML attributes of aria- * class do not have corresponding DOM properties.

Similarly, not all DOM properties have corresponding HTML attributes, for example, you can use el.textContent to set the text content of an element, but there is no corresponding HTML attributes to do the same job.

There is a correlation between the value of HTML attributes and the value of DOM properties, such as the following HTML snippet:

01 < **div** id = "foo" > </**div** >

This snippet describes a div tag with an id attribute. The DOM properties with id = "foo" are el.id, and the value is the string "foo." We treat such HTML attributes as direct mappings to attributes with the same name (i.e., id) as DOM properties. But not all HTML attributes and DOM properties are directly mapped, for example:

```
01 < input value = "foo"/>
```

This is an input tag with a value attribute. If the user does not modify the content of the textbox, then reading the value of the corresponding DOM properties through el.value is the string "foo." And if the user modifies the value of the textbox, then the value of el.value is the value of the current textbox. For example, if the user changes the content of the text box to "bar," then:

```
01 console.log (el.value) //' bar '
```

But if you run the following code, a "strange" phenomenon will occur:

```
01 console.log (el.getAttribute (' value ')) // is still 'foo '
02 console.log (el.value) //' bar '
```

You can find that the user's modification of the content of the text box will not affect the return value of el.getAttribute ("value"), which implies the meaning of HTML attributes. In fact, the role of HTML attributes is to set the initial value of the corresponding DOM properties. Once the value changes, the DOM properties always store the current value, and the getAttribute function still gets the initial value.

But we can still access the initial value through el.defaultValue, as shown in the following code:

```
01 el.getAttribute ('value')//still 'foo '
02 el.value//' bar '
03 el.defaultValue//' foo '
```

This means that HTML attributes may be associated with multiple DOM prop-erties. For example, in the above example, value = "foo" is associated with both el. value and el.defaultValue.

Although we can think of HTML attributes as setting the initial value of the corresponding DOM properties, some values are restricted, as if the default value was checked internally by the browser. If the default value you provide via HTML attributes is illegal, then the browser will use the built-in legal value as the default value for the corresponding DOM properties, for example:

```
01 < input type = "foo"/>
```

We know that specifying the string "foo" for the type attribute of the < input/> tag is illegal, so the browser will correct this illegal value. So when we try to read el. type, we actually get the corrected value, that is, string "text," rather than string "foo":

```
01 console.log (el.type)//'text'
```

From the above analysis, the relationship between HTML attributes and DOM properties is very complicated, but in fact we only need to remember one core principle: the role of HTML attributes is to set the initial value of corresponding DOM properties.

8.3   Setting Element Properties Correctly

We discussed HTML attributes and DOM properties in detail in the previous section because HTML attributes and DOM properties affect how DOM attributes are added. For ordinary HTML files, the viewer will automatically analyze HTML attributes and set appropriate DOM properties after parsing the HTML code. But templates written by users in Vue.js single-file components are not parsed by the browser, which means that work that originally required the browser to do now requires the framework to do it.

Let's take a disabled button as an example, as shown in the following HTML code:

```
01 < button disabled > Button </button >
```

When the browser parses this HTML code, it finds that there is an HTML attributes called disabled for this button, so the browser will set the button to disabled state and set its DOM properties value, el.disabled, to true, all of which are handled by the browser for us. But if the same code appears in Vue.js template, the situation will be different. First of all, this HTML template will be compiled to vnode, which is equivalent to

```
01 const button = {
02 type: 'button',
03 props: {
04 disabled: "
05 }
06 }
```

Note that the value of the props.disabled here is the string empty; if you call the setAttribute function in the renderer to set the attribute, it is equivalent to

```
01 el.setAttribute('disabled', '')
```

This is indeed no problem. The browser will disable the button. But consider the following template:

```
01 < button: disabled = "false" > Button </button >
```

Its corresponding vnode is as follows:

```
01 const button = {
02 type: 'button',
03 props: {
04 disabled: false
05 }
06 }
```

The user's original intention is to "not disable" the button. But if the renderer still uses the setAttribute function to set the property value, it will have an unexpected effect, that is, the button is disabled:

```
01 el.setAttribute('disabled', false)
```

Running the above code in the browser, we find that the browser still disables the button. This is because the value set by the setAttribute function is always stringed, so the above code is equivalent to

```
01 el.setAttribute ('disabled', 'false')
```

For the button, its el.disabled attribute value is Boolean, and it does not care what the specific value of HTML attributes. The button will be disabled as long as the disabled attribute exists. So we found that the renderer should not always use the setAttribute function to set the attributes in the vnode.props object to the element. So what should be done? A natural idea is that we can set DOM properties first, for example:

```
01 el.disabled = false
```

This works correctly, but introduces new problems. Let's also use the above code as the example:

```
01 < button disabled > Button </button >
```

The vnode corresponding to this template is as follows:

```
01 const button = {
02 type: 'button',
03 props: {
04 disabled: "
05 }
06 }
```

We notice that in the vnode object obtained after the template is compiled, the value props.disabled is an empty string. If you use it to set the DOM properties of the element directly, it is equivalent to

```
01 el.disabled = ''
```

Since el.disabled is a Boolean value, when we try to set it to an empty string, the browser will correct its value to a Boolean value, which is false. So the execution result of the above code is equivalent to

```
01 el.disabled = false
```

This is against the user's intention because the user wants to disable the button, and el.disabled = false means not disabling.

In this way, whether it is using the setAttribute function or directly setting the DOM properties of the element, there are defects. To completely solve this problem, we can only do special treatment, that is, set the DOM properties of the element first; but when the value is empty string, manually correct the value to true. Only in this way can we ensure that the behavior of the code is as expected. The following mountElement function gives the specific implementation:

```
01 function mountElement (vnode, container) {
02 const el = createElement (vnode.type)
03 // omit the processing of children
04
05 if (vnode.props) {
```

```
06 for (const key in vnode.props) {
07 // use the in operator to determine whether the corresponding DOM
Properties exist for the key
08 if (key in el) {
09 // get the DOM Properties' type
10 const type = typeof el[key]
11 const value = vnode.props[key]
12 // Correct the value to true if it is of Boolean type and is an empty
string
13 if (type === 'boolean' && value === '') {
14 el[key] = true
15 } else {
16 el[key] = value
17 }
18 } else {
19 // If the property to be set does not have the corresponding DOM
Properties, use the setAttribute function to set the property
20 el.setAttribute(key, vnode.props[key])
21 }
22 }
23 }
24
25 insert(el, container)
26 }
```

As shown in the above code, we check the properties in each vnode.props to see if
the corresponding DOM properties exist, and if so, set the DOM properties first. At
the same time, we correct the value of the DOM properties of the Boolean type, that
is, when the value to be set is an empty string, correct it to the Boolean value true. Of
course, if vnode.props, the attribute does not have the corresponding DOM properties, the setAttribute function is still used to complete the setting of the attribute.

But the implementation given above is still problematic, because some DOM
properties are read-only, as shown in the following code:

```
01 < form id = "form1" > </form >
02 < input form = "form1"/>
```

In this code, we set the form attribute (HTML attributes) for the < input/> tag. Its
corresponding DOM properties are el.form; but el.form is read-only, so we can only
set it through the setAttribute function.

```
01 function shouldSetAsProps(el, key, value) {
02 // special handling
03 if (key === 'form' && el.tagName === 'INPUT') return false
04 // fallback
05 return key in el
06 }
07
08 function mountElement(vnode, container) {
09 const el = createElement(vnode.type)
```

```
10 // omit children's Handling
11
12 if (vnode.props) {
13 for (const key in vnode.props) {
14 const value = vnode.props[key]
15 // Use shouldSetAsProps function to determine whether it should be
set as DOM Properties
16 if (shouldSetAsProps(el, key, value)) {
17 const type = typeof el[key]
18 if (type === 'boolean' && value === '') {
19 el[key] = true
20 } else {
21 el[key] = value
22 }
23 } else {
24 el.setAttribute(key, value)
25 }
26 }
27 }
28
29 insert(el, container)
30 }
```

As shown in the code above, for the readability of the code, we extracted a shouldSetAsProps function. The function will return a Boolean value representing whether the property should be set as DOM properties. If it returns true, it should be set as DOM properties, otherwise it should be set using the setAttribute function. Within the shouldSetAsProps function, we do special treatment for < input form = "xxx"/>, that is, the form attribute of the < input/> tag must be set using the setAttribute function. In fact, not just < input/> tags, all form elements have form attributes, and they should all be set as HTML attributes.

Of course, < input form = "xxx"/> is a special case, and there are some other cases like this that require special treatment. We will not go through all the situations, because it is more important to know how to deal with the problem. Also, we may not remember all the places that need special treatment, not to mention that sometimes we do not even know what situations need special treatment. So, the above solutions are essentially empirical. Do not be afraid to write imperfect code. As long as you "see tricks" in subsequent iterations, the code will become more and more perfect, and the framework will become more and more robust.

Finally, we need to make the property settings platform independent, so we need to extract the property settings related operations into the renderer options, as shown in the following code:

```
01 const renderer = createRenderer({
02 createElement(tag) {
03 return document.createElement(tag)
04 },
05 setElementText(el, text) {
06 el.textContent = text
```

```
07 },
08 insert (el, parent, anchor = null) {
09 parent.insertBefore (el, anchor)
10 },
11 // Encapsulate property setting related operations into the
patchProps function and pass them as renderer options
12 patchProps (el, key, prevValue, nextValue) {
13 if (shouldSetAsProps (el, key, nextValue)) {
14 const type = typeof el [key]
15 if (type === 'boolean' && nextValue === '') {
16 el [key] = true
17 } else {
18 el [key] = nextValue
19 }
20 } else {
21 el.setAttribute (key, nextValue)
22 }
23 }
24 })
```

In the mountElement function, you only need to call the patchProps function and pass the relevant parameters to it:

```
01 function mountElement (vnode, container) {
02 const el = createElement (vnode.type)
03 if (typeof vnode.children === 'string') {
04 setElementText (el, vnode.children)
05 } else if (Array.isArray (vnode.children)) {
06 vnode.children.forEach (child => {
07 patch (null, child, el)
08 })
09 }
10
11 if (vnode.props) {
12 for (const key in vnode.props) {
13 // Just call patchProps function
14 patchProps (el, key, null, vnode.props [key])
15 }
16 }
17
18 insert (el, container)
19 }
```

In this way, we have extracted the rendering logic related to properties from the core of the renderer.

8.4   Class Processing

In the previous section, we explained how to properly set the properties defined in the vnode.props to DOM elements. However, in Vue.js, there are still some properties that need special treatment, such as the class attribute. Why do you need special treatment for the class attribute? This is because Vue.js enhanced the class attribute. There are several ways to set the class name for the element in the Vue.js.

Method 1: Specify the class as a string value.

```
01 < p class = "foo bar" > </p >
```

The vnode corresponding to this template is as follows:

```
01 const vnode = {
02 type: 'p',
03 props: {
04 class: 'foo bar'
05 }
06 }
```

Method 2: Specify class as an object value.

```
01 < p: class = "cls" > </p >
```

Suppose the contents of the object cls are as follows:

```
01 const cls = {foo: true, bar: false}
```

Then the vnode corresponding to this template is as follows:

```
01 const vnode = {
02 type: 'p',
03 props: {
04 class: {foo: true, bar: false}
05 }
06 }
```

Method 3: class is an array containing the above two types.

```
01 < p: class = "arr" > </p >
```

This array can be a combination of string value and object value:

```
01 const arr = [
02 //string
03 'foo bar ',
```

```
04//objects
05 {
06 baz: true
07}
08]
```

Then the vnode corresponding to this template is as follows:

```
01 const vnode = {
02 type:' p ',
03 props: {
04 class: [
05'foo bar ',
06 {baz: true}
07]
08}
09}
```

As you can see, since the value of class can be of multiple types, we must unify the value into a uniform string before setting the element's class, and then set the string as the element's class value. Therefore, we need to encapsulate the normalizeClass function to normalize different types of class values into strings, for example:

```
01 const vnode = {
02 type: 'p',
03 props: {
04//Serialize values with the normalizeClass function
05 class: normalizeClass ([
06'foo bar ',
07 {baz: true}
08])
09}
10}
```

The final result is equivalent to

```
01 const vnode = {
02 type: 'p',
03 props: {
04//The result after serialization
05 class: 'foo bar baz'
06}
07}
```

As for the implementation of the normalizeClass function, we will not explain it in detail here, because it is essentially a small algorithm for data structure conversion, and it is not complicated to implement.

Suppose that now we have been able to normalize the class value. Next, we will discuss how to set the normalized class value to the element. In fact, our current

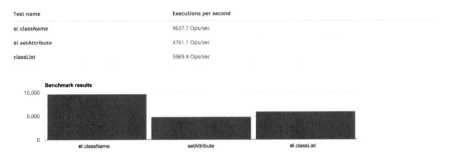

Fig. 8.2 Performance comparison of el.className, setAttribute, and el.classList

implementation of the renderer has been able to complete the rendering of the class. Observing the code of the function above, since the DOM properties corresponding to the class attribute are el.className, the value of the expression "class" in el will be false. Therefore, the patchProps function will use the setAttribute function to complete the class setting. But we know that there are three ways to set the class for an element in the browser, that is, using setAttribute, el.className, or el. classList. So which method has better performance? Figure 8.2 compares the performance of these three ways to set a class for an element 1000 times.

You can see that el.className has the best performance. Therefore, we need to adjust the implementation of the patchProps function as shown in the following code:

```
01 const renderer = createRenderer({
02 // Omit other options
03
04 patchProps(el, key, prevValue, nextValue) {
05 // Special handling of class
06 if (key === 'class') {
07 el.className = nextValue || ''
08 } else if (shouldSetAsProps(el, key, nextValue)) {
09 const type = typeof el[key]
10 if (type === 'boolean' && nextValue === '') {
11 el[key] = true
12 } else {
13 el[key] = nextValue
14 }
15 } else {
16 el.setAttribute(key, nextValue)
17 }
18 }
19 })
```

From the code above we can see that we have a special treatment for class, that is, using el.className instead of the setAttribute function. In fact, in addition to the class attribute, the Vue.js has also enhanced the style attribute, so we need to do similar treatment for style.

By dealing with *class*, we can realize that the types of attribute values defined in vnode.props objects are not always consistent with the data structure of DOM element attributes, depending on the design of the upper-level API. Vue.js allowing values of object types as classes is for the convenience of developers, and in the low-level implementation, the value must be normalized before use. In addition, the process of normalizing values comes at a cost, and if a lot of normalization operations are required, it will consume more performance.

8.5 Unloading Operations

Mounting operations were mainly discussed earlier. Next, we will discuss unloading operations. The uninstall operation occurs in the update phase. The update means that after the initial mount is completed, the subsequent rendering will trigger the update, as shown in the following code:

```
01 //initial mount
02 renderer.render(vnode, document.querySelector('#app'))
03 //mount the new vnode again, which will trigger the update
04 renderer.render(newVNode, document.querySelector('#app'))
```

There are several cases of update. We will look at them one by one. When the subsequent call to the render function renders empty content (i.e., null), as shown in the following code:

```
01 //Initial mount
02 renderer.render(vnode, document.querySelector('#app'))
03 //The new vnode is null, which means that the previously rendered
content is unmounted
04 renderer.render(null, document.querySelector('#app'))
```

After the first mount is completed, if null is passed as the new vnode during subsequent rendering, it means that nothing is rendered. In this case, we need to uninstall the previously rendered content:

```
01 function render(vnode, container) {
02 if (vnode) {
03 patch(container._vnode, vnode, container)
04 } else {
05 if (container._vnode) {
06 // Uninstall, empty container
07 container.innerHTML = ''
08 }
09 }
10 container._vnode = vnode
11 }
```

You can see that when vnode is null, and the container element's container. _vnode attribute exists, we empty the container directly through innerHTML. But this is not rigorous, for three reasons.

- The contents of a container may be rendered by one or more components. When an unmounting operation occurs, the component's beforeUnmount, unmounted, and other lifecycle functions should be called correctly.
- Even if the content is not rendered by a component and some elements have custom instructions, we should properly execute the corresponding instruction hook function when the unload operation occurs.
- Another drawback of using innerHTML to empty the contents of container elements is that it does not remove event handlers bound to DOM elements.

For the above three reasons, we cannot simply use innerHTML to complete the uninstall operation. The correct way to uninstall is to get the real DOM element associated with the vnode object based on it, and then use the native DOM manipulation method to remove the DOM element. To do this, we need to establish a connection between the vnode and the real DOM element, modifying the mountElement function, as shown in the following code:

```
01 function mountElement(vnode, container) {
02 // Let vnode.el reference the real DOM element
03 const el = vnode.el = createElement(vnode.type)
04 if (typeof vnode.children === 'string') {
05 setElementText(el, vnode.children)
06 } else if (Array.isArray(vnode.children)) {
07 vnode.children.forEach(child => {
08 patch(null, child, el)
09 })
10 }
11
12 if (vnode.props) {
13 for (const key in vnode.props) {
14 patchProps(el, key, null, vnode.props[key])
15 }
16 }
17
18 insert(el, container)
19 }
```

As you can see, when we call the createElement function to create a real DOM element, we will assign the real DOM element to the vnode.el attribute. In this way, a connection is established between the vnode and the real DOM element, and we can get the real DOM element corresponding to the virtual node through vnode.el. With these, when the unload operation occurs, we only need to obtain the real DOM element according to the virtual node object vnode.el, and then remove it from the parent element:

```
01 function render (vnode, container) {
02 if (vnode) {
03 patch(container._vnode, vnode, container)
04 } else {
05 if (container._vnode) {
06 // Get the real DOM Element to be unloaded according to vnode
07 const el = container._vnode.el
08 // Get the parent element of el
09 const parent = el.parentNode
10 // Call removeChild to remove elements
11 if (parent) parent.removeChild(el)
12 }
13 }
14 container._vnode = vnode
15 }
```

As shown in the code above, where container._vnode stands for the old vnode, which is the vnode to be unloaded. Then get the real DOM element through the container._vnode.el and call the removeChild function to remove it from the parent element.

Since the unmount operation is a common and basic operation, we should wrap it in the unmount function so that subsequent code can reuse it, as shown in the following code:

```
01 function unmount (vnode) {
02 const parent = vnode.el.parentNode
03 if (parent) {
04 parent.removeChild(vnode.el)
05 }
06 }
```

The *unmount* function takes a virtual node as an argument and removes the real DOM element corresponding to the virtual node from the parent element. The code of the *unmount* function is still very simple, and we will gradually enrich it and make it more perfect. Yes, after the unmount function, you can call it directly in the render function to complete the unmount task:

```
01 function render(vnode, container) {
02 if (vnode) {
03 patch(container._vnode, vnode, container)
04 } else {
05 if (container._vnode) {
06 // call the unmount function to unmount vnode
07 unmount(container._vnode)
08 }
09 }
10 container._vnode = vnode
11 }
```

Finally, encapsulating the unmount operation into unmount has two additional benefits.

- Inside the unmount function, we have the opportunity to call the instruction hook function bound to the DOM element, such as beforeUnmount, unmounted, etc.
- When the *unmount* function executes, we have the opportunity to detect the type of the virtual node vnode. If the virtual node describes a component, we have the opportunity to call the component-related lifecycle function.

8.6 Distinguishing the Type of Vnode

In the previous section, we learned that when the subsequent call to the render function renders empty content (i.e., null), the unload operation will be performed. If a new vnode is passed to the render function during subsequent rendering, the unload operation will not be performed, but the old and new vnodes will be passed to the patch function for patching operation.

```
01 function patch(n1, n2, container) {
02 if (!n1) {
03 mountElement(n2, container)
04 } else {
05 // Update
06 }
07 }
```

The two parameters n1 and n2 of the patch function represent the old vnode and the new vnode, respectively. If the old vnode exists, you need to patch between the old and new vnodes. But before we actually perform the patch operation, we need to ensure that the content described by the old and new vnodes is the same. What does this mean? For example, suppose the first rendered vnode is a p element:

```
01 const vnode = {
02 type: 'p'
03 }
04 renderer.render(vnode, document.querySelector('#app'))
```

Then render an input element:

```
01 const vnode = {
02 type: 'input'
03 }
04 renderer.render(vnode, document.querySelector('#app'))
```

This will cause the content described by the old and new vnodes to be different, that is, the value of vnode.type attribute is different. For the above example, there is no sense of patching between the p element and the input element, because each element has a unique attribute for different elements, for example:

```
01 <p id="foo" />
02 <! -- The type attribute is specific to the input tag, but the p tag
does not have this attribute --
03 <input type="submit" />
```

In this case, the correct update operation is to unload the p element first, and then mount the input element to the container. Therefore, we need to adjust the code of the patch function:

```
01 function patch(n1, n2, container) {
02 // If n1 exists, compare the types of n1 and n2
03 if (n1 && n1.type !== n2.type) {
04 // If the old and new vnodes are of different types, unmount the old
vnode directly
05 unmount(n1)
06 n1 = null
07 }
08
09 if (!n1) {
10 mountElement(n2, container)
11 } else {
12 // Update
13 }
14 }
```

As shown in the above code, before actually performing the update operation, we first check whether the content described by the old and new vnodes is the same. If it is different, we directly call the unmount function to unmount the old vnode. It should be noted here that after the unmount is completed, we should reset the value of the parameter n1 to null, so as to ensure that subsequent mount operations are performed correctly.

Even if the contents of the old and new vnodes are the same, we still need to further confirm whether their types are the same. We know that a vnode can be used to describe ordinary tags, components, fragments, etc. For different types of vnodes, we need to provide different ways of mounting or patching. Therefore, we need to continue to modify the code of the patch function to meet the requirements, as shown in the following code:

```
01 function patch(n1, n2, container) {
02 if (n1 && n1.type !== n2.type) {
03 unmount(n1)
04 n1 = null
05 }
06 // The code runs here to prove that n1 and n2 describe the same
07 const { type } = n2
08 // If the value of n2.type is of type string, it describes the normal
label element
```

```
09 if (typeof type === 'string') {
10 if (!n1) {
11 mountElement(n2, container)
12 } else {
13 patchElement(n1, n2)
14 }
15 } else if (typeof type === 'object') {
16 // if the value of n2.type is an object, it describes a component
17 } else if (type === 'xxx') {
18 // handles other types of vnode
19 }
20 }
```

In fact, in the previous explanation, we have always assumed that the type of vnode is a normal label element. But the strict practice is to further confirm what their type is according to vnode.type, so as to use the corresponding handler function to process it. For example, if the value of vnode.type is of type string, it describes the normal tag element, then we will call mountElement or patchElement to complete the mount and update operation; if the value of vnode.type is of type object, it describes the component, then we will call the mount and update methods related to the component.

8.7 Handling of Events

In this section, we will discuss how to handle events, including how to describe events in virtual nodes, how to add events to DOM elements, and how to update events.

Let's solve the first problem, which is how to describe events in virtual nodes. Events can be treated as a special property, so we can agree that in the vnode.props object, any property that begins with the string on is treated as an event. For example:

```
01 const vnode = {
02 type: 'p',
03 props: {
04 // Describe events using onXxx
05 onClick: () => {
06 alert('clicked')
07 }
08 },
09 children: 'text'
10 }
```

After solving the problem of describing events at the virtual node level, let's look at how to add events to DOM elements. This is very simple, just call the addEventListener function in patchProps to bind the event, as shown in the following code:

```
01 patchProps(el, key, prevValue, nextValue) {
02 // Match the property starting with on; treat it as an event
03 if (/^on/.test(key)) {
04 // Get the corresponding event name according to the property name,
such as onClick ---> click
05 const name = key.slice(2).toLowerCase()
06 // bind the event; nextValue is the event handler function
07 el.addEventListener(name, nextValue)
08 } else if (key === 'class') {
09 // omit part of the code
10 } else if (shouldSetAsProps(el, key, nextValue)) {
11 // omit part of the code
12 } else {
13 // omit part of the code
14 }
15 }
```

So, how do we handle the update event? In general, we need to remove the previously added event handler, and then bind the new event handler to the DOM element, as shown in the following code:

```
01 patchProps(el, key, prevValue, nextValue) {
02 if (/^on/.test(key)) {
03 const name = key.slice(2).toLowerCase()
04 // Remove the last bound event handler
05 prevValue && el.removeEventListener(name, prevValue)
06 // Bind the new event handler
07 el.addEventListener(name, nextValue)
08 } else if (key === 'class') {
09 // Omit part of the code
10 } else if (shouldSetAsProps(el, key, nextValue)) {
11 // omit part of the code
12 } else {
13 // omit part of the code
14 }
15 }
```

Doing this enables code to work as expected, but in fact, there is a better performance way to complete event updates. When binding an event, we can bind a fake event handler invoker, and then set the real event handler to the value of the invoker.value property. In this way, when updating the event, we will no longer need to call the removeEventListener function to remove the last bound event, but only need to update the value of invoker.value, as shown in the following code:

```
01 patchProps(el, key, prevValue, nextValue) {
02 if (/^on/.test(key)) {
03 // Get the event handler forged for this element invoker
```

```
04 let invoker = el._vei
05 const name = key.slice(2).toLowerCase()
06 if (nextValue) {
07 if (!invoker) {
08 // cache a fake invoker to el._vei if there is no invoker
09 // vei is an acronym for vue event invoker
10 invoker = el._vei = (e) => {
11 // the real event handler is executed when the fake event handler
executes
12 invoker.value(e)
13 }
14 // assign the real event handler to invoker.value
15 invoker.value = nextValue
16 // Bind invoker as event handler
17 el.addEventListener(name, invoker)
18 } else {
19 // If the invoker exists, it means to update, and only need to update
the value of the invoker.value
20 invoker.value = nextValue
21 }
22 } else if (invoker) {
23 // The new event binding function does not exist, and the
previously bound invoker exists, so remove the binding
24 el.removeEventListener(name, invoker)
25 }
26 } else if (key === 'class') {
27 // Omit part of the code
28 } else if (shouldSetAsProps(el, key, nextValue)) {
29 // Omit part of the code
30 } else {
31 // Omit part of the code
32 }
33 }
```

Observing the above code, event binding is mainly divided into two steps.

- First read the corresponding invoker from el._vei; if the invoker does not exist, the fake invoker is used as the event handler and cached in the el._vei property.
- Assign the real event handler to the invoker.value property, then bind the fake invoker function as an event and the handler to the element. You can see that when the event fires, the fake event handler is actually executed, and the real event handler function invoker.value(e) is indirectly executed inside.

When updating the event, since the el._vei already exists, we only need to modify the value of the invoker.value to the new event handler function. In this way, a call to the removeEventListener function can be avoided when updating the event, which improves the performance. In fact, the fake event handler function does more than that: it can also solve the problem of the interaction between event bubbling and event updating, which will be explained in detail below.

But the current implementation still has problems. Now that we have event handlers cached in the el._vei property, the problem is that only one event handler can be cached at a time. This means that if an element is bound to multiple events at the same time, there will be an event overwriting phenomenon. For instance, bind *click* and *contextmenu* events to elements at the same time:

```
01 const vnode = {
02 type: 'p',
03 props: {
04 onClick: () => {
05 alert('clicked')
06 },
07 onContextmenu: () => {
08 alert('contextmenu')
09 }
10 },
11 children: 'text'
12 }
13 renderer.render(vnode, document.querySelector('#app'))
```

When the renderer tries to render the vnode given in the above code, the click event will be bound first, and then the contextmenu event will be bound. The handler of the late-bound contextmenu event will override the handler of the first-bound click event. To solve the problem of event overwriting, we need to redesign the data structure of el._vei. We should design el._vei as an object whose key is the event name and whose value is the corresponding event handler, so that the phenomenon of event overwriting does not occur, as shown in the following code:

```
01 patchProps(el, key, prevValue, nextValue) {
02 if (/^on/.test(key)) {
03 // Define el._vei as an object; there is a mapping of event name to
event handler
04 const invokers = el._vei || (el._vei = {})
05 // get invoker by event name
06 let invoker = invokers[key]
07 const name = key.slice(2).toLowerCase()
08 if (nextValue) {
09 if (!invoker) {
10 // Cache event handlers under el._vei[key] to avoid overwriting
11 invoker = el._vei[key] = (e) => {
12 invoker.value(e)
13 }
14 invoker.value = nextValue
15 el.addEventListener(name, invoker)
16 } else {
17 invoker.value = nextValue
18 }
19 } else if (invoker) {
20 el.removeEventListener(name, invoker)
21 }
22 } else if (key === 'class') {
23 // Omit some code
24 } else if (shouldSetAsProps(el, key, nextValue)) {
```

```
25 // Omit some code
26 } else {
27 // Omit some code
28 }
29 }
```

In addition, an element can bind not only multiple types of events, but also the same type of events multiple, event handler functions. We know that in native DOM programming, when the addEventListener function is called multiple times for element binding, multiple event handlers can coexist when the same type of event, for example:

```
01 el.addEventListener('click', fn1)
02 el.addEventListener('click', fn2)
```

When the element is clicked, the event handlers fn1 and fn2 will be executed. Therefore, in order to describe multiple event handlers for the same event, we need to adjust the data structure of the event in the vnode.props object, as shown in the following code:

```
01 const vnode = {
02 type: 'p',
03 props: {
04 onClick: [
05 // first event handler
06 () => {
07 alert('clicked 1')
08 },
09 // second event handler
10 () => {
11 alert('clicked 2')
12 }
13 ]
14 },
15 children: 'text'
16 }
17 renderer.render(vnode, document.querySelector('#app'))
```

In the above code, we use an array to describe events; each element in the array is an independent event handler, and these event handlers are properly bound to the corresponding element. In order to implement this function, we need to modify the code related to event handling in the patchProps function, as shown in the following code:

```
01 patchProps(el, key, prevValue, nextValue) {
02 if (/^on/.test(key)) {
03 const invokers = el._vei || (el._vei = {})
04 let invoker = invokers[key]
05 const name = key.slice(2).toLowerCase()
```

```
06 if (nextValue) {
07 if (!invoker) {
08 invoker = el._vei[key] = (e) => {
09 // //If  is an array, iterate over it and call event handlers one by
one
10 if (Array.isArray(invoker.value)) {
11 invoker.value.forEach(fn => fn(e))
12 } else {
13 // Otherwise call as the function
14 invoker.value(e)
15 }
16 }
17 invoker.value = nextValue
18 el.addEventListener(name, invoker)
19 } else {
20 invoker.value = nextValue
21 }
22 } else if (invoker) {
23 el.removeEventListener(name, invoker)
24 }
25 } else if (key === 'class') {
26 // omit part of the code
27 } else if (shouldSetAsProps(el, key, nextValue)) {
28 // omit part of the code
29 } else {
30 // omit part of the code
31 }
32 }
```

In this code, we modify the implementation of the invoker function. When the invoker function executes, before calling the real event handler function, it is necessary to check whether the data structure of the invoker.value is an array. If it is an array, it is traversed and the event handlers defined in the array are called one by one.

8.8 Event Bubbling and Update Timing Issues

In the previous section, we introduced basic event handling. In this section, we will discuss the problems caused by the combination of event bubbling and update timing. To better illustrate the situation, we need to create an example.

```
01 const { effect, ref } = VueReactivity
02
03 const bol = ref(false)
04
05 effect(() => {
06 // create vnode
07 const vnode = {
```

```
08 type: 'div',
09 props: bol.value ? {
10 onClick: () => {
11 alert('parent element clicked')
12 }
13 } : {},
14 children: [
15 {
16 type: 'p',
17 props: {
18 onClick: () => {
19 bol.value = true
20 }
21 },
22 children: 'text'
23 }
24 ]
25 }
26 // Rendering vnode
27 renderer.render(vnode, document.querySelector('#app'))
28 })
```

This example is more complicated. In the above code, we create a reactive data bol, which is a ref. with an initial value of false. Next, we create an effect and call renderer.render function inside the side effect function to render the vnode. The focus here is on the vnode object, which describes a div element, and the div element has a p element, as sub-node. Let's take a closer look at the div element and the characteristics of the p element.

- div element
  the value of its props object is determined by a ternary expression. At first rendering, since bol.value is false, its props value is an empty object.
- p element
  has a click event, and when it is clicked, the event handler will set the value of the bol.value to true.

Combining the above characteristics, let's think about a question: When the p element is clicked with the mouse after the first rendering is completed, will the event handler of the click event of the parent div element be executed?

The answer is actually obvious. After the first rendering is completed, since the bol.value is false, the renderer will not bind the click event to the div element. When you click the p element with the mouse, even though the click event can bubble from the p element to the parent div element, nothing happens because the div element has no event handler bound to the click event. But the truth is, when you try to run the above code and click the p element, you will find that the event handler of the click event of the parent div element is executed. Why does such a strange phenomenon happen? This is actually related to the update mechanism. Let's analyze what happens when the p element is clicked.

Fig. 8.3 Update and event
triggering flowchart

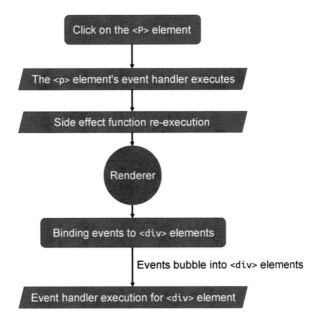

When the p element is clicked, the click event handler bound to it will execute, so the value of bol.value is changed to true. The next step is very critical. Since bol is a reactive data, when its value changes, it will be triggered, and the side effect function will be re-executed. Since the bol.value has become true, the renderer will bind the click event handler to the parent div element during the update phase. When the update is complete, the click event bubbles up from the p element to the parent div element. The above strange phenomenon occurs because the div element has already bound the handler of the click event. Figure 8.3 shows the flow chart of the entire update and event triggering when the p element is clicked.

According to Fig. 8.3, we can see that the above strange phenomenon occurs because the update operation occurs before the event bubble, that is, the binding event handler for the div element occurs before the event bubble. So how do we avoid this problem? A natural idea is can the action of binding events be moved after the event bubble? But this idea is unreliable, because we have no way of knowing whether and to what extent the event bubble is completed. You might be wondering, isn't Vue.js update happening in an asynchronous micro-task queue? Is it natural to avoid this problem? In fact, it is not. In other words, micro-tasks will be executed interspersed between multiple event handlers triggered by event bubbling. Therefore, even if the action of binding events is placed in micro-tasks, it will not avoid this problem.

So how do we solve it? In fact, if you look closely at Fig. 8.3, you will find that there is a relationship between the time when the event is triggered and the time when the event is bound, as shown in Fig. 8.4.

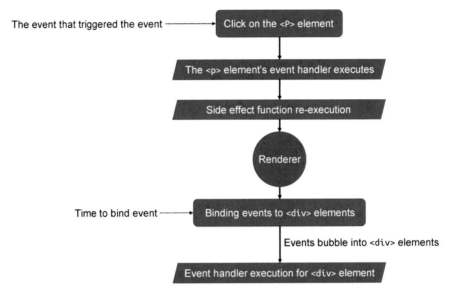

Fig. 8.4 The relationship between the time when the event is triggered and the time when the event is bound

It can be found in Fig. 8.4 that the event is triggered earlier than the time the event handler is bound. This means that when an event is triggered, there is no binding related event handler on the target element. We can solve the problem according to this feature: block the execution of all event handlers whose binding time is later than the event triggering time. Based on this, we can adjust the code about the event in the patchProps function as follows:

```
01 patchProps(el, key, prevValue, nextValue) {
02 if (/^on/.test(key)) {
03 const invokers = el._vei || (el._vei = {})
04 let invoker = invokers[key]
05 const name = key.slice(2).toLowerCase()
06 if (nextValue) {
07 if (!invoker) {
08 invoker = el._vei[key] = (e) => {
09 // e.timeStamp is the time the event occurred
10 // If the event occurred earlier than the time the event handler
bound, the event handler is not executed
11 if (e.timeStamp < invoker.attached) return
12 if (Array.isArray(invoker.value)) {
13 invoker.value.forEach(fn => fn(e))
14 } else {
15 invoker.value(e)
16 }
17 }
18 invoker.value = nextValue
```

```
19 // Add the invoker.attached property to store the time the event
handler was bound
20 invoker.attached = performance.now()
21 el.addEventListener(name, invoker)
22 } else {
23 invoker.value = nextValue
24 }
25 } else if (invoker) {
26 el.removeEventListener(name, invoker)
27 }
28 } else if (key === 'class') {
29 // omit partial code
30 } else if (shouldSetAsProps(el, key, nextValue)) {
31 // omit partial code
32 } else {
33 // omit partial code
34 }
35 }
```

As shown in the above code, we only added two lines of code to the original.
First, we add invoker.attached property to the fake event handling function to store
the time the event handler is bound. Then, when the invoker executes, we get the
time of the event occurrence through the e.timeStamp of the event object. Finally,
compare the two. If the event is handled and the function is bound later than the time
the event occurred, the event handler is not executed.

It is necessary to point out here that in terms of storage and comparison of time,
we use high-precision time, which is performance.now. But depending on the
browser, e, the value of e. timeStamp will also vary. It can be either high-precision
or non-high-precision time. Therefore, strictly speaking, compatibility is required
here. However, in Chrome 49, Firefox 54, Opera 36, and later versions, the value of
e.timeStamp is high- precision time.

8.9 Updating Sub-nodes

In the previous sections, we explained the update of element properties, including
common label properties and events. Next, we will discuss how to update the
sub-node of an element. First, let's review how sub-nodes are mounted, as shown
in the following code:

```
01 function mountElement(vnode, container) {
02 const el = vnode.el = createElement(vnode.type)
03
04 // mount sub-node; first determine the type of children
05 // If it is a string type, it means the text sub-node
06 if (typeof vnode.children === 'string') {
07 setElementText(el, vnode.children)
08 } else if (Array.isArray(vnode.children)) {
```

```
09 // If it is an array, it means that there are multiple sub-nodes
10 vnode.children.forEach(child => {
11 patch(null, child, el)
12 })
13 }
14
15 if (vnode.props) {
16 for (const key in vnode.props) {
17 patchProps(el, key, null, vnode.props[key])
18 }
19 }
20
21 insert(el, container)
22 }
```

When mounting a sub-node, first distinguish its type:

- if the vnode.children is a string, the element has the text sub-node
- if the vnode.children is an array, the element has multiple sub-nodes

What needs to be considered here is why we should distinguish the types of child nodes? In fact, this is a normative problem, because only the type of sub-node is normalized, which is conducive to our writing update logic. Therefore, before discussing how to update sub-node, we need to normalize vnode.children. What kind of specification should be set? To figure this out, we need to first figure out what happens to sub-nodes of elements in an HTML page, as shown in the following HTML code:

```
01 <!-- no sub-node -->
02 <div></div>
03 <!-- text sub-node -->
04 <div>Some Text</div>
05 <!-- multiple sub-nodes -->
06 <div>
07 <p/>
08 <p/>
09 </div>
```

For an element, its sub-node has nothing more than the following three cases.

- There is no sub-node, and the value of the vnode.children is null
- There is a text sub-node, and the value of the vnode.children is string, which represents the content of the text
- In other cases, either a single element sub-node, or multiple sub-nodes (possibly a mix of text and elements), can be represented by an array

As shown in the following code:

```
01 // No sub-node
02 vnode = {
03 type: 'div',
```

Fig. 8.5 The relationship
between the old and new
sub-nodes

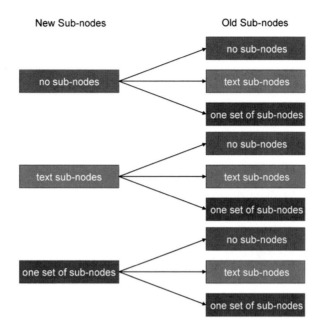

```
04 children: null
05 }
06 // Text sub-node
07 vnode = {
08 type: 'div',
09 children: 'Some Text'
10 }
11 // Otherwise, sub-node uses an array to represent
12 vnode = {
13 type: 'div',
14 children: [
15 { type: 'p' },
16 'Some Text'
17 ]
18 }
```

Now, we have normalized the types of vnode.children. Since there are three
possible cases for a vnode's sub-node, both old and new sub-nodes are one of
three cases when the renderer performs the update. So, we can summarize all nine
possibilities for updating child nodes, as shown in Fig. 8.5.

But when we implement the code, we will find that we do not need to completely
cover these nine possibilities. Now let's implement it, as in the following
patchElement function:

```
01 function patchElement(n1, n2) {
02 const el = n2.el = n1.el
03 const oldProps = n1.props
04 const newProps = n2.props
05 // Step 1: Update props
06 for (const key in newProps) {
07 if (newProps[key] !== oldProps[key]) {
08 patchProps(el, key, oldProps[key], newProps[key])
09 }
10 }
11 for (const key in oldProps) {
12 if (!(key in newProps)) {
13 patchProps(el, key, oldProps[key], null)
14 }
15 }
16
17 // Step 2: Update children
18 patchChildren(n1, n2, el)
19 }
```

As shown in the code above, updating sub-node is the last step in patching an element. We encapsulate it in the patchChildren function and pass it as arguments the old and new vnodes, as well as the DOM element el that is currently being patched.

The patchChildren function is implemented as follows:

```
01 function patchChildren(n1, n2, container) {
02 // Determine whether the new sub-node is a text node
03 if (typeof n2.children === 'string') {
04 // There are three possible types of the old sub-node: no sub-node,
text sub-node, and a set of sub-nodes
05 // Only if the old sub-node is a set of sub-nodes, it is necessary to
unmount one by one; otherwise, this is not necessary
06 if (Array.isArray(n1.children)) {
07 n1.children.forEach((c) => unmount(c))
08 }
09 // Finally set the content of the new text node to the container
element
10 setElementText(container, n2.children)
11 }
```

As shown in the above code, first, we check whether the type of the new sub-node is a text node, and if so, we also check the type of the old sub-node. There are three possible cases of the old sub-node type, namely no sub-node, text sub-node, or a set of sub-nodes. If there is no old sub-node or the type of the old sub-node is text sub-node, then we only need to set the new text content to the container element. If the old sub-node exists and is not a text sub-node, it means that its type is a set of sub-nodes. At this time, we need to loop through them and call the unmount function one by one to unmount.

If the type of the new sub-node is not text sub-node, we need to add another judgment branch to determine whether it is a set of child nodes, as shown in the following code:

```
01 function patchChildren(n1, n2, container) {
02 if (typeof n2.children === 'string') {
03 // omit part of the code
04 } else if (Array.isArray(n2.children)) {
05 // Describe the new sub -node is a set of sub-nodes
06
07 // Determine whether the old sub-node is also a set of sub-nodes
08 if (Array.isArray(n1.children)) {
09 // The code runs here; then the old and new sub-nodes are a set of
sub-nodes, which involves the core Diff algorithm
10 } else {
11 // 此时:
12 // The old sub-node is either a text sub-node or does not exist
13 // But In either case, we just need to empty the container and mount
a new set of sub-nodes one by one
14 setElementText(container, '')
15 n2.children.forEach(c => patch(null, c, container))
16 }
17 }
18 }
```

In the above code, we have added a new determination of the type of n2.children: check if it is a set of sub-nodes, and if so, then check the type of the old sub-node. Similarly, there are three possibilities for the old sub-node: no sub-node, text sub-node, and a set of sub-nodes. For the case where there is no old sub-node or the old sub-node is a text sub-node, we just need to empty the container elements and mount a new set of sub-nodes into the container one by one. If the old sub-node is also a set of sub-nodes, it involves the comparison of the old and new sub-nodes, which involves the Diff algorithm we often call. However, since we have not yet explained how the Diff algorithm works, we can temporarily use a relatively fool-like method to ensure that the function is available. This method is very simple, that is, to unload all the old set of sub-nodes, and then mount all the new set of sub-nodes, as shown in the following code:

```
01 function patchChildren(n1, n2, container) {
02 if (typeof n2.children === 'string') {
03 if (Array.isArray(n1.children)) {
04 n1.children.forEach((c) => unmount(c))
05 }
06 setElementText(container, n2.children)
07 } else if (Array.isArray(n2.children)) {
08 if (Array.isArray(n1.children)) {
09 //unmount the old set of sub-nodes all
10 n1.children.forEach(c => unmount(c))
11 // mount the new set of sub-nodes all into the container
12 n2.children.forEach(c => patch(null, c, container))
```

```
13 } else {
14 setElementText(container, '')
15 n2.children.forEach(c => patch(null, c, container))
16 }
17 }
18 }
```

This achieves the requirements, but is not the optimal solution. We will explain how to use the Diff algorithm to efficiently update two sets of sub-nodes in the next chapter. Now, for the new sub-node, there is one last case left, that is, the new sub-node does not exist, as shown in the following code:

```
01 function patchChildren(n1, n2, container) {
02 if (typeof n2.children === 'string') {
03 if (Array.isArray(n1.children)) {
04 n1.children.forEach((c) => unmount(c))
05 }
06 setElementText(container, n2.children)
07 } else if (Array.isArray(n2.children)) {
08 if (Array.isArray(n1.children)) {
09 //
10 } else {
11 setElementText(container, '')
12 n2.children.forEach(c => patch(null, c, container))
13 }
14 } else {
15 // The code runs here, indicating that the new sub-node does not
exist
16 // The old sub-node is a set of sub-nodes
17 if (Array.isArray(n1.children)) {
18 n1.children.forEach(c => unmount(c))
19 } else if (typeof n1.children === 'string') {
20 // The old sub-node is a text sub-node, and the content can be
emptied
21 setElementText(container, '')
22 }
23 // If there is no old sub-node, then nothing needs to be done
24 }
25 }
```

As you can see, if the code goes to the else branch, it means that the new sub-node does not exist. At this time, for the old sub-node, there are still three possibilities: no sub-node, text sub-node, and a set of sub-nodes. If the old sub-node does not exist either, nothing needs to be done; if the old sub-node is a set of sub-nodes, you can uninstall them one by one; if the old sub-node is a text sub-node, you can empty the text content.

8.10 Text Nodes and Comment Nodes

In the previous chapter, we only explained one type of vnode, that is, a vnode used to describe a common label, as shown in the code below:

```
01 const vnode = {
02 type: 'div'
03}
```

We use vnode.type to describe the name of an element, which is a value of type string.

Next, we discuss how to use virtual DOM to describe more types of real DOM. The two most common types of nodes are text nodes and comment nodes, as shown in the following HTML code:

```
01 < div > <! -- comment node -- > I am a text node </div >
```

< div > is an element node, which contains a comment node and a text node. So, how to use vnode to describe comments, nodes and text nodes?

We know that vnode.type attribute can represent the type of a vnode. If vnode. type value is of type string, it describes a normal tag, and the value represents the name of the tag. But comment nodes and text nodes are different from ordinary label nodes, they do not have label names, so we need to artificially create some unique identifiers and use them as the type attribute value of comment nodes and text nodes, as shown in the following code:

```
01 // type identification of a text node
02 const Text = Symbol ()
03 const newVNode = {
04 // description text nodes
05 type: Text,
06 children: ''I am text content '
07 }
08
09 // type identifier of comment nodes
10 const Comment = Symbol ()
11 const newVNode = {
12 // Describe comment nodes
13 type: Comment,
14 children: 'I am commenting content'
15 }
```

As you can see, we create a symbol type value for the text node and the comment node, respectively, and use it as the value of the vnode.type property. This allows vnode to describe the text node and the comment node. Since the text node and the comment node only care about the text content, we use vnode.children to store their corresponding text content.

Once we have vnode objects that describe the text and comment nodes, we can use the renderer to render them, as shown in the following code:

```
01 function patch(n1, n2, container) {
02 if (n1 && n1.type !== n2.type) {
03 unmount(n1)
04 n1 = null
05 }
06
07 const { type } = n2
08
09 if (typeof type === 'string') {
10 if (!n1) {
11 mountElement(n2, container)
12 } else {
13 patchElement(n1, n2)
14 }
15 } else if (type === Text) { // If the new vnode is of type Text, it
means that the vnode describes a text node
16 // If there is no old node, mount
17 if (!n1) {
18 // Create text node with createTextNode
19 const el = n2.el = document.createTextNode(n2.children)
20 // Insert text node into container
21 insert(el, container)
22 } else {
23 // If the old vnode exists, just update the old text node with the
text content of the new text node
24 const el = n2.el = n1.el
25 if (n2.children !== n1.children) {
26 el.nodeValue = n2.children
27 }
28 }
29 }
30 }
```

Observing the above code, we add a judgment condition, that is, to determine whether the expression type === Text is true. If so, it means that the node to be processed is a text node. Next, we need to determine whether the old virtual node (n1) exists. If not, we directly mount the new virtual node (n2). Here we use the createTextNode function to create the text node and insert it into the container element. If the old virtual node (n1) exists, the text content needs to be updated. Here we use the nodeValue property of the text node to complete the update of the text content.

In addition, from the above code we can also notice that the patch function relies on browser platform-specific APIs, namely createTextNode and el.nodeValue. In order to ensure the cross-platform capability of the renderer core, we need to encapsulate these two DOM APIs into the renderer options, as shown in the following code:

```
01 const renderer = createRenderer({
02 createElement(tag) {
03 // Omit some code
04 },
05 setElementText(el, text) {
06 // Omit some code
07 },
08 insert(el, parent, anchor = null) {
09 // Omit some code
10 },
11 createText(text) {
12 return document.createTextNode(text)
13 },
14 setText(el, text) {
15 el.nodeValue = text
16 },
17 patchProps(el, key, prevValue, nextValue) {
18 // Omit some code
19 }
20 })
```

In the above code, we encapsulate the createText function and setText function in the option parameter passed when calling the createRenderer function to create the renderer. These two functions are used to create text nodes and set the content of text nodes, respectively. We can replace the browser-specific API that the renderer core code depends on with these two functions, as shown in the following code:

```
01 function patch(n1, n2, container) {
02 if (n1 && n1.type !== n2.type) {
03 unmount(n1)
04 n1 = null
05 }
06
07 const { type } = n2
08
09 if (typeof type === 'string') {
10 if (!n1) {
11 mountElement(n2, container)
12 } else {
13 patchElement(n1, n2)
14 }
15 } else if (type === Text) {
16 if (!n1) {
17 // call createText function to create text node
18 const el = n2.el = createText(n2.children)
19 insert(el, container)
20 } else {
21 const el = n2.el = n1.el
22 if (n2.children !== n1.children) {
23 // Call the setText function to update the contents of the text node
24 setText(el, n2.children)
25 }
```

```
26 }
27 }
28 }
```

Annotation nodes are handled similarly to text nodes. The difference is that we need to use the document.createComment function to create the annotation node element.

8.11   Fragment

Fragment is a new vnode type in Vue.js 3. Before discussing the implementation of Fragment in detail, it is necessary to understand why we need Fragment. Consider such a scenario, suppose we want to encapsulate a set of list components:

```
01 < List >
02 < Items/>
03 </List >
```

The whole consists of two components, namely the < List > component and the < Items > component. The < List > component renders a < ul > tag as the wrapping layer:

```
01 <!-- List.vue -->
02 <template>
03 <ul>
04 <slot />
05 </ul>
06 </template>
while the < Items > component renders a set of < li > lists:
01 <!-- Items.vue -->
02 <template>
03 <li>1</li>
04 <li>2</li>
05 <li>3</li>
06 </template>
```

This is not possible in Vue.js 2. In Vue.js 2, templates for components are not allowed to have multiple root nodes. This means that an < Items > component can only render at most one < li > tag:

```
01 <!-- Item.vue -->
02 <template>
03 <li>1</li>
04 </template>
```

So in Vue.js 2, we usually need to use the v-for directive to achieve the purpose:

```
01 < List >
02 < Items v-for = "item in list"/>
03 </List >
```

Similar combinations are also < select > Tags and < option > tags.

And Vue.js 3 supports multiple root node templates, so the above problems do not exist. So, how does Vue.js 3 use vnode to describe multi-root node templates?

```
01 const Fragment = Symbol ()
02 const vnode = {
03 type: Fragment,
04 children: [
05 { type: 'li', children: 'text 1' },
06 { type: 'li', children: 'text 2' },
07 { type: 'li', children: 'text 3' }
08 ]
09 }
```

Similar to text nodes and comment nodes, fragments do not have so-called tag names, so we also need to create a unique identifier for fragments, that is, Fragment. For vnodes of type Fragment, its children store the contents of all root nodes in the template. With Fragment, we can use it to describe the template of the Items.vue component:

```
01 <!-- Items.vue -->
02 <template>
03 <li>1</li>
04 <li>2</li>
05 <li>3</li>
06 </template>
```

The virtual node corresponding to this template is as follows:

```
01 const vnode = {
02 type: Fragment,
03 children: [
04 { type: 'li', children: '1' },
05 { type: 'li', children: '2' },
06 { type: 'li', children: '3' }
07 ]
08 }
```

Similarly, for the following template:

```
01 < List >
02 < Items/>
03 </List >
```

We can describe it with the following virtual node:

```
01 const vnode = {
02 type: 'ul',
03 children: [
04 {
05 type: Fragment,
06 children: [
07 { type: 'li', children: '1' },
08 { type: 'li', children: '2' },
09 { type: 'li', children: '3' }
10 ]
11 }
12 ]
13 }
```

As you can see, the vnode.children array contains a type of The virtual node of the fragment. When the renderer renders a virtual node of type Fragment, since the fragment itself does not render anything, the renderer only renders the sub-node of the fragment, as shown in the following code:

```
01 function patch(n1, n2, container) {
02 if (n1 && n1.type !== n2.type) {
03 unmount(n1)
04 n1 = null
05 }
06
07 const { type } = n2
08
09 if (typeof type === 'string') {
10 // omit some code
11 } else if (type === Text) {
12 // omit some code
13 } else if (type === Fragment) { // Handling vnode of Fragment type
14 if (!n1) {
15 // If the old vnode does not exist, you only need to mount the
children of the fragment one by one
16 n2.children.forEach(c => patch(null, c, container))
17 } else {
18 // If the old vnode exists, you only need to update the children of
the fragment
19 patchChildren(n1, n2, container)
20 }
21 }
22 }
```

Observing the above code, we added handling of virtual nodes of Fragment type in the patch function. The logic of rendering a fragment is much simpler than expected, because in essence, the difference between rendering a fragment and rendering a normal element is that the fragment itself does not render anything, so it only needs to process its sub-node.

However, it is still important to note that the unmount function also needs to support the unmounting of virtual nodes of type Fragment, as shown in the code of the following unmount function:

```
01 function unmount(vnode) {
02 // When unmounting, if the unmounted vnode type is Fragment, you
need to unmount its children
03 if (vnode.type === Fragment) {
04 vnode.children.forEach(c => unmount(c))
05 return
06 }
07 const parent = vnode.el.parentNode
08 if (parent) {
09 parent.removeChild(vnode.el)
10 }
11 }
```

When unmounting a virtual node of type Fragment, since the fragment itself does not render any real DOM, you only need to traverse its children array and unload the nodes one by one.

8.12 Summary

In this chapter, we first discussed how to mount sub-nodes and the properties of nodes. For sub-nodes, you only need to recursively call the patch function to complete the mount. While the attributes of nodes are more complicated than expected, it involves two important concepts: HTML attributes and DOM properties. When setting attributes for elements, we cannot always use the setAttribute function, nor can we always set them through the element's DOM properties. As for how to correctly set attributes for elements, it depends on the characteristics of the set attributes. For example, the el.form attribute of a form element is read-only, so it can only be set using the setAttribute function.

Next, we discussed the handling of special attributes. Taking class as an example, Vue.js has made enhancements to the class attribute, which allows us to specify different types of values for the class. But before setting these values to DOM elements, we need to normalize the values. We also discussed three ways to set the class for elements and their performance. Among them, el.className has the best performance, so we chose to use el.className in the patchProps function to complete the setting of the class attribute. In addition to the class attribute, Vue.js has also made enhancements to the style attribute, so the style attribute needs to be treated similarly.

Then, we discussed the uninstall operation. At first, we directly used innerHTML to empty the container elements, but there are many problems.

- The content of the container may be rendered by one or more components. When the uninstall operation occurs, the component's beforeUnmount, unmounted and other lifecycle functions should be called correctly
- Even if the content is not rendered by the component, some elements have custom instructions; we should execute the corresponding instruction hook function correctly when the unmount operation occurs
- Another drawback of using innerHTML to empty the container element content is that it does not remove the event handler bound to the DOM element

Therefore, we cannot use innerHTML directly to complete the unmount task. To solve these problems, we encapsulate the unmount function. This function takes the dimension of a vnode to unload; it will get the real DOM corresponding to the virtual node according to the vnode.el property, and then call the native DOM API to complete the unloading of the DOM element. There are two additional benefits to doing this.

- Inside the unmount function, we have the opportunity to call the instruction hook function bound to the DOM element, such as beforeUnmount, unmounted, etc.
- When the unmount function executes, we have the opportunity to detect the type of the virtual node vnode. If the virtual node describes a component, then we also have the opportunity to call the component-related lifecycle functions.

Then, we discussed the distinction between vnode types. When the renderer performs updates, it needs to check whether the content described by the old and new vnodes is the same. Patching is necessary only if the content they describe is the same. In addition, even if the content they describe is the same, we need to further check their types, that is, check the type of the vnode.type attribute value, and determine what the specific content it describes is. If the type is a string, it describes a normal tag element. In this case, we will call mountElement and patchElement to complete the mount and patch. If the type is an object, it describes a component. In this case, we need to call mountComponent and patchComponent to complete the mount and patch.

We also explained the handling of events. First, we introduced how to describe events in virtual nodes. We treated the properties starting with string on in the vnode. props object as events. Next, we explained how to bind and update events. In order to improve the performance, we fake the invoker function and store the real event handler function in the invoker.value property. When the event needs to be updated, only the value of invoker.value can be updated, so as to avoid a call to the removeEventListener function.

We also explained how to deal with the issue of event and update timing. The solution is to use the difference between the time when the event handler is bound to the DOM element and the time when the event fires. We need to block the execution of all event handlers whose binding time is later than the event firing time.

After that, we discussed sub-node updates. We normalized the children attribute in virtual nodes, specifying that the vnode.children attribute can only have the following three types.

- String type: The representative element has a text sub-node
- Array type: The representative element has a set of sub-nodes
- null: The representative element has no sub-nodes

When updating, the sub-nodes of both the old and new vnodes may be one of the above three situations, so we need to consider a total of nine possibilities when executing the update, that is, as shown in Fig. 8.5. But in the code, we do not need to list all the cases. In addition, when both the old and new vnodes have a set of sub-nodes, we adopt a relatively stupid way to complete the update, that is, uninstall all the old sub-nodes, and then mount all the new sub-nodes. A better approach is to try to maximize the reuse of DOM elements by comparing the old and new sets of sub-nodes through the Diff algorithm. We will explain how the Diff algorithm works in detail in subsequent chapters.

We also discussed how to use virtual nodes to describe text nodes and comment nodes. We took advantage of the uniqueness of symbol type values to create unique identifiers for text nodes and comment nodes, respectively, as the value of the vnode. type attribute.

Finally, we discussed Fragments and their uses. The renderer renders a fragment in a similar way to normal tags, except that the fragment itself does not render any DOM elements. So, you only need to render all sub-nodes of a fragment.

Chapter 9
Simple Diff Algorithms

Starting from this chapter, we will introduce the core Diff algorithm of the renderer. Simply put, when the sub-nodes of the old and new vnodes are a group of nodes, in order to complete the update operation with the minimum performance overhead, the two groups of sub-nodes need to be compared. The algorithm used for comparison is called the Diff algorithm. We know that the performance overhead of manipulating the DOM is usually relatively large, and the core Diff algorithm of the renderer was born to solve this problem.

9.1 Reducing Performance Overhead for DOM Operations

Core Diff only cares about the existence of a set of sub-nodes in both old and new virtual nodes. In the previous chapter, we adopted a simple and straightforward method for updating two sets of child nodes, that is, uninstall all old sub-nodes, and then mount all new sub-nodes. Doing so can indeed complete the update, but since no DOM elements are reused, it will incur a huge performance overhead. We now use the following old virtual nodes as an example:

```
01 // the old vnode
02 const oldVNode = {
03 type: 'div',
04 children: [
05 { type: 'p', children: '1' },
06 { type: 'p', children: '2' },
07 { type: 'p', children: '3' }
08 ]
09 }
10
11 // the new vnode
12 const newVNode = {
13 type: 'div',
```

© The Author(s), under exclusive license to Springer Nature Singapore Pte Ltd. 2023
H. Yang, *Vue. JS Framework*, https://doi.org/10.1007/978-981-99-4947-2_9

```
14 children: [
15 { type: 'p', children: '4' },
16 { type: 'p', children: '5' },
17 { type: 'p', children: '6' }
18 ]
19 }
```

As before, we need to perform 6 DOM operations when updating sub-node:

- Unmounting all old sub-nodes requires 3 DOM delete operations
- Mounting all new sub-nodes requires 3 DOM add operations

However, by observing the sub-nodes of the old and new vnodes above, we can find that

- All sub-nodes before and after the update are p-tags, that is, the label elements are unchanged
- Only the sub-nodes (text nodes) of the p-tag will change

For example, the first sub-node of oldVNode is a p-tag, and the sub-node type of the p-tag is a text node with the content of "1." The first sub-node of newVNode is also a p-tag, and its sub-node type is also a text node with the content of "4." It can be found that only the content of the p-tag text node changes before and after updating. Therefore, the most ideal update method is to directly update the content of the p-tag text node. This only requires a DOM operation to complete a p-tag update. Both new and old virtual nodes have 3 p-tags as sub-nodes, so it only takes 3 DOM operations to complete the update of all nodes. Compared with the original method that requires 6 DOM operations to complete the update, its performance has doubled.

In this way, we can reimplement the update logic of two sets of sub-nodes, as shown in the code of the patchChildren function below:

```
01 function patchChildren(n1, n2, container) {
02 if (typeof n2.children === 'string') {
03 // omit some code
04 } else if (Array.isArray(n2.children)) {
05 // re-implement the update method of two sets of sub-nodes
06 // new and old children
07 const oldChildren = n1.children
08 const newChildren = n2.children
09 // traverse the old children
10 for (let i = 0; i < oldChildren.length; i++) {
11 // call the patch function to update sub-node
12 patch(oldChildren[i], newChildren[i])
13 }
14 } else {
15 // omit part of the code
16 }
17 }
```

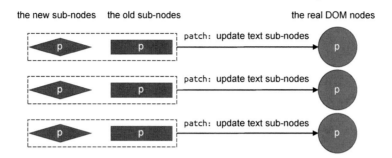

Fig. 9.1 Only update the text sub-nodes

In this code, oldChildren and newChildren are the old set of sub-nodes and the new set of sub-nodes, respectively. We iterate over the former and pass the nodes in the corresponding positions in the two to the patch function for updating. When the patch function performs the update, it finds that the new and old sub-nodes only have different text content, so it only updates the content of its text nodes. In this way, we successfully reduced the number of DOM operations from 6 to 3. Figure 9.1 is a schematic diagram of the entire update process, where the rhombus represents the new sub-node, the rectangle represents the old sub-node, and the circle represents the real DOM node.

Although this approach can reduce the number of DOM operations, the problem is also obvious. In the above code, we iterate through the old set of sub-nodes and assume that the new set has the same number of sub-nodes. Only in this case will this code work correctly. However, the number of new and old sets of sub-nodes may not be the same. When the number of new set of sub-nodes is less than the number of old set of sub-nodes, it means that some nodes should be unloaded after the update, as shown in Fig. 9.2.

In Fig. 9.2, the old set of sub-nodes has a total of 4 p-tags, while the new set of sub-nodes has only 3 p-tags. This means that during the update process, non-existing p-tags need to be unloaded. Similarly, the number of new sub-nodes may also be larger than the number of old sub-nodes, as shown in Fig. 9.3.

In Fig. 9.3, the new set of sub-nodes has one more p-tag than the old set of sub-nodes. In this case, we should mount the new node. From the above analysis, we realized that when updating the old and new sets of sub-nodes, we should not always traverse the old set of sub-nodes or traverse the new set of sub-nodes, but should traverse the shorter group. In this way, we can call the patch function as many times as possible to update. Then, compare the length of the new and old two sets of sub-nodes. If the new set of sub-nodes is longer, it means that there is a new sub-node that needs to be mounted, otherwise it means that there is an old sub-node that needs to be uninstalled. The final implementation method is as follows:

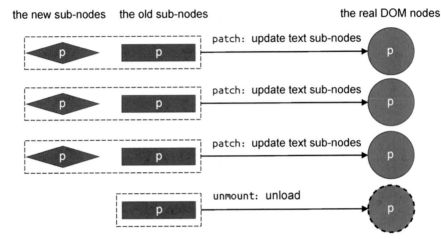

Fig. 9.2 Unloading nodes that no longer exist

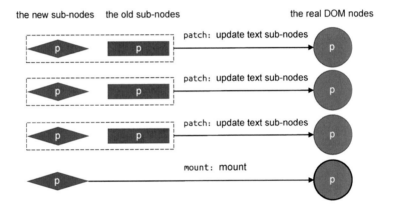

Fig. 9.3 Mounting new nodes

```
01 function patchChildren(n1, n2, container) {
02 if (typeof n2.children === 'string') {
03 // omit some code
04 } else if (Array.isArray(n2.children)) {
05 const oldChildren = n1.children
06 const newChildren = n2.children
07 // length of an old set of sub-nodes
08 const oldLen = oldChildren.length
09 // length of a new set of sub-nodes
10 const newLen = newChildren.length
11 // The common length of the two sets of sub-nodes, that is, the length
of the shorter set of sub-nodes
12 const commonLength = Math.min(oldLen, newLen)
13 // Traverse commonLength times
14 for (let i = 0; i < commonLength; i++) {
```

```
15 patch(oldChildren[i], newChildren[i], container)
16 }
17 // If newLen > oldLen, there is a new sub-node that needs to be
mounted
18 if (newLen > oldLen) {
19 for (let i = commonLength; i < newLen; i++) {
20 patch(null, newChildren[i], container)
21 }
22 } else if (oldLen > newLen) {
23 // if oldLen > newLen, there is an old sub-node that needs to be
unmounted
24 for (let i = commonLength; i < oldLen; i++) {
25 unmount(oldChildren[i])
26 }
27 }
28 } else {
29 // omit some code
30 }
31 }
```

This way, the renderer can mount or unmount both sets of sub-nodes correctly, regardless of the number of new and old sub-nodes.

9.2   DOM Replication and the Role of Key

In the previous section, we improved update performance by reducing the number of DOM operations. But there is still room for optimization in this way. As an example, suppose the contents of the old and new sets of sub-nodes are as follows:

```
01 // oldChildren
02 [
03 { type: 'p' },
04 { type: 'div' },
05 { type: 'span' }
06 ]
07
08 // newChildren
09 [
10 { type: 'span' },
11 { type: 'p' },
12 { type: 'div' }
13 ]
```

If you use the algorithm described in the previous section to complete the above two sets of sub-node updates, it will take 6 DOM operations.

• Call the patch function to patch between the old sub-node {type: 'p'} and the new sub-node {type: 'span'}. Since the two are different labels, the patch function will

unload {type: 'p'} and then mount {type: 'span'}, which requires 2 DOM operations.
- Similar to step 1, unmounting the old sub-node {type: 'div'} and then mounting the new sub-node {type: 'p'} requires 2 DOM operations.
- Similar to step 1, unmounting the old sub-node {type: 'span'} and then mounting the new sub-node {type: 'div'} also requires 2 DOM operations.

Therefore, a total of 6 DOM operations can be performed to complete the update of the above case. However, observing the new and old two sets of sub-nodes, it is easy to find that the two are just in different order. So, the optimal way to deal with it is to complete the update of the sub-node through the movement of the DOM, which is better than constantly performing the unloading and mounting of the sub-node. However, if you want to complete the update through the movement of the DOM, you must ensure one premise: there are indeed reusable nodes in the new and old two sets of sub-nodes. This is easy to understand. If the new sub-node does not appear in the old set of sub-nodes, it cannot be updated by moving the nodes. So now the question becomes: how to determine whether the new sub-node appears in the old set of sub-nodes? Taking the above example, how to determine that the first child node {type: 'span'} in the new set of sub-nodes is the same as the third child node in the old set of sub-nodes? One solution is to judge by vnode.type; as long as vnode.type has the same value, we consider both to be the same node. This method, however, is not reliable. Please consider the following example:

```
01 // oldChildren
02 [
03 { type: 'p', children: '1', key: 1 },
04 { type: 'p', children: '2', key: 2 },
05 { type: 'p', children: '3', key: 3 }
06 ]
07
08 // newChildren
09 [
10 { type: 'p', children: '3', key: 3 },
11 { type: 'p', children: '1', key: 1 },
12 { type: 'p', children: '2', key: 2 }
13 ]
```

Observing the above two sets of sub-nodes, we found that this case can be updated by moving the DOM. However, the vnode.type attribute values of all nodes are the same, which makes it impossible to determine the corresponding relationship between the nodes in the old and new two sets of sub-nodes, and it is impossible to know what DOM movement should be made to complete the update. So, we need to introduce extra keys as the marks of vnode, as in the following code:

```
01 // oldChildren
02 [
03 { type: 'p', children: '1', key: 1 },
04 { type: 'p', children: '2', key: 2 },
```

without key   with key

the new sub-nodes / the old sub-nodes   the new sub-nodes / the old sub-nodes

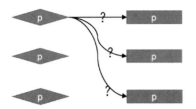   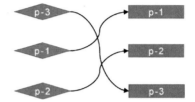

Fig. 9.4   With and without key

```
05 { type: 'p', children: '3', key: 3 }
06 ]
07
08 // newChildren
09 [
10 { type: 'p', children: '3', key: 3 },
11 { type: 'p', children: '1', key: 1 },
12 { type: 'p', children: '2', key: 2 }
13 ]
```

The key attribute is like the "ID" number of the virtual node, as long as the type attribute value and key attribute of the two virtual nodes are the same, then we consider them to be the same, that is, we can reuse the DOM. Figure 9.4 shows the mapping of the old and new sub-nodes with key and no key.

It can be seen from Fig. 9.4 that without the key, we cannot know the mapping relationship between the new sub-node and the old sub-node, and we cannot know how to move the node. If there is a key, the situation is different. According to the key attribute of the sub-node, we can clearly know the position of the new sub-node in the old sub-node, so that the corresponding DOM movement operation can be performed.

It is important to emphasize that DOM reusability does not mean that there is no need to update, as shown in the following two virtual nodes:

```
01 const oldVNode = { type: 'p', key: 1, children: 'text 1' }
02 const newVNode = { type: 'p', key: 1, children: 'text 2' }
```

These two virtual nodes have the same key value and vnode.type attribute value. This means that DOM elements can be reused at update time, i.e., only the move operation is required to complete the update. However, the two virtual nodes still need to be patched because the content of the text sub-node of the new virtual node (newVNode) has changed (from 'text 1 'to'text 2'). Therefore, before discussing how to move the DOM, we need to complete the patch operation, as shown in the following patchChildren function code:

```
01 function patchChildren(n1, n2, container) {
02 if (typeof n2.children === 'string') {
03 // omit some code
04 } else if (Array.isArray(n2.children)) {
05 const oldChildren = n1.children
06 const newChildren = n2.children
07
08 // traverse the new children
09 for (let i = 0; i < newChildren.length; i++) {
10 const newVNode = newChildren[i]
11 // traverse the old children
12 for (let j = 0; j < oldChildren.length; j++) {
13 const oldVNode = oldChildren[j]
14 // If two nodes with the same key value are found, it is possible to
reuse, but still the patch function is still needed to be called to update
15 if (newVNode.key === oldVNode.key) {
16 patch(oldVNode, newVNode, container)
17 break // here needs break
18 }
19 }
20 }
21
22 } else {
23 // omit some code
24 }
25 }
```

In the above code, we reimplement the update logic of the old and new sets of sub-nodes. As you can see, we use two layers of for loops, the outer loop is used to traverse the new set of sub-nodes, and the inner loop is used to traverse the old set of sub-nodes. In the inner loop, we compare the key values of the old and new sub-nodes one by one, trying to find reusable nodes in the old sub-nodes. Once found, we call the patch function to patch. After this step, we can ensure that all reusable nodes themselves have been updated.

```
01 const oldVNode = {
02 type: 'div',
03 children: [
04 { type: 'p', children: '1', key: 1 },
05 { type: 'p', children: '2', key: 2 },
06 { type: 'p', children: 'hello', key: 3 }
07 ]
08 }
09
10 const newVNode = {
11 type: 'div',
12 children: [
13 { type: 'p', children: 'world', key: 3 },
14 { type: 'p', children: '1', key: 1 },
15 { type: 'p', children: '2', key: 2 }
16 ]
```

```
17 }
18
19 // First mount
20 renderer.render(oldVNode, document.querySelector('#app'))
21 setTimeout(() => {
22 // Update after 1 second
23 renderer.render(newVNode, document.querySelector('#app'))
24 }, 1000);
```

Run the above code. After 1 s, the text content of the real DOM corresponding to the sub-node with key value 3 will be updated from the string "hello" to string "world." Let's analyze in detail what happens when the above code performs the update operation.

- The first step is to take the first sub-node in the new set of sub-nodes, that is, the node with key value 3. Try to find nodes with the same key value in the old set of sub-nodes. We find that the old sub-node oldVNode [2] has key value 3, so we call the patch function to patch. After this step is completed, the renderer will update the text content of the real DOM corresponding to the virtual node with key value 3 from string "hello" to string "world."
- In the second step, take the second sub-node in the new set of sub-nodes, that is, the node with key value 1. Try to find the node with the same key value in the old set of sub-nodes. We find that the old sub-node oldVNode [0] has a key value of 1, so we call the patch function to patch it. Since there is no difference between the old and new sub-nodes with a key value equal to 1, nothing will be done.
- In the third step, we take the last sub-node in the new set of sub-nodes, that is, the node with a key value of 2, and the final result is the same as in the second step.

After the above update operation, the real DOM elements corresponding to all nodes are updated. But the real DOM still maintains the order of the old set of sub-nodes, that is, the real DOM corresponding to the node with key value 3 is still the last sub-node. Since the node with key value 3 has become the first sub-node in the new set of sub-nodes, we still need to move the nodes to complete the update of the real DOM order.

9.3   Finding the Elements that Need to Be Moved

Now, we have been able to find reusable nodes by key value. The next thing to think about is how to determine whether a node needs to move and how to move. For the first question, we can use reverse thinking. First, think about when nodes do not need to move? The answer is very simple. When the node order of the old and new groups of sub-nodes remains the same, no additional move operations are required, as shown in Fig. 9.5.

In Fig. 9.5, the order of the new and old two sets of sub-nodes does not change. The figure also shows the indices of each node in the old set of sub-nodes:

Fig. 9.5 The order of nodes
remains unchanged

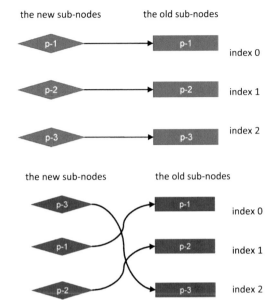

Fig. 9.6 Node order
changes

- A node with a key value of 1 has an index of 0 in the old children's array
- A node with a key value of 2 has an index of 1 in the old children's array
- A node with a key value of 3 has an index of 2 in the old children's array

Next, we use the update algorithm introduced in the previous section for the new and old two sets of sub-nodes to see what the update algorithm has when the order of the new and old two sets of sub-nodes does not change.

- Step 1: Take the first node in the new set of sub-nodes, p-1, whose key is 1. Try to find a reusable node with the same key value in the old set of sub-nodes, and find that it can be found, and the node has an index of 0 in the old set of sub-nodes.
- Step 2: Take the second node in the new set of sub-nodes, p-2, whose key is 2. Try to find a reusable node with the same key value in the old set of sub-nodes, and find that it can be found, and the node in the old set of sub-nodes has an index of 1.
- Step 3: Take the third node in the new set of sub-nodes, p-3, whose key is 3. Try to find a reusable node with the same key value in the old set of sub-nodes, and find that it can be found, and the node has an index of 2 in the old set of sub-nodes.

In this process, every time a reusable node is found, the position index of the reusable node in the old set of sub-nodes is recorded. If the position index values are arranged in order, you can get a sequence: 0, 1, 2. This is an increasing sequence, in which case no nodes need to be moved.

Let's look at another example again, as shown in Fig. 9.6.

Again, we execute the update algorithm again according to the example given in Fig. 9.6 to see how it will be different this time.

- Step 1: Take the first node p-3 in a new set of sub-nodes, which has key 3. Try to find a reusable node with the same key value in the old set of sub-nodes, and find that it can be found, and the node in the old set of sub-nodes has an index of 2.
- Step 2: Take the second node in the new set of sub-nodes, p-1, whose key is 1. Try to find a reusable node with the same key value in the old set of sub-nodes, and find that it can be found, and the node has an index of 0 in the old set of sub-nodes.

At this point we find that the order of increasing index values is broken. The index of node p-1 in the old children is 0, which is smaller than the index 2 of node p-3 in the old children. This shows that node p-1 is ahead of node p-3 in the old children, but behind node p-3 in the new children. Therefore, we are able to draw a conclusion: the real DOM corresponding to node p-1 needs to be moved.

- Step 3: Take the third node p-2 in the new set of sub-nodes, which has key 2. Try to find a reusable node with the same key value in the old set of sub-nodes, and find that it can be found, and the node has an index of 1 in the old set of sub-nodes.

At this point we find that the index 1 of node p-2 in the old children is smaller than the index 2 of node p-3 in the old children. This means that node p-2 is ahead of node p-3 in the old children, but behind node p-3 in the new children. Therefore, the real DOM corresponding to node p-2 also needs to be moved.

The above is how the Diff algorithm determines whether the node needs to move during the update process. In the above example, we conclude that nodes p-1 and p-2 need to move. This is because their index in the old children is smaller than the index of node p-3 in the old children. If we record the position indexes encountered during the node search in order, we will get a sequence: 2, 0, 1. It can be found that this sequence does not have an increasing trend.

In fact, we can define the index of node p-3 in the old children as the maximum index value encountered in the process of finding nodes with the same key value in the old children. If in the subsequent search process, there is a node whose index value is smaller than the maximum index value currently encountered, which means that the node needs to move.

We can use the lastIndex variable to store the maximum index value encountered during the entire search, as shown in the following code:

```
01 function patchChildren(n1, n2, container) {
02 if (typeof n2.children === 'string') {
03 // omit some code
04 } else if (Array.isArray(n2.children)) {
05 const oldChildren = n1.children
06 const newChildren = n2.children
07
08 // to store the maximum index value encountered during the search
```

```
09 let lastIndex = 0
10 for (let i = 0; i < newChildren.length; i++) {
11 const newVNode = newChildren[i]
12 for (let j = 0; j < oldChildren.length; j++) {
13 const oldVNode = oldChildren[j]
14 if (newVNode.key === oldVNode.key) {
15 patch(oldVNode, newVNode, container)
16 if (j < lastIndex) {
17 // If the index of the currently found node in the old children is
less than the maximum index value lastIndex,
18 // Indicate that the real DOM corresponding to the node needs to be
moved
19 } else {
20 // If the index of the currently found node in the old children is not
less than the maximum index value,
21 // Update the value of lastIndex
22 lastIndex = j
23 }
24 break // This requires break
25 }
26 }
27 }
28
29 } else {
30 // Omit some code
31 }
32 }
```

As shown in the above code and comments, if the key values of the old and new nodes are the same, it means that we have found a node that can reuse the DOM in the old children. At this time, we use the index j of the node in the old children to compare with lastIndex. If j is less than lastIndex, it means that the real DOM corresponding to the current oldVNode needs to be moved, otherwise it means that no move is required. But at this time, the value of the variable j should be assigned to the variable lastIndex to ensure that during the process of finding a node, the variable lastIndex always stores the maximum index value currently encountered.

Now that we have found the node that needs to be moved, we will discuss how to move the node to complete the update of the node order in the next section.

9.4   How to Move Elements

In the previous section, we discussed how to determine whether a node needs to be moved. Mobile node refers to moving a virtual node corresponding to the real DOM node, not moving the virtual node itself. Since we are moving a real DOM node, we need to get a reference to it. We know that when a virtual node is mounted, its corresponding real DOM node will be stored in its vnode.el attributes, as shown in Fig. 9.7.

Fig. 9.7 The virtual node in refers to the real DOM element

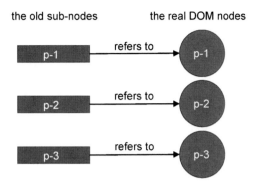

the old sub-nodes   the real DOM nodes

p-1 — refers to → p-1

p-2 — refers to → p-2

p-3 — refers to → p-3

So in the code, we can get its corresponding real DOM node through the vnode.el attribute of the old sub-node.

When the update operation occurs, the renderer calls the patchElement function to patch between the old and new virtual nodes. Review the code of the patchElement function, as follows:

```
01 function patchElement (n1, n2) {
02 //The new vnode also references the real DOM element
03 const el = n2.el = n1.el
04 //Omit part of the code
05 }
```

As you can see, the patchElement function first assigns the n1.el properties of the old node to the n2.el properties of the new node. The real meaning of this assignment statement is actually the reuse of DOM elements. After reusing the DOM elements, the new node will also hold a reference to the real DOM, as shown in Fig. 9.8.

You can see that both the new sub-node and the old sub-node have references to the real DOM. On this basis, we can perform DOM moving operations.

In order to illustrate how to move DOM nodes, we still refer to the update case in the previous section, as shown in Fig. 9.9.

The update steps are as follows.

- Step 1: Take the first node p-3 in the new set of sub-nodes; its key is 3 and try to find a reusable node with the same key value in the old set of sub-nodes. Find that it can be found, and the node is in the old set of sub-nodes, with index 2. At this point, the value of the variable lastIndex is 0, and the index 2 is not less than 0, so the real DOM corresponding to node p-3 does not need to be moved, but the value of the variable lastIndex needs to be updated to be 2.
- Step 2: Take the second node in the new group of sub-nodes, p-1, whose key is 1, and try to find a reusable node with the same key value in the old group of sub-nodes. It is found that it can be found, and the node is in the old group of sub-nodes, and the index is 0. At this point, the value of the variable lastIndex is 2, and the index 0 is less than 2, so the real DOM corresponding to node p-1 needs to be moved.

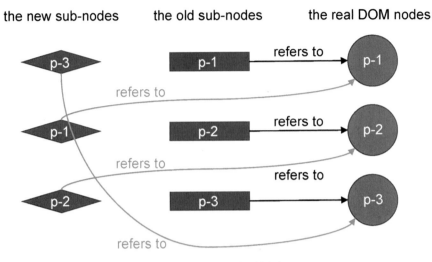

Fig. 9.8 Make the new sub-node also refer to the real DOM element

Fig. 9.9 The relationship between the old and new sub-nodes

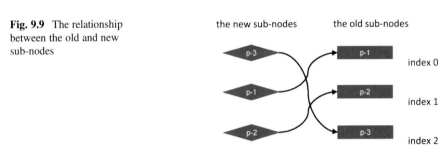

At this step, we find that the real DOM corresponding to node p-1 needs to be moved, but where should it be moved? We know that the order of new children is actually the order of the real DOM nodes after the update. Therefore, the position of node p-1 in the new children represents the position of the real DOM after the update. Since node p-1 is behind node p-3 in the new children, we should move the real DOM corresponding to node p-1 to the real DOM corresponding to node p-3. The result after moving is shown in Fig. 9.10.

You can see that after this operation, the order of the real DOM at this time is p-2, p-3, and p-1.

- Step 3: Take the third node in the new set of sub-nodes, p-2, whose key is 2. Try to find a reusable node with the same key value in the old set of sub-nodes. It is found that it can be found, and the node is in the old set of sub-nodes, and the index is 1. At this time, the value of the variable lastIndex is 2, and the index 1 is less than 2, so the real DOM corresponding to node p-2 needs to be moved.

The third step is similar to the second step, and the real DOM of node p-2 also needs to be moved. Similarly, since node p-2 ranks behind node p-1 in the new children, we should move the real DOM of node p-2 to the real DOM of node p-1. The result of the move is shown in Fig. 9.11.

the new sub-nodes   the old sub-nodes   the real DOM nodes

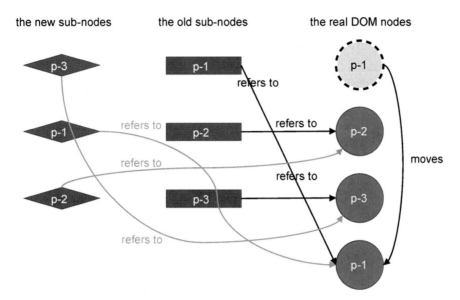

Fig. 9.10 Move the real DOM of node p-1 to the real DOM of node p-3

After this move operation, we find that the order of the real DOM is the same as that of the new set of sub-nodes: p-3, p-1, p-2. At this point, the update operation is completed.

Next, we start to implement the code. It is not complex, as shown in the following patchChildren function code:

```
01 function patchChildren(n1, n2, container) {
02 if (typeof n2.children === 'string') {
03 // omit part of the code
04 } else if (Array.isArray(n2.children)) {
05 const oldChildren = n1.children
06 const newChildren = n2.children
07
08 let lastIndex = 0
09 for (let i = 0; i < newChildren.length; i++) {
10 const newVNode = newChildren[i]
11 let j = 0
12 for (j; j < oldChildren.length; j++) {
13 const oldVNode = oldChildren[j]
14 if (newVNode.key === oldVNode.key) {
15 patch(oldVNode, newVNode, container)
16 if (j < lastIndex) {
17 // The code runs here, indicating that the real DOM corresponding to
newVNode needs to be moved
18 // Get the previous vnode of newVNode first, that is, prevVNode
19 const prevVNode = newChildren[i - 1]
20 // If prevVNode does not exist, it means that the current newVNode is
the first node, and it does not need to move
```

the new sub-nodes   the old sub-nodes   the real DOM nodes

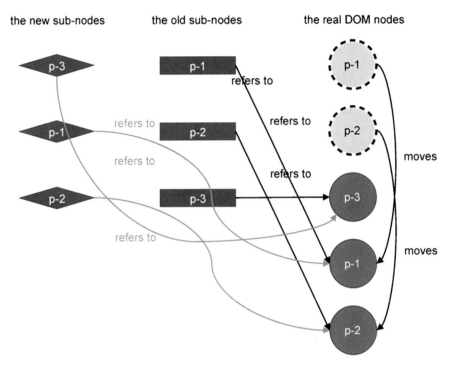

Fig. 9.11 Move the real DOM corresponding to node p-2 to the real DOM corresponding to node p-1

```
21 if (prevVNode) {
22 // Since we want to move the real DOM corresponding to newVNode to the
back of the real DOM corresponding to prevVNode,
23 // So we need to take the next sibling node of the real DOM
corresponding to the prevVNode and use it as an anchor point
24 const anchor = prevVNode.el.nextSibling
25 // call the insert method to insert the real DOM corresponding to
newVNode in front of the anchor element,
26 // that is, behind prevVNode corresponding to the real DOM
27 insert(newVNode.el, container, anchor)
28 }
29 } else {
30 lastIndex = j
31 }
32 break
33 }
34 }
35 }
36
37 } else {
38 // omit part of the code
39 }
40 }
```

In the above code, if the condition j < lastIndex is true, it means that the real DOM corresponding to the current newVNode needs to be moved. According to the previous analysis, we need to get the previous virtual node of the current newVNode node, that is, newChildren [i - 1], and then use the insert function to complete the movement of the node, where the insert function relies on the insertBefore function of the browser native, as shown in the following code:

```
01 const renderer = createRenderer({
02 // omit part of the code
03
04 insert(el, parent, anchor = null) {
05 // insertBefore requires element anchor
06 parent.insertBefore(el, anchor)
07 }
08
09 // omit part of the code
10 })
```

9.5   Adding New Elements

In this section, we will discuss the case of adding new nodes, as shown in Fig. 9.12.

Observing Fig. 9.12, we can see that in the new group of sub-nodes, there is an extra node p-4 with a key value of 4. This node does not exist in the old group of sub-nodes, so it should be regarded as a new node. For new nodes, we should mount it correctly during update. This is mainly divided into two steps:

- Find a way to find the new node
- Mount the new node to the correct location

First, let's take a look at how to find the new node. To figure this out, we need to simulate the logic of executing the simple Diff algorithm according to the example given in Fig. 9.12. Before that, we need to figure out the current state of the new and old two sets of sub-nodes and real DOM elements, as shown in Fig. 9.13.

Fig. 9.12 New node p-4

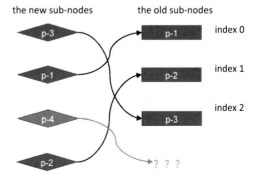

the new sub-nodes   the old sub-nodes   the real DOM nodes

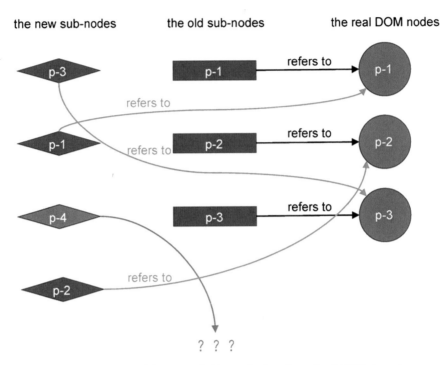

Fig. 9.13 The current state of the new and old sets of sub-nodes and real DOM elements

Next, we start to simulate the update logic of executing the simple Diff algorithm.

- Step 1: Take the first node in the new set of sub-nodes, p-3, with a key value of 3, and try to find a reusable node in the old set of sub-nodes. It is found that it can be found, and the node has an index value of 2 in the old set of sub-nodes. At this point, the value of the variable lastIndex is 0, and the index value 2 is not less than the value of lastIndex, so the node p-3 corresponding to the real DOM does not need to move, but the value of the variable lastIndex needs to be updated to 2.
- Step 2: Take the second node in the new set of sub-nodes, p-1; its key value is 1, and try to find a reusable node in the old set of sub-nodes. It is found that it can be found, and the index value of this node in the old set of sub-nodes is 0. At this time, the value of the variable lastIndex is 2, and the index value 0 is less than the value of lastIndex 2, so the real DOM corresponding to node p-1 needs to be moved, and it should be moved behind the real DOM corresponding to node p-3. After this move operation, the state of the real DOM is shown in Fig. 9.14.

  In this case, the order of the real DOM is p-2, p-3, p-1.
- Step 3: Take the third node in the new set of sub-nodes, p-4, whose key value is 4, and try to find reusable nodes in the old set of sub-nodes. Since there is no node with key value 4 in the old set of sub-nodes, the renderer will regard node p-4 as a new node and mount it. So, where should it be mounted? To figure this out, we

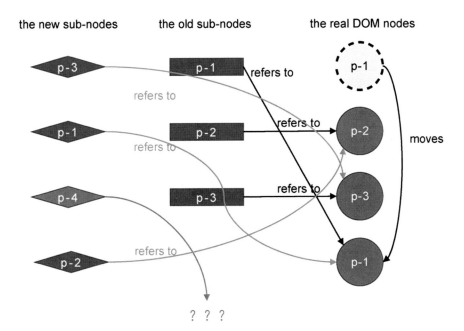

Fig. 9.14 The current state of the real DOM

need to observe the position of node p-4 in a new set of sub-nodes. Since node p-4 appears after node p-1, we should mount node p-4 behind the real DOM corresponding to node p-1. After this step, after the mount operation, the state of the real DOM is shown in Fig. 9.15.

The order of the real DOM at this time is p-2, p-3, p-1, p-4, where p-4 is just mounted.

- Step 4: Take the fourth node in the new set of sub-nodes, p-2, whose key value is 2, and try to find a reusable node in the old set of sub-nodes. It is found that it can be found, and the index value of this node in the old group of sub-nodes is 1.

  At this time, the value of the variable lastIndex is 2, and the index value 1 is less than the value 2 of lastIndex, so the real DOM corresponding to node p-2 needs to be moved and should be moved behind the real DOM corresponding to node p-4. After this step of moving operation, the state of the real DOM is shown in Fig. 9.16.

At this time, the order of the real DOM is p-3, p-1, p-4, p-2. At this point, the order of the real DOM is the same as that of the new set of sub-nodes, and the update is completed.

Then, we need to implement the code, as shown in the following patchChildren function code:

the new sub-nodes   the old sub-nodes   the real DOM nodes

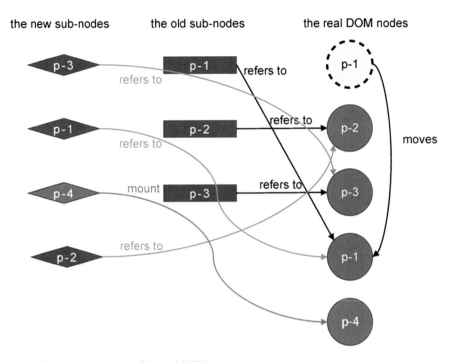

Fig. 9.15 The current state of the real DOM

```
01 function patchChildren(n1, n2, container) {
02 if (typeof n2.children === 'string') {
03 // omit part of the code
04 } else if (Array.isArray(n2.children)) {
05 const oldChildren = n1.children
06 const newChildren = n2.children
07
08 let lastIndex = 0
09 for (let i = 0; i < newChildren.length; i++) {
10 const newVNode = newChildren[i]
11 let j = 0
12 // Define the variable find in the first-level loop,
representing whether to find reusable nodes in the old set of sub-nodes,
13 // The initial value is false, representing not found
14 let find = false
15 for (j; j < oldChildren.length; j++) {
16 const oldVNode = oldChildren[j]
17 if (newVNode.key === oldVNode.key) {
18 // Set the value of the variable find to true once a reusable
node is found
19 find = true
20 patch(oldVNode, newVNode, container)
21 if (j < lastIndex) {
22 const prevVNode = newChildren[i - 1]
```

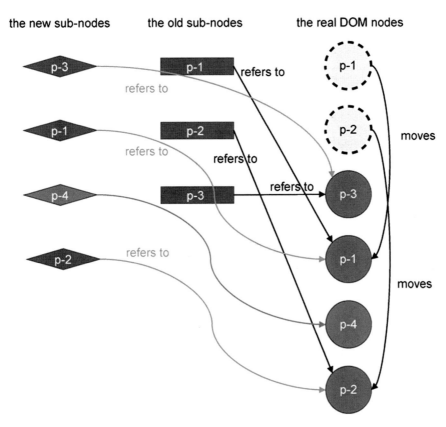

Fig. 9.16   The current state of the real DOM

```
23 if (prevVNode) {
24 const anchor = prevVNode.el.nextSibling
25 insert(newVNode.el, container, anchor)
26 }
27 } else {
28 lastIndex = j
29 }
30 break
31 }
32 }
33 // If the code runs here, find is still false,
34 // Indicate that the current newVNode has not found a
reusable node in the old set of sub-nodes
35 // That is, the current newVNode is a new node and needs to
mount
36 if (!find) {
37 // In order to mount the node to the correct position,
we need to get the anchor element first
38 // First get the previous vnode of the current newVNode
39 const prevVNode = newChildren[i - 1]
40 let anchor = null
```

```
41 if (prevVNode) {
42 // If there is a previous vnode, use its next sibling as the
anchor element
43 anchor = prevVNode.el.nextSibling
44 } else {
45 // If there is no previous vnode, it means that the new node
to be mounted is the first sub-node
46 // In this case we use the firstChild of the container
element as the anchor
47 anchor = container.firstChild
48 }
49 // mounting newVNode
50 patch(null, newVNode, container, anchor)
51 }
52 }
53
54 } else {
55 // omit part of the code
56 }
57 }
```

Observe the above code. First, we define a variable called find in the outer loop, which represents whether the renderer can find reusable nodes in the old set of sub-nodes. The initial value of the variable find is false, and once a reusable node is found, the value of the variable find is set to true. If the value of the variable find is still false after the inner loop ends, then the current newVNode is a brand-new node and needs to be mounted. In order to mount the node to the correct position, we need to get the anchor element first: find the previous virtual node of newVNode, that is, prevVNode, if it exists, use its corresponding next brother node of the real DOM as the anchor element; if it does not exist, it means that the newVNode node to be mounted is the first sub-node of the container element, and in this case, the container. firstChild of the container element should be used as the anchor element. Finally, use the anchor element as the fourth parameter of the patch function, and call the patch function to complete the mounting of the node.

However, since the currently implemented patch function does not support passing the fourth parameter, we need to adjust the code of the patch function as follows:

```
01 // The patch function needs to receive the fourth parameter, that
is, the anchor element
02 function patch(n1, n2, container, anchor) {
03 // omit some code
04
05 if (typeof type === 'string') {
06 if (!n1) {
07 // pass anchor element as third argument to mountElement function
on mount
08 mountElement(n2, container, anchor)
09 } else {
10 patchElement(n1, n2)
```

```
11 }
12 } else if (type === Text) {
13 // omit some code
14 } else if (type === Fragment) {
15 // omit some code
16 }
17 }
18
19 // The mountElement function needs to add a third parameter, that
is, the anchor element
20 function mountElement (vnode, container, anchor) {
21 // omit some code
22
23 // 在When inserting a node, pass the anchor element through to the
insert function
24 insert (el, container, anchor)
25 }
```

9.6   Removing Non-existent Elements

When updating a sub-node, not only new elements will be encountered, but elements will also be deleted, as shown in Fig. 9.17.

In a new set of sub-nodes, node p-2 no longer exists, which means that the node has been deleted. The renderer should be able to find the nodes that need to be deleted and delete them correctly.

How do we do it specifically? First, let's discuss how to find the nodes that need to be deleted. Taking Fig. 9.17 as an example, let's analyze its update step. Before simulating the update logic, we need to know the current state of the old and new sub-nodes and the real DOM nodes, as shown in Fig. 9.18.

Next, we start to simulate the process of performing the update.

• Step 1: Take the first node in the new set of sub-nodes, p-3, whose key value is 3. Try to find reusable nodes in the old set of child nodes. It is found that it can be found, and the index value of the node in the old set of sub-nodes is 2. At this time, the value of the variable lastIndex is 0, and the index 2 is not less than the

Fig. 9.17 Node deletion

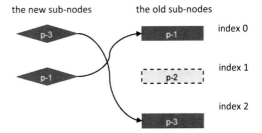

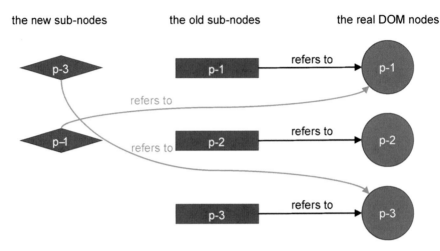

the new sub-nodes   the old sub-nodes   the real DOM nodes

Fig. 9.18 The current state of the old and new sub-nodes and the real DOM nodes

value of lastIndex, so the node p-3 corresponds to the real DOM, but the value of the variable lastIndex needs to be updated to be 2.

- Step 2: Take the second node p-1 in the new set of sub-nodes, and its key value is 1. Try to find a reusable node in the old set of child nodes. It is found that it can be found, and the index value of this node in the old set of sub-nodes is 0. At this time, the value of the variable lastIndex is 2, and the index 0 is less than the value of lastIndex 2, so the real DOM corresponding to node p-1 needs to be moved, and it should be moved behind the real DOM corresponding to node p-3. After this step of movement, the state of the real DOM is shown in Fig. 9.19.

At this point, the update is over. We found that the real DOM corresponding to node p-2 still exists, so we need to add extra logic to delete the legacy nodes. The idea is very simple. When the basic update is over, we need to traverse the old set of sub-nodes, and then go to the new set of sub-nodes to find nodes with the same key value. If not, the node should be removed, as shown in the following code for the patchChildren function:

```
01 function patchChildren(n1, n2, container) {
02 if (typeof n2.children === 'string') {
03 // omit some code
04 } else if (Array.isArray(n2.children)) {
05 const oldChildren = n1.children
06 const newChildren = n2.children
07
08 let lastIndex = 0
09 for (let i = 0; i < newChildren.length; i++) {
10 // omit some code
11 }
12
13 // After the previous update operation completes
```

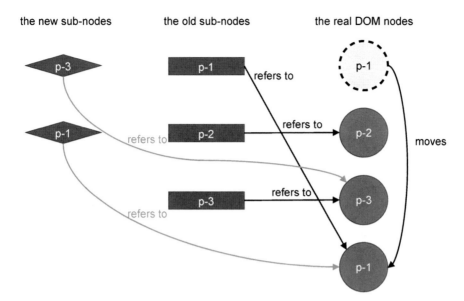

Fig. 9.19 The current state of the real DOM

```
14 // Traverse the old set of sub-nodes
15 for (let i = 0; i < oldChildren.length; i++) {
16 const oldVNode = oldChildren[i]
17 // Take the old sub-node oldVNode to the new set of sub-nodes to find
nodes with the same key value
18 const has = newChildren.find(
19 vnode => vnode.key === oldVNode.key
20 )
21 if (!has) {
22 // If no node with the same key value is found, the node needs to be
removed
23 // Call the unmount function to unmount it
24 unmount(oldVNode)
25 }
26 }
27
28 } else {
29 // omit some code
30 }
31 }
```

As shown in the above code and comments, after the update operation in the previous step is completed, we also need to traverse the old set of sub-nodes. The purpose is to check whether the old sub-node still exists in the new set of sub-nodes. If it no longer exists, call the unmount function to unmount it.

9.7   Summary

In this chapter, we first discussed the role of the Diff algorithm. The Diff algorithm is used to calculate the differences between two sets of sub-nodes and try to reuse DOM elements to the greatest extent possible. In the previous chapter, we adopted a simple way to update sub-nodes, that is, unmount all old sub-nodes, and then mount all new sub-nodes. However, this update method cannot reuse DOM elements and requires a lot of DOM operations to complete the update, which is very performance-consuming. So, we improved it. The improved scheme is to iterate over the small number of sub-nodes in the old and new groups and call the patch function one by one to patch, and then compare the number of sub-nodes in the old and new groups. If the number of sub-nodes in the new group is more, it means that there are new sub-nodes that need to be mounted; otherwise, it means that there are nodes in the old group of sub-nodes that need to be uninstalled.

Then, we discussed the role of the key attribute in the virtual node, which is like the "ID number" of the virtual node. When updating, the renderer finds reusable nodes through the key attribute, and then uses the DOM move operation as much as possible to complete the update, avoiding excessive destruction and reconstruction of DOM elements.

Next, we discussed how the simple Diff algorithm found nodes that needed to be moved. The core logic of the simple Diff algorithm is to take the nodes in a new set of sub-nodes and find the reusable nodes in the old set of sub-nodes. If it is found, the location index of the node is recorded. We call this position index the maximum index. During the whole update process, if the index of a node is less than the maximum index, it means that the real DOM element corresponding to the node needs to be moved.

Finally, we explained how the renderer moves, adds, and removes the DOM element corresponding to the virtual node through several examples.

Chapter 10
Double-Ended Diff Algorithms

In the previous chapter, we introduced the implementation principle of the simple Diff algorithm. The simple Diff algorithm uses the key attributes of virtual nodes to reuse DOM elements as much as possible and updates the DOM by moving the DOM, thereby reducing the performance overhead caused by constantly creating and destroying DOM elements. However, the simple Diff algorithm still has many shortcomings, which can be solved by the double-ended Diff algorithm introduced in this chapter.

10.1   Principles of Double-Ended Comparison

The problem with the simple Diff algorithm is that it is not optimal for moving the DOM. Let's take the example from the previous chapter, as shown in Fig. 10.1.

In this example, if the simple Diff algorithm is used to update it, two DOM moving operations will occur, as shown in Fig. 10.2.

The first DOM move moves the real DOM node p-1 behind the real DOM node p-3. The second move moves the real DOM node p-2 behind the real DOM node p-1. Eventually, the order of the real DOM nodes is the same as the new set of sub-nodes: p-3, p-1, p-2.

However, the above update process is not the optimal solution. In this example, the update can be completed only by moving the DOM node in one step, that is, only the real DOM node p-3 needs to be moved in front of the real DOM node p-1, as shown in Fig. 10.3.

You can see that in theory, only one DOM move operation is required to complete the update. However, the simple Diff algorithm cannot do this, but the double-ended Diff algorithm will be introduced in this chapter. Next, we will discuss the principle of the double-ended Diff algorithm.

As the name suggests, the double-ended Diff algorithm is an algorithm that compares two endpoints of the old and new groups of sub-nodes at the same time.

Fig. 10.1 The old and new sets of sub-nodes and indexes

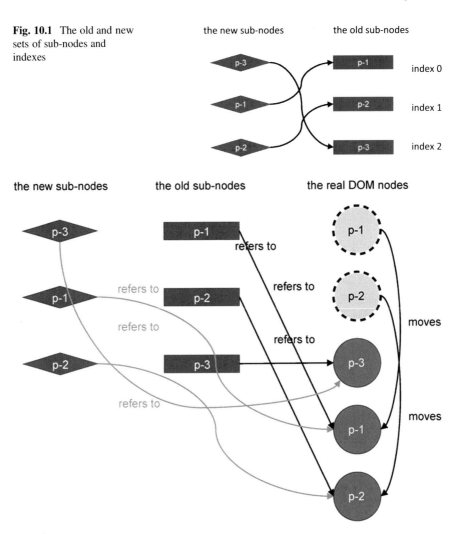

Fig. 10.2 Two DOM movement operations complete the update

Therefore, we need four index values, pointing to the endpoints of the old and new groups of sub-nodes, as shown in Fig. 10.4.

Expressing the four endpoints with code, as shown in the code of the patchChildren and patchKeyedChildren functions below:

```
01 function patchChildren(n1, n2, container) {
02 if (typeof n2.children === 'string') {
03 // omit some code
04 } else if (Array.isArray(n2.children)) {
05 // encapsulate the patchKeyedChildren function to handle two sets
of sub- node
```

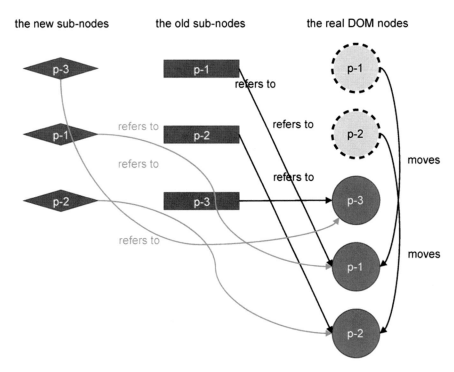

Fig. 10.3 Move the real DOM node p-3 in front of the real DOM node p-1

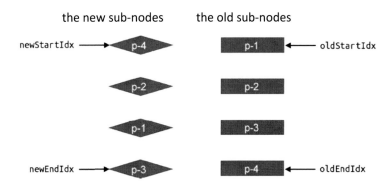

Fig. 10.4 Four index values, pointing to the endpoints of the new and old sets of sub-nodes

```
06 patchKeyedChildren(n1, n2, container)
07 } else {
08 // omit some code
09 }
10 }
11
12 function patchKeyedChildren(n1, n2, container) {
13 const oldChildren = n1.children
```

Fig. 10.5 The way of
double-ended comparison

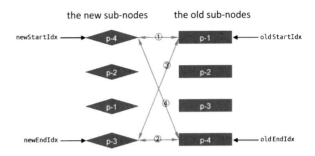

```
14 const newChildren = n2.children
15 // four index values
16 let oldStartIdx = 0
17 let oldEndIdx = oldChildren.length - 1
18 let newStartIdx = 0
19 let newEndIdx = newChildren.length - 1
20 }
```

In the above code, we encapsulated two sets of sub-node patches into the patchKeyedChildren function. In this function, first get the old and new sets of sub-node oldChildren and newChildren, and then create four index values, respectively, pointing to the head and tail of old and new sets of sub-node, namely oldStartIdx, oldEndIdx, newStartIdx, and newEndIdx. With the index, you can find the virtual node it points to, as shown in the following code:

```
01 function patchKeyedChildren(n1, n2, container) {
02 const oldChildren = n1.children
03 const newChildren = n2.children
04 // four index values
05 let oldStartIdx = 0
06 let oldEndIdx = oldChildren.length - 1
07 let newStartIdx = 0
08 let newEndIdx = newChildren.length - 1
09 // Four indexed vnodes
10 let oldStartVNode = oldChildren[oldStartIdx]
11 let oldEndVNode = oldChildren[oldEndIdx]
12 let newStartVNode = newChildren[newStartIdx]
13 let newEndVNode = newChildren[newEndIdx]
14 }
```

Here, oldStartVNode and oldEndVNode are the first and last nodes in the old set of sub-nodes, and newStartVNode and newEndVNode are the first and last nodes in the new set of sub-nodes. With this information, we can start the double-ended comparison. How do we compare? As shown in Fig. 10.5.

In double-ended comparison, each round of comparison is divided into four steps, as shown by the connection in Fig. 10.5.

- Step 1: Compare the first sub-node p-1 in the old group of sub-nodes with the first child node p-4 in the new group of sub-nodes to see if they are the same. Since the key values of the two are different, they are not the same and cannot be reused, so nothing is done.
- Step 2: Compare the last sub-node p-4 in the old set of sub-nodes with the last sub-node p-3 in the new set of sub-nodes to see if they are the same. Since the key values of the two are different, they are not the same and cannot be reused, so nothing is done.
- Step 3: Compare the first sub-node p-1 in the old set of sub-nodes with the last child in the new set of sub-nodes, node p-3, to see if they are the same. Since the key values of the two are different, they are not the same and cannot be reused, so nothing is done.
- Step 4: Compare the last sub-node p-4 in the old set of sub-nodes with the first child in the new set of sub-nodes, node p-4. Since their key values are the same, DOM multiplexing can be performed.

You can see that we found the same nodes in the fourth step, which means that their corresponding real DOM nodes can be reused. For reusable DOM nodes, we only need to complete the update through the DOM move operation. So how should DOM elements be moved? In order to figure out this problem, we need to analyze the details in the fourth step comparison process. We notice that the fourth step is to compare the last sub-node of the old set of sub-nodes with the first sub-node of the new set of sub-nodes and find that both are the same. This means that node p-4 was originally the last sub-node, but in the new order, it becomes the first sub-node. In other words, node p-4 should be the first sub-node after the update. The logic corresponding to the program can be translated as: move the real DOM corresponding to the virtual node pointed to by the index oldEndIdx to the front of the real DOM corresponding to the virtual node pointed to by the index oldStartIdx.

```
01 function patchKeyedChildren(n1, n2, container) {
02 const oldChildren = n1.children
03 const newChildren = n2.children
04 // four indexed values
05 let oldStartIdx = 0
06 let oldEndIdx = oldChildren.length - 1
07 let newStartIdx = 0
08 let newEndIdx = newChildren.length - 1
09 // four indexed vnodes
10 let oldStartVNode = oldChildren[oldStartIdx]
11 let oldEndVNode = oldChildren[oldEndIdx]
12 let newStartVNode = newChildren[newStartIdx]
13 let newEndVNode = newChildren[newEndIdx]
14
15 if (oldStartVNode.key === newStartVNode.key) {
16 // Step 1: oldStartVNode vs newStartVNode
17 } else if (oldEndVNode.key === newEndVNode.key) {
18 // Step 2: oldEndVNode vs newEndVNode
19 } else if (oldStartVNode.key === newEndVNode.key) {
```

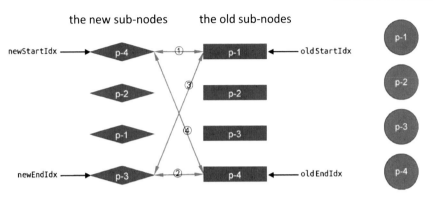

Fig. 10.6 State of the new and old groups of sub-nodes and real DOM nodes

```
20 // Step 3 : oldStartVNode vs newEndVNode
21 } else if (oldEndVNode.key === newStartVNode.key) {
22 // Step 4 : oldEndVNode vs newStartVNode
23 // still need to call patch function to patch
24 patch(oldEndVNode, newStartVNode, container)
25 // move DOM operations
26 // oldEndVNode.el moves to the front oldStartVNode.el
27 insert(oldEndVNode.el, container, oldStartVNode.el)
28
29 // After moving the DOM, update the index value and point to the next
position
30 oldEndVNode = oldChildren[--oldEndIdx]
31 newStartVNode = newChildren[++newStartIdx]
32 }
33 }
```

In this code, we add a series of if … else if … statements to perform the comparison between the virtual nodes pointed to by the four indexes. Taking the above example, in the fourth step, we find the node with the same key value. This means that the node at the tail should be at the head in the new order. Therefore, we only need to use the head element oldStartVNode.el as the anchor point and move the tail element oldEndVNode.el in front of the anchor point. However, it should be noted that before performing the DOM shift operation, we still need to call the patch function to patch the old and new virtual nodes.

After the DOM move operation is completed in this step, the next critical step is to update the index value. Since the two indexes involved in step 4 are oldEndIdx and newStartIdx, we need to update the values of both so that each of them takes a step in the right direction and points to the next node. Figure 10.6 shows the status of the old and new sub-nodes and the real DOM nodes before the update.

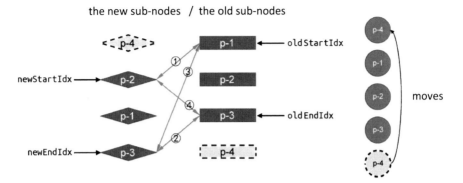

Fig. 10.7 State of the new and old groups of sub-nodes and real DOM nodes

Figure 10.7 shows the state of the new and old groups of sub-nodes and real DOM nodes in the comparison of the fourth step, after the first step DOM move operation is completed.

At this time, the real DOM node order is p-4, p-1, p-2, p-3, which is inconsistent with the new set of sub-node order. This is because the Diff algorithm is not over yet, and the next round of updates is needed. Therefore, we need to encapsulate the update logic into a while loop, as shown in the following code:

```
01 while (oldStartIdx <= oldEndIdx && newStartIdx <= newEndIdx) {
02 if (oldStartVNode.key === newStartVNode.key) {
03 // Step 1: oldStartVNode vs newStartVNode
04 } else if (oldEndVNode.key === newEndVNode.key) {
05 // Step 2: oldEndVNode vs newEndVNode
06 } else if (oldStartVNode.key === newEndVNode.key) {
07 // Step 3: oldStartVNode vs newEndVNode
08 } else if (oldEndVNode.key === newStartVNode.key) {
09 // Step 4: oldEndVNode vs newStartVNode
10 // still need to call the patch function to patch
11 patch(oldEndVNode, newStartVNode, container)
12 // Move DOM operation
13 // oldEndVNode.el moves to the front of oldStartVNode.el
14 insert(oldEndVNode.el, container, oldStartVNode.el)
15
16 // After moving DOM, update index values, pointing to the next
position
17 oldEndVNode = oldChildren[--oldEndIdx]
18 newStartVNode = newChildren[++newStartIdx]
19 }
20 }
```

Since after each round of updates, the indexes of the four indexes associated with the current update round are updated, the entire while loop executes with the condition that the head index value is less than or equal to the tail index value.

After the end of the first round of updates, the loop condition still holds, so the next round of comparison needs to be made, as shown in Fig. 10.7.

- Step 1: Compare the head node p-1 in the old set of sub-nodes with the head node p-2 in the new set of sub-nodes to see if they are the same. Since the key values of the two are different and not reusable, nothing is done

  Here, we use the new noun: head node. It refers to the node pointed to by the head indexes oldStartIdx and newStartIdx.
- Step 2: Compare the tail node p-3 in the old set of sub-nodes with the tail node p-3 in the new set of sub-nodes, both of which have the same key value and can be reused. In addition, since both are in the tail, there is no need to move the real DOM, just patch it, as shown in the following code:

```
01 while (oldStartIdx <= oldEndIdx && newStartIdx <= newEndIdx) {
02 if (oldStartVNode.key === newStartVNode.key) {
03 // Step 1: oldStartVNode vs newStartVNode
04 } else if (oldEndVNode.key === newEndVNode.key) {
05 // Step 2: oldEndVNode vs newEndVNode
06 // Node is still at the tail in the new order and does not need to be
moved, but still needs to be patched
07 patch(oldEndVNode, newEndVNode, container)
08 // Update index and variables of head and tail nodes
09 oldEndVNode = oldChildren[--oldEndIdx]
10 newEndVNode = newChildren[--newEndIdx]
11 } else if (oldStartVNode.key === newEndVNode.key) {
12 // Step 3: oldStartVNode vs newEndVNode
13 } else if (oldEndVNode.key === newStartVNode.key) {
14 // Step 4: oldEndVNode vs newStartVNode
15 patch(oldEndVNode, newStartVNode, container)
16 insert(oldEndVNode.el, container, oldStartVNode.el)
17 oldEndVNode = oldChildren[--oldEndIdx]
18 newStartVNode = newChildren[++newStartIdx]
19 }
20 }
```

After this round of updates, the status of the old and new sub-nodes and the real DOM nodes is shown in Fig. 10.8.

The order of the real DOM does not change from the previous round, because no DOM nodes are moved in this round of comparison, only p-3 nodes are patched. Next, we perform the next round of comparison according to the state shown in Fig. 10.8.

- Step 1: Compare the head node p-1 in the old set of sub-nodes with the head node p-2 in the new set of sub-nodes to see if they are the same. Since the key values of the two are different and cannot be reused, nothing is done
- Step 2: Compare the tail node p-2 in the old set of sub-nodes with the tail node p-1 in the new set of sub-nodes to see if they are the same. Since the key values of the two are different, they cannot be reused, so we do nothing

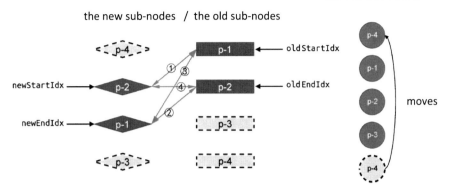

Fig. 10.8 The status of the old and new sub-nodes and the real DOM nodes

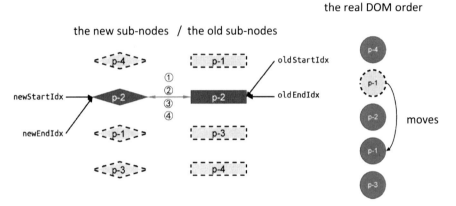

Fig. 10.9 The state of the old and new sets of sub-nodes and the real DOM nodes

• Step 3: Compare the head node p-1 in the old set of sub-nodes with the tail node p-1 in the new set of sub-nodes. Both have the same key value and can be reused

In the third step of comparison, we find the same node, which means: node p-1 was originally the head node, but in the new order, it becomes the tail node. Therefore, we need to move the real DOM corresponding to node p-1 to the old set of the tail node of the sub-node behind the real DOM corresponding to node p-2, and also need to update the corresponding index to the next position, as shown in Fig. 10.9.

The code implementation of this step is as follows:

```
01 while (oldStartIdx <= oldEndIdx && newStartIdx <= newEndIdx) {
02 if (oldStartVNode.key === newStartVNode.key) {
03 } else if (oldEndVNode.key === newEndVNode.key) {
04 patch(oldEndVNode, newEndVNode, container)
```

```
05 oldEndVNode = oldChildren[--oldEndIdx]
06 newEndVNode = newChildren[--newEndIdx]
07 } else if (oldStartVNode.key === newEndVNode.key) {
08 // Call patch function to patch between oldStartVNode and
newEndVNode
09 patch(oldStartVNode, newEndVNode, container)
10 // Move the real DOM node corresponding to the head node of the old
set of sub-nodes, oldStartVNode.el,
11 // to the real DOM node corresponding to the tail node of the old set
of sub-nodes
12 insert(oldStartVNode.el, container, oldEndVNode.el.
nextSibling)
13 // Update related index to next location
14 oldStartVNode = oldChildren[++oldStartIdx]
15 newEndVNode = newChildren[--newEndIdx]
16 } else if (oldEndVNode.key === newStartVNode.key) {
17 patch(oldEndVNode, newStartVNode, container)
18 insert(oldEndVNode.el, container, oldStartVNode.el)
19
20 oldEndVNode = oldChildren[--oldEndIdx]
21 newStartVNode = newChildren[++newStartIdx]
22 }
23 }
```

As shown in the above code, if the head node of the old set of sub-nodes matches the tail node of the new set of sub-nodes, then the real DOM node corresponding to the old node needs to be moved to the tail. Therefore, we need to get the next brother node of the current tail node as the anchor point, that is, oldEndVNode.el. nextSibling. Finally, update the relevant index to the next position.

As can be seen from Fig. 10.9, at this time, the head index and tail index of the old and new sub-nodes coincide, but still meet the conditions of the loop, so the next round of updates will be carried out. In the next round of updates, the update steps also coincide.

Step 1: Compare the head node p-2 in the old group of sub-nodes with the head node p-2 in the new group of sub-nodes. It is found that the key values of the two are the same and can be reused. But both are head nodes in the old and new groups of sub-nodes, so there is no need to move, just call the patch function to patch.

The code implementation is as follows:

```
01 while (oldStartIdx <= oldEndIdx && newStartIdx <= newEndIdx) {
02 if (oldStartVNode.key === newStartVNode.key) {
03 // Call the patch function to patch between oldStartVNode and
newStartVNode
04 patch(oldStartVNode, newStartVNode, container)
05 // Update the relevant index to the next location
06 oldStartVNode = oldChildren[++oldStartIdx]
07 newStartVNode = newChildren[++newStartIdx]
08 } else if (oldEndVNode.key === newEndVNode.key) {
09 patch(oldEndVNode, newEndVNode, container)
10 oldEndVNode = oldChildren[--oldEndIdx]
```

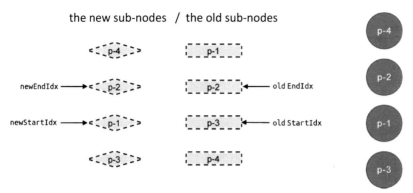

Fig. 10.10 The state of the old and new sets of sub-nodes and the real DOM nodes

```
11 newEndVNode = newChildren[--newEndIdx]
12 } else if (oldStartVNode.key === newEndVNode.key) {
13 patch(oldStartVNode, newEndVNode, container)
14 insert(oldStartVNode.el, container, oldEndVNode.el.
nextSibling)
15
16 oldStartVNode = oldChildren[++oldStartIdx]
17 newEndVNode = newChildren[--newEndIdx]
18 } else if (oldEndVNode.key === newStartVNode.key) {
19 patch(oldEndVNode, newStartVNode, container)
20 insert(oldEndVNode.el, container, oldStartVNode.el)
21
22 oldEndVNode = oldChildren[--oldEndIdx]
23 newStartVNode = newChildren[++newStartIdx]
24 }
25 }
```

After this round of updates, the status of the new and old two sets of sub-nodes and the real DOM nodes is shown in Fig. 10.10.

At this time, the order of the real DOM nodes is the same as the order of the new set of sub-nodes: p-4, p-2, p-1, p-3. In addition, after this round of updates is completed, the values of the index newStartIdx and the index oldStartIdx are both smaller than newEndIdx and oldEndIdx, so the loop terminates and the double-ended Diff algorithm is executed.

10.2   Advantages of Double-Ended Comparison

After understanding the principle of double-ended comparison, let's take a look at the advantages of double-ended Diff algorithm compared with simple Diff algorithm. Let's take the example from Chap. 9, as shown in Fig. 10.11.

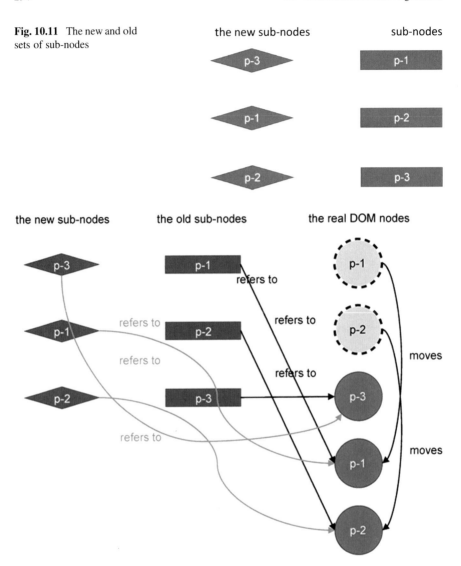

Fig. 10.11 The new and old sets of sub-nodes

Fig. 10.12 Two DOM movements

Figure 10.11 shows the node order of the new and old sets of sub-nodes. When the simple Diff algorithm is used to update this example, two DOM movement operations will occur, as shown in Fig. 10.12.

If the double-ended Diff algorithm is used to update this example, how will the performance be? Next, we complete the update of this example with the idea of double-ended comparison, and see if the double-ended Diff algorithm can reduce the number of DOM movement operations.

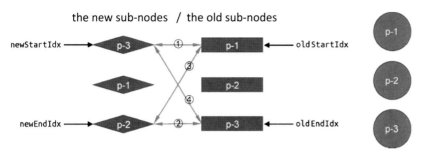

Fig. 10.13 The state of the old and new groups of sub-nodes and the real DOM nodes

Figure 10.13 shows the state of the old and new groups of sub-nodes and the real DOM nodes before the algorithm is executed.

Next, we perform the update according to the steps of double-ended comparison.

- Step 1: Compare the head node p-1 in the old group of sub-nodes with the head node p-3 in the new group of sub-nodes. The key values of the two are different and cannot be reused.
- Step 2: Compare the tail node p-3 in the old group of sub-nodes with the tail node p-2 in the new group of sub-nodes. The key values of the two are different and cannot be reused.
- Step 3: Compare the head node p-1 in the old group of sub-nodes with the tail node p-2 in the new group of sub-nodes. The key values of the two are different and cannot be reused.
- Step 4: Compare the tail node p-3 in the old set of sub-nodes with the head node p-3 in the new set of sub-nodes and find that it can be multiplexed.

As you can see, in the comparison of step 4, we found the reusable node p-3. This node was originally at the tail of all sub-nodes, but it is at the head of the new set of sub-nodes. Therefore, it is only necessary to make the real DOM corresponding to node p-3 become the new head node. After this move operation, the status of the old and new sub-nodes and the real DOM nodes is shown in Fig. 10.14.

It can be found by observing Fig. 10.14 that after this round of comparison, the order of the real DOM nodes has been aligned with the order of the new set of sub-nodes. In other words, we completed the update, but the algorithm will continue to execute. Start the next round of comparison.

Step 1: Compare the head node p-1 in the old set of sub-nodes with the head node p-1 in the new set of sub-nodes. Both have the same key value and can be reused. But since both are in the head, there is no need to move, just patch it.

After this round of comparison, the status of the new and old sub-nodes and the real DOM nodes is shown in Fig. 10.15. At this point, the double-ended Diff algorithm still does not stop and starts a new round of comparison.

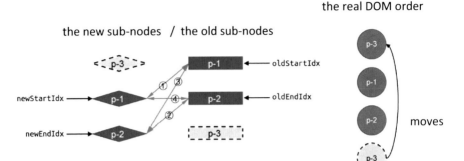

Fig. 10.14 The status of the old and new sub-nodes and the real DOM nodes

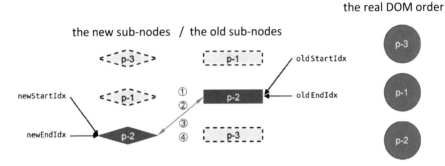

Fig. 10.15 The status of the old and new sub-nodes and the real DOM nodes

Step 1: Compare the head node p-2 in the old group of sub-nodes with the head node p-2 in the new group of sub-nodes. The key values of the two are the same and can be reused. But since both are in the head, there is no need to move, only patches are needed.

After this round of comparison, the status of the old and new sub-nodes and the real DOM nodes is shown in Fig. 10.16.

After this step, the values of the indexes newStartIdx and oldStartIdx are larger than the values of the indexes newEndIdx and oldEndIdx, so the update ends. As you can see, for the same example, the simple Diff algorithm requires two DOM moves to complete the update, while the double-ended Diff algorithm only needs one DOM move to complete the update.

10.3   Treatment of Non-ideal Conditions

In the explanation in the previous section, we used an ideal example. We know that the process of each round of comparison of the double-ended Diff algorithm is divided into four steps. In the example in the previous section, each round of

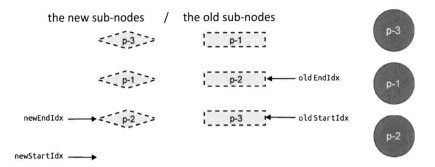

Fig. 10.16 The status of the old and new sub-nodes and the real DOM nodes

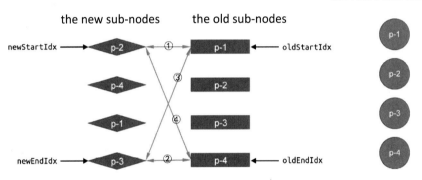

Fig. 10.17 None of the first-round comparisons hit

comparison will hit one of the four steps, which is an ideal situation. But in reality, not all cases are so ideal, as shown in Fig. 10.17.

In this example, the order of the old and new sets of sub-nodes is as follows.

- The old set of sub-nodes: p-1, p-2, p-3, p-4
- A new set of sub-nodes: p-2, p-4, p-1, p-3

When we try to perform the first round of comparison along the lines of the double-ended Diff algorithm, we will find that we cannot hit any of the four steps.

- Step 1: Compare the head node p-1 in the old set of sub-nodes with the head node p-2 in the new set of sub-nodes, which is not reusable.
- Step 2: Compare the tail node p-4 in the old set of sub-nodes with the tail node p-3 in the new set of sub-nodes, which are not reusable.
- Step 3: Compare the head node p-1 in the old set of sub-nodes with the tail node p-3 in the new set of sub-nodes, which are not reusable.

- Step 4: Compare the tail node p-4 in the old set of sub-nodes with the head node p-2 in the new set of sub-nodes, which are not reusable.

In the four-step comparison process, no reusable node can be found. What should we do? At this time, we can only deal with this non-ideal situation by adding additional processing steps. Since there are no reusable nodes in the four nodes of the two heads and two tails, let's try to see if the non-head and non-tail nodes can be reused.

```
01 while (oldStartIdx <= oldEndIdx && newStartIdx <= newEndIdx) {
02 if (oldStartVNode.key === newStartVNode.key) {
03 // omit some code
04 } else if (oldEndVNode.key === newEndVNode.key) {
05 // omit some code
06 } else if (oldStartVNode.key === newEndVNode.key) {
07 // omit some code
08 } else if (oldEndVNode.key === newStartVNode.key) {
09 // omit some code
10 } else {
11 // traverse the old set of sub-nodes, trying to find the node with the
same key value as newStartVNode
12 // idxInOld is the index of the head node of the new set of sub-nodes
in the old set of sub-nodes
13 const idxInOld = oldChildren.findIndex(
14 node => node.key === newStartVNode.key
15 )
16 }
17 }
```

In the above code, we iterate over the old set of sub-nodes, try to find the node in it that has the same key value as the head node of the new set of sub-nodes, and store the index of this node in the old set of sub-nodes in the variable idxInOld. What is the purpose of doing so? To understand this problem, we essentially need to figure out: in the old set of sub-nodes, what does it mean to find a node with the same key value as the head node of the new set of sub-nodes? As shown in Fig. 10.18.

Observing Fig. 10.18, when we take the head node p-2 of a new set of sub-nodes and look in the old set of sub-nodes, we will find the reusable node at index 1. This means that node p-2 was not originally a head node, but after updating, it should become a head node. So we need to move the real DOM node corresponding to node p-2 before the real DOM node corresponding to the head node p-1 of the current old set of sub-nodes. The specific implementation is as follows:

```
01 while (oldStartIdx <= oldEndIdx && newStartIdx <= newEndIdx) {
02 if (oldStartVNode.key === newStartVNode.key) {
03 // omit some code
04 } else if (oldEndVNode.key === newEndVNode.key) {
05 // omit some code
06 } else if (oldStartVNode.key === newEndVNode.key) {
07 // omit some code
```

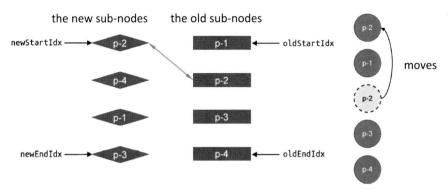

Fig. 10.18 Finding reusable nodes in old sub-nodes

```
08 } else if (oldEndVNode.key === newStartVNode.key) {
09 // omit some code
10 } else {
11 // traverse old children, trying to find owned with newStartVNode
Elements with the same key value
12 const idxInOld = oldChildren.findIndex(
13 node => node.key === newStartVNode.key
14 )
15 // idxInOld is greater than 0, indicating that a reusable node has
been found and its corresponding real DOM needs to be moved to the head
16 if (idxInOld > 0) {
17 // the vnode corresponding to the idxInOld position is the node
that needs to be moved
18 const vnodeToMove = oldChildren[idxInOld]
19 // Do not forget to remove the move operation
20 patch(vnodeToMove, newStartVNode, container)
21 // Move vnodeToMove.el in front of the head node, so use the latter
as an anchor
22 insert(vnodeToMove.el, container, oldStartVNode.el)
23 // Set it to undefined since the real DOM corresponding to the nodes
at idxInOld has been moved
24 oldChildren[idxInOld] = undefined
25 // Last, update newStartIdx to the next position
26 newStartVNode = newChildren[++newStartIdx]
27 }
28 }
29 }
```

In the above code, first determine whether idxInOld is greater than 0. If the condition is true, it means that a reusable node has been found, and then move the real DOM corresponding to the node to the head. To do this, we first need to get the node that needs to be moved. Here, the node pointed to by oldChildren [idxInOld] is the node that needs to be moved. Before moving the node, do not forget to call the

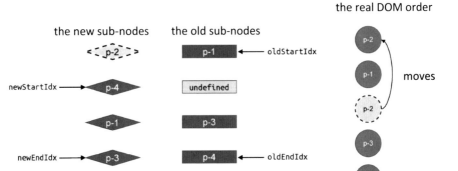

Fig. 10.19 The state of the old and new sub-nodes and the real DOM nodes

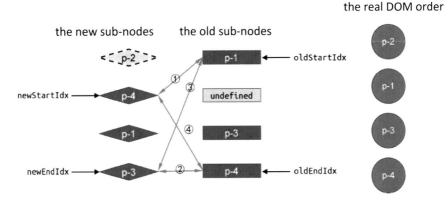

Fig. 10.20 The state of the old and new sub-nodes and the real DOM nodes

patch function to patch it. Next, call the insert function and use the real DOM node oldStartVNode.el corresponding to the current head node as the anchor parameter to complete the node movement operation. When the node movement is completed, there are two more steps to do.

- Since the node at idxInOld has already been processed (the corresponding real DOM has been moved elsewhere), we should set oldChildren [idxInOld] to undefined.
- The head nodes in the new set of sub-nodes have been processed, so newStartIdx is advanced to the next position.

After the above two steps, the state of the new and old sets of sub-nodes and the real DOM nodes is shown in Fig. 10.19.

At this time, the order of the real DOM is p-2, p-1, p-3, p-4. Then, the double-ended Diff algorithm will continue, as shown in Fig. 10.20.

- Step 1: Compare the head node p-1 in the old group of sub-nodes with the head node p-4 in the new group of sub-nodes. The key values of the two are different and cannot be reused.
- Step 2: Compare the tail node p-4 in the old group of sub-nodes with the tail node p-3 in the new group of sub-nodes. The key values of the two are different and cannot be reused.
- Step 3: Compare the head node p-1 in the old group of sub-nodes with the tail node p-3 in the new group of sub-nodes. The key values of the two are different and cannot be reused.
- Step 4: Compare the tail node p-4 in the old group of sub-nodes with the head node p-4 in the new group of sub-nodes. The key values of the two are the same and can be reused.

In the fourth step of this round of comparison, we find reusable nodes. Therefore, we move the real DOM according to the logic of the double-ended Diff algorithm, that is, move the real DOM corresponding to node p-4 to the old set of sub-nodes corresponding to the head node p-1, in front of the real DOM, as shown in Fig. 10.21.

At this point, the order of the real DOM nodes is p-2, p-4, p-1, p-3. Next, start the next round of comparison.

Step 1: Compare the head node p-1 in the old group of sub-nodes with the head node p-1 in the new group of sub-nodes. Both have the same key value and can be multiplexed.

In this round of comparison, the first step finds the reusable node. Since both are in the head, there is no need to move the real DOM, just patch it. After this step, the status of the new and old groups of sub-nodes and the real DOM nodes is shown in Fig. 10.22.

Now the order of real DOM nodes is p-2, p-4, p-1, p-3. Then, the next round of comparison is carried out. One thing to note is that the head node of the old set of sub-nodes is undefined at this time. This means that the node has already been

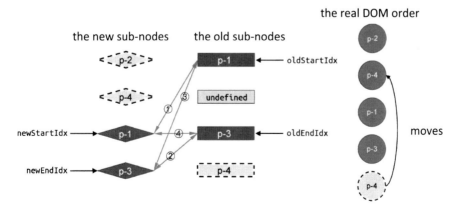

Fig. 10.21 Mobile node p-4

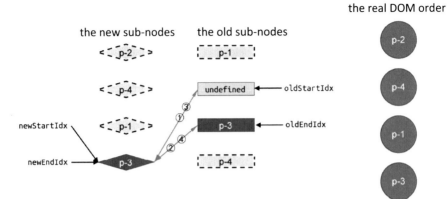

Fig. 10.22 The status of the new and old groups of sub-nodes and the real DOM nodes

processed, so there is no need to process it anymore, just skip it. To this end, we need to add this part of the logic code, the specific implementation is as follows:

```
01 while (oldStartIdx <= oldEndIdx && newStartIdx <= newEndIdx) {
02 // Add two judgment branches; if the head and tail node is undefined,
it means that the node has been processed; skip directly to the next
position
03 if (!oldStartVNode) {
04 oldStartVNode = oldChildren[++oldStartIdx]
05 } else if (!oldEndVNode) {
06 oldEndVNode = oldChildren[--oldEndIdx]
07 } else if (oldStartVNode.key === newStartVNode.key) {
08 // omit some code
09 } else if (oldEndVNode.key === newEndVNode.key) {
10 // omit some code
11 } else if (oldStartVNode.key === newEndVNode.key) {
12 // omit some code
13 } else if (oldEndVNode.key === newStartVNode.key) {
14 // omit some code
15 } else {
16 const idxInOld = oldChildren.findIndex(
17 node => node.key === newStartVNode.key
18 )
19 if (idxInOld > 0) {
20 const vnodeToMove = oldChildren[idxInOld]
21 patch(vnodeToMove, newStartVNode, container)
22 insert(vnodeToMove.el, container, oldStartVNode.el)
23 oldChildren[idxInOld] = undefined
24 newStartVNode = newChildren[++newStartIdx]
25 }
26
27 }
28 }
```

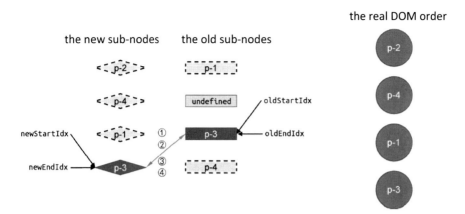

Fig. 10.23 The status of the new and old groups of sub-nodes and the real DOM nodes

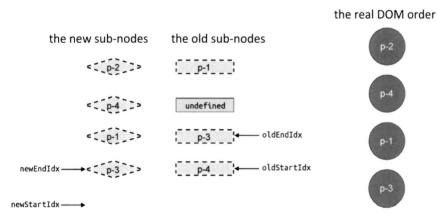

Fig. 10.24 The state of the old and new sub-nodes and the real DOM nodes

Looking at the code above. At the start of the loop, we prioritize the existence of the head and tail nodes. If they do not exist, it means that they have been processed; just jump to the next position. After this round of comparison, the status of the new and old groups of sub-nodes and the real DOM nodes is shown in Fig. 10.23.

Now the four steps are overlapped, and the final round of comparison is carried out.

Step 1: Compare the head node p-3 in the old group of sub-nodes with the head node p-3 in the new group of sub-nodes. Both have the same key value and can be reused.

In the first step, the reusable node is found. Since both are head nodes, there is no need to perform DOM movement operations; just patch it directly. After this round of comparison, the final state is shown in Fig. 10.24.

At this time, the condition of the loop stopping is satisfied, so the update is completed. Finally, the order of the real DOM nodes is the same as the order of the new set of child nodes, which are p-2, p-4, p-1, p-3.

10.4   Adding New Elements

In Sect. 10.3, we explained the handling of the non-ideal case, that is, during a round of comparison, no one of the four steps will be hit. In this case, we will take the head nodes of the new set of sub-nodes and look for reusable nodes in the old set of sub-nodes, but it is not always possible to find them, as shown in the example in Fig. 10.25.

In this example, the order of the new and old sets of sub-nodes is as follows. The old set of sub-nodes: p-1, p-2, p-3. A new set of sub-nodes: p-4, p-1, p-3, p-2.

First, we try to do the first round of comparison and find that no reusable nodes can be found in the four-step comparison. So, we try to take the head node p-4 in the new set of sub-nodes and look for nodes with the same key value in the old set of sub-nodes, but there is no p-4 node in the old set of sub-nodes at all, as shown in Fig. 10.26.

This shows that node p-4 is a new node, and we should mount it to the correct location. So where should it be mounted? Simple. Because node p-4 is the head node in the new set of sub-nodes, it only needs to be mounted before the current head node. "The current" head node refers to the real DOM node p-1 corresponding to the head nodes in the old set of sub-nodes. The following is the code used to complete the mount operation:

```
01 while (oldStartIdx <= oldEndIdx && newStartIdx <= newEndIdx) {
02 // Add two judgment branches. If the head and tail nodes are
undefined, it means that the node has been processed and jumps directly to
the next position
03 if (!oldStartVNode) {
```

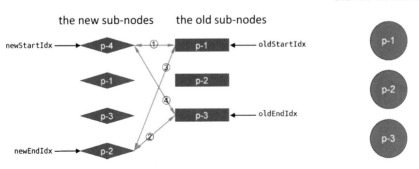

Fig. 10.25   The situation of the new nodes

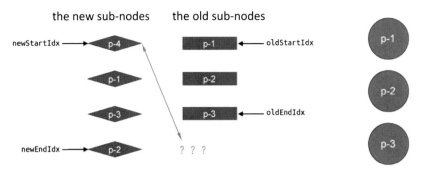

Fig. 10.26 No reusable node found in the old set of sub-nodes

```
04 oldStartVNode = oldChildren[++oldStartIdx]
05 } else if (!oldEndVNode) {
06 oldEndVNode = newChildren[--oldEndIdx]
07 } else if (oldStartVNode.key === newStartVNode.key) {
08 // omit some code
09 } else if (oldEndVNode.key === newEndVNode.key) {
10 // omit some code
11 } else if (oldStartVNode.key === newEndVNode.key) {
12 // omit some code
13 } else if (oldEndVNode.key === newStartVNode.key) {
14 // omit some code
15 } else {
16 const idxInOld = oldChildren.findIndex(
17 node => node.key === newStartVNode.key
18 )
19 if (idxInOld > 0) {
20 const vnodeToMove = oldChildren[idxInOld]
21 patch(vnodeToMove, newStartVNode, container)
22 insert(vnodeToMove.el, container, oldStartVNode.el)
23 oldChildren[idxInOld] = undefined
24 } else {
25 // make newStartVNode a new node Mount to the head and use the
current head node oldStartVNode.el as the anchor
26 patch(null, newStartVNode, container, oldStartVNode.el)
27 }
28 newStartVNode = newChildren[++newStartIdx]
29 }
30 }
```

As shown in the above code, when the condition idxInOld >0 does not hold, it means that the newStartVNode node is a brand-new node. And since the newStartVNode node is the head node, we should mount it as the new head node. So, when calling the patch function to mount the node, we use oldStartVNode.el as the anchor point. After this step is completed, the status of the new and old two sets of sub-nodes and the real DOM node is shown in Fig. 10.27.

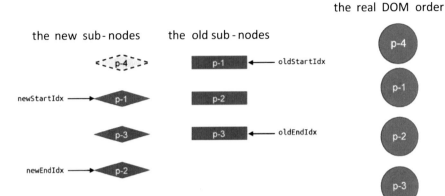

Fig. 10.27   The state of the old and new sub-nodes and the real DOM nodes

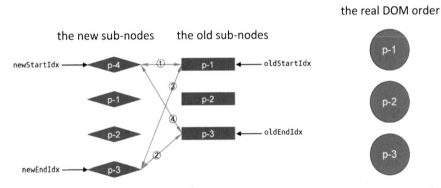

Fig. 10.28   The state of the old and new sub-nodes and the real DOM nodes

When the new node p-4 is mounted, subsequent updates will be made until all updates are completed. But is this perfect? The answer is no. Let's look at another example, as shown in Fig. 10.28.

The difference between this example and the previous example is that we adjusted the order of the new set of sub-nodes: p-4, p-1, p-2, p-3. Let's perform the update according to the idea of the double-ended Diff algorithm and see what happens.

- Step 1: Compare the head node p-1 in the old group of sub-nodes with the head node p-4 in the new group of sub-nodes. The key values of the two are different and cannot be reused.
- Step 2: Compare the tail node p-3 in the old group of sub-nodes with the tail node p-3 in the new group of sub-nodes. Both have the same key value and can be reused.

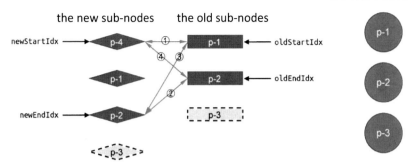

Fig. 10.29 The state of the old and new sub-nodes and the real DOM nodes

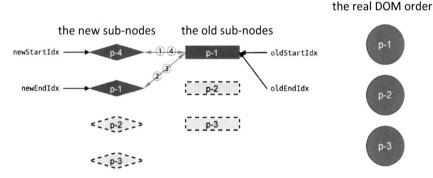

Fig. 10.30 The status of the old and new sub-nodes and the real DOM nodes

In the second step, the reusable node is found, so the update is made. The updated state of the old and new sub-nodes and the real DOM nodes is shown in Fig. 10.29. Now is the next round of comparison.

- Step 1: The head node p-1 in the old group of sub-nodes and the head node p-4 in the new group of sub-nodes have different key values and cannot be reused.
- Step 2: The tail node p-2 in the old group of sub-nodes and the tail node p-2 in the new group of sub-nodes have the same key value and can be reused.

We found the reusable node in the second step, so we updated again. The status of the old and new sub-nodes and the real DOM nodes after the update is shown in Fig. 10.30.

And then the next round of updates is carried out.

- Step 1: Compare the head node p-1 in the old group of sub-nodes with the head node p-4 in the new group of sub-nodes. The key values of the two are different and cannot be reused.

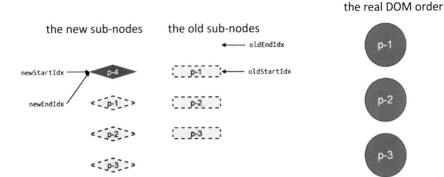

Fig. 10.31 The status of the old and new sub-nodes and the real DOM nodes

- Step 2: Compare the tail node p-1 in the old group of sub-nodes with the tail node p-1 in the new group of sub-nodes. Both have the same key value and can be reused.

We also found the reusable node in the second step and updated again. The state of the updated new and old groups of sub-nodes and the real DOM node is shown in Fig. 10.31.

After this round of update is completed, the update stops because the value of the variable oldStartIdx is greater than the value of oldEndIdx, which satisfies the condition of update stop. However, it can be seen from observation that node p-4 is missed during the whole update process and has not been processed, which shows that our algorithm is flawed. To make up for this shortcoming, we need to add extra processing code, as in the following:

```
01 while (oldStartIdx <= oldEndIdx && newStartIdx <= newEndIdx) {
02 // Omit part of the code
03 }
04
05 // Check the index value after the loop ends,
06 if (oldEndIdx < oldStartIdx && newStartIdx <= newEndIdx) {
07 // If the condition is met, there are new nodes left behind and they
need to be mounted
08 for (let i = newStartIdx; i <= newEndIdx; i++) {
09 const anchor = newChildren[newEndIdx + 1] ? newChildren
[newEndIdx + 1].el : null;
10 patch(null, newChildren[i], container, anchor);
11 }
12 }
```

We add an if conditional statement after the while loop ends to check the four index values. According to Fig. 10.31, if the condition oldEndIdx < oldStartIdx & & newStartIdx < = newEndIdx is right, it means that there are legacy nodes in the new set of child nodes that need to be mounted as new nodes. Which nodes are new nodes? Nodes with index values in the interval newStartIdx and newEndIdx are new nodes. So we start a for loop to traverse the nodes in this interval and mount them one by one. The anchor point at mount time still uses the current head node oldStartVNode.el, thus completing the processing of new elements.

10.5 Removing Non-existent Elements

After solving the problem of new nodes, let's discuss the case of removing elements, as shown in the example in Fig. 10.32.

In this example, the order of the old and new groups of sub-nodes is as follows.

- The old group of sub-nodes: p-1, p-2, p-3.
- The new group of sub-nodes: p-1, p-3.

As you can see, the p-2 node no longer exists in the new group of sub-nodes. In order to figure out how to handle the case of nodes being removed, we still perform the update along the lines of the double-ended Diff algorithm.

Step 1: Compare the head node p-1 in the old group of sub-nodes with the head node p-1 in the new group of sub-nodes. Both have the same key value and can be reused.

In the first step of comparison, the reusable node is found, so the update is performed. After this round of comparison, the status of the new and old groups of child nodes and the real DOM node is shown in Fig. 10.33.

Next, perform the next round of updates.

- Step 1: Compare the head node p-2 in the old group of sub-nodes with the head node p-3 in the new group of sub-nodes. The key values of the two are different and cannot be reused.
- Step 2: Compare the tail node p-3 in the old group of sub-nodes with the tail node p-3 in the new group of sub-nodes. Both have the same key value and can be reused.

In the second step, the reusable nodes are found, so the update is performed. The state of the updated new and old groups of sub-nodes and the real DOM nodes is shown in Fig. 10.34.

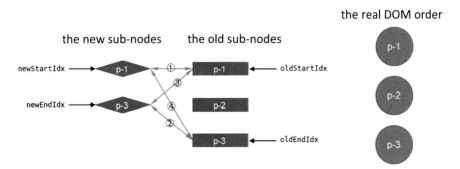

Fig. 10.32 The case of removing nodes

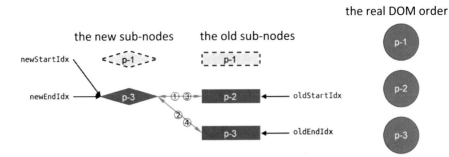

Fig. 10.33 Status of old and new sub-nodes and real DOM nodes

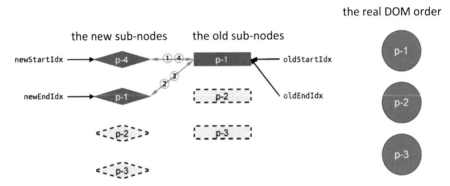

Fig. 10.34 The status of the old and new sub-nodes and the real DOM nodes

In this case, the value of the variable newStartIdx is greater than the value of the variable newEndIdx, which satisfies the condition that the update stops, so the update ends. However, observing Fig. 10.34, it can be seen that there are unprocessed nodes in the old set of sub-nodes, which should be removed. Therefore, we need to add additional code to handle it, as follows:

```
01 while (oldStartIdx <= oldEndIdx && newStartIdx <= newEndIdx) {
02 // omit some code
03 }
04
05 if (oldEndIdx < oldStartIdx && newStartIdx <= newEndIdx) {
06 // add new nodes
07 // omit some code
08 } else if (newEndIdx < newStartIdx && oldStartIdx <= oldEndIdx) {
09 // removing operation
10 for (let i = oldStartIdx; i <= oldEndIdx; i++) {
11 unmount (oldChildren[i])
12 }
13 }
```

Similar to handling new nodes, we add an *else* ... *if* branch after the *while* loop ends to unload nodes that no longer exist. As can be seen from Fig. 10.34, the nodes with index values in the interval oldStartIdx and oldEndIdx should be unloaded, so we start a for loop to unload them one by one.

10.6   Summary

In this chapter, we introduced the principle and advantages of double-ended Diff algorithms. As the name suggests, double-ended Diff algorithms refer to comparing the four endpoints of the old and new groups of sub-nodes and trying to find reusable nodes. Compared with simple Diff algorithms, the advantage of double-ended Diff algorithms is that fewer DOM moves are performed for the same update scenario.

Chapter 11
Fast Diff Algorithms

In this chapter, we will discuss a third way to compare the old and new sets of sub-nodes: the fast Diff algorithm. As the name suggests, this algorithm is very fast. This algorithm was first applied to the ivi and inferno frameworks, and Vue.js 3 draws on and extends it. Figure 11.1 compares the performance of ivi, inferno, and Vue.js 2.

Figure 11.1 is from js-framework-benchmark. It can be seen that the fast Diff algorithm used by ivi and inferno performs slightly better than the double-ended Diff algorithm used by Vue.js 2 in all aspects of DOM manipulation. Since the fast Diff algorithm is so efficient, it is necessary for us to understand its thinking. Next, we will focus on the implementation principle of the fast Diff algorithm.

11.1 Same Precondition and Postcondition Elements

Different from simple Diff algorithm and double-ended Diff algorithm, fast Diff algorithm contains preprocessing steps, which is actually borrowed from the idea of plain text Diff algorithm. In plain text Diff algorithm, there is a process of preprocessing two pieces of text. For example, before Diff two pieces of text, you can compare them congruently:

```
01 if (text1 === text2) return
```

This is also called a shortcut path. If the two pieces of text are identical, then there is no need to enter the steps of the core Diff algorithm. In addition, the preprocessing process will also process the same prefix and suffix of the two pieces of text. Suppose there are the following two paragraphs of text:

```
01 TEXT1: I use vue for app development
02 TEXT2: I use react for app development
```

© The Author(s), under exclusive license to Springer Nature Singapore Pte Ltd. 2023
H. Yang, *Vue. JS Framework*, https://doi.org/10.1007/978-981-99-4947-2_11

Fig. 11.1 Performance comparison

Name Duration for...	ivi-v0.20.0-keyed	inferno-v7.1.2-keyed	vue-v2.6.2-keyed
create rows creating 1,000 rows	118.1 ± 4.3 (1.00)	124.2 ± 3.9 (1.05)	163.1 ± 5.6 (1.38)
replace all rows updating all 1,000 rows (5 warmup runs).	123.6 ± 1.4 (1.00)	126.8 ± 11.3 (1.03)	151.6 ± 6.8 (1.23)
partial update updating every 10th row for 1,000 rows (3 warmup runs). 16x CPU slowdown.	202.7 ± 6.9 (1.00)	223.2 ± 18.8 (1.10)	336.4 ± 12.1 (1.66)
select row highlighting a selected row. (5 warmup runs). 16x CPU slowdown.	40.9 ± 2.2 (1.00)	44.0 ± 2.8 (1.08)	190.5 ± 22.2 (4.66)
swap rows swap 2 rows for table with 1,000 rows. (5 warmup runs). 4x CPU slowdown.	67.5 ± 3.4 (1.00)	67.4 ± 4.1 (1.00)	97.4 ± 4.2 (1.44)
remove row removing one row. (5 warmup runs).	50.1 ± 0.8 (1.04)	48.1 ± 0.6 (1.00)	57.7 ± 1.3 (1.20)
create many rows creating 10,000 rows	1,147.1 ± 25.8 (1.00)	1,185.1 ± 65.7 (1.03)	1,385.4 ± 50.5 (1.21)
append rows to large table appending 1,000 to a table of 10,000 rows. 2x CPU slowdown	310.0 ± 4.3 (1.08)	286.1 ± 4.8 (1.00)	380.4 ± 4.9 (1.33)
clear rows clearing a table with 1,000 rows. 8x CPU slowdown	137.1 ± 5.5 (1.00)	162.2 ± 5.1 (1.18)	230.1 ± 5.8 (1.68)
slowdown geometric mean	1.01	1.05	1.58

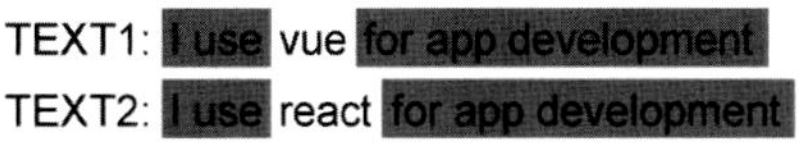

Fig. 11.2 Text preprocessing

TEXT1: I use vue for app development
TEXT2: I use react for app development

It can be easily found by the naked eyes that the head and tail of these two paragraphs of text have the same content, as shown in Fig. 11.2.

Figure 11.2 highlights the same content in TEXT1 and TEXT2. For problems with the same content, there is no need for core diff manipulation. So, for TEXT1 and TEXT2, the part that really needs to diff is as follows:

```
01 TEXT1: vue
02 TEXT2: react
```

This is actually a way to simplify the problem. The advantage of this is that we can easily determine the insertion and deletion of text under certain circumstances, for example:

```
01 TEXT1: I like you
02 TEXT2: I like you too
```

After preprocessing, remove the same prefix and suffix content in these two pieces of text, it will become

```
01 TEXT1:
02 TEXT2: too
```

You can see that after preprocessing, the content of TEXT1 is empty. This shows that TEXT2 adds the string too on the basis of TEXT1. Instead, we can also swap the positions of the two texts:

```
01 TEXT1: I like you too
02 TEXT2: I like you
```

The two texts will become

```
01 TEXT1: too
02 TEXT2:
```

It can be seen that TEXT2 deletes the string *too* on the basis of TEXT1. The fast Diff algorithm borrows from the preprocessing steps of the plain text Diff algorithm. Take the two sets of sub-nodes shown in Fig. 11.3 as an example.

The order of these two sets of sub-nodes is as follows.

- The old set of sub-nodes: p-1, p-2, p-3.
- The new set of sub-nodes: p-1, p-4, p-2, p-3.

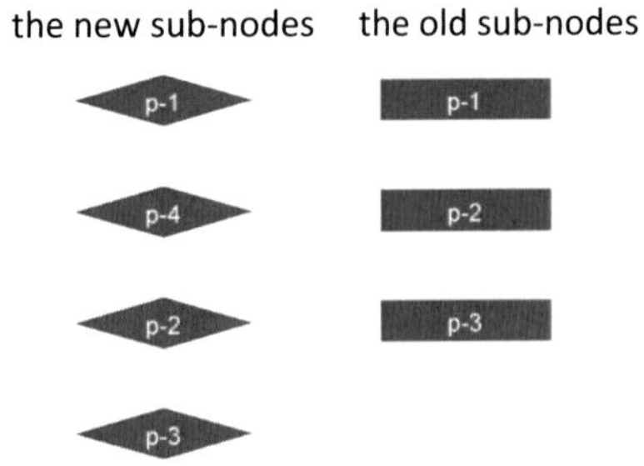

Fig. 11.3 The new and old
sets of sub-nodes

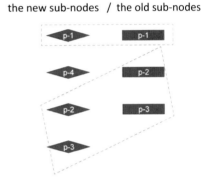

Fig. 11.4 The same pre-
and post-nodes

Fig. 11.5 Create an index J
pointing to the beginning of
two sets of sub-nodes

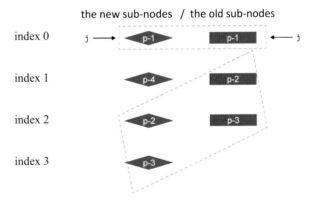

By observation, it can be found that the two sets of sub-nodes have the same pre-node p-1, and the identical post-nodes p-2 and p-3, as shown in Fig. 11.4.

For identical pre- and post-nodes, since their relative positions in the old and new sets of sub-nodes do not change, we do not need to move them, but still need to patch between them.

For the pre-nodes, we can create an index j with an initial value of 0, which is used to point to the beginning of the two sets of sub-nodes, as shown in Fig. 11.5.

Then, start a while loop, so that the index j is incremented until a different node is encountered, as shown in the code of the patchKeyedChildren function below:

Fig. 11.6 The state after the previous node is processed

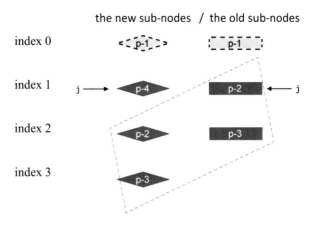

the new sub-nodes / the old sub-nodes

index 0

index 1

index 2

index 3

```
01 function patchKeyedChildren(n1, n2, container) {
02 const newChildren = n2.children
03 const oldChildren = n1.children
04 // handle the same pre- node
05 // index j points to the beginning of the old and new sets of
sub-nodes
06 let j = 0
07 let oldVNode = oldChildren[j]
08 let newVNode = newChildren[j]
09 // while loop traverses backwards until it encounters a node with a
different key value
10 while (oldVNode.key === newVNode.key) {
11 // call patch function to update
12 patch(oldVNode, newVNode, container)
13 // update index j and let it increment
14 j++
15 oldVNode = oldChildren[j]
16 newVNode = newChildren[j]
17 }
18
19 }
```

In the above code, we use the while loop to find all the same predecessor nodes, and call the patch function to patch until we encounter nodes with different key values. In this way, we have completed the update of the predecessor nodes. After the new operation, the state of the new and old sets of sub-nodes is shown in Fig. 11.6.

It should be noted here that when the while loop terminates, the index j has a value of 1. Next, we need to deal with the same, post-nodes. Since the number of sub-nodes in the old and new groups may be different, we need two indexes, newEnd and oldEnd, pointing to the last node in the old and new groups of sub-nodes, respectively, as shown in Fig. 11.7.

Fig. 11.7 Indexing and pointing to the last node of the two sets of sub-nodes

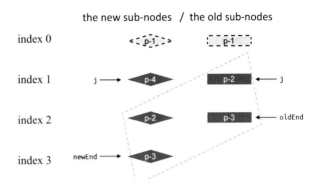

Then, start a while loop and traversing the two sets of sub-nodes backwards and forwards until a node with a different key value is encountered, as shown in the following code:

```
01 function patchKeyedChildren(n1, n2, container) {
02 const newChildren = n2.children
03 const oldChildren = n1.children
04 // Update the same pre- node
05 let j = 0
06 let oldVNode = oldChildren[j]
07 let newVNode = newChildren[j]
08 while (oldVNode.key === newVNode.key) {
09 patch(oldVNode, newVNode, container)
10 j++
11 oldVNode = oldChildren[j]
12 newVNode = newChildren[j]
13 }
14
15 // update the same postnode
16 // index oldEnd points to the last node of the old set of sub-nodes
17 let oldEnd = oldChildren.length - 1
18 // index newEnd points to the last node of the new set of sub-nodes
19 let newEnd = newChildren.length - 1
20
21 oldVNode = oldChildren[oldEnd]
22 newVNode = newChildren[newEnd]
23
24 // while loop traverses backwards and forwards until it encounters
a node with a different key value
25 while (oldVNode.key === newVNode.key) {
26 // Call the patch function to update
27 patch(oldVNode, newVNode, container)
28 // Decrement oldEnd and nextEnd
29 oldEnd--
30 newEnd--
31 oldVNode = oldChildren[oldEnd]
32 newVNode = newChildren[newEnd]
```

Fig. 11.8 Status after processing post-nodes

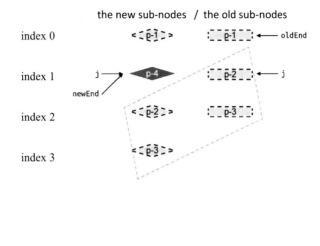

```
33 }
34
35 }
```

Just like dealing with the same predecessor node, in the while loop, you need to call the patch function to patch, and then decrement the values of the two indexes oldEnd and newEnd. After this update operation, the status of the new and old two sets of sub-nodes is shown in Fig. 11.8.

From Fig. 11.8, it can be seen that when the same pre-node and post-node are processed, the old group of sub-nodes has all been processed, and in the new group of sub-nodes, there is still an unprocessed node p-4. In fact, it is not difficult to find that node p-4 is a new node. So, how can we use the program to draw the conclusion that "node p-4 is a new node"? This requires us to observe the relationship between three indexes j, newEnd, and oldEnd.

- Condition 1 oldEnd < j holds: indicating that during the preprocessing process, all old sub-nodes have been processed.
- Condition 2 newEnd >= j holds: indicating that after the preprocessing, there are still unprocessed nodes in the new set of sub-nodes, and these legacy nodes will be regarded as new nodes.

If condition 1 and condition 2 are true at the same time, it means that there are legacy nodes in the new set of sub-nodes, and these nodes are new nodes. Therefore, we need to mount them to the correct position, as shown in Fig. 11.9.

In the case of newly added nodes in the new set of sub-nodes, any node whose index value is between j and newEnd needs to be mounted as a new sub-node. So, how should these nodes be mounted to the correct position? This requires us to find the correct anchor element. Looking at the new set of sub-nodes in Fig. 11.9, we can see that the new node should be mounted in front of the real DOM corresponding to node p-2. Therefore, the real DOM node corresponding to node p-2 is the anchor element of the mount operation. With these information, we can give the detail code implementation, as shown below:

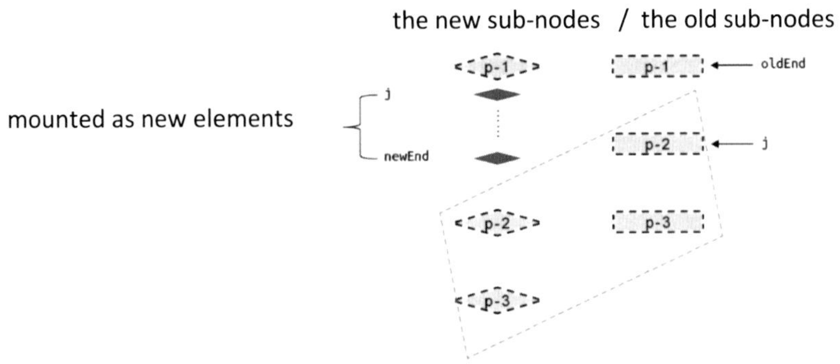

the new sub-nodes / the old sub-nodes

Fig. 11.9 Conditions of new nodes

```
01 function patchKeyedChildren(n1, n2, container) {
02 const newChildren = n2.children
03 const oldChildren = n1.children
04 // Update the same pre-node
05 // omit some code
06
07 // Update the same post-node
08 // omit some code
09
10 // After preprocessing, if the following conditions are met, the
node between j--> newEnd should be inserted as a new node
11 if (j > oldEnd && j <= newEnd) {
12 // anchor index
13 const anchorIndex = newEnd + 1
14 // anchor element
15 const anchor = anchorIndex < newChildren.length ? newChildren
[anchorIndex].el : null
16 // Using a while loop, call the patch function to mount new nodes one
by one
17 while (j <= newEnd) {
18 patch(null, newChildren[j++], container, anchor)
19 }
20 }
21
22 }
```

In the above code, the index value of the anchor point (that is, anchorIndex) is first calculated as newEnd +1. If it is less than the number of new sub-nodes, it means that the anchor element is in a new set of sub-nodes, so use newChildren [anchorIndex].el as the anchor element directly; otherwise, the node corresponding to the index newEnd is already a tail node, and there is no need to provide an anchor element. With the anchor element, we start a while loop to traverse the nodes between index j and index newEnd, and call the patch function to mount them.

The above example shows the case of adding new nodes. Let's take a look at the case of deleting nodes, as shown in Fig. 11.10.

Fig. 11.10 Delete nodes

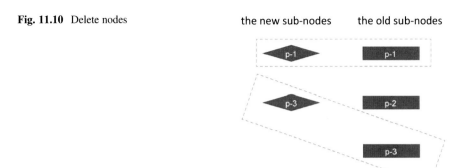

Fig. 11.11 In the case of deleting nodes, the relationship of indexes

In this example, the order of the new and old two sets of sub-nodes is as follows:

- The old set of sub-nodes: p-1, p-2, p-3.
- The new set of sub-nodes: p-1, p-3.

We also use indices j, oldEnd, and newEnd to mark, as shown in Fig. 11.11.

Next, the same predecessor node is preprocessed, and the processed state is shown in Fig. 11.12.

Then, the same post-node is preprocessed, and the processed state is shown in Fig. 11.13.

From Fig. 11.13, it can be seen that when the same pre-node and post-node are all processed, the new set of sub-nodes has all been processed, and the old set of sub-nodes has left a node p-2. This means that node p-2 should be uninstalled. In fact, there may be multiple remaining nodes, as shown in Fig. 11.14.

Any node between index j and index oldEnd should be unloaded as follows:

```
01 function patchKeyedChildren(n1, n2, container) {
02 const newChildren = n2.children
03 const oldChildren = n1.children
04 // update the same pre-node
```

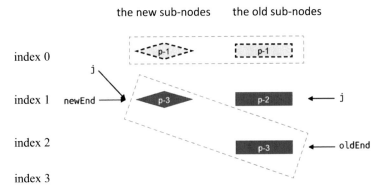

Fig. 11.12 After the pre-node is processed, the relationship of indexes

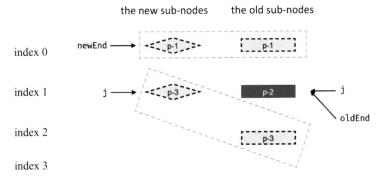

Fig. 11.13 After the post-node is processed, the relationship of indexes

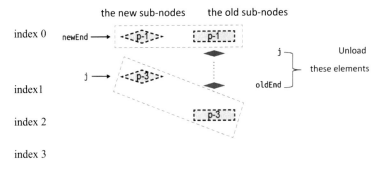

Fig. 11.14 There may be multiple legacy nodes

```
05 // omit part of the code
06
07 // update the same postnode
08 // omit part of the code
09
10 if (j > oldEnd && j <= newEnd) {
11 // omit part of the code
12 } else if (j > newEnd && j <= oldEnd) {
13 // Nodes between j -> oldEnd should be unmounted
14 while (j <= oldEnd) {
15 unmount(oldChildren[j++])
16 }
17 }
18
19 }
```

In the above code, we add an else … if branch. When the condition $j > newEnd$ & & $j < = oldEnd$ is satisfied, a while loop is opened and the unmount function is called to unmount these legacy nodes one by one.

11.2 Determining Whether DOM Movement Operation Is Required

In the previous section, we explained the preprocessing process of the fast Diff algorithm, that is, to deal with the same pre- and post-nodes. However, the example given in the previous section is idealized. After processing the same pre-node or post-node, there will always be a group of sub-nodes in the old and new groups. In this case, you only need to simply mount and unload nodes. However, the situation is more complicated, as shown in the example given in Fig. 11.15.

In this example, the order of the old and new groups of sub-nodes is as follows.

Fig. 11.15 New and old two sets of sub-nodes in the complex case

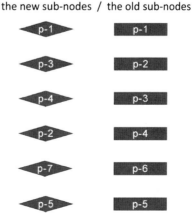

Fig. 11.16 In the complex
case, there are only a few
identical pre- and post-
nodes

the new sub-nodes / the old sub-nodes

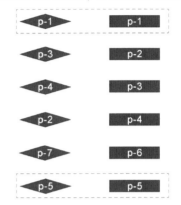

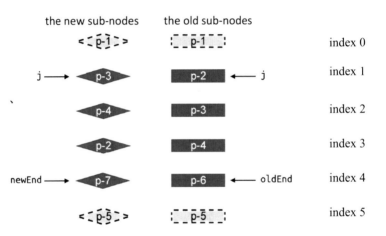

Fig. 11.17 Status after processing the pre-node and post-node

- The old set of sub-nodes: p-1, p-2, p-3, p-4, p-6, p-5.
- The new set of sub-nodes: p-1, p-3, p-4, p-2, p-7, p-5.

It can be seen that compared with the old set of sub-nodes, the new set of sub-nodes has one more node p-7 and lacks one node p-6. This example is not as idealistic as the example given in the previous section, and we cannot simply complete the update through the preprocessing process. In this example, the same pre-node has only p-1, while the same post-node has only p-5, as shown in Fig. 11.16.

Figure 11.17 shows the state of the two sets of sub-nodes after preprocessing.

You can see that after preprocessing, some nodes are not processed, whether it is a new group of sub-nodes or an old group of sub-nodes. At this time, we need further processing. How to deal with it? In fact, whether it is a simple Diff algorithm, a double-ended Diff algorithm, or a fast Diff algorithm introduced in this chapter, they all follow the same processing rules:

- Determine whether a node needs to move, and how it should move
- Find out which nodes need to be added or removed

So, our next task is to determine which nodes need to move, and how to move. Figure 11.17 shows that in this non-ideal situation, when the same pre- and post-nodes are processed, the indexes j, newEnd, and oldEnd do not satisfy either of the following two conditions:

- $j > oldEnd \ \& \ \& \ j < = newEnd$
- $j > newEnd \ \& \ \& \ j < = oldEnd$

Therefore, we need to add a new *else* branch to handle the situation shown in Fig. 11.17, as shown in the following code:

```
01 function patchKeyedChildren(n1, n2, container) {
02 const newChildren = n2.children
03 const oldChildren = n1.children
04 // update the same prefix
05 // omit some code
06
07 // update the same postfix
08 // omit some code
09
10 if (j > oldEnd && j <= newEnd) {
11 // omit some code
12 } else if (j > newEnd && j <= oldEnd) {
13 // omit some code
14 } else {
15 // Add an else branch to handle non-ideal cases
16 }
17
18 }
```

Subsequent processing logic will be written in this else branch. Knowing where to write processing code, let's explain the specific processing ideas. First, we need to construct an array source whose length is equal to the number of unprocessed nodes left in the new set of sub-nodes after preprocessing, and whose initial value for each element in source is −1, as shown in Fig. 11.18.

We can complete the construction of the source array with the following code:

```
01 if (j > oldEnd && j <= newEnd) {
02 // omit some code
03 } else if (j > newEnd && j <= oldEnd) {
04 // omit some code
05 } else {
06 // Construct the source array
07 // The number of remaining unprocessed nodes in the new set of
sub-nodes
```

```
08 const count = newEnd - j + 1
09 const source = new Array(count)
10 source.fill(-1)
11 }
```

As shown in the code above. First, we need to calculate the number of remaining unprocessed nodes in the new set of sub-nodes, which is newEnd - j + 1, then create an array source of the same length, and finally use the fill function to complete the filling of the array. So, what is the role of the array source? Looking at Fig. 11.18, we can see that each element in the array source corresponds to the remaining unprocessed nodes in the new set of sub-nodes. In fact, the source array will be used to store the position index of the nodes of the new set of sub-nodes in the old set of sub-nodes, which will be used later to calculate the longest incrementing subsequence and used to assist in the DOM movement operation, as shown in Fig. 11.19.

Figure 11.19 shows the process of filling the source array. Since the source array stores the position index of the new sub-node in the old set of sub-nodes, there are as follows:

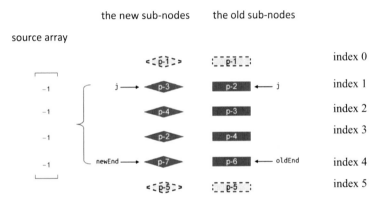

Fig. 11.18 Constructing the source array

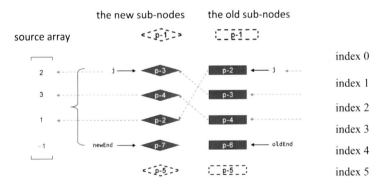

Fig. 11.19 Filling the source array

- node p-3 in the new set of sub-nodes has an index of 2 in the old set of sub-nodes, so the first element of the source array has a value of 2
- node p-4 in the new set of sub-nodes has an index of 3 in the old set of sub-nodes, so the second element of the source array has a value of 3
- node p-2 in the new set sub-node has an index of 1 in the old group of sub-nodes, so the third element of the source array has a value of 1
- node p-7 in the new group of sub-nodes is special because there is no node equal to its key value in the old group of sub-nodes, so the fourth element value of the source array retains the original −1

We can fill the source array with two layers of *for* loops; the outer loop is used to traverse the old set of child nodes, and the inner loop is used to traverse the new set of sub-nodes:

```
01 if (j > oldEnd && j <= newEnd) {
02 // omit some code
03 } else if (j > newEnd && j <= oldEnd) {
04 // omit some code
05 } else {
06 const count = newEnd - j + 1
07 const source = new Array(count)
08 source.fill(-1)
09
10 // oldStart and newStart are the starting indexes respectively,
i.e. j
11 const oldStart = j
12 const newStart = j
13 // Traverse an old set of sub-nodes
14 for (let i = oldStart; i <= oldEnd; i++) {
15 const oldVNode = oldChildren[i]
16 // Traverse a new set of sub-nodes
17 for (let k = newStart; k <= newEnd; k++) {
18 const newVNode = newChildren[k]
19 // find a reusable node with the same key value
20 if (oldVNode.key === newVNode.key) {
21 // call patch to update
22 patch(oldVNode, newVNode, container)
23 // Finally fill the source array
24 source[k - newStart] = i
25 }
26 }
27 }
28 }
```

It should be noted here that since the index of the array source starts from 0, and the index of the unprocessed node does not necessarily start from 0, the value of the expression k - newStart needs to be used as the index value of the array when filling the array. The variable i in the outer loop is the position index of the current node in the old set of sub-nodes, so directly assign the value of variable i to source [k - newStart].

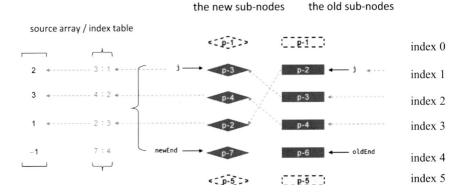

Fig. 11.20 Use the index table to populate the source array

Now that the source array has been filled; we will use it later. But before we go any further, we need to think about the problem with the code used to fill the source array above. In this code, we use two layers of nested loops with a time complexity of O (n1 * n2), where n1 and n2 are the number of new and old two sets of sub-nodes. We can also use O (n ^ 2) to represent. When the number of new and old two sets of sub-nodes is large, two layers of nested loops will cause performance problems. For optimization purposes, we can build an index table for a new set of sub-nodes to store the mapping between the node's key and the node location index, as shown in Fig. 11.20.

With the index table, we can use it to quickly populate the source array, as shown in the following code:

```
01 if (j > oldEnd && j <= newEnd) {
02 // omit some code
03 } else if (j > newEnd && j <= oldEnd) {
04 // omit some code
05 } else {
06 const count = newEnd - j + 1
07 const source = new Array(count)
08 source.fill(-1)
09
10 // oldStart and newStart are the starting indexes respectively,
i.e. j
11 const oldStart = j
12 const newStart = j
13 // build index table
14 const keyIndex = {}
15 for(let i = newStart; i <= newEnd; i++) {
16 keyIndex[newChildren[i].key] = i
17 }
18 // traverse the remaining unprocessed nodes in the old set of
sub-nodes
19 for(let i = oldStart; i <= oldEnd; i++) {
```

```
20 oldVNode = oldChildren[i]
21 // Quickly find the node positions with the same key value in the new
set of sub-nodes through the index table
22 const k = keyIndex[oldVNode.key]
23
24 if (typeof k !== 'undefined') {
25 newVNode = newChildren[k]
26 // Call the patch function to complete the update
27 patch(oldVNode, newVNode, container)
28 // fill the source array
29 source[k - newStart] = i
30 } else {
31 // not found
32 unmount(oldVNode)
33 }
34 }
35 }
```

In the above code, two *for* loops are also used, but they are no longer a nested relationship, so the time complexity of the code can be reduced to O (n). Among them, the first *for* loop is used to build the index table, which stores the mapping between the node's key value and the node's position index in the new set of sub-nodes, and the second for loop is used to traverse the old set of sub-nodes. As you can see, we take the key value of the old sub-node to the index table keyIndex to find the position of the node in the new set of sub-nodes, and store the search result in a variable k. If k exists, it means that the node is reusable, so we call the patch function to patch and fill the source array; otherwise, it means that the node no longer exists in the new set of sub-nodes. At this time, we need to call the unmount function to unmount it.

After the above process is completed, the source array has been filled. Next, we should think about how to determine whether the node needs to be moved. In fact, the fast Diff algorithm determines whether a node needs to move in a similar way to the simple Diff algorithm, as shown in the following code:

```
01 if (j > oldEnd && j <= newEnd) {
02 // omit some code
03 } else if (j > newEnd && j <= oldEnd) {
04 // omit some code
05 } else {
06 // Construct the source array
07 const count = newEnd - j + 1 // number of remaining unprocessed
nodes in new set of sub-nodes
08 const source = new Array(count)
09 source.fill(-1)
10
11 const oldStart = j
12 const newStart = j
13 // add two variables, moved and pos
14 let moved = false
15 let pos = 0
```

```
16
17 const keyIndex = {}
18 for(let i = newStart; i <= newEnd; i++) {
19 keyIndex[newChildren[i].key] = i
20 }
21 for(let i = oldStart; i <= oldEnd; i++) {
22 oldVNode = oldChildren[i]
23 const k = keyIndex[oldVNode.key]
24
25 if (typeof k !== 'undefined') {
26 newVNode = newChildren[k]
27 patch(oldVNode, newVNode, container)
28 source[k - newStart] = i
29 // Determine if the node needs to be moved
30 if (k < pos) {
31 moved = true
32 } else {
33 pos = k
34 }
35 } else {
36 unmount(oldVNode)
37 }
38 }
39 }
```

In the above code, we added two variables moved and pos. The initial value of the former is false, representing whether the mobile node is needed, and the initial value of the latter is 0, representing the maximum index value k encountered in the process of traversing the old set of sub-nodes. We mentioned in the simple Diff algorithm that if the index value encountered during the traversal shows an increasing trend, it means that the mobile node is not needed, and the reverse is needed. So, in the second for loop, we judge whether the mobile node is needed by comparing the value of the variable k with the variable pos.

In addition to this, we also need a quantity identifier representing the number of nodes that have been updated. We know that the number of nodes that have been updated should be less than the number of nodes that need to be updated in the new set of sub-nodes. Once the former exceeds the latter, it means that there are redundant nodes, we should unload them, as shown in the following code:

```
01 if (j > oldEnd && j <= newEnd) {
02 // omit some code
03 } else if (j > newEnd && j <= oldEnd) {
04 // omit some code
05 } else {
06 // construct the source array
07 const count = newEnd - j + 1
08 const source = new Array(count)
09 source.fill(-1)
10
11 const oldStart = j
```

```
12 const newStart = j
13 let moved = false
14 let pos = 0
15 const keyIndex = {}
16 for (let i = newStart; i <= newEnd; i++) {
17 keyIndex[newChildren[i].key] = i
18 }
19 // Add patched variable representing the number of nodes updated
20 let patched = 0
21 for (let i = oldStart; i <= oldEnd; i++) {
22 oldVNode = oldChildren[i]
23 // If the number of nodes updated is less than or equal to the number
of nodes that need to be updated, update
24 if (patched <= count) {
25 const k = keyIndex[oldVNode.key]
26 if (typeof k !== 'undefined') {
27 newVNode = newChildren[k]
28 patch(oldVNode, newVNode, container)
29 // each time a node is updated, add + 1 to patched variable
30 patched++
31 source[k - newStart] = i
32 if (k < pos) {
33 moved = true
34 } else {
35 pos = k
36 }
37 } else {
38 // not found
39 unmount(oldVNode)
40 }
41 } else {
42 // If the number of nodes updated is greater than the number of nodes
that need to be updated, unmount the redundant nodes
43 unmount(oldVNode)
44 }
45 }
46 }
```

In the above code, we add the patched variable, whose initial value is 0, which represents the number of nodes updated. Then, in the second *for* loop, we add the judgment patched < = count. If this condition is true, the update is performed normally, and the variable patched is incremented after each update; otherwise, the remaining nodes are redundant, so call the unmount function to unmount them.

Now, by judging the value of the variable moved, we have been able to know whether we need to move the node, and also deal with a lot, boundary conditions. Next, we discuss how to move the node.

11.3   How to Move Elements

In the previous section, we achieved two goals.

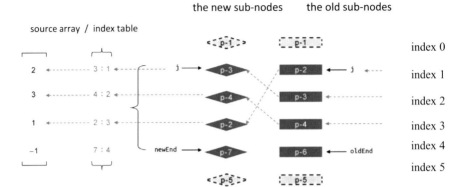

Fig. 11.21 An example of calculating the incrementing subsequence of the source array

- Determined whether a DOM move operation was required. We created the variable moved as an identifier. When its value is true, it indicates that a DOM move operation is required.
- Built the source array. The length of this array is equal to the number of remaining unprocessed nodes after a new set of sub-nodes removes the same pre/post nodes. The source array stores the positions of the nodes of the new set of sub-nodes in the old set of sub-nodes. Later we will calculate the longest incrementing subsequence based on the source array for DOM move operations.

Next, we will discuss how to do the DOM move operation, as shown in the following code:

```
01 if (j > oldEnd && j <= newEnd) {
02 // omit part of the code
03 } else if (j > newEnd && j <= oldEnd) {
04 // omit part of the code
05 } else {
06 // omit part of the code
07 for(let i = oldStart; i <= oldEnd; i++) {
08 // omit part of the code
09 }
10
11 if (moved) {
12 // If moved is true, we need to do a DOM move operation
13 }
14 }
```

In the above code, we added an *if* branch after the *for* loop. If the variable *moved* evaluates to true, the DOM move operation is required, so the logic for the DOM move operation is written inside the *if* block.

To perform the DOM move operation, we first compute its longest incrementing subsequence from the source array. The source array still takes the example given in Sect. 11.2, as shown in Fig. 11.21.

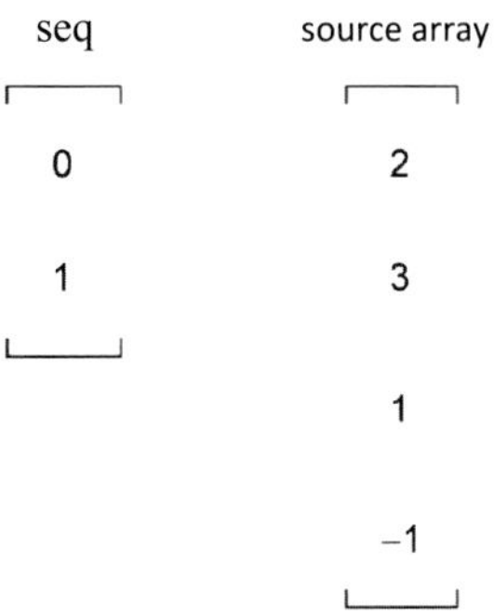

Fig. 11.22 The
incrementing subsequence
stores the position index of
the elements in the source
array

seq	source array
0	2
1	3
	1
	−1

In this example, we calculate the source array as $[2, 3, 1, -1]$. So, what is the longest incrementing subsequence of this array? This requires us to understand the concept of the longest incrementing subsequence. To do this, we must first figure out what is a sequence of incrementing subsequences. Simply put, given a sequence of values, find one of its subsequences, and the values in the subsequence are increasing. The elements in the subsequence are not necessarily continuous in the original sequence. A sequence may have many increasing subsequences, and the longest one is called the longest increasing subsequence. For example, given a sequence of values $[0, 8, 4, 12]$, its longest increasing subsequence is $[0, 8, 12]$. Of course, for the same numeric sequence, there may be multiple longest incrementing subsequences, and $[0, 4, 12]$ is also one of the answers in this example.

Understanding what the longest incrementing subsequence is, we can then solve for the longest incrementing subsequence of the source array, as shown in the following code:

```
01 if (moved) {
02 //Calculate the longest incrementing subsequence
03 const seq = lis (sources ) // [ 0,1]
04 }
```

In the above code, we use the lis function to calculate the longest incrementing subsequence of an array. The lis function takes an array of sources as an argument and returns one of the longest incrementing subsequences of the source array. In the example above, you may be wondering why the value calculated by the lis function is $[0, 1]$? In fact, the longest incrementing subsequence of the source array $[2, 3, 1, -1]$ should be $[2, 3]$, but we get $[0, 1]$, why? This is because the lis function returns the position index of the element in the source array of the longest incrementing subsequence, as shown in Fig. 11.22.

Because the longest incrementing subsequence of the source array is $[2, 3]$, where the index of element 2 in the array is 0, and the index of array 3 in the array is 1, the final result is $[0, 1]$.

With the index information for the longest incrementing subsequence, the next step is to renumber the nodes, as shown in Fig. 11.23.

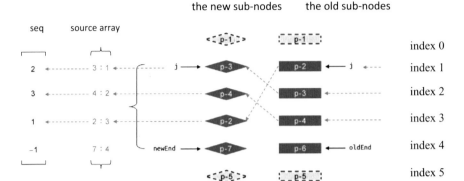

Fig. 11.23 Status after renumbering the nodes

Observing Fig. 11.23, when numbering, we ignore the preprocessed nodes p-1 and p-5. So, the node with index 0 is p-2, the node with index 1 is p-3, and so on. Renumbering is to make the subsequence seq correspond to the new index value. In fact, the longest incrementing subsequence seq has a very important meaning. In the above example, the value of the subsequence seq is [0,1], which means that in a new set of sub-nodes, the two nodes with index values 0 and 1 are updated after renumbering, and the order has not changed. In other words, after renumbering, the nodes with index values 0 and 1 do not need to move. In the new set of sub-nodes, node p-3 has an index of 0 and node p-4 has an index of 1, so the real DOM corresponding to nodes p-3 and p-4 does not need to be moved. In other words, only nodes p-2 and p-7 may need to be moved.

In order to complete the node movement, we also need to create two index values i and s:

- Index i points to the last node in the new set of sub-nodes
- Index s points to the last element in the longest incrementing subsequence

As shown in Fig. 11.24.

Observing Fig. 11.24, to simplify the illustration, we have removed the old set of sub-nodes and extraneous lines and variables. Next, we will start a *for* loop and move the variables i and s in the direction of the arrows in Fig. 11.24, as shown in the following code:

```
01 if (moved) {
02 const seq = lis(sources)
03
04 // s points to the last element of the longest incrementing
subsequence
05 let s = seq.length - 1
06 // i points to the last element of a new set of sub-nodes
07 let i = count - 1
08 // for cycle such that i is decremented, i.e. moving in the
direction of the arrow in FIG. 11-24
```

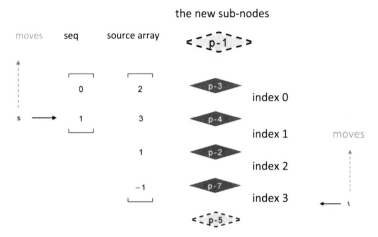

Fig. 11.24 Create indexes s and i pointing to the last position of the sequence and index, respectively

```
09 for (i; i >= 0; i--) {
10 if (i !== seq[s]) {
11 // If the index i of the node is not equal to the value of seq [s], it
means that the node needs to move
12 } else {
13 // When i === seq [s] , it means that the node at this position does
not need to move
14 // just need to make the s point to the next position
15 s--
16 }
17 }
18 }
```

The purpose of the loop is to make the variable i moves according to the direction of the arrow in Fig. 11.24, so that the nodes in a new set of sub-nodes can be accessed one by one, where the variable i is the index of the node. Inside the *for* loop, determine the condition i! == seq [s]; if the index i of the node is not equal to the value of seq [s], it means that the real DOM corresponding to the node needs to be moved, otherwise it means that the node of the current visit does not need to be moved, but then the variable's needs to be moved in the direction of the arrow in Fig. 11.24, that is, the variable s needs to be decremented.

Next, we perform the update according to the above idea. Initially, the index i points to node p-7. Since the element at the same position in the source array corresponding to node p-7 is −1, we should mount node p-7 as a brand-new node, as shown in the following code:

```
01 if (moved) {
02 const seq = lis (sources)
```

```
03
04 // s points to the last element of the longest incrementing
subsequence
05 let s = seq.length - 1
06 // //i points to the last element of the new set of sub-nodes
07 let i = count - 1
08 // for loop so that i is decremented, that is, move in the direction
of the arrow in Figure 11-24
09 for (i; i >= 0; i--) {
10 if (source[i] === -1) {
11 // Indicates that the node with index i is a brand new node and
should be mounted
12 // The index of the node's true position in the new children
13 const pos = i + newStart
14 const newVNode = newChildren[pos]
15 // position index of the next node of this node
16 const nextPos = pos + 1
17 // anchor
18 const anchor = nextPos < newChildren.length
19 ? newChildren[nextPos].el
20 : null
21 // mount
22 patch(null, newVNode, container, anchor)
23 } else if (i !== seq[s]) {
24 // If the index i of a node is not equal to the value of seq[s], it
means that the node needs to move
25 } else {
26 // When i === seq[s], it means that the node at this position does
not need to move
27 // Just let s point to the next position
28 s--
29 }
30 }
31 }
```

If the value of source [i] is −1, it means that the node with index i is a brand-new node, so we call the patch function to mount it into the container. It should be noted here that since the index i is renumbered, in order to get the real index value, we need to calculate the value of the expression i + newStart.

After the new node is created, the *for* loop has been executed once, and the index i is moved up one step to point to node p-2, as shown in Fig. 11.25.

And then, the next *for* loop is carried out; the steps are as follows.

- Step 1: Is source [i] equal to −1? Obviously, the value of index i is 2 at this time, and the value of source [2] is equal to 1, so node p-2 is not a brand-new node. There is no need to mount it, and the next step is to judge.
- Step 2: Does i! == seq [s] hold? At this time, the value of index i is 2, and the value of index s is 1. Therefore, 2! == seq [1] holds, and the real DOM corresponding to node p-2 needs to be moved.

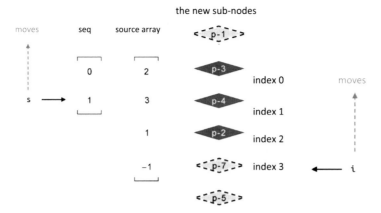

Fig. 11.25 The current state of the node and the index

In the second step, we know that the real DOM corresponding to node p-2 should move. The code is as follows:

```
01 if (moved) {
02 const seq = lis(sources)
03
04 // s points to the last element of the longest incrementing
sequence
05 let s = seq.length - 1
06 let i = count - 1
07 for (i; i >= 0; i--) {
08 if (source[i] === -1) {
09 // omit some code
10 } else if (i !== seq[s]) {
11 // indicates that the node needs to move
12 // the true position index of the node in a new set of sub-node
13 const pos = i + newStart
14 const newVNode = newChildren[pos]
15 //the next node of the node position index
16 const nextPos = pos + 1
17 // anchor
18 const anchor = nextPos < newChildren.length
19 ? newChildren[nextPos].el
20 : null
21 // move
22 insert(newVNode.el, container, anchor)
23 } else {
24 // When i === seq[s], it means that the node at this position does
not need to move
25 // and let s points to the next position
26 s--
27 }
```

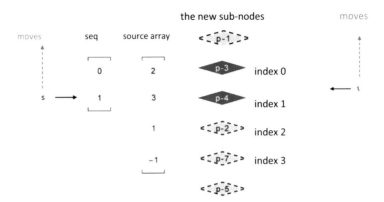

Fig. 11.26 Node and the current state of the index

```
28 }
29 }
```

As you can see, the implementation idea of moving a node is similar to mounting a brand-new node. The difference is that the mobile node is done through the insert function.

Next, the next round of the loop is performed. At this time, the index i points to the node p-4, as shown in Fig. 11.26.

The update process is still divided into three steps.

- Step 1: Determine whether the value of the expression source [i] is equal to −1. Obviously, the value of index i is 1, and the value of the expression source [1] is equal to 3. The condition does not hold. So, node p-4 is not a brand-new node and does not need to be mounted. Then proceed to the next step.
- Step 2: Determine whether the expression i! == seq [s] holds. At this time, the value of index i is 1, and the value of index s is 1. At this time, the expression 1 === seq [1] is true, so the condition i! == seq [s] does not hold either.
- Step 3: Since the conditions in step 1 and step 2 are not true, the code executes the final else branch. This means that the real DOM corresponding to node p-4 does not need to be moved, but we still need to decrement the value of index s, that is, s--.

After three steps of judgment, we conclude that node p-4 does not need to be moved. So, we proceed to the next round of the loop, and the state at this time is shown in Fig. 11.27.

From Fig. 11.27, we can see that the index i points to node p-3 at this time. We continue to determine in three steps.

- Step 1: Determine whether the value of the expression source [i] is equal to −1. Obviously, the value of index i is 0 at this time, and the value of the expression

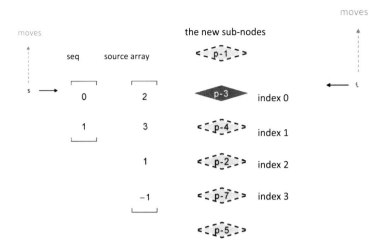

Fig. 11.27 The current state of the node and the index

source [0] is equal to 2, so node p-3 is not a brand-new node. We do not need to mount it. Then proceed to the next step.

- Step 2: Determine whether the expression i! == seq [s] holds. At this time, the value of index i is 0, and the value of index s is also 0. At this time, the expression 0 == seq [0] is true, so the condition is not true, and the code of the else branch will be executed eventually, which is the third step.
- Step 3: When you get here, it means that the real DOM corresponding to node p-3 does not need to be moved either.

After this round of updates is complete, the loop will stop and the update will complete.

It should be emphasized that the method of finding the incrementing subsequences of a given sequence is not within the scope of this book. There are a large number of articles on the Internet that explain this content, and readers can check it out for themselves. The following is the code for solving the longest incrementing subsequence of a given sequence, taken from Vue.js 3:

```
01 function getSequence(arr) {
02 const p = arr.slice()
03 const result = [0]
04 let i, j, u, v, c
05 const len = arr.length
06 for (i = 0; i < len; i++) {
07 const arrI = arr[i]
08 if (arrI !== 0) {
09 j = result[result.length - 1]
10 if (arr[j] < arrI) {
11 p[i] = j
12 result.push(i)
```

```
13 continue
14 }
15 u = 0
16 v = result.length - 1
17 while (u < v) {
18 c = ((u + v) / 2) | 0
19 if (arr[result[c]] < arrI) {
20 u = c + 1
21 } else {
22 v = c
23 }
24 }
25 if (arrI < arr[result[u]]) {
26 if (u > 0) {
27 p[i] = result[u - 1]
28 }
29 result[u] = i
30 }
31 }
32 }
33 u = result.length
34 v = result[u - 1]
35 while (u-- > 0) {
36 result[u] = v
37 v = p[v]
38 }
39 return result
40 }
```

11.4   Summary

Fast Diff algorithm has the best performance in the test. It draws on the preprocessing idea in the text Diff and first deals with the old and new groups of children, with the same pre-node and the same post-node in the node. After the pre-nodes and the post-nodes are all processed, if the update cannot be completed simply by mounting a new node or unloading a node that no longer exists, it is necessary to construct a longest incrementing subsequence according to the index relationship of the nodes. The node pointed to by the longest incrementing subsequence is the node that does not need to be moved.

Part IV
Componentization

Chapter 12
Implementation Principles of Components

In the previous article, we focused on the basic principle and implementation of the renderer. The renderer is mainly responsible for rendering the virtual DOM as the real DOM. We only need to use the virtual DOM to describe the final rendered content. But when we write more complex pages, the amount of code used to describe the virtual DOM of the page structure will become more and more, or the page template will become larger and larger. This is where we need the ability to componentize. With components, we can split a large page into multiple parts. Each part can be used as a separate component, which together make up the complete page. The implementation of component also requires the support of renderer. From the beginning of this chapter, we will discuss component in Vue.js in detail.

12.1 Rendering Components

From the user's perspective, a stateful component is an option object, as shown in the following code:

```
01 // MyComponent is a component whose value is an option object
02 const MyComponent = {
03 name: 'MyComponent',
04 data() {
05 return { foo: 1 }
06 }
07 }
```

However, from the internal implementation of the renderer, a component is a special type of virtual DOM node. For example, to describe a normal label, we use the vnode.type attribute of the virtual node to store the label name, as shown in the following code:

```
01 // This vnode is used to describe the normal label
02 const vnode = {
03 type: 'div'
04 // ...
05 }
```

To describe the fragment, let the value of the virtual node's vnode.type attribute be Fragment, for example:

```
01//The vnode is used to describe the fragment
02 const vnode = {
03 type: Fragment
04//...
05 }
```

In order to describe the text, we set the value of the vnode.type attribute of the virtual node to be Text, for example:

```
01//The vnode is used to describe the text node
02 const vnode = {
03 type: Text
04//...
05}
```

The renderer's patch function proves the above, and here is the code for the patch function we implemented in Part 3:

```
01 function patch(n1, n2, container, anchor) {
02 if (n1 && n1.type !== n2.type) {
03 unmount(n1)
04 n1 = null
05 }
06
07 const { type } = n2
08
09 if (typeof type === 'string') {
10 // Handle as normal element
11 } else if (type === Text) {
12 // Handle as text node
13 } else if (type === Fragment) {
14 // Handle as fragment
15 }
16 }
```

As you can see, the renderer uses the type attribute of virtual nodes to distinguish their types. For different types of nodes, different methods of handling are required to complete mounting and updating.

In fact, the same is true for components. In order to use the virtual node to describe the component, we can use the vnode.type attribute of the virtual node to store the option object of the component, for example:

```
01//The vnode is used to describe the component; the type attribute
stores the option object of the component
02 const vnode = {
03 type: MyComponent
04//...
05}
```

In order for the renderer to handle virtual nodes of component type, we also need to process virtual nodes of component type in the patch function, as shown in the following code:

```
01 function patch(n1, n2, container, anchor) {
02 if (n1 && n1.type !== n2.type) {
03 unmount(n1)
04 n1 = null
05 }
06
07 const { type } = n2
08
09 if (typeof type === 'string') {
10 // Handling as a normal element
11 } else if (type === Text) {
12 // Handling as a text node
13 } else if (type === Fragment) {
14 // processed as fragment
15 } else if (typeof type === 'object') {
16 // vnode.type value is an option object, processed as a component
17 if (!n1) {
18 // mount component
19 mountComponent(n2, container, anchor)
20 } else {
21 // update component
22 patchComponent(n1, n2, anchor)
23 }
24 }
25 }
```

In the above code, we added an else if branch to handle the vnode.type attribute value of the virtual node, in the case of an object, that is, to treat the virtual node as a description of the component, and call the mountComponent and patchonCompent functions to complete the mounting and update of components.

After the renderer has the ability to handle the component, the next step is to design the interface of the component at the user level. This includes: how should the user write the component? what must the component's option object contain? and what capabilities does the component have? and so on. In fact, the component itself is the encapsulation of the page content, which is used to describe the part of the page content. Therefore, a component must contain a render function, that is, the render function, and the return value of the render function should be a virtual DOM. In other words, component rendering, the function is used to describe the component of the rendered content interface, as shown in the following code:

```
01 const MyComponent = {
02 // component name, optional
03 name: 'MyComponent',
04 // component rendering function, its return value must be virtual
DOM
05 render() {
06 // return virtual DOM
07 return {
08 type: 'div',
09 children: `I am text content'
10 }
11 }
12 }
```

This is the simplest example of a component. With the basic component structure, the renderer can complete the rendering of the component, as shown in the following code:

```
01 // VNode object used to describe the component; the type attribute
value is the option object of the component
02 const CompVNode = {
03 type: MyComponent
04 }
05 // Call the renderer to render the component
06 renderer.render(CompVNode, document.querySelector('#app'))
```

The real thing in the renderer that does the component rendering task is the mountComponent function, which is implemented as follows:

```
01 function mountComponent(vnode, container, anchor) {
02 // Get the option object of the component through vnode, that is,
vnode.type
03 const componentOptions = vnode.type
04 // Get the rendering function of the component render
05 const { render } = componentOptions
06 // Execute the rendering function to get the content of the
component to be rendered, that is, the virtual DOM returned by the render
function
07 const subTree = render()
08 // Finally, we call the patch function to mount the content
described by the component, namely subTree
09 patch(null, subTree, container, anchor)
10 }
```

In this way, we have implemented the most basic component scheme.

12.2 Component Status and Self-Updating

In the previous section, we completed the initial rendering of the component. Next, we try to design our own state for the component, as shown in the following code:

```
01 const MyComponent = {
02 name: 'MyComponent',
03 // Use the data function to define the state of the component itself
04 data() {
05 return {
06 foo: 'hello world'
07 }
08 },
09 render() {
10 return {
11 type: 'div',
12 children: `value of foo is: ${this.foo}` // use the component state
inside the render function
13 }
14 }
15 }
```

In the above code, we agreed that the user must use the data function to define the state of the component itself, and at the same time, the state data returned by the data function can be accessed through this in the render function.

The following code implements the initialization of the component's own state:

```
01 function mountComponent(vnode, container, anchor) {
02 const componentOptions = vnode.type
03 const { render, data } = componentOptions
04
05 // Call the data function to get the original data source and call the
reactive function to wrap it as responsive data
06 const state = reactive(data())
07 // When the render function is called, set this to be state,
08 // so, inside the render function, you can access the component's
own state data through this
09 const subTree = render.call(state, state)
10 patch(null, subTree, container, anchor)
11 }
```

As shown in the above code, to realize the initialization of the component's own state requires two steps:

- Obtain the data function through the option object of the component and execute it, and then call the reactive function to wrap the state returned by the data function as reactive data
- When the render function is called, its *this* pointer is set to the reactive data state, and the state is passed as the first parameter of the render function.

After the above two steps, we have implemented the support for the component's own state and the ability to access the component's own state within the render function.

When the state of the component itself changes, we need to have the ability to trigger component updates, that is, self-updating of the component.

To do this, we need to wrap the entire rendering task into an effect, as shown in the following code:

```
01 function mountComponent (vnode, container, anchor) {
02 const componentOptions = vnode.type
03 const { render, data } = componentOptions
04
05 const state = reactive(data())
06
07 // Wrap the component's render function call into effect
08 effect(() => {
09 const subTree = render.call(state, state)
10 patch(null, subTree, container, anchor)
11 })
12 }
```

In this way, once the component's own responsive data changes, the component will automatically re-execute the rendering function to complete the update. However, since the execution of effect is synchronous, when the responsive data changes, the side effect functions associated with it will be executed synchronously. In other words, if the value of the responsive data is modified multiple times, the rendering function will be executed multiple times, which is actually unnecessary. Therefore, we need to design a mechanism so that no matter how many times the responsive data is modified, the side effect function will only be re-executed once. To do this, we need to implement a scheduler. When the side effect function needs to be re-executed, we do not execute it immediately, but buffer it into a microtask queue, wait until the execution stack is empty, then remove it from the microtask queue and execute it. With the caching mechanism, we have the opportunity to deduplicate the task, thus avoiding the performance overhead caused by executing the side effect function multiple times. The specific implementation is as follows:

```
01 // Task cache queue, represented by a Set data structure, so that
tasks can be automatically deduplicated
02 const queue = new Set()
03 // A flag representing whether the task queue is being refreshed
04 let isFlushing = false
05 // Create a Promise instance that resolves immediately
```

```
06 const p = Promise.resolve()
07
08 // The main function of the scheduler, used to add a task to the
buffer queue, and Start flush queue
09 function queueJob(job) {
10 // Add job to task queue queue
11 queue.add(job)
12 // If the queue has not been refreshed, then do the refresh
13 if (!isFlushing) {
14 // Set this flag to true to avoid repeated flushing
15 isFlushing = true
16 // Flush buffer queue in microtasks
17 p.then(() => {
18 try {
19 // Execute tasks in task queue
20 queue.forEach(job => job())
21 } finally {
22 // Reset state
23 isFlushing = false
24 queue.clear = 0
25 }
26 })
27 }
28 }
```

The above is the minimal implementation of the scheduler, which essentially utilizes the asynchronous execution mechanism of microtasks to achieve buffering of side effect functions. The queueJob function is the main function of the scheduler, which is used to add a task or side effect function to the buffer queue and start flushing the queue. With the queueJob function, we can use it when creating render side effects, as shown in the following code:

```
01 function mountComponent(vnode, container, anchor) {
02 const componentOptions = vnode.type
03 const { render, data } = componentOptions
04
05 const state = reactive(data())
06
07 effect(() => {
08 const subTree = render.call(state, state)
09 patch(null, subTree, container, anchor)
10 }, {
11 // Specify the scheduler for the side effect function as queueJob
12 scheduler: queueJob
13 })
14 }
```

In this way, when the responsive data changes, the side effect function will not be executed synchronously immediately, but will be scheduled by the queueJob function, and finally executed in a microtask.

However, the above code is flawed. As you can see, when we call the patch function in the effect function to complete the rendering, the first parameter is always null. This means that every time an update occurs, a new mount will be performed without patching, which is incorrect. The correct way is every time an update occurs, the new subTree will be patched with the subTree rendered by the previous component. To do this, we need to implement the component instance and use it to maintain the state of the component throughout its life cycle, so that the renderer can perform the right operation at the right time.

12.3   Component Instances and Component Lifetime

A component instance is essentially a state set (or an object), which maintains all the information in the process of running the component, such as the life cycle function registered to the component, the component rendering subtree (subTree), whether the component has been mounted, the component itself, the state (data), and so on. In order to solve the problem of component update in the previous section, we need to introduce the concept of component instance, and related state information, as shown in the following code:

```
01 function mountComponent (vnode, container, anchor) {
02 const componentOptions = vnode.type
03 const { render, data } = componentOptions
04
05 const state = reactive(data())
06
07 // Define component instance; a component instance is essentially an
object, which contains component-related state information
08 const instance = {
09 // The component's own state data, that is, data
10 state,
11 // A boolean value used to indicate whether the component has been
mounted, the initial value is false
12 isMounted: false,
13 // The content rendered by the component, that is, the subtree
(subTree)
14 subTree: null
15 }
16
17 // Set the component instance to the vnode for subsequent updates
18 vnode.component = instance
19
20 effect(() => {
21 // Call the component's render function to get the subtree
22 const subTree = render.call(state, state)
23 // Check if the component has been mounted
24 if (!instance.isMounted) {
25 // Initial mount - call the patch function with null
```

```
26 patch(null, subTree, container, anchor)
27 // Important: Set the isMounted of the component instance to true so
that when the update occurs it will not be mounted again,
28 // Instead, update
29 instance.isMounted = true
30 } else {
31 // When isMounted is true, it means that the component has been
mounted and only needs to be completed
32 // So when calling the patch function, the first parameter is the
subtree of the last rendering of the component,
33 // indicating that the new subtree is used to patch the last rendered
subtree
34 patch(instance.subTree, subTree, container, anchor)
35 }
36 // Update the subtree of the component instance
37 instance.subTree = subTree
38 }, { scheduler: queueJob })
39 }
```

In the above code, we use an object to represent a component instance, which has three attributes.

- State: The state data of the component itself, that is, data.
- isMounted: A Boolean value used to indicate whether the component is mounted.
- SubTree: Store the virtual DOM returned by the component's render function, that is, the component's subtree (subTree).

In fact, we can arbitrarily add the required properties to the component instance when needed. However, it should be noted that we should keep the component instance as light as possible to reduce memory consumption.

In the above implementation, the instance.isMounted properties of the component instance can be used to distinguish the mounting and updating of the component. Therefore, we can call the corresponding lifecycle hook of the component at the right time, as shown in the following code:

```
01 function mountComponent(vnode, container, anchor) {
02 const componentOptions = vnode.type
03 // Get the lifecycle function of the component from the component
option object
04 const { render, data, beforeCreate, created, beforeMount, mounted,
beforeUpdate,
     updated } = componentOptions
05
06 // Call the beforeCreate hook here
07 beforeCreate && beforeCreate()
08
09 const state = reactive(data())
10
11 const instance = {
12 state,
13 isMounted: false,
```

```
14 subTree: null
15 }
16 vnode.component = instance
17
18 // call created hook here
19 created && created.call(state)
20
21 effect((() => {
22 const subTree = render.call(state, state)
23 if (!instance.isMounted) {
24 // call beforeMount hook here
25 beforeMount && beforeMount.call(state)
26 patch(null, subTree, container, anchor)
27 instance.isMounted = true
28 // call mounted hook here
29 mounted && mounted.call(state)
30 } else {
31 // call beforeUpdate hook here
32 beforeUpdate && beforeUpdate.call(state)
33 patch(instance.subTree, subTree, container, anchor)
34 // call updated hook here
35 updated && updated.call(state)
36 }
37 instance.subTree = subTree
38 }, { scheduler: queueJob })
39 }
```

In the above code, we first got the lifecycle functions registered to the component from the option object of the component, and then call them at the right time, which is actually the implementation principle of the component lifecycle. But in fact, since there may be multiple identical component lifecycle hooks, such as the lifecycle hook function from mixins, we usually need to serialize the component lifecycle hooks into an array, but the core principle remains unchanged.

12.4   Passive Update of Props and Components

At the virtual DOM level, the props of components are not much different from the attributes of ordinary HTML tags. Suppose we have the following template:

```
01 < MyComponent title = "A Big Title": other = "val"/>
   The virtual DOM corresponding to this template is:
01 const vnode = {
02 type: MyComponent,
03 props: {
04 title: 'A big Title',
05 other: this.val
06 }
07 }
```

As you can see, the template and the virtual DOM are almost "isomorphic." In addition, when writing the component, we need to explicitly specify which props the component will receive, as shown in the following code:

```
01 const MyComponent = {
02 name: 'MyComponent',
03 // The component receives a props named title, and the props type is String
04 props: {
05 title: String
06 },
07 render() {
08 return {
09 type: 'div',
10 children: `count is: ${this.title}` // access props data
11 }
12 }
13}
```

So, for a component, there are two parts about props we need to care about:

- The props data passed for the component, that is, the vnode.props object of the component
- The props options defined in the component options object, that is, the MyComponent.props object

We need to combine these two options to resolve the props data that the component needs to use when rendering, the specific implementation is as follows:

```
01 function mountComponent(vnode, container, anchor) {
02 const componentOptions = vnode.type
03 // Remove the props definition from the component option object, that is, propsOption
04 const { render, data, props: propsOption /* others omitted */ } = componentOptions
05
06 beforeCreate && beforeCreate()
07
08 const state = reactive(data())
09 // Call resolveProps function to parse out the final props data with attrs data
10 const [props, attrs] = resolveProps(propsOption, vnode.props)
11
12 const instance = {
13 state,
14 // Wrap the parsed props data as shallowReactive and define it on the component instance
15 props: shallowReactive(props),
16 isMounted: false,
17 subTree: null
18 }
```

```
19 vnode.component = instance
20
21 // omit some code
22 }
23
24 // resolveProps function is used to parse component props and attrs
data
25 function resolveProps(options, propsData) {
26 const props = {}
27 const attrs = {}
28 // traverse the props data passed for the component
29 for (const key in propsData) {
30 if (key in options) {
31 // If the props data passed to the component is defined in the
component's own props options, it is considered a valid props
32 props[key] = propsData[key]
33 } else {
34 // otherwise it is passed as attrs
35 attrs[key] = propsData[key]
36 }
37 }
38
39 // Finally return props and attrs data
40 return [ props, attrs ]
41 }
```

In the above code, we combine the MyComponent.props objects defined in the component options and the vnode.props objects passed to the component, and finally resolve the props and attrs data that the component needs to use when rendering. Here, pay attention to two points.

- In Vue.js 3, props data that is not defined in the MyComponent.props options will be stored in the attrs object.
- The above implementation does not include the processing of default values, type verification, etc. In fact, these contents are also around MyComponent.props and vnode.props objects, which is not complicated to implement.

After processing the props data, let's talk about the problem of props data changes. Props is essentially the parent component, data; when the props changes, it will trigger the parent component to re-render. Suppose the parent component's template is as follows:

```
01 < template >
02 < MyComponent : title = "title"/>
03 </template >
```

Here the initial value of the responsive data title is the string "A big Title," so the virtual DOM of the parent component is as follows:

```
01 // The content to be rendered by the parent component
02 const vnode = {
03 type: MyComponent,
04 props: {
05 title: 'A Big Title'
06 }
07 }
```

When the responsive data title changes, the parent component's render function will re-execute. Assuming the value of title becomes the string "A Small Title," then the newly generated virtual DOM is as follows:

```
01 // content to be rendered by the parent component
02 const vnode = {
03 type: MyComponent,
04 props: {
05 title: 'A Small Title'
06 }
07 }
```

Next, the parent component will self-update. During the update process, the renderer finds that the subTree of the parent component contains virtual nodes of the component type, so it will call the patchComponent function to complete the update of the child component, as shown in the code of the patch function below:

```
01 function patch(n1, n2, container, anchor) {
02 if (n1 && n1.type !== n2.type) {
03 unmount(n1)
04 n1 = null
05 }
06
07 const { type } = n2
08
09 if (typeof type === 'string') {
10 // omit some code
11 } else if (type === Text) {
12 // omit some code
13 } else if (type === Fragment) {
14 // omit some code
15 } else if (typeof type === 'object') {
16 // The value of vnode.type is an option object, processed as a
component
17 if (!n1) {
18 mountComponent(n2, container, anchor)
19 } else {
20 // Update components
21 patchComponent(n1, n2, anchor)
22 }
23 }
24 }
```

The patchComponent function is used to complete the update of the child component. We call the passive update of the child component caused by the self-update of the parent component as the passive update of the child component. When the subcomponent is passively updated, what we need to do is:

- Detect whether the subcomponent really needs to be updated, because the props of the subcomponent may be unchanged
- If it needs to be updated, update the props, slots, etc. of the subcomponent.

The specific implementation of the patchComponent function is as follows:

```
01 function patchComponent (n1, n2, anchor) {
02 // Get the component instance, that is, n1.component, and let the
new component virtual node n2.component also point to the component
instance
03 const instance = (n2.component = n1.component)
04 // Get the current props data
05 const { props } = instance
06 // Call hasPropsChanged to check whether the props passed for the
subcomponent have changed; if not, there is no need to update
07 if (hasPropsChanged (n1.props, n2.props)) {
08 // Call resolveProps function to retrieve props data
09 const [ nextProps ] = resolveProps (n2.type.props, n2.props)
10 // update props
11 for (const k in nextProps) {
12 props [k] = nextProps [k]
13 }
14 // remove props not existing
15 for (const k in props) {
16 if (! (k in nextProps)) delete props [k]
17 }
18 }
19 }
20
21 function hasPropsChanged (
22 prevProps,
23 nextProps
24 ) {
25 const nextKeys = Object.keys (nextProps)
26 // If the number of old and new props has changed, then there is a
change
27 if (nextKeys.length !== Object.keys (prevProps).length) {
28 return true
29 }
30 // Only
31 for (let i = 0; i < nextKeys.length; i++) {
32 const key = nextKeys [i]
33 // There are unequal props, then there is a change
34 if (nextProps [key] !== prevProps [key]) return true
35 }
36 return false
37 }
```

The above is the minimum implementation of passive component update. There are two points to note:

- The component instance needs to be added to the new component vnode object, that is, n2.component = n1.component, otherwise, the next update will not get the component instance
- The instance.props object itself is shallow response (that is, shallowReactive). Therefore, when updating the props of the component, you only need to set the property value under the instance.props object to trigger the component to re-render.

In the above implementation, we did not deal with the update of attrs and slots. The update of attrs is essentially similar to the update of props. For slots, we will explain in subsequent chapters. In fact, to fully implement the props mechanism in Vue.js, you need to write a lot of boundary code. But in essence, the principle is processed according to the definition of the component's props option and the props data passed for the component.

Because the props data and the component's own state data need to be exposed to the rendering function and the render function can access them through this, so we need to encapsulate a render context object as shown in the following code:

```
01 function mountComponent (vnode, container, anchor) {
02 // omit some code
03
04 const instance = {
05 state,
06 props: shallowReactive(props),
07 isMounted: false,
08 subTree: null
09 }
10
11 vnode.component = instance
12
13 // create a render context object, which is essentially a group
14 const renderContext = new Proxy(instance, {
15 get (t, k, r) {
16 // get the component's own state and props data
17 const { state, props } = t
18 // first try to read its own state data
19 if (state && k in state) {
20 return state[k]
21 } else if (k in props) { //If the component itself does not have this data, try to read from props
22 return props[k]
23 } else {
24 console.error('does not exist')
25 }
26 },
27 set (t, k, v, r) {
28 const { state, props } = t
29 if (state && k in state) {
30 state[k] = v
```

```
31 } else if (k in props) {
32 console.warn(`Attempting to mutate prop "${k}". Props are
readonly.`)
33 } else {
34 console.error('does not exist')
35 }
36 }
37 })
38
39 // Bind the rendering context object when calling the lifecycle
function
40 created && created.call(renderContext)
41
42 // omit some code
43 }
```

In the above code, we created a proxy object for the component instance, which was the rendering context object. Its significance is to intercept the read and set operations of the data state. Whenever the data is read through this in the render function or lifecycle hook, the data will be preferentially read from the component's own state. If the component itself has no corresponding data, it will be read from the props data. Finally, we can use the rendering context as the *this* value of the render function and lifecycle hook.

In fact, in addition to the component's own data and props data, the complete component also contains methods, computed, etc., the data and methods defined in the options, which should be handled in the rendering context object.

12.5 The Role and Implementation of Setup Functions

The component's setup function is a new component option in Vue.js 3, which is different from other component options that exist in Vue.js 2. This is because the setup function is mainly used in conjunction with the composite API, providing users with a place to build combinatorial logic, create, responsive data, create generic functions, register lifecycle hooks, etc. During the entire life cycle of the component, the setup function will only be executed once when it is mounted, and its return value can have two cases.

Return a function that will act as the component's render function:

```
01 const Comp = {
02 setup() {
03 // The setup function can return a function that will act as the
component's render function
04 return () => {
05 return { type: 'div', children: 'hello' }
06 }
07 }
08 }
```

This method is often used when the component does not express its rendered content as a template. If the component uses a template to express its rendered content, the setup function cannot return a function, otherwise it will conflict with the render function generated by template compilation.

Return an object; the data contained in the object will be exposed to the template:

```
01 const Comp = {
02 setup () {
03 const count = ref (0)
04 // Return an object; the data in the object will be exposed to the
render function
05 return {
06 count
07 }
08 },
09 render () {
10 // This allows access to the responsive data exposed by the setup
11 return { type: 'div', children: `count is: ${this.count}` }
12 }
13 }
```

As you can see, the data exposed by the setup function can be accessed via this in the render function.

In addition, the setup function takes two arguments. The first parameter is the props data object, and the second parameter is also an object, usually called setupContext, as shown in the following code:

```
01 const Comp = {
02 props: {
03 foo: String
04 },
05 setup (props, setupContext) {
06 props.foo // Access the incoming props data
07 // setupContext contains important data related to the component
interface
08 const { slots, emit, attrs, expose } = setupContext
09 // ...
10 }
11 }
```

As can be seen from the above code, we can get the props data object passed externally for the component through the first parameter of the setup function. At the same time, the setup function also receives a second parameter setupContext object, which holds the data and methods related to the component's interface, as shown below.

- slots: The slots received by the component, which we will explain in subsequent chapters.

- emit: A function to emit custom events. attrs: We introduced the attrs object in Sect. 12.4. When passing props to the component, those properties that are not explicitly declared as props are stored in the attrs object.
- expose: A function that explicitly exposes component data. At the time of writing this book, the API design related to expose is still under discussion, see the specific RFC for details.

In general, it is not recommended to mix setup with other component options in Vue.js 2, for example, options such as data, watch, methods, etc., which are called "traditional" component options. This is because in the Vue.js 3 scenario, composite APIs are more advocated, and the setup function is born for composite APIs. Mixing the setup option of the combined API with the "traditional" component option is not a wise choice, because it will bring a burden on semantics and understanding.

Next, we will try to implement the setup component options around these capabilities, as shown in the following code:

```
01 function mountComponent(vnode, container, anchor) {
02 const componentOptions = vnode.type
03 // Remove the setup function from the component options
04 let { render, data, setup, /* omit other options */ } =
componentOptions
05
06 beforeCreate && beforeCreate()
07
08 const state = data ? reactive(data()) : null
09 const [props, attrs] = resolveProps(propsOption, vnode.props)
10
11 const instance = {
12 state,
13 props: shallowReactive(props),
14 isMounted: false,
15 subTree: null
16 }
17
18 // setupContext; since we haven't explained emit and slots, we only
need attrs
19 const setupContext = { attrs }
20 // Call the setup function to pass the read-only version of props as
the first parameter to prevent users from accidentally modifying the
value of props,
21 // pass setupContext setupContext as the second parameter
22 const setupResult = setup(shallowReadonly(instance.props),
setupContext)
23 // setupState is used to store the data returned by setup
24 let setupState = null
25 // If the return value of the setup function is a function, it is
used as the render function
26 if (typeof setupResult === 'function') {
27 // report conflict
28 if (render) console.error('setup function returns the render
function, the render option will be ignored')
```

```
29 // setupResult as render function
30 render = setupResult
31 } else {
32 //if the valued returned by setup is not a function, it will be given
to setupState as the data state value
33 setupState = setupResult
34 }
35
36 vnode.component = instance
37
38 const renderContext = new Proxy(instance, {
39 get(t, k, r) {
40 const { state, props } = t
41 if (state && k in state) {
42 return state[k]
43 } else if (k in props) {
44 return props[k]
45 } else if (setupState && k in setupState) {
46 // Rendering context needs to add support for setupState
47 return setupState[k]
48 } else {
49 console.error('does not exist')
50 }
51 },
52 set(t, k, v, r) {
53 const { state, props } = t
54 if (state && k in state) {
55 state[k] = v
56 } else if (k in props) {
57 console.warn(`Attempting to mutate prop "${k}". Props are
readonly.`)
58 } else if (setupState && k in setupState) {
59 // Rendering context needs to add support for setupState
60 setupState[k] = v
61 } else {
62 console.error(''does not exist')
63 }
64 }
65 })
66
67 // omit some code
68 }
```

The above is the minimal implementation of setup. Here are a few things to note.

- A setupContext is an object, and since we haven't covered emit and slots yet, setupContext only contains attrs for now.
- We decide what to do with it by detecting the return type of the setup function. If its return value is a function, it is directly rendered as the component's function. It should be noted here that to avoid ambiguity, we need to check whether the render option already exists in the component option, and if so, we need to print a warning message.

• The renderContext should handle setupState correctly, because the data state returned by the setup function should also be exposed to the rendering environment.

12.6   Implementation of Component Events and Emit

Emit is used to emit the custom event of the component, as shown in the following code:

```
01 const MyComponent = {
02 name: 'MyComponent',
03 setup (props, { emit }) {
04 // emit the change event and pass two parameters to the event
handler
05 emit ('change', 1, 2)
06
07 return () => {
08 return // ...
09 }
10 }
11 }
```

When using this component, we can listen to the custom event emitted by the emit function:

```
01 < MyComponent @change = "handler"/>
```

The virtual DOM corresponding to the template above is:

```
01 const CompVNode = {
02 type: MyComponent,
03 props: {
04 onChange: handler
05}
06}
```

As you can see, the custom event change is compiled into a property named onChange and stored in the props data object. This is actually a convention. As a framework designer, you can also design the compilation result of events in the way you expect.

In the specific implementation, the essence of sending custom event is to find the corresponding one in the props data object according to the event name and execute the event handler function, as shown in the following code:

```
01 function mountComponent (vnode, container, anchor) {
02 // omit some code
03
04 const instance = {
05 state,
06 props: shallowReactive (props),
07 isMounted: false,
08 subTree: null
09 }
10
11 // Define the emit function, which takes two arguments
12 // event: name of the event
13 // payload: parameter passed to the event handler
14 function emit (event, ...payload) {
15 // Handle event names by convention, e.g. change -- > onChange
16 const eventName = `on${event [0] .toUpperCase () + event .slice (1) }
17 // According to the name of the event processed, go to props to find
the corresponding event handler
18 const handler = instance.props [eventName]
19 if (handler) {
20 // Call the event handler and pass the parameter
21 handler (...payload)
22 } else {
23 console.error ('event does not exist')
24 }
25 }
26
27 // add emit to setupContext; users can get eimt from setupContext
28 const setupContext = { attrs, emit }
29
30 // omit some code
31 }
```

The overall implementation is not complicated—just need to implement an emit function and add it to the setupContext object, so that users can get the emit function through setupContext. In addition, when the emit function is called, we will convert the event name according to the convention, so that we can find the corresponding event handler function in the props data object. Finally, call the event handler function and pass-through parameters. One additional point to note here is that when we explained props, we mentioned that any properties that are not explicitly declared as props will be stored in attrs. In other words, any props of event type, that is, properties of the onXxx class, will not appear in props. As a result, we cannot find the corresponding event handler in the instance.props based on the event name. To solve this problem, we need to do special handling of props of event type when parsing props data, as shown in the following code:

```
01 function resolveProps (options, propsData) {
02 const props = {}
03 const attrs = {}
```

```
04 for (const key in propsData) {
05 // Props starting with string on, whether explicitly declared or
not, are added to the props data, not to attrs
06 if (key in options || key.startsWith('on')) {
07 props[key] = propsData[key]
08 } else {
09 attrs[key] = propsData[key]
10 }
11 }
12
13 return [ props, attrs ]
14 }
```

The processing method is very simple, by detecting the key value of propsData to determine whether it begins with a string "on." If it is, the property is the component's custom event. In this case, even if the component does not explicitly declare it as props, we will add it to the final resolved props data object instead of adding it to the attrs object.

12.7   Working Principles and Implementation of Slots

As the name suggests, the slot of the component means that the component will reserve a slot, and the specific content of the slot to be rendered is inserted by the user, as shown in the template of the MyComponent component given below:

```
01 <template>
02 <header><slot name="header" /></header>
03 <div>
04 <slot name="body" />
05 </div>
06 <footer><slot name="footer" /></footer>
07 </template>
```

When using the < MyComponent > component in the parent component, you can insert custom content based on the name of the slot:

```
01 <MyComponent>
02 <template #header>
03 <h1> I am the title </h1>
04 </template>
05 <template #body>
06 <section> I am the content </section>
07 </template>
08 <template #footer>
09 <p> I am the footer </p>
10 </template>
11 </MyComponent>
```

The template of the parent component above will be compiled into the following rendering function:

```
01 // The parent component's rendering function
02 function render() {
03 return {
04 type: MyComponent,
05 // The children of the component will be compiled into an object
06 children: {
07 header() {
08 return { type: 'h1', children: 'I am the title' }
09 },
10 body() {
11 return { type: 'section', children: 'I am the content'}
12 },
13 footer() {
14 return { type: 'p', children: 'I am the footnote'}
15 }
16 }
17 }
18 }
```

As you can see, the content of the slots in the component template are compiled into a slot function, and the return value of the slot function is the specific slot contents. The template of the component MyComponent will be compiled into the following rendering function:

```
01 // The result of the compilation of the component template of
MyComponent
02 function render() {
03 return [
04 {
05 type: 'header',
06 children: [this.$slots.header()]
07 },
08 {
09 type: 'body',
10 children: [this.$slots.body()]
11 },
12 {
13 type: 'footer',
14 children: [this.$slots.footer()]
15 }
16 ]
17 }
```

As you can see, the process of rendering the content of the slot is the process of calling the slot function and rendering the content returned by it. This is very similar to the concept of render props in React.

In the runtime implementation, the slot depends on the slots object in the setupContext, as shown in the following code:

```
01 function mountComponent(vnode, container, anchor) {
02 // omit some code
03
04 // directly use the compiled vnode.children object as the slots
object
05 const slots = vnode.children || {}
06
07 // add the slots object to the setupContext
08 const setupContext = { attrs, emit, slots }
09
10 }
```

As you can see, the most basic slots implementation is very simple. Just add the compiled vnode.children as a slots object, and then add the slots object to the setupContext object. In order to be able to access the content of the slot via *this. $slots* inside the render function and the lifecycle hook function, we also need to treat the $slots property specially in the renderContext, as shown in the following code:

```
01 function mountComponent(vnode, container, anchor) {
02 // omit some code
03
04 const slots = vnode.children || {}
05
06 const instance = {
07 state,
08 props: shallowReactive(props),
09 isMounted: false,
10 subTree: null,
11 // Add slots to component instances
12 slots
13 }
14
15 // omit some code
16
17 const renderContext = new Proxy(instance, {
18 get(t, k, r) {
19 const { state, props, slots } = t
20 // When the value of k is $slots, return the slots on the component
instance directly
21 if (k === '$slots') return slots
22
23 // omit some code
24 },
25 set(t, k, v, r) {
26 // omit some code
27 }
28 })
29
30 // omit some code
31 }
```

We do special treatment for the get interceptor function of the renderContext proxy object in the rendering context. When the key read is $slots, it directly returns the slots object on the component instance, so that the user can access the slot content through *this. $slots*.

12.8 Registration Lifetime

In Vue.js 3, a part of the combined API is used to register the lifecycle hook functions, such as onMounted, onUpdated, etc., as shown in the following code:

```
01 import { onMounted } from 'vue'
02
03 const MyComponent = {
04 setup() {
05 onMounted(() => {
06 console.log('mounted 1')
07 })
08 // can register more than one
09 onMounted(() => {
10 console.log('mounted 2')
11 })
12
13 // ...
14 }
15 }
```

The mounted lifecycle hook function can be registered by calling the onMounted function in the setup function, and multiple hook functions can be registered by calling the onMounted function multiple times, which will be executed after the component is mounted. The question here is that calling the onMounted function in the setup function of component A will register the hook function to component A; and calling the onMounted function in the setup function of group B will register the hook function to component B. How is this achieved? In fact, we need to maintain a variable currentInstance, which is used to store the current component instance. Whenever the component is initialized and the component's setup function is executed, the currentInstance is set to the current component instance, and then the component's setup function is executed, so that we can get the currently initialized component instance through currentInstance, so as to associate those hook functions registered with the component instance through the onMounted function.

Next, we work on the implementation. First of all, you need to design a mainte-nance method for the current instance, as shown in the following code:

```
01 // global variable, store the component instance currently being
initialized
02 let currentInstance = null
03 // The method receives the component instance as a parameter, and
sets the instance to currentInstance
04 function setCurrentInstance(instance) {
05 currentInstance = instance
06 }
```

With the currentInstance variable, and the setCurrentInstance function used to set the variable, we can start modifying the mounteComponent function, as shown in the following code:

```
01 function mountComponent(vnode, container, anchor) {
02 // omit some code
03
04 const instance = {
05 state,
06 props: shallowReactive(props),
07 isMounted: false,
08 subTree: null,
09 slots,
10 // Add mounted array to component instance to store lifecycle hook
function registered with onMounted function
11 mounted: []
12 }
13
14 // omit some code
15
16 // setup
17 const setupContext = { attrs, emit, slots }
18
19 // Set the current component instance before calling the setup
function
20 setCurrentInstance(instance)
21 // Execute the setup function
22 const setupResult = setup(shallowReadonly(instance.props),
setupContext)
23 // Reset the current component instance after setup function is
executed
24 setCurrentInstance(null)
25
26 // omit some code
27 }
```

The above code takes the onMounted function as an example for illustration. In order to store the lifecycle registered by the onMounted function, hook, we need to add instance.mounted array on the component instance object. The reason why instance.mounted data type is array is because in the setup function, the onMounted function can be called multiple times to register different lifecycle functions, and these lifecycle functions will be stored in the array instance.mounted.

Next, consider the implementation of the onMounted function itself, as shown in the following code:

```
01 function onMounted(fn) {
02 if (currentInstance) {
03 // Add the lifecycle function to the instance.mounted array
04 currentInstance.mounted.push(fn)
05 } else {
06 console.error('onMounted function can only be called in setup')
07 }
08 }
```

As you can see, the overall implementation is very simple and intuitive. You just need to get the current component instance through currentInstance and add the lifecycle hook function to the instance.mounted array of the current instance object. In addition, if the current instance does not exist, it means that the user did not call the onMounted function in the setup function, which is wrong usage, so we should throw the error and its reason.

The last step is to call these lifecycle hook functions registered in the instance. mounted array at the right time, as shown in the following code:

```
01 function mountComponent(vnode, container, anchor) {
02 // omit some code
03
04 effect(() => {
05 const subTree = render.call(renderContext, renderContext)
06 if (!instance.isMounted) {
07 // omit some code
08
09 // traverse instance.mounted array and execute one by one
10 instance.mounted && instance.mounted.forEach(hook => hook.call
(renderContext))
11 } else {
12 // omit some code
13 }
14 instance.subTree = subTree
15 }, {
16 scheduler: queueJob
17 })
18 }
```

As you can see, we just need to traverse instance.mounted array at the right time and execute the lifecycle hook function in the array.

For lifecycle hook functions other than mounted, the principle is the same as above.

12.9 Summary

In this chapter, we first discussed how to use virtual nodes to describe components. The vnode.type property of the virtual node is used to store the component object, and the renderer determines whether it is a component or not based on the type of this property of the virtual node. If it is a component, then the renderer uses mountComponent and patchComponent to complete the mounting and updating of the component.

Next, we discussed the self-updating of the component. We know that during the component mount phase, a side effect function is created for the component to render its contents. The side effect function will establish a response relationship with the component's own reactive data. When the component's own reactive data changes, it will trigger the rendering side effect function to re-execute, that is, re-render. However, since re-rendering is performed synchronously by default, it is impossible to deduplicate the task, so we specified a custom caller when creating the rendering side effect function. The role of this scheduler is to buffer the rendering side effect function into the micro task queue when the component's own reactive data changes. With the buffer queue, we can deduplicate the rendering task, thus avoiding the extra performance overhead caused by useless re-rendering.

Then, we introduced the component instance. It is essentially an object that contains the state of the component during operation, such as whether the component is mounted, the component's own responsive data, and the content rendered by the component (i.e., subtree). With the component instance, after that, in the render side effect function, we can decide whether to mount a new one or patch it based on the state identifier on the component instance.

Then, we discussed the component's props and passive update of the component. Subcomponent updates caused by side effect self-update are called passive updates of subcomponents. We also introduced the renderContext, which is actually a proxy object for the component instance. Accessing the component instance within the render function exposes the data through this proxy object.

After that, we discussed the setup function. This function is built for composite APIs, so we want to avoid mixing it with the "traditional" component options in Vue.js. The return value of the setup function can be of two types. If it returns a function, the function is used as the component's rendering function; if it returns a data object, the object is exposed to the rendering context.

The emit function is contained in the setupContext object, and the component's custom event can be emitted through the emit function. The events bound to the component through the v-on directive are compiled and stored in the props object as onXxx. When the emit function executes, it looks for the corresponding event handler in the props object and executes it.

Then, we discussed the component's slot. It borrows the concept of the < slot > tag in the Web Component. The slot content is compiled into the slot function, and the return value of the slot function is the content filled into the slot. The < slot > tag will be compiled into a slot, and the call to the function, by executing the corresponding slot function, gets the content (that is, the virtual DOM) to fill the slot externally, and finally renders the content into the slot.

Finally, we discussed the implementation of methods such as onMounted for registering lifecycle hook functions. The lifecycle function registered through onMounted will be registered in the instance.mounted array of the current component instance. To maintain the component instance currently being initialized, we define the global variable currentInstance, and the setCurrentInstance function that sets the variable.

Chapter 13
Asynchronous Components and Functional Components

In Chap. 12, we discussed the basic meaning and implementation of components in detail. In this chapter, we will continue to discuss two important concepts of components, namely asynchronous components and functional components. In asynchronous components, the word "asynchronous" refers to loading and rendering a component asynchronously. This is especially important in scenarios such as code segmentation and server level distribution of components. Functional components allow a component to be defined using an ordinary function and use the return value of the function as the content to be rendered by the component. The characteristics of functional components are none, state, simple, and intuitive to write. In Vue.js 2, compared with stateful components, functional components have obvious performance advantages. But in Vue.js 3, the performance gap between functional components and stateful components is not big, and both are very good. As Vue.js RFC said in the original text: "Functional components are used in Vue.js 3 mainly because of their simplicity, not because of their performance."

13.1 Problems to Be Solved by Asynchronous Components

The problem to be solved by asynchronous components is that, fundamentally speaking, the implementation of asynchronous components does not require any framework-level support, and users can implement it by themselves. An example of rendering an App component to a page is as follows:

```
01 import App from 'App.vue'
02 createApp(App).mount('#app')
```

The above code shows synchronous rendering. We can easily change this to asynchronous rendering, as shown in the following code:

© The Author(s), under exclusive license to Springer Nature Singapore Pte Ltd. 2023   373
H. Yang, *Vue. JS Framework*, https://doi.org/10.1007/978-981-99-4947-2_13

```
01 const loader = () => import('App.vue')
02 loader().then(App => {
03 createApp(App).mount('#app')
04 })
```

Here we load the component with the dynamic import statement import (), which returns a *promise* instance. After the component is loaded successfully, it will call the createApp function to complete the mount, which realizes the asynchronous rendering of the page.

The above example realizes the asynchronous rendering of the entire page. Usually a page is composed of multiple components; each component is responsible for rendering part of the page. So, what should I do if I only want to asynchronous render part of the page? At this time, I only need the ability to load a certain component asynchronously. Assume the following code is App.vue component:

```
01 <template>
02 <CompA />
03 <component :is="asyncComp" />
04 </template>
05 <script>
06 import { shallowRef } from 'vue'
07 import CompA from 'CompA.vue'
08
09 export default {
10 components: { CompA },
11 setup() {
12 const asyncComp = shallowRef(null)
13
14 // asynchronous loading of CompB components
15 import('CompB.vue').then(CompB => asyncComp.value = CompB)
16
17 return {
18 asyncComp
19 }
20 }
21 }
22 </script>
```

As you can see from the template in this code, the page consists of < CompA/> components and dynamic < components >. Among them, the CompA component is rendered synchronously, and the dynamic component binds the asyncComp variable. Looking at the script block, we load the CompB component asynchronously through dynamic import and the statement import (). When the loading is successful, the value of the asyncComp variable is set to CompB. This realizes the asynchronous loading and rendering of the CompB component.

However, although users can achieve asynchronous loading and rendering of components by themselves, the overall implementation is more complicated, because the implementation of a complete asynchronous component involves much more complicated content than the above example. Usually when loading components asynchronously, we also consider the following aspects.

- If the component fails to load or load timeout, do you want to render the Error component?
- When the component is loaded, do you want to display placeholder content? For example, render a Loading component.
- The loading speed of the component may be very fast or very slow. Do you want to set a delay time to display the Loading component? If the component does not load successfully within 200 ms, the Loading component will be displayed only, which can avoid flickering caused by the component loading too fast.
- Do you need to retry after the component fails to load?

In order to better solve the above problems for users, we need to provide better encapsulation support for asynchronous components at the framework level. The corresponding capabilities are as follows.

- Allow the user to specify the component to be rendered when loading errors.
- Allow the user to specify the delay time of the Loading component and display the component.
- Allow the user to set the timeout period for loading the component.
- Provide the user with the ability to retry when the component fails to load.

These are the problems that asynchronous components really solve.

13.2   Implementation Principles of Asynchronous Components

13.2.1   Encapsulation of DefineAsyncComponent Function

Asynchronous components are essentially through encapsulation means to achieve a friendly user interface, thereby reducing the complexity of user-level use, as shown in the following user code:

```
01 <template>
02 <AsyncComp />
03 </template>
04 <script>
05 export default {
06 components: {
07 // Use defineAsyncComponent to define an asynchronous component,
which receives a loader as a parameter
08 AsyncComp: defineAsyncComponent(() => import('CompA'))
09 }
10 }
11 </script>
```

In the above code, we use defineAsyncComponent to define the asynchronous component and register it directly with the components option. In this way, the asynchronous component can be used in the template as if it were a normal component. As you can see, using the defineAsyncComponent function to define asynchronous components is much simpler and more straightforward than the asynchronous component scheme we implemented ourselves in Sect. 13.1.

defineAsyncComponent is a higher order component; its most basic implementation is as follows:

```
01 // defineAsyncComponent function is used to define an asynchronous
component, receiving an asynchronous component loader as a parameter
02 function defineAsyncComponent(loader) {
03 // A variable is used to store asynchronously loaded components
04 let InnerComp = null
05 // Return a wrapper component
06 return {
07 name: 'AsyncComponentWrapper',
08 setup() {
09 // Whether the asynchronous component loads successfully
10 const loaded = ref(false)
11 // Execute the loader function and return a Promise instance
12 // After the load is successful, assign the successfully loaded
component to InnerComp and mark the loaded as true, which means the load
is successful
13 loader().then(c => {
14 InnerComp = c
15 loaded.value = true
16 })
17
18 return () => {
19 // Render the asynchronous component if it loads successfully,
otherwise render a placeholder
20 return loaded.value ? { type: InnerComp } : { type: Text, children:
'' }
21 }
22 }
23 }
24 }
```

Here are a few key points.

- defineAsyncComponent function is essentially a higher order component, and its return value is a wrapper component.
- The wrapper component decides what content to render based on the state of the loader. If the loader successfully loads the component, it renders the loaded component, otherwise it renders a placeholder.
- Usually, the placeholder content is a comment node. When the component is not loaded successfully, a comment node will be rendered in the page to occupy the placeholder. But here we use an empty text node to occupy the placeholder.

13.2.2   Timeout and Error Components

Asynchronous components are usually loaded as network requests. The front end sends an HTTP request to download the JavaScript resources of the component or directly obtain the component data from the server level. Since there is a network request, it is necessary to consider the situation of slow network speed, especially in the weak connection environment; it may take a long time to load a component. Therefore, we need to provide the user with the ability to specify the timeout period. When the loading time of the component exceeds the specified time period, a timeout error will be triggered. In this case, if the user configures the Error component, the component will be rendered.

First, let's design the user interface. In order for the user to specify the timeout, the defineAsyncComponent function needs to receive a configuration object as an argument:

```
01 const AsyncComp = defineAsyncComponent({
02 loader: () => import('CompA.vue'),
03 timeout: 2000, // timeout in ms
04 errorComponent: MyErrorComp // specifying the component to render
in case of an error
05 })
```

- loader: Specify the loader of the asynchronous component.
- timeout: The unit is ms, specifying the timeout duration.
- errorComponent: Specify an Error component that will be rendered when an error occurs.

After designing the user interface, we can give the specific implementation, as shown in the following code:

```
01 function defineAsyncComponent(options) {
02 // options can be a configuration item or a loader
03 if (typeof options === 'function') {
04 // If options is a loader, it is formatted as a configuration item
05 options = {
06 loader: options
07 }
08 }
09
10 const { loader } = options
11
12 let InnerComp = null
13
14 return {
15 name: 'AsyncComponentWrapper',
16 setup() {
17 const loaded = ref(false)
```

```
18 // means whether to time out, the default is false, that is, no
timeout
19 const timeout = ref(false)
20
21 loader().then(c => {
22 InnerComp = c
23 loaded.value = true
24 })
25
26 let timer = null
27 if (options.timeout) {
28 // start a timer if timeout is specified
29 timer = setTimeout(() => {
30 // set timeout to true after timeout
31 timeout.value = true
32 }, options.timeout)
33 }
34 // The packing component is removed when the timer is removed
35 onUmounted(() => clearTimeout(timer))
36
37 // placeholder
38 const placeholder = { type: Text, children: '' }
39
40 return () => {
41 if (loaded.value) {
42 // If the component loads successfully asynchronously, the loaded
component is rendered
43 return { type: InnerComp }
44 } else if (timeout.value) {
45 // If the load times out and the user specifies an Error component, the
component is rendered
46 return options.errorComponent ? { type: options.errorComponent }
: placeholder
47 }
48 return placeholder
49 }
50 }
51 }
52 }
```

The overall implementation is not complicated. The key points are as follows.

- A flag variable is required to identify whether the load of the asynchronous component has timed out, that is, timeout.value.
- Start loading the component and start a timer to count. When the load times out, set the timeout.value value to true, which means that the load has timed out. It should be noted here that when the wrapper component is uninstalled, the timer needs to be cleared.
- The wrapper component determines the specific rendering content according to the value of the loaded variable and the value of the timeout variable. If the asynchronous component loads successfully, the loaded component is rendered;

if the asynchronous component loads out of time, and the user specifies the Error component, the Error component is rendered.

In this way, we achieve compatibility with load timeouts and support for Error components. In addition, we hope to have a more complete mechanism to handle errors that occur during asynchronous component loading, and timeout is only one of the causes of errors. Based on this, we also hope to provide users with the following capabilities.

- When an error occurs, the error object is passed as the props of the Error component, so that the user can perform more fine-grained processing on its own
- In addition to timeout, it has the ability to handle loading errors caused by other reasons, such as network failures

To achieve both of these goals, we need to make some adjustments to the code as follows:

```
01 function defineAsyncComponent(options) {
02 if (typeof options === 'function') {
03 options = {
04 loader: options
05 }
06 }
07
08 const { loader } = options
09
10 let InnerComp = null
11
12 return {
13 name: 'AsyncComponentWrapper',
14 setup() {
15 const loaded = ref(false)
16 // Define error; when an error occurs, store the error object
17 const error = shallowRef(null)
18
19 loader()
20 .then(c => {
21 InnerComp = c
22 loaded.value = true
23 })
24 // Add catch statement to catch errors during loading
25 .catch((err) => error.value = err)
26
27 let timer = null
28 if (options.timeout) {
29 timer = setTimeout(() => {
30 // create an error object after timeout and copy it to error.value
31 const err = new Error(`Async component timed out after ${options.timeout}ms.`)
32 error.value = err
33 }, options.timeout)
34 }
```

```
35
36 const placeholder = { type: Text, children: '' }
37
38 return () => {
39 if (loaded.value) {
40 return { type: InnerComp }
41 } else if (error.value && options.errorComponent) {
42 // The Error component is only displayed if the error exists and the
user has configured errorComponent, and the passes error as props
43 return { type: options.errorComponent, props: { error: error.value
} }
44 } else {
45 return placeholder
46 }
47 }
48 }
49 }
50 }
```

Observing the above code, we made some adjustments to the previous implementation. First, add a catch statement to the loader to catch all load errors. Then, when the load times out, we create a new error object and assign it to the error.value variable. When the component is rendered, as long as the error.value value exists and the user has configured the errorComponent component, it is directly rendered and the errorComponent component error.value value is passed as the component's props. In this way, users can receive error objects on their own Error components by defining props named error, so as to achieve fine grain control.

13.2.3   Delay and Loading Components

Components loaded asynchronously are greatly affected by the network, and the loading process may be slow or fast. At this time, we will naturally think, for the first case, whether we can provide a better user experience by displaying the Loading component. In this way, users will not feel "stuck." This is a good idea, but the timing of displaying the Loading component is a problem that needs to be carefully considered. Usually, we will display the Loading component from the moment it is loaded. But in the case of good network conditions, the loading speed of the asynchronous component will be very fast, which will cause the Loading component to enter the uninstall stage immediately after rendering, so there is a flicker situation. This is a very bad experience for the user. Therefore, we need to set a delayed display time for the Loading component. For example, the Loading component is only shown when the load is not completed for more than 200 ms. In this way, the flicker problem is avoided for the case where the load can be completed within 200 ms.

However, the first thing to consider is still the design of the user interface, as shown in the following code:

```
01 defineAsyncComponent ({
02 loader: () => new Promise (r => { /* ... */ }),
03 // Delay 200ms to show the Loading component
04 delay: 200,
05 // Loading component
06 loadingComponent: {
07 setup () {
08 return () => {
09 return { type: 'h2', children: 'Loading...' }
10 }
11 }
12 }
13 })
```

- delay, which is used to specify the duration of the delay to display the Loading component
- loadingComponent, similar to the errorComponent option, is used to configure the Loading component

After the user interface design is completed, we can start to implement it. The specific implementation of the delay time and Loading component is as follows:

```
01 function defineAsyncComponent (options) {
02 if (typeof options === 'function') {
03 options = {
04 loader: options
05 }
06 }
07
08 const { loader } = options
09
10 let InnerComp = null
11
12 return {
13 name: 'AsyncComponentWrapper',
14 setup () {
15 const loaded = ref (false)
16 const error = shallowRef (null)
17 // A flag that indicates whether it is loading, which defaults to false
18 const loading = ref (false)
19
20 let loadingTimer = null
21 // If there is a delay in the configuration item, turn on a timer timer and set loading.value to true when the delay arrives
22 if (options.delay) {
23 loadingTimer = setTimeout (() => {
24 loading.value = true
25 }, options.delay);
26 } else {
```

```
27 // If there is no delay in the configuration item, it is directly
marked as loading
28 loading.value = true
29 }
30 loader()
31 .then(c => {
32 InnerComp = c
33 loaded.value = true
34 })
35 .catch((err) => error.value = err)
36 .finally(() => {
37 loading.value = false
38 // After the load is complete, the delay timer is cleared regardless
of success or failure
39 clearTimeout(loadingTimer)
40 })
41
42 let timer = null
43 if (options.timeout) {
44 timer = setTimeout(() => {
45 const err = new Error(`Async component timed out after ${options.
timeout}ms.`)
46 error.value = err
47 }, options.timeout)
48 }
49
50 const placeholder = { type: Text, children: '' }
51
52 return () => {
53 if (loaded.value) {
54 return { type: InnerComp }
55 } else if (error.value && options.errorComponent) {
56 return { type: options.errorComponent, props: { error: error.value
} }
57 } else if (loading.value && options.loadingComponent) {
58 // If the asynchronous component is loading and the user specifies a
Loading component, render the Loading component
59 return { type: options.loadingComponent }
60 } else {
61 return placeholder
62 }
63 }
64 }
65 }
66 }
```

The overall implementation idea is similar to the timeout and Error components, with the following key points.

- A marker variable loading is required to indicate whether the component is loading.

- If the user specifies a delay time, turn on the delay timer. After the timer expires, set the loading.value to true.
- Clear the delay timer regardless of whether the component is loaded successfully or not, otherwise there will be a problem that the component has been loaded successfully, but still shows the Loading component.
- In the render function, if the component is loading and the user specifies a Loading component, the Loading component is rendered.

Another thing to note is that when the asynchronous component loads successfully, the Loading component is unloaded and the asynchronously loaded component is rendered. In order to support the unmounting of Loading components, we need to modify the unmount function, as shown in the following code:

```
01 function unmount(vnode) {
02 if (vnode.type === Fragment) {
03 vnode.children.forEach(c => unmount(c))
04 return
05 } else if (typeof vnode.type === 'object') {
06 // For the unmounting of components, it is essentially to unmount
the content rendered by the component, that is, subTree
07 unmount(vnode.component.subTree)
08 return
09 }
10 const parent = vnode.el.parentNode
11 if (parent) {
12 parent.removeChild(vnode.el)
13 }
14 }
```

For component unloading, it is essentially to uninstall the content rendered by the component, that is, subTree. So in the above code, we get the component instance through the vnode.component of the component instance, and then recursively call the unmount function to complete the unloading of vnode. component.subTree.

13.2.4   Retry Mechanism

Retry refers to the ability to re-initiate a request to load a component when a loading error occurs. It is very common for an error to occur during the loading of a component, especially when the network is unstable. Therefore, providing an out-of-the-box retry mechanism will improve the user's development experience.

The retry mechanism after an asynchronous component fails to load is the same as the retry mechanism after a failed request to the server level interface. Therefore, let's discuss how the retry mechanism after an interface request fails is implemented. To do this, we need to encapsulate a fetch function to simulate an interface request:

```
01 function fetch() {
02 return new Promise((resolve, reject) => {
03 // request will fail after 1 sec
04 setTimeout(() => {
05 reject('err')
06 }, 1000);
07 })
08 }
```

Assume that the fetch function is called to send an HTTP request, and the request will be sent in 1 s after failure. In order to achieve retry after failure, we need to wrap a load function, as shown in the following code:

```
01 // load function receives an onError callback function
02 function load(onError) {
03 // request interface; get Promise instance
04 const p = fetch()
05 // catch error
06 return p.catch(err => {
07 // when the error occurs, return a new Promise instance and call the
onError callback,
08 // also take the retry function as an argument to the onError
callback
09 return new Promise((resolve, reject) => {
10 // retry function, the function used to perform the retry, the
execution of the function will call the load function again and send the
request
11 const retry = () => resolve(load(onError))
12 const fail = () => reject(err)
13 onError(retry, fail)
14 })
15 })
16 }
```

The fetch function is called inside the load function to send the request and get a Promise instance. Next, a catch block is added to catch the error of that instance. When an error is caught, we have two options: either throw an error or return a new Promise instance and expose the instance's resolve and reject methods to the user, allowing the user to decide what to do next. Here, we encapsulate the resolve and reject of the new Promise instance as retry and fail functions, respectively, and use them as arguments to the onError callback function. This allows the user to actively choose to retry or throw the error when it occurs. The following code shows how the user retries loading:

```
01 // Call the load function to load the resource
02 load(
03 // onError callback
04 (retry) => {
05 // retry after failure
06 retry()
```

```
07 }
08 ).then(res => {
09 // success
10 console.log(res)
11 })
```

Based on this principle, we can easily integrate it into the loading process of asynchronous components. It is implemented as the following:

```
01 function defineAsyncComponent(options) {
02 if (typeof options === 'function') {
03 options = {
04 loader: options
05 }
06 }
07
08 const { loader } = options
09
10 let InnerComp = null
11
12 // Record the number of retries
13 let retries = 0
14 // Encapsulate the load function to load asynchronous components
15 function load() {
16 return loader()
17 // Catch errors for the loader
18 .catch((err) => {
19 // If the user specifies the onError callback, control is given to the
user
20 if (options.onError) {
21 // Return a new instance of the Promise
22 return new Promise((resolve, reject) => {
23 // retry
24 const retry = () => {
25 resolve(load())
26 retries++
27 }
28 // fail
29 const fail = () => reject(err)
30 // As a parameter to the onError callback function, let the user
decide what to do next
31 options.onError(retry, fail, retries)
32 })
33 } else {
34 throw error
35 }
36 })
37 }
38
39 return {
40 name: 'AsyncComponentWrapper',
41 setup() {
```

```
42 const loaded = ref(false)
43 const error = shallowRef(null)
44 const loading = ref(false)
45
46 let loadingTimer = null
47 if (options.delay) {
48 loadingTimer = setTimeout((() => {
49 loading.value = true
50 }, options.delay);
51 } else {
52 loading.value = true
53 }
54 // Call the load function to load the component
55 load()
56 .then(c => {
57 InnerComp = c
58 loaded.value = true
59 })
60 .catch((err) => {
61 error.value = err
62 })
63 .finally(() => {
64 loading.value = false
65 clearTimeout(loadingTimer)
66 })
67
68 // omit some code
69 }
70 }
71 }
```

As shown in the code and comments above, the overall idea is similar to the retry mechanism of ordinary interface requests.

13.3 Functional Components

A functional component is essentially a normal function whose return value is a virtual DOM. As mentioned at the beginning of this chapter: "Functional components are used in Vue.js 3 mainly because of their simplicity, not because of their good performance." This is because in Vue.js 3, even stateful components have very little initialization performance consumption.

At the user interface level, a functional component is a function that returns a virtual DOM, as shown in the following code:

```
01 function MyFuncComp(props) {
02 return { type: 'h1', children: props.title }
03 }
```

Functional components have no state of their own, but it can still receive incoming props from outside. In order to define props for functional components, we need to add static props properties to component functions, as shown in the following code:

```
01 function MyFuncComp(props) {
02 return { type: 'h1', children: props.title }
03 }
04 // define props
05 MyFuncComp.props = {
06 title: String
07 }
```

On the basis of stateful components, implementing functional components will become very simple, because the logic of mounting components can be reused mountComponent Function. To do this, we need vnode.type that supports function types inside the patch function, as shown in the code for the patch function below:

```
01 function patch(n1, n2, container, anchor) {
02 if (n1 && n1.type !== n2.type) {
03 unmount(n1)
04 n1 = null
05 }
06
07 const { type } = n2
08
09 if (typeof type === 'string') {
10 // omit some code
11 } else if (type === Text) {
12 // omit some code
13 } else if (type === Fragment) {
14 // omit some code
15 } else if (
16 // type is an object -- > stateful component
17 // type is a function -- > functional component
18 typeof type === 'object' || typeof type === 'function'
19 ) {
20 // component
21 if (!n1) {
22 mountComponent(n2, container, anchor)
23 } else {
24 patchComponent(n1, n2, anchor)
25 }
26 }
27 }
```

Inside the patch function, determine the type of a component by checking the type of vnode.type:

- if vnode.type is an object, it is a stateful component, and vnode.type is a component option object;
- if vnode.type is a function, it is a functional component.

But whether it is a stateful component or a functional component, we can mount it through the mountComponent function, and we can also update it through the patchComponent function.

The following is a modified mountComponent function that supports mounting functional components:

```
01 function mountComponent(vnode, container, anchor) {
02 // Check if it is a functional component
03 const isFunctional = typeof vnode.type === 'function'
04
05 let componentOptions = vnode.type
06 if (isFunctional) {
07 // If it is a functional component, vnode.type is the render
function and vnode.type.props is the props option
08 componentOptions = {
09 render: vnode.type,
10 props: vnode.type.props
11 }
12 }
13
14 // omit some code
15 }
```

As you can see, it is very simple to achieve compatibility with functional components. First, check the type of the component in the mountComponent function. If it is a functional component, directly use the component function as the render option of the component option object, and use the static props property of the component function as the component's props option. Other logic remains unchanged. Of course, for more serious considerations, we need to implement the initialization logic selectively through isFunctional variables, because for functional components, it does not need to initialize data and lifecycle hooks. From this point, it can be seen that the initialization performance consumption of functional components is less than that of stateful components.

13.4 Summary

In this chapter, we first discussed the problems to be solved by asynchronous components. Asynchronous components are especially important in scenarios such as page performance, unpacking, and server level distribution of components. Basically, the implementation of asynchronous components can be completely implemented at the user level without the need for framework support. However, a complete asynchronous component still needs to consider many issues, such as

- Allowing the user to specify the component to be rendered when loading errors
- Allowing the user to specify the delay time of the Loading component and displaying the component
- Allowing the user to set the timeout time for loading the component
- Providing the user with the ability to retry when the component fails to load

Therefore, it is necessary for the framework to build the implementation of asynchronous components.

Vue.js 3 provides the defineAsyncComponent function to define asynchronous components.

Next, we explained the load timeout problem of asynchronous components and how to specify the Error component when a load error occurs. By specifying the option parameter for the defineAsyncComponent function, the user is allowed to set the timeout duration through the timeout option. When the load timeout is triggered, a load error will be triggered, which will render the Error component specified by the user through the errorComponent option.

During the loading of asynchronous components, it is greatly affected by network conditions. When network conditions are poor, the loading process can be lengthy. To provide a better user experience, we need to display the Loading Component at load time. Therefore, we designed the loadingComponent option to allow users to configure custom Loading Components. But the timing of displaying Loading Components is an issue that requires careful consideration. In order to avoid the flicker problem caused by the Loading component, we also need to design an interface that allows the user to specify the delay time to display the Loading component, that is, the delay option.

During the process of loading the component, errors occur very often. Therefore, we designed a retry mechanism after the component loading error occurs. When explaining the retry loading mechanism of asynchronous components, we compared the retry mechanism when the interface request fails, and the two ideas are similar.

Finally, we discussed functional components. It is essentially a function whose internal implementation logic can reuse the implementation logic of stateful components. To define props for functional components, we allow developers to add static, props properties to the main function of functional components. For more serious considerations, functional components have no own state and no concept of life cycle. Therefore, when initializing functional components, it is necessary to selectively reuse the initialization logic of stateful components.

Chapter 14
Built-In Components and Modules

In Chaps. 12 and 13, we discussed how Vue.js achieved the ability of components based on the renderer. In this chapter, we will discuss several very important built-in components and modules in the Vue.js, such as KeepAlive components, Teleport components, Transition components, etc., all of which require low-level support at the renderer level. In addition, the capabilities provided by these built-in components are very important and useful for developers, and understanding how they work will help us use them correctly.

14.1 Implementation Principles of KeepAlive Component

14.1.1 Activation and Deactivation of Components

The term KeepAlive is borrowed from the HTTP protocol. In the HTTP protocol, KeepAlive is also known as HTTP persistent connection (HTTP persistent connection), which allows multiple requests or responses to share a TCP connection. Without KeepAlive, an HTTP connection is closed after each request/response, and a new HTTP connection is established when the next request occurs. Frequent destruction and creation of HTTP connections introduce additional performance overhead, and KeepAlive is built to solve this problem.

KeepAlive in HTTP avoids frequent destruction/creation of connections. Similar to KeepAlive in HTTP, Vue.js built-in KeepAlive components can prevent a component from being destroyed/rebuilt frequently. Suppose we have a set of < Tab > components in our page, as shown in the following code:

```
01 <template>
02 <Tab v-if="currentTab === 1">...</Tab>
03 <Tab v-if="currentTab === 2">...</Tab>
```

```
04 <Tab v-if="currentTab === 3">...</Tab>
05 </template>
```

As you can see, different < Tab > components are rendered depending on the value of the variable currentTab. When users switch tabs frequently, it will cause the corresponding < Tab > components to be uninstalled and rebuilt non-stop. To avoid the resulting performance overhead, you can use the KeepAlive component to solve this problem, as shown in the following code:

```
01 <template>
02 <!-- Wrapped with the KeepAlive component -->
03 <KeepAlive>
04 <Tab v-if="currentTab === 1">...</Tab>
05 <Tab v-if="currentTab === 2">...</Tab>
06 <Tab v-if="currentTab === 3">...</Tab>
07 </KeepAlive>
08 </template>
```

In this way, no matter how the user switches < Tab > components, frequent creation and destruction will not occur, thus greatly optimizing the response to user actions, especially in large component scenarios, where advantage will be more obvious. So, what is the implementation principle of KeepAlive components? In fact, the essence of KeepAlive is cache management, coupled with special mount/ unload logic.

First of all, the implementation of KeepAlive components needs renderer-level support. This is because when the KeepAlive component is uninstalled, we cannot really uninstall it, otherwise the current state of the component cannot be maintained. The correct way is to move the KeepAlive component from the original container to another hidden container to achieve "fake unloading." When a component moved into a hidden container needs to be "mounted" again, we cannot perform the real mount logic, but should move the component from the hidden container to the original container. This process corresponds to the life cycle of the component, which is actually activated and deactivated.

Figure 14.1 depicts the process of "unmounting" and "mounting" a KeepAlive component.

The process of "unmounting" and "mounting" a KeepAlive component is shown in Fig. 14.1. When "unmounting" a KeepAlive component, it is not actually unmounted, but moved to a hidden container. When the component is "mounted" again, it is not actually mounted, but is removed from the hidden container and "put back" in the original container, that is, the page.

A basic KeepAlive component is not complicated to implement, as shown in the following code:

```
01 const KeepAlive = {
02 // unique properties of KeepAlive component, used as identification
03 __isKeepAlive: true,
```

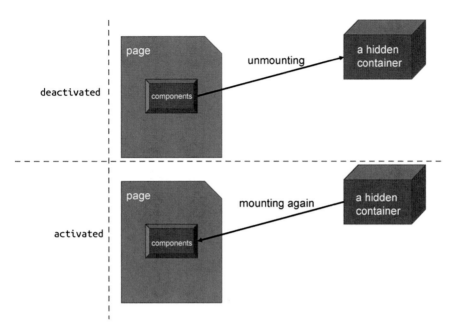

Fig. 14.1 The process of "Unmounting" and "Mounting" a KeepAlive component

```
04 setup(props, { slots }) {
05 // Create a cache object
06 // key: vnode.type
07 // value: vnode
08 const cache = new Map()
09 // An instance of the current KeepAlive component
10 const instance = currentInstance
11 // For the KeepAlive component, there is a special startAliveCtx
object on its instance, which is injected by the renderer
12 // This object exposes some internal methods of the renderer, where
the move function is used to move a piece of DOM into another container
13 const { move, createElement } = instance.keepAliveCtx
14
15 // Create a hidden container
16 const storageContainer = createElement('div')
17
18 // Two internal functions are added to the instance of the KeepAlive
component, _deActivate and _activate
19 // These two functions are called in the renderer
20 instance._deActivate = (vnode) => {
21 move(vnode, storageContainer)
22 }
23 instance._activate = (vnode, container, anchor) => {
24 move(vnode, container, anchor)
25 }
26
27 return () => {
```

```
28 // KeepAlive's default slot is to be KeepAlive's component
29 let rawVNode = slots.default()
30 // If it is not a component, it is sufficient to render directly,
because virtual nodes that are not components cannot be KeepAlive
31 if (typeof rawVNode.type !== 'object') {
32 return rawVNode
33 }
34
35 // If it is not a component, it can be rendered directly, because
non-component virtual nodes cannot be KeepAlive
36 const cachedVNode = cache.get(rawVNode.type)
37 if (cachedVNode) {
38 // If there is cached content, it means that the mount should not be
performed, but should be activated
39 // Inherit component instance
40 rawVNode.component = cachedVNode.component
41 // Add the keptAlive property on the vnode, mark it true, avoid
renderer to remount it
42 rawVNode.keptAlive = true
43 } else {
44 // If there is no cache, add it to the cache so no new mount action is
performed the next time the component is activated
45 cache.set(rawVNode.type, rawVNode)
46 }
47
48 // Add shouldKeepAlive property on component vnode and mark it true
to avoid the renderer actually unloading the component
49 rawVNode.shouldKeepAlive = true
50 // Add instance of KeepAlive component to vnode as well to access
51 rawVNode.keepAliveInstance = instance
52
53 // Render component vnode
54 return rawVNode
55 }
56 }
57 }
```

As can be seen from the implementation of KeepAlive above, a big difference from ordinary components is that the combination of KeepAlive components and renderers is very deep. First of all, the KeepAlive component itself does not render additional content. Its render function only returns the component that needs to be KeepAlive. We call this component that needs to be KeepAlive as an "internal component." The KeepAlive component will operate on the "internal component," mainly adding some markup properties on the vnode object of the "internal component," so that the renderer can perform specific logic accordingly. These markup properties include the following.

- shouldKeepAlive: This property will be added to the vnode object of the "internal component," so that when the renderer uninstalls the "internal component," it can be checked that the "internal component" needs to be KeepAlive. As a result, the renderer will not actually unmount the "internal component," but will call the _deActivate function to complete the handling, as shown in the following code:

```
01 // unmount operation
02 function unmount (vnode) {
03 if (vnode.type === Fragment) {
04 vnode.children.forEach(c => unmount(c))
05 return
06 } else if (typeof vnode.type === 'object') {
07 // vnode.shouldKeepAlive is a boolean, which is used to identify
whether the component should be KeepAlive
08 if (vnode.shouldKeepAlive) {
09 // For components that need to be KeepAlive, we should not actually
unmount it, but call the parent component of the component
10 // That is, the _deActivate function of the KeepAlive component
deactivates it
11 vnode.keepAliveInstance._deActivate(vnode)
12 } else {
13 unmount (vnode.component.subTree)
14 }
15 return
16 }
17 const parent = vnode.el.parentNode
18 if (parent) {
19 parent.removeChild(vnode.el)
20 }
21 }
```

As you can see, the unmount function detects whether the component should be KeepAlive when unmounting the component, so as to perform different operations.

- keepAliveInstance: The vnode object of the "internal component" will hold the KeepAlive component instance, and the _deActivate function will be accessed through keepAliveInstance in the unmount function.
- keptAlive: If the "internal component" is already cached, it will also add a keptAlive flag to it. In this way, when the "internal component" needs to be re-rendered, the renderer will not remount it, but will activate it, as shown in the code of the patch function below:

```
01 function patch(n1, n2, container, anchor) {
02 if (n1 && n1.type !== n2.type) {
03 unmount(n1)
04 n1 = null
05 }
06
07 const { type } = n2
08
09 if (typeof type === 'string') {
10 // omit some code
11 } else if (type === Text) {
```

```
12 // omit some code
13 } else if (type === Fragment) {
14 // omit some code
15 } else if (typeof type === 'object' || typeof type ===
'function') {
16 // component
17 if (!n1) {
18 // If the component is already KeepAlive, it is not remounted, but
_activate is called to activate it
19 if (n2.keptAlive) {
20 n2.keepAliveInstance._activate(n2, container, anchor)
21 } else {
22 mountComponent(n2, container, anchor)
23 }
24 } else {
25 patchComponent(n1, n2, anchor)
26 }
27 }
28 }
```

You can see if the keptAlive flag is present in the object of the vnode of the component, the renderer does not remount it, but activates it via the keepAliveInstance._activate function.

Let's look at the two functions used to activate and inactivate components:

```
01 const { move, createElement } = instance.keepAliveCtx
02
03 instance._deActivate = (vnode) => {
04 move(vnode, storageContainer)
05 }
06 instance._activate = (vnode, container, anchor) => {
07 move(vnode, container, anchor)
08 }
```

As you can see, the essence of deactivation is to move the content rendered by the component into a hidden container, and the essence of activation is to transport the content rendered by the component from the hidden container back to the original container. In addition, the move function involved in the above code is injected by the renderer, as shown in the code of the mountComponent function below:

```
01 function mountComponent(vnode, container, anchor) {
02 // Omit part of the code
03
04 const instance = {
05 state,
06 props: shallowReactive(props),
07 isMounted: false,
08 subTree: null,
09 slots,
10 mounted: [],
```

```
11 // Only KeepAlive component instances will have a reservAliveCtx
property
12 keepAliveCtx: null
13 }
14
15 // Check whether the current component to be mounted is a
KeepAlive component
16 const isKeepAlive = vnode.type.__isKeepAlive
17 if (isKeepAlive) {
18 // Add a reservAliveCtx object to the KeepAlive component instance
19 instance.keepAliveCtx = {
20 // move function to move a vnode
21 move(vnode, container, anchor) {
22 // Essentially, it is to move the rendered content of the
component into the specified container, that is, hide the container
23 insert(vnode.component.subTree.el, container, anchor)
24 },
25 createElement
26 }
27 }
28
29 // omit some code
30 }
```

At this point, a basic KeepAlive component is complete.

14.1.2   Include and Exclude

By default, the KeepAlive component will cache all "internal components." But sometimes the user expects only specific components to be cached. To enable users to customize caching rules, we need to make the KeepAlive component support two props, include and exclude. Among them, include is used to explicitly configure the components that should be cached, and exclude is used to explicitly configure the components that should not be cached.

The props for the KeepAlive component are defined as follows:

```
01 const KeepAlive = {
02 __isKeepAlive: true,
03 // Define include and exclude
04 props: {
05 include: RegExp,
06 exclude: RegExp
07 },
08 setup(props, { slots }) {
09 // omit some code
10 }
11 }
```

   To simplify matters, we only allow regular type values for include and exclude. When the KeepAlive component is mounted, it is matched according to the name of the "internal component" (i.e., the name option), as shown in the following code:

```
01 const cache = new Map()
02 const KeepAlive = {
03 __isKeepAlive: true,
04 props: {
05 include: RegExp,
06 exclude: RegExp
07 },
08 setup(props, { slots }) {
09 // omit some code
10
11 return () => {
12 let rawVNode = slots.default()
13 if (typeof rawVNode.type !== 'object') {
14 return rawVNode
15 }
16 // get the name of "internal component"
17 const name = rawVNode.type.name
18 // match name
19 if (
20 name &&
21 (
22 // if name cannot be matched by include
23 (props.include && !props.include.test(name)) ||
24 // or be matched by excluded
25 (props.exclude && props.exclude.test(name))
26 )
27 ) {
28 // render "internal components" directly without subsequent
caching operations
29 return rawVNode
30 }
31
32 // omit some code
33 }
34 }
35 }
```

   We match the names of the "internal components" according to the user-specified include and exclude regularities, and judge whether to cache the "internal components" based on the matching results. On this basis, we can arbitrarily expand the matching capabilities. For example, we can design include and exclude as multiple types of values, allowing the user to specify strings or functions, thus providing a more flexible matching mechanism. In addition, when making matching, it is not limited to the name of the "internal component," and we can even let users specify the matching element by themselves. But in any case, the principle remains unchanged.

14.1.3   Cache Management

In the implementation given above, we use a Map object to cache components:

```
01 const cache = new Map()
```

The key of the Map object is the component option object, that is, the value of the vnode.type property, and the value of the Map object is the vnode object used to describe the component. Since the vnode object used to describe the component has a reference to the component instance (i.e., vnode.component property), caching the vnode object used to describe the component is equivalent to caching the component instance.

Review the current KeepAlive component on the cache implementation, the following is part of the component rendering function code:

```
01 // KeepAlive component rendering function on the cache
implementation
02
03 // Use the component option object rawVNode.type as the key to find
the cache
04 const cachedVNode = cache.get(rawVNode.type)
05 if (cachedVNode) {
06 // If the cache exists, you do not need to re-create the component
instance; just need to inherit
07 rawVNode.component = cachedVNode.component
08 rawVNode.keptAlive = true
09 } else {
10 // Set cache if cache does not exist
11 cache.set(rawVNode.type, rawVNode)
12 }
```

The processing logic of cache can be summarized as:

- If cache exists, inherit component instance and mark vnode object used to describe component as keptAlive, so that renderer does not recreate new component instance
- If cache does not exist, set cache

The problem here is that when cache does not exist, new cache is always set. This causes cache to keep growing, which in extreme cases takes up a lot of memory. To solve this problem, we have to set a cache threshold and prune the cache when the number of caches exceeds the specified threshold. But this begs another question: how should we prune the cache? In other words, when the cache needs to be pruned, what strategy should it be pruned with? Which part should be pruned first?

The current pruning strategy of Vue.js is called "latest access." First, you need to set the maximum cache capacity, which is set by the max property of the KeepAlive component, for example:

```
01 <KeepAlive :max="2">
02 <component :is="dynamicComp"/>
03 </KeepAlive>
```

In the above code, we set the cache capacity to 2. Suppose we have three components Comp1, Comp2, Comp3, and they will all be cached. Then, we start to simulate the cache change during the component switching process, as shown below.

- Initially render Comp1 and cache it. At this time, the cache queue is [Comp1], and the latest accessed (or rendered) component is Comp1.
- Switch to Comp2 and cache it. At this time, the cache queue is [Comp1, Comp2], and the latest accessed (or rendered) component is Comp2.
- Switch to Comp3. At this time, the cache capacity is full and needs to be pruned. Who should be pruned? Because the last component accessed (or rendered) is Comp2, it is "safe," that is, it will not be pruned. Therefore, the component that will be pruned will be Comp1. When the cache is pruned, there will be free cache space to store Comp3. So, now, the cache queue is [Comp2, Comp3], and the last rendered component becomes Comp3.

We can also switch components another way, as shown below.

- Initially render Comp1 and cache it. At this point, the cache queue is [Comp1], and the latest component accessed (or rendered) is Comp1.
- Switch to Comp2 and cache it. At this point, the cache queue is [Comp1, Comp2], and the latest component accessed (or rendered) is Comp2.
- Switch back to Comp1. Since Comp1 is already in the cache queue, there is no need to prune the cache, just activate the component, but set the latest rendered component to Comp1.
- When switching to Comp3, the cache capacity is full and needs to be trimmed. Who should be trimmed? Since Comp1 is the latest rendered, it is "safe," that is, it will not be trimmed, so it is Comp2 that will eventually be trimmed. Therefore, the current cache queue is [Comp1, Comp3], and the latest rendered component becomes Comp3.

It can be seen that the final cache result will be different under different simulation strategies. The core of the cache pruning strategy is that the currently accessed (or rendered) component needs to be the latest rendered component, and the component is always safe during the cache pruning process, that is, it will not be pruned.

Implementing Vue.js built-in cache strategy is not difficult, which is essentially equivalent to a small algorithm problem. Our concern is whether the cache policy can be changed. Even allow users to customize the cache policy? In fact, there are already relevant proposals in the official RFCs ①. This proposal allows users to implement custom cache policies, and at the user interface level, the KeepAlive component adds a new cache interface that allows users to specify cache instances:

```
01 <KeepAlive :cache="cache">
02 <Comp />
03 </KeepAlive>
```

Cache instances need to meet a fixed format, a basic cache instance implementation is as follows:

```
01 // Custom implementation
02 const _cache = new Map()
03 const cache: KeepAliveCache = {
04 get(key) {
05 _cache.get(key)
06 },
07 set(key, value) {
08 _cache.set(key, value)
09 },
10 delete(key) {
11 _cache.delete(key)
12 },
13 forEach(fn) {
14 _cache.forEach(fn)
15 }
16 }
```

In the internal implementation of the KeepAlive component, if the user provides a custom cache instance, the cache instance is used directly to manage the cache. In essence, this is equivalent to transferring management rights for the cache from the KeepAlive component to the user.

14.2   Implementation Principles of Teleport Components

14.2.1   Problems to Be Solved by Teleport Components

The Teleport component is a built-in component added in Vue.js 3. Let's first discuss what problems it wants to solve. Usually, when rendering a virtual DOM as a real DOM, the hierarchy of the final rendered real DOM is the same as that of the virtual DOM. Take the following template as an example:

```
01 < template >
02 < div id = "box" style = "z-index: -1;" >
03 < Overlay/>
04 </div >
05 </template >
```

In this template, the content of the < Overlay > component will be rendered under the div tag with id box. However, sometimes this is not what we expect.

Suppose $<$ Overlay $>$ is an "overlay" component that renders an "overlay" and requires the "overlay" to be able to occlude any element on the page. In other words, we require the $<$ Overlay $>$ component to have the highest level of z-index to achieve occlusion. But the problem is that if the content of the $<$ Overlay $>$ component cannot be rendered across the DOM hierarchy, this goal cannot be achieved. Take the above template as an example. The div tag with id box has an internal connection style: z-index: -1, which makes it impossible to achieve occlusion even if we set the z-index value of the content rendered by the $<$ Overlay $>$ component to infinity.

Usually, when facing the above scenario, we will choose to render the "overlay" content directly under the $<$ body $>$ tag. In Vue.js 2, we can only manually handle the DOM element implementation requirements through the native DOM API. The disadvantage of this is that manually manipulating DOM elements can make the rendering of elements out of touch with the Vue.js rendering mechanism and cause various foreseeable or unforeseeable problems. Considering that this requirement is indeed very common, and users are eager to expect it, Vue.js 3 has a built-in Teleport component. This component can render specified content into a specific container without being restricted by the DOM hierarchy.

Let's first look at how the Teleport component solves this problem. The following is the template of the $<$ Overlay $>$ component based on the Teleport component:

```
01 < template >
02 < Teleport to = "body" >
03 < div class = "overlay" > </div >
04 </Teleport >
05 </template >
06 < style scoped >
07 .overlay {
08 z-index: 9999;
09 }
10 </style >
```

You can see that the content that needs to be rendered by the $<$ Overlay $>$ component is contained in the Teleport component, which is the slot of the Teleport component. By specifying the value of the render target body, that is, the value of the to attribute for the Teleport component, the component will directly render its slot content under the body, instead of rendering according to the DOM level of the template, thus achieving cross-DOM level rendering. Finally, the z-index value of the $<$ Overlay $>$ component will also work as expected and block all content in the page.

14.2.2   Implementing Teleport Components

Like the KeepAlive component, the Teleport component also needs the underlying support of the renderer. First of all, we need to separate the rendering logic of the Teleport component from the renderer, which has two advantages:

- It can avoid the "bloat" of the renderer logic code
- When the user does not use the Teleport component, because the rendering logic of the Teleport is separated, we can use the TreeShaking mechanism to remove the Teleport-related code in the final bundle, making the final build package smaller.

To accomplish the logical separation, first modify the patch function, as shown in the following code:

```
01 function patch(n1, n2, container, anchor) {
02 if (n1 && n1.type !== n2.type) {
03 unmount(n1)
04 n1 = null
05 }
06
07 const { type } = n2
08
09 if (typeof type === 'string') {
10 // omit some code
11 } else if (type === Text) {
12 // omit some code
13 } else if (type === Fragment) {
14 // omit some code
15 } else if (typeof type === 'object' && type.__isTeleport) {
16 // If there is a __isTeleport identifier in the component option, it is a Teleport component,
17 // Call the process function in the Teleport component option to hand over control
18 // The fifth parameter passed to the process function is some internal method of the renderer
19 type.process(n1, n2, container, anchor, {
20 patch,
21 patchChildren,
22 unmount,
23 move(vnode, container, anchor) {
24 insert(vnode.component ? vnode.component.subTree.el : vnode.el, container, anchor)
25 }
26 })
27 } else if (typeof type === 'object' || typeof type === 'function') {
28 // omit some code
29 }
30 }
```

As you can see, we passUse the __isTeleport identifier of the component option to determine whether the component is a Teleport component. If yes, directly call the process function defined in the component option to completely hand over the rendering control, thus achieving the separation of rendering and logic.

The definition of the Teleport component is as follows:

```
01 const Teleport = {
02 __isTeleport: true,
03 process (n1, n2, container, anchor) {
04 //handle rendering logic here
05 }
06 }
```

As you can see, the Teleport component is not a normal component; it has special options __isTeleport and process.

Next, we design the structure of the virtual DOM. Suppose the user writes the following template:

```
01 < Teleport to = "body" >
02 < h1 > Title </h1 >
03 < p > content </p >
04 </Teleport >
```

So, what kind of virtual DOM should it be compiled into? Although Teleport is a built-in component to the user, in fact, the nature of whether Teleport has components is determined by the framework itself. Normally, a component's sub-node is compiled as the contents of the slot, but for Teleport components, the sub-node is directly compiled into an array, as shown in the following code:

```
01 function render() {
02 return {
03 type: Teleport,
04 // Represent the content of the Teleport in the form of ordinary children
05 children: [
06 { type: 'h1', children: 'Title' },
07 { type: 'p', children: 'content' }
08 ]
09 }
10 }
```

After designing the structure of the virtual DOM, we can start implementing the Teleport component, as in the following code:

```
01 const Teleport = {
02 __isTeleport: true,
03 process(n1, n2, container, anchor, internals) {
04 // Get the internal method of the renderer through the internals parameter
05 const { patch } = internals
06 // If the old VNode n1 does not exist, it is a brand new mount, otherwise Perform update
07 if (!n1) {
08 // mount
09 // get the container, that is, mount point
```

```
10 const target = typeof n2.props.to === 'string'
11 ? document.querySelector(n2.props.to)
12 : n2.props.to
13 // Render n2.children to the specified mount point
14 n2.children.forEach(c => patch(null, c, target, anchor))
15 } else {
16 // Update
17 }
18 }
19 }
```

As you can see, even if the Teleport rendering logic is separated separately, its rendering ideas are still consistent with the rendering ideas of the renderer itself. Determine whether to mount or update by judging whether the old virtual node (n1) exists. If you want to perform a mount, you need to get the real mount point based on the value of the props.to property. Finally, iterate through the children property of the Teleport component and call the patch function one by one to complete the sub-node mount.

The handling of updates is simpler, as shown in the following code:

```
01 const Teleport = {
02 __isTeleport: true,
03 process(n1, n2, container, anchor, internals) {
04 const { patch, patchChildren } = internals
05 if (!n1) {
06 // Omit some code
07 } else {
08 // update
09 patchChildren(n1, n2, container)
10 }
11 }
12 }
```

Just call the patchChildren function to complete the update operation. However, it is important to note that the update operation may be caused by a change in the value of the to attribute of the Teleport component, so we should consider this situation when updating.

```
01 const Teleport = {
02 __isTeleport: true,
03 process(n1, n2, container, anchor, internals) {
04 const { patch, patchChildren, move } = internals
05 if (!n1) {
06 // omit some code
07 } else {
08 // update
09 patchChildren(n1, n2, container)
10 // if the old and new to parameters have different values, you need
to move the content
11 if (n2.props.to !== n1.props.to) {
```

```
12 // get new containers
13 const newTarget = typeof n2.props.to === 'string'
14 ? document.querySelector(n2.props.to)
15 : n2.props.to
16 // Move to a new container
17 n2.children.forEach(c => move(c, newTarget))
18 }
19 }
20 }
21 }
```

The implementation of the move function used to perform the move operation is as follows:

```
01 else if (typeof type === 'object' && type.__isTeleport) {
02 type.process(n1, n2, container, anchor, {
03 patch,
04 patchChildren,
05 // Used to move the content of Teleport
06 move(vnode, container, anchor) {
07 insert(
08 vnode.component
09 ? vnode.component.subTree.el // Move a component
10 : vnode.el, // Move a normal element
11 container,
12 anchor
13 )
14 }
15 })
16 }
```

In the above code, we only consider moving components and normal elements. We know that there are many types of virtual nodes, such as text type, fragment type, etc. A perfect implementation should consider the types of all these virtual nodes.

14.3 Implementation Principles of Transition Components

Through the explanation of KeepAlive components and Teleport components, we can realize that Vue.js built-in components are usually very closely integrated with the core logic of the renderer. The Transition component discussed in this section is no exception, and it is even more closely integrated with the renderer.

In fact, the implementation of the Transition component is much simpler than expected. Its core principle is as follows:

- When a DOM element is mounted, attach motion graphics to the DOM element
- When a DOM element is unmounted, do not uninstall the DOM element immediately, but wait until the dynamic attached to the DOM element is completed before uninstalling it.

Of course, the rules mainly follow the above two elements. However, we only need to understand its core principle. As for the details, you can add or improve it as needed on the basis of the basic implementation.

14.3.1   *Transition of Native DOM*

In order to better understand the implementation principle of Transition components, it is necessary to first discuss how to create transition motion graphics for native DOM. The transition effect is essentially a switch between two states of a DOM element, and the browser will complete the transition of the DOM element according to the transition effect. The transition effect here refers to the duration, motion curve, attributes to be transitioned, etc.

Let's start with an example. Suppose we have a div element with width and height of 100px, as shown in the following code:

```
01 < div class = "box" > </div >
```

Next, add the corresponding CSS style to it:

```
01 .box {
02 width: 100px;
03 height: 100px;
04 background-color: red;
05 }
```

Now, suppose we want to add an entry motion graphics to the element. We can describe the motion graphics as follows: Moving from a position of 200px from the left to a position of 0px from the left in 1 s. In this description, the initial state is "200px from the left," so we can use the following style to describe the initial state:

```
01 enter-from {
02 transform: translateX (200px);
03 }
```

and the end state is "0px from the left," which is the initial position, which can be described by the following CSS code:

```
01 enter-to {
02 transform: translateX (0);
03 }
```

The initial state and the end state have been described. Finally, we also describe the motion process, such as duration, motion curve, etc. For this, we can use the following CSS code to describe:

```
01 enter-active {
02 transition: transform 1s ease-in-out;
03 }
```

Here we specify that the motion property is transform, duration is 1 s, and the motion curve is ease-in-out.

After defining the initial state, end state, and motion process of the motion, we can add motion graphics to the DOM element, as shown in the following code:

```
01 // Create a DOM element with class box
02 const el = document.createElement('div')
03 el.classList.add('box')
04
05 // Before the DOM element is added to the page, define the initial
state and motion process to elements
06 el.classList.add('enter-from') // the initial state
07 el.classList.add('enter-active') // motion process
08
09 // add elements to pages
10 document.body.appendChild(el)
```

The above code mainly does three things:

- Create DOM elements
- Define the initial state of transition and motion process to the element, that is, put enter-from, enter-active—these two classes—to the element
- Add elements to the page, that is, mount

After these three steps, the initial state of the element will take effect. When the page is rendered, the DOM element will be displayed in the initial state and the defined style. Next, we need to switch the state of the element so that the element starts to move. So, what should be done? In theory, we just need to remove the enter-from class from the DOM element and add the enter-to class to the DOM element, as shown in the following code:

```
01 // Create a DOM element with class box
02 const el = document.createElement('div')
03 el.classList.add('box')
04
05 // Define the initial state and motion process to the DOM element
before it is added to the page
```

```
06 el.classList.add('enter-from') // 初始状态
07 el.classList.add('enter-active') // Initial state
08
09 // add element to page
10 document.body.appendChild(el)
11
12 // toggle element state
13 el.classList.remove('enter-from') // remove enter-from
14 el.classList.add('enter-to') // add enter-to
```

However, the above code does not perform as expected. This is because the browser will draw the DOM element in the current frame, and the end result is that the browser will draw the style of the enter-to class instead of the style of the enter-from class. To solve this problem, we need to perform state switching in the next frame, as shown in the following code:

```
01 // Create DOM element with class box
02 const el = document.createElement('div')
03 el.classList.add('box')
04
05 // Before DOM element is added to the page, define the initial state
and motion process to the element
06 el.classList.add('enter-from') // initial state
07 el.classList.add('enter-active') // motion process
08
09 // add the element to the page
10 document.body.appendChild(el)
11
12 // switch the state of the element in the next frame
13 requestAnimationFrame(() => {
14 el.classList.remove('enter-from') // remove enter-from
15 el.classList.add('enter-to') // add enter-to
16 })
```

You can see that we use requestAnimationFrame to register a callback function, which will theoretically be executed in the next frame. In this way, the browser will draw the initial state of the element in the current frame, and then switch the state of the element in the next frame, so that the transition takes effect. But if you try to run the above code in Chrome or Safari browser, you will find that the transition still does not take effect. Why? In fact, this is caused by a browser implementation bug. See Issue 675795: Interop: mismatch in when animations are started between different browsers for a detailed description of the bug. The gist of this is that the registration callback using the requestAnimationFrame function executes in the current frame unless other code has already called the requestAnimationFrame function once. This is obviously incorrect, so we need a workaround, as shown in the following code:

```
01 // Create a DOM element with class box
02 const el = document.createElement('div')
03 el.classList.add('box')
04
 05 // Define the initial state and motion process on the element before
the DOM element is added to the page
06 el.classList.add('enter-from') // Initial state
07 el.classList.add('enter-active') // motion process
08
09 // Add elements to pages
10 document.body.appendChild(el)
11
12 // Nested calls requestAnimationFrame
13 requestAnimationFrame(() => {
14 requestAnimationFrame(() => {
15 el.classList.remove('enter-from') // Remove enter-from
16 el.classList.add('enter-to') // Add enter-to
17 })
18 })
```

The above problem can be solved by nesting a call to the requestAnimationFrame function. Now, if you try to run the code in the browser again, you will find that the incoming motion graphics can be displayed normally.

The last thing we need to do is, when the transition is complete, remove the enter-to and enter-active classes from the DOM element, as shown in the following code:

```
01 // Create a DOM element with class box
02 const el = document.createElement('div')
03 el.classList.add('box')
04
 05 // Define the initial state and motion process before the DOM
element is added to the page
06 el.classList.add('enter-from') // initial state
07 el.classList.add('enter-active') // motion process
08
09 // add element to pages
10 document.body.appendChild(el)
11
12 // nested call requestAnimationFrame
13 requestAnimationFrame(() => {
14 requestAnimationFrame(() => {
15 el.classList.remove('enter-from') // remove enter-from
16 el.classList.add('enter-to') // add enter-to
17
 18 // listen for transitionend event to complete the finishing touches
19 el.addEventListener('transitionend', () => {
20 el.classList.remove('enter-to')
21 el.classList.remove('enter-active')
22 })
23 })
24 })
```

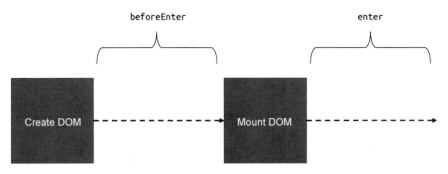

Fig. 14.2 The abstraction of the entry transition process

Finish the work by listening for the element's transitionend event. In fact, we can abstract the above process of adding the entry transition to the DOM element, as shown in Fig. 14.2.

It can be regarded as the beforeEnter stage from the time the DOM element is created to the time the DOM element is added to the body. After the DOM element is added to the body, it can be regarded as the enter stage. Perform different operations in different stages to complete the implementation of the entire entry-to transition.

- beforeEnter stage: add enter-from and enter-active classes.
- enter stage: remove enter-from and add enter-to in the next frame.
- End of entry motion graphics: remove enter-to and enter-active classes.

After understanding the implementation principle of the entry transition, next we discuss the exit transition effect of DOM elements. As with the approach transition, we need to define the initial state, end state, and transition process of the exit transition, as shown in the following CSS code:

```
01 /* Initial state */
02 .leave-from {
03 transform: translateX(0);
04 }
05 /* End state */
06 .leave-to {
07 transform: translateX(200px);
08 }
09 /* Transition process */
10 .leave-active {
11 transition: transform 2s ease-out;
12 }
```

You can see that the initial state and the end state of the exit transition correspond exactly to the end state and the initial state of the incoming transition. Of course, we can completely break this correspondence, and you can use any transition effect.

Exit dynamic effect graphics usually happens when the DOM element is unloaded, as shown in the following code:

```
01//Uninstall Element
02 el.addEventListener ('click ', () => {
03 el.parentNode.removeChild(el)
04})
```

When an element is clicked, the element will be removed, thus achieving
unloading. However, as can be seen from the code, the element will be unloaded
the moment it is clicked, so if only this is done, the element will have no chance to
perform the transition at all. So, a very natural idea arises: when an element is
unloaded, do not unload it immediately, but wait for the transition effect to end
before unloading it. To achieve this, we need to encapsulate the code for unloading
DOM elements into a function that waits for the transition to be called, as shown in
the following code:

```
01 el.addEventListener('click', () => {
02 // encapsulate the unloading action into the performRemove
function
03 const performRemove = () => el.parentNode.removeChild(el)
04 })
```

In the above code, we encapsulate the unloading action into the performRemove
function, which will wait for the transition effect to end before executing.

The specific implementation of the exit dynamic effect is as follows:

```
01 el.addEventListener('click', () => {
02 // encapsulate the unloading action into the performRemove
function
03 const performRemove = () => el.parentNode.removeChild(el)
04
05 // Set initial state: add leave-from and leave-active classes
06 el.classList.add('leave-from')
07 el.classList.add('leave-active')
08
09 // Force reflow: make initial status effective
10 document.body.offsetHeight
11
12 // switch state in the next frame
13 requestAnimationFrame(() => {
14 requestAnimationFrame(() => {
15 // Next, toggle to end state
16 el.classList.remove('leave-from')
17 el.classList.add('leave-to')
18
19 // Listen transitionend event for finishing work
20 el.addEventListener('transitionend', () => {
21 el.classList.remove('leave-to')
22 el.classList.remove('leave-active')
23 // When the transition is complete, remember to call the
performRemove function to remove DOM elements
24 performRemove()
```

```
25 })
26 })
27 })
28 })
```

As you can see from the above code, the exit transition is handled in a very similar way to the entry transition, that is, first set the initial state, and then switch to the end state in the next frame, so that the transition takes effect. It should be noted that when the exit transition is completed, the performRemove function needs to be executed to actually unload the DOM element.

14.3.2   Implementation of Transition Components

The implementation principle of the Transition component is the same as the transition principle of the native DOM introduced in Sect. 14.3.1. However, the Transition component is implemented based on the virtual DOM. In Sect. 14.3.1, when creating incoming motion graphics and outgoing motion for native DOM elements, we noticed that the entire transition process can be abstracted into several stages, which can be abstracted into specific callback functions. For example, beforeEnter, enter, leave, etc. In fact, virtual DOM-based implementations also need to divide the life cycle of DOM elements into such stages and execute the corresponding callback functions at specific stages.

In order to implement the Transition component, we need to design its representation at the virtual DOM level first. Assume that the template content of the component is as follows:

```
01 <template>
02 <Transition>
03 <div> I am the element that needs to transition </div>
04 </Transition>
05 </template>
```

We can design the virtual DOM after this template is compiled as:

```
01 function render() {
02 return {
03 type: Transition,
04 children: {
05 default() {
06 return { type: 'div', children: 'I am Elements that require
transitions'}
07 }
08 }
09 }
10 }
```

As you can see, the sub-node of the Transition component is compiled as the default slot, which is consistent with the behavior of ordinary components. The representation of the virtual DOM level has been designed. Next, we proceed to implement the Transition component, as shown in the following code:

```
01 const Transition = {
02 name: 'Transition',
03 setup(props, { slots }) {
04 return () => {
05 // Get the element that needs to be transitioned through the
default slot
06 const innerVNode = slots.default()
07
08 // Add the transition corresponding to the VNode object of the
transition element Hook function
09 innerVNode.transition = {
10 beforeEnter(el) {
11 // Omit some code
12 },
13 enter(el) {
14 // Omit some code
15 },
16 leave(el, performRemove) {
17 // Omit some code
18 }
19 }
20
21 // Rendering elements that need transition
22 return innerVNode
23 }
24 }
25 }
```

Looking at the above code, we can find several important information:

- The Transition component itself does not render any additional content; it just reads the transition elements through the default slot and renders the elements that need to transition
- The role of the Transition component is to add transition-related hook functions on the virtual nodes of the transition elements.

As you can see, after the Transition component is wrapped, a vnode.transition object will be added to the virtual node object that needs to be transitioned internally. There are some hook functions related to the transition of DOM elements under this object, such as beforeEnter, enter, leave, etc. These hook functions are the same as the hook functions we introduced in Sect. 14.3.1. When the renderer renders a virtual node that needs to transition, it will call the transition-related lifecycle hook function attached to the virtual node at the appropriate time, which is embodied in the mountElement function and the unmount function, as shown in the following code:

```
01 function mountElement(vnode, container, anchor) {
02 const el = vnode.el = createElement(vnode.type)
03
04 if (typeof vnode.children === 'string') {
05 setElementText(el, vnode.children)
06 } else if (Array.isArray(vnode.children)) {
07 vnode.children.forEach(child => {
08 patch(null, child, el)
09 })
10 }
11
12 if (vnode.props) {
13 for (const key in vnode.props) {
14 patchProps(el, key, null, vnode.props[key])
15 }
16 }
17
18 // Determine whether a VNode needs a transition
19 const needTransition = vnode.transition
20 if (needTransition) {
21 // Call transition.beforeEnter hook and pass the DOM element as an
argument
22 vnode.transition.beforeEnter(el)
23 }
24
25 insert(el, container, anchor)
26 if (needTransition) {
27 // Call transition.enter hook and pass the DOM element as an
argument
28 vnode.transition.enter(el)
29 }
30 }
```

The above code is a modified mountElement function, which we added transition hook handling. As you can see, before mounting the DOM element, the transition. beforeEnter hook is called; after mounting the element, the transition.enter hook is called, and both hook functions receive the DOM element object that needs to be transitioned as the first parameter. In addition to mounting, we should also call the transition.leave hook function when unmounting elements, as shown in the following code:

```
01 function unmount(vnode) {
02 // Determine whether VNode needs transition processing
03 const needTransition = vnode.transition
04 if (vnode.type === Fragment) {
05 vnode.children.forEach(c => unmount(c))
06 return
07 } else if (typeof vnode.type === 'object') {
08 if (vnode.shouldKeepAlive) {
09 vnode.keepAliveInstance._deActivate(vnode)
10 } else {
```

```
11 unmount(vnode.component.subTree)
12 }
13 return
14 }
15 const parent = vnode.el.parentNode
16 if (parent) {
17 // encapsulate the uninstall action into the performRemove
function
18 const performRemove = () => parent.removeChild(vnode.el)
19 if (needTransition) {
20 // if a transition is required Process, then call the transition.
leave hook,
21 // pass both the DOM element and the performRemove function as
arguments
22 vnode.transition.leave(vnode.el, performRemove)
23 } else {
24 // If no transition processing is required, the uninstall
operation is directly performed
25 performRemove()
26 }
27 }
28 }
```

The above code is the implementation of the modified unmount function, and we also added processing for the transition. First of all, you need to encapsulate the unloading action into the performRemove function. If the DOM element needs to be transitioned, then you need to wait and execute the performRemove function to complete the unloading after the transition is over. Otherwise, you can directly call the function to complete the unloading.

With mountElement and unmount support, we can easily implement a basic Transition component, as shown in the following code:

```
01 const Transition = {
02 name: 'Transition',
03 setup(props, { slots }) {
04 return () => {
05 const innerVNode = slots.default()
06
07 innerVNode.transition = {
08 beforeEnter(el) {
09 // Set the initial state: add enter-from and enter-active classes
10 el.classList.add('enter-from')
11 el.classList.add('enter-active')
12 },
13 enter(el) {
14 // switch to end state in next frame
15 nextFrame(() => {
16 // remove enter-from class; add enter-to class
17 el.classList.remove('enter-from')
18 el.classList.add('enter-to')
19 // listento  transitionend event to finish work
```

```
20 el.addEventListener('transitionend', () => {
21 el.classList.remove('enter-to')
22 el.classList.remove('enter-active')
23 })
24 })
25 },
26 leave(el, performRemove) {
27 // Set initial state of exit transition: add leave-from and leave-
active classes
28 el.classList.add('leave-from')
29 el.classList.add('leave-active')
30 // Force reflow so that initial status takes effect
31 document.body.offsetHeight
32 // Modify status in the next frame
33 nextFrame(() => {
34 // Remove leave-from class, add leave-to class
35 el.classList.remove('leave-from')
36 el.classList.add('leave-to')
37
38 // Listen to  transitionend event to finish work
39 el.addEventListener('transitionend', () => {
40 el.classList.remove('leave-to')
41 el.classList.remove('leave-active')
42 // Call the second parameter of the transition.leave hook function
to complete the unloading of DOM elements
43 performRemove()
44 })
45 })
46 }
47 }
48
49 return innerVNode
50 }
51 }
52 }
```

In the above code, we completed the specific implementation of each hook function in vnode.transition. As you can see, the implementation idea is the same as that we discussed in Sect. 14.3.1 about the native DOM transition.

In the above implementation, we hardcoded the class name of the transition state, such as enter-from, enter-to, etc. In fact, we can easily implement the ability to allow users to customize the class name through props, thus implementing a more flexible Transition component. In addition, we do not implement the concept of "pattern," that is, in-out or last-in-first-out (out-in). In fact, the concept of pattern just adds control over the transition timing of nodes. In principle, just like encapsulating the unloading action into the performRemove function, you only need to hand over control in the form of callbacks at specific moments.

14.4 Summary

In this chapter, we introduced three components built into Vue.js, namely KeepAlive component, Teleport component and Transition component. Their common feature is that they are very tightly integrated with the renderer, so the framework needs to provide low-level implementation and support.

The KeepAlive component acts like a persistent link in HTTP. It avoids component instances from being destroyed and rebuilt constantly. The basic implementation of KeepAlive is not complicated. When "unmounted" by a KeepAlive component, the renderer does not actually unmount it, but moves the component into a hidden container, so that the component can maintain its current state. When "mounted" by a KeepAlive component, the renderer does not actually mount it, but moves it from the hidden container to the original container.

We also discussed other capabilities of KeepAlive, such as matching policies and caching policies. The include and exclude options are used to specify which components need to be KeepAlive and which components do not need to be KeepAlive. By default, include and exclude will match the component's name option. However, in specific implementations, we can extend the matching ability. For caching policies, Vue.js defaults to "latest access." In order to allow users to implement caching policies themselves, we also introduced proposals under discussion.

Next, we discussed the problem that the Teleport component aims to solve and its implementation principle. Teleport components can render across the DOM hierarchy, which is very useful in many scenarios. When implementing Teleport, we separate the rendering logic of the Teleport component from the renderer, which has two advantages:

• It avoids the "bloat" of the renderer logic code
• It can use the TreeShaking mechanism to remove the Teleport-related code in the final bundle, making the final build smaller

The Teleport component is a special component. Compared with normal components, its component options are very special, such as __isTeleport selection and process options. This is because Teleport is essentially a reasonable abstraction of the renderer logic, it can exist as part of the renderer.

Finally, we discussed the principle and implementation of the Transition component. We started with the native DOM transition and explained how to use JavaScript to add in-field motion graphics and out-of-field motion graphics to DOM elements. In this process, we divide the process of implementing motion graphics into multiple stages, namely beforeEnter, enter, leave, etc. The implementation principle of the Transition component is similar to the principle of adding transition effects to the native DOM. We define the transition-related hook function into the vnode.transition object of the virtual node. When performing mount and unload operations, the renderer will preferentially check whether the virtual node needs to make a transition, and if so, it will execute the transition-related hook function defined in the vnode.transition object at the right time.

Part V
Compilers

Chapter 15
Overview of Core Technologies of Compilers

Compilation technology is a huge subject, and we cannot fully explain it in a few chapters. However, the difficulty of compilers or compilation technologies for different purposes may vary greatly, and the knowledge requirements will vary greatly. If you want to implement a general-purpose language such as C and JavaScript, then you need to master more knowledge of compilation technology. For example, understanding context-free grammars, writing grammar rules using Bacos Normal Form (BNF), Extending Bacos Normal Form (EBNF), performing grammar derivation, understanding and eliminating left recursion, recursive descent algorithms, and even knowledge of type systems. But as front-end engineers, the scenarios where we apply compilation techniques are usually custom formula calculators in tables, reports, designing a domain-specific language (DSL), etc. Among them, the implementation of the formula calculator even involves only the compilation front-end technology, and the difficulty of domain-specific languages will vary according to their specific usage scenarios and target platforms. Vue.js templates and JSX are domain-specific languages, and their implementation difficulty is medium and low, as long as you master the basic compilation technology theory, you can achieve these functions.

15.1 Compilers for Template DSL

The compiler is actually just a program; it is used to translate "one language A" into "another language B." Among them, language A is usually called source code, and language B is usually called object code (object code or target code). The process of translating source code into object code by the compiler is called compiling. The complete compilation process usually includes steps such as lexical analysis, syntax analysis, semantic analysis, intermediate code generation, optimization, and object code generation, as shown in Fig. 15.1.

H. Yang, *Vue. JS Framework*, https://doi.org/10.1007/978-981-99-4947-2_15

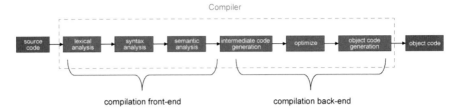

Fig. 15.1 Complete compilation process

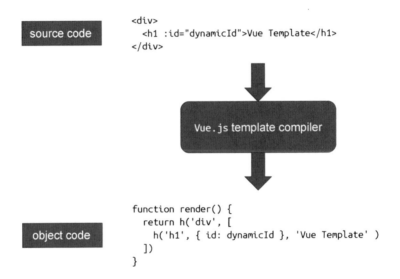

Fig. 15.2 The object code of the Vue.js. Template compiler is javascript code

You can see that the entire compilation process is divided into compilation front-end and compilation back-end. The compilation front-end includes lexical analysis, syntax analysis, and semantic analysis. It is usually independent of the target platform and is only responsible for analyzing the source code. The compilation back-end is usually related to the target platform. The compilation back-end involves intermediate code generation and optimization and object code generation. However, the compilation back-end does not necessarily contain intermediate code generation and optimization, depending on the specific scenario and implementation. The intermediate code generation and optimization are sometimes referred to as the "middle end."

Figure 15.1 shows the "textbook" compilation model, but Vue.js template is compiled differently as a DSL. For the Vue.js template compiler, the source code is the template of the component, and the object code is the JavaScript code that can be run on the browser platform, or other platform code with a JavaScript runtime, as shown in Fig. 15.2.

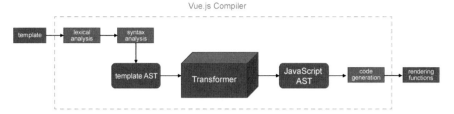

Fig. 15.3 Vue.js workflow of template compiler

You can see that the object code of the Vue.js template compiler is actually the rendering function. In detail, template compiler will first perform lexical analysis and syntax analysis on the template to obtain the template AST. Then, the template AST is transformed into a JavaScript AST. Finally, the JavaScript code is generated from the JavaScript AST, that is, the rendering function code. Figure 15.3 shows the workflow of the Vue.js template compiler.

AST is an acronym for abstract syntax tree. The so-called template AST is actually an abstract syntax tree used to describe templates. For example, suppose we have the following template:

```
01 < div >
02 < h1 v-if = "ok" > Vue Template </h1 >
03 </div >
```

This template will be compiled to the AST as follows:

```
01 const ast = {
02 // Logical root node
03 type: 'Root',
04 children: [
05 // div tag node
06 {
07 type: 'Element',
08 tag: 'div',
09 children: [
10 // h1 tag node
11 {
12 type: 'Element',
13 tag: 'h1',
14 props: [
15 // v-if instruction node
16 {
17 type: 'Directive', // The type Directive stands for Directive
18 name: 'if', // instruction name if without prefix v- 19 exp: {
20 // Expression node
21 type: 'Expression',
22 content: 'ok'
23 }
24 }
```

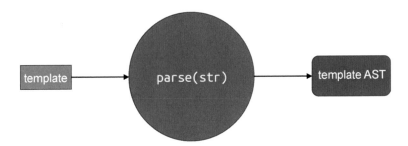

Fig. 15.4 The role of the parse function

```
25 ]
26 }
27 ]
28 }
29 ]
30 }
```

As you can see, the AST is actually an object with a hierarchical structure. Template AST has a nested structure that is isomorphic to templates. Each AST has a logical root node of type Root. The real root node in the template exists as the children of the Root node. Observing the AST above, we can draw the following conclusions.

- Different types of nodes are distinguished by the *type* attribute of the node. For example, the *type* value of a label node is "Element"
- The sub-node of the label node is stored in its children array
- The attribute nodes and instruction nodes of the label node are stored in the props array
- Different types of nodes are described with different object attributes. For example, the instruction node has the name attribute, which is used to express the name of the instruction, and the expression node has the content attribute, which is used to describe the content of the expression

We can complete the lexical analysis and syntax analysis of the template by encapsulating the parse function to obtain the template AST, as shown in Fig. 15.4.

We can also use the following code to express the process of template parsing:

```
01 const template = `
02 <div>
03 <h1 v-if="ok">Vue Template</h1>
04 </div>
05 `
06
07 const templateAST = parse(template)
```

Fig. 15.5 The role of the transform function

Fig. 15.6 The role of the generate function

As you can see, the parse function receives a string template as a parameter and returns the AST obtained after parsing as a return value.

After we have the template AST, we can perform semantic analysis on it and transform the template AST. What is semantic analysis? To give a few examples.

- Check whether there is a matching v-if instruction for the v-else directive
- Analyze whether the property value is static, whether it is a constant, etc.
- Whether the slot will refer to the variables in the upper scope

On the basis of semantic analysis, we can get the template AST. Next, we also need to convert the template AST to JavaScript AST. Because the ultimate goal of Vue.js template compiler is to generate rendering functions, which are essentially JavaScript code, we need to convert the template AST into a JavaScript AST that describes the rendering function.

We can wrap the transform function to do the conversion from template AST to JavaScript AST, as shown in Fig. 15.5.

Again, we can also express it with the following code:

```
01 const templateAST = parse (template)
02 const jsAST = transform (templateAST)
```

We will explain the structure of the JavaScript AST in detail in the next chapter.

With the JavaScript AST, we can generate the rendering function from it. This step can be done by wrapping the generate function, as shown in Fig. 15.6.

We can also express the code generation process with the following code:

```
01 const templateAST = parse (template)
02 const jsAST = transform (templateAST)
03 const code = generate (jsAST)
```

In the above code, the generate function returns the code of the render function as a string and stores it in the code constant. Figure 15.7 shows the complete process.

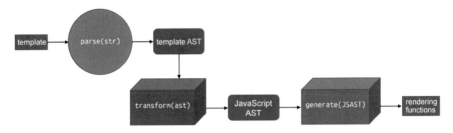

Fig. 15.7 The complete process of compiling. Vue.js templates into rendering functions

15.2   Implementation Principles of Parsers and Finite-State Machines

In the previous section, we explained the basic structure and workflow of template compiler, which mainly consists of three parts:

- A parser used to parse template strings into template AST
- A transformer used to convert template AST into JavaScript AST
- A generator used to generate AST rendering function code based on JavaScript.

In this section, we will discuss the implementation principle of the parser in detail.

The imported parameter of the parser is the string template, and the parser will read the characters in the string template one by one, and cut the entire string into tokens according to certain rules. The tokens here can be regarded as lexical tokens. We will use the word Token to represent lexical tokens in the future. For example, suppose there is such a template:

```
01 < p > Vue </p >
```

The parser will cut this string template into three tokens.

- Start tag: $< p >$.
- Text node: Vue.
- End tag: $</p >$.

So, how does the parser cut the template? According to what rules? This has to mention the finite-state automatic machine. Do not be intimidated by this term; it is not difficult to understand. The so-called finite state refers to a finite number of states, and "automaton" means that as characters are input; the parser will automatically migrate between different states. Take the template above, for example, when we analyze this template string, the parse function will read characters one by one. The state chance has an initial state, which we denote as "initial state 1." Figure 15.8 shows the state transition process.

We use natural language to describe the state transition process given in Fig. 15.8.

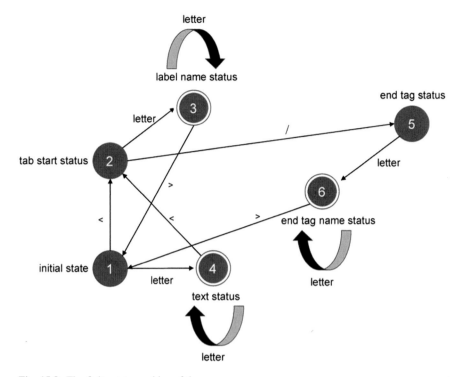

Fig. 15.8 The finite-state machine of the parser

- The finite-state machine starts in "initial state 1"
- In "initial state 1," the first character < of the template is read, and the state opportunity goes to the next state, which is "label start state 2"
- In "label start state 2," the next character p is read. Since the character p is a letter, the state opportunity enters "Label Name State 3"
- Under "Label Name State 3," the next character > is read. At this time, the state opportunity transitions from "Label Name State 3" to "Initial State 1" and records the label name p generated under "Label Name State"
- Under "Initial State 1," the next character V is read, and the state opportunity enters "Text State 4"
- Under "Text State 4," continue reading subsequent characters until the character < is encountered, the state opportunity enters "Label Start State 2" again, and records the text content generated under "Text State 4," that is, the string "Vue"
- Under "Label Start State 2," the next character/is read, and the state opportunity enters "End Label State 5"
- Under "End Label State 5," the next character p is read, and the state opportunity enters "End Label Name State 6"
- Under "End Tag Name State 6," the last character > is read, which is the closing character of the end tag, so the state machine transitions back to "Initial State 1" and records the end tag name generated under "End Tag Name State 6"

§   **13.2.5.1 Data state**

Consume the next input character:

↳ **U+0026 AMPERSAND (&)**

Set the *return state* to the data state. Switch to the character reference state.

↳ **U+003C LESS-THAN SIGN (<)**

Switch to the tag open state.

↳ **U+0000 NULL**

This is an unexpected-null-character parse error. Emit the current input character as a character token.

↳ **EOF**

Emit an end-of-file token.

↳ **Anything else**

Emit the current input character as a character token.

Fig. 15.9   Data state

After such a series of state transition processes, we can finally get the corresponding token. Observing Fig. 15.8, we can see that some circles are single-line, while others are double-line. The two lines indicate that the finite-state machine is a valid token at this time.

In addition, the finite-state machine shown in Fig. 15.8 is not rigorous. In fact, the process of parsing HTML and constructing tokens is standardized and can be followed. The state transition process of the finite-state machine in the "initial state" defined in the specification is elaborated in the WHATWG's specification on browser parsing HTML. Figure15.9 captures the state transition process of the finite-state machine in the "initial state" defined in the specification.

You can see that in the "initial state" (Data State), when the character < is encountered, the state will migrate to the tag open state, that is, the "tag start state." If a character other than the character < is encountered, there are corresponding instructions in the specification: which state should be migrate to the finite-state machine. However, Vue.js template is a DSL and does not have to comply with this specification. But Vue.js template is an HTML-like implementation after all, so it does not hurt to follow the specification as much as possible. More importantly, the specification already defines a very detailed state transition process, which is very helpful for us to write parsers.

According to the state transition process of finite-state automata, we can easily write corresponding code implementations. Therefore, finite-state automata can help us complete the tokenization of templates, and eventually we will get a series of Tokens. The implementation of the finite-state machine depicted in Fig. 15.8 is as follows:

```
01 // Define the state of the finite-state machine
02 const State = {
03 initial: 1, // initial state
04 tagOpen: 2, // tag start state
05 tagName: 3, // tag name state
```

```
06 text: 4, // text state
07 tagEnd: 5, // end tag state
08 tagEndName: 6 // end tag name state
09 }
10 // An auxiliary function that determines whether it is a letter
11 function isAlpha(char) {
12 return char >= 'a' && char <= 'z' || char >= 'A' && char <= 'Z'
13 }
14
15 // Receive the template string as an argument and slices the
template back as a token
16 function tokenize(str) {
17 // The current state of the state machine: The initial state
18 let currentState = State.initial
19 // Used to cache characters
20 const chars = []
21 // The resulting token is stored in an array of tokens and returned
as the return value of the function
22 const tokens = []
23 // Use the while loop to turn on the automaton, which runs as long as
the template string is not consumed
24 while(str) {
25 // Look at the first character, note that here is just viewing, not
consuming that character
26 const char = str[0]
27 // The switch statement matches the current state
28 switch (currentState) {
29 // The state machine is currently in an initial state
30 case State.initial:
31 // A character was encountered <
32 if (char === '<') {
33 // 1. The state machine switches to the label start state
34 currentState = State.tagOpen
35 // 2. Consume characters <
36 str = str.slice(1)
37 } else if (isAlpha(char)) {
38 // 1. Letters are encountered and switch to the text state
39 currentState = State.text
40 // 2. Cache the current letter to the chars array
41 chars.push(char)
42 // 3. Consume the current character
43 str = str.slice(1)
44 }
45 break
46 // The state machine is currently in the label start state
47 case State.tagOpen:
48 if (isAlpha(char)) {
49 // 1. Letters are encountered, switching to the label name status
50 currentState = State.tagName
51 // 2. Cache the current character to the chars array
52 chars.push(char)
53 // 3. Consume the current character
54 str = str.slice(1)
```

```
55 } else if (char === '/') {
56 // 1. The character / is encountered and switch to the end label
state
57 currentState = State.tagEnd
58 // 2. Consume characters /
59 str = str.slice(1)
60 }
61 break
62 // The state machine is currently in the label name state
63 case State.tagName:
64 if (isAlpha(char)) {
65 // 1. Letters are encountered, and since they are currently in the
label name state, there is no need to switch states,
66 // However, you need to cache the current characters to the chars
array
67 chars.push(char)
68 // 2. Consume the current character
69 str = str.slice(1)
70 } else if (char === '>') {
71 // 1. The character > is encountered and switch to the initial state
72 currentState = State.initial
73 // 2. At the same time, a tag Token is created and added to the tokens
array
74 // Note that the characters cached in the chars array are the label
names
75 tokens.push({
76 type: 'tag',
77 name: chars.join('')
78 })
79 // 3. The content of the chars array have been consumed; empty it
80 chars.length = 0
81 // 4. Consumes the current character > at the same time
82 str = str.slice(1)
83 }
84 break
85 // The state machine is currently in the text state
86 case State.text:
87 if (isAlpha(char)) {
88 // 1. Letters are encountered, leaving the state unchanged, but the
current character should be cached to the chars array
89 chars.push(char)
90 // 2. Consume the current character
91 str = str.slice(1)
92 } else if (char === '<') {
93 // 1. When the character < is encountered, switch to the label start
state
94 currentState = State.tagOpen
95 // 2. Starting from the Text State --> label, a text token should be
created and added to the tokens array
96 // Note that the characters in the chars array are the text contents
97 tokens.push({
98 type: 'text',
99 content: chars.join('')
```

```
100 })
101 // 3. The content of the chars array have been consumed; empty it
102 chars.length = 0
103 // 4. Consume the current character
104 str = str.slice(1)
105 }
106 break
107 // The state machine is currently in the end-of-label state
108 case State.tagEnd:
109 if (isAlpha(char)) {
110 // 1. Letters are encountered and switch to the end label name
state
111 currentState = State.tagEndName
112 // 2. Cache the current character to the chars array
113 chars.push(char)
114 // 3. Consume the current character
115 str = str.slice(1)
116 }
117 break
118 // The state machine is currently in the end label name state
119 case State.tagEndName:
120 if (isAlpha(char)) {
121 // 1. When letters are encountered, there is no need to switch
states, but the current characters need to be cached to the chars array
122 chars.push(char)
123 // 2. Consume the current character
124 str = str.slice(1)
125 } else if (char === '>') {
126 // 1. The character > encountered and switches to the initial
state
127 currentState = State.initial
128 // 2. From the end tag name state --> the initial state, the end tag
name Token should be saved
129 // Note that the contents cached in the chars array are the label
names
130 tokens.push({
131 type: 'tagEnd',
132 name: chars.join('')
133 })
134 // 3. The content of the chars array have been consumed, emptied it
135 chars.length = 0
136 // 4. Consume the current character
137 str = str.slice(1)
138 }
139 break
140 }
141 }
142
143 // finally, return tokens
144 return tokens
145 }
```

The above code seems to be verbose and there are many points that can be optimized. This code highly restores the finite-state machine shown in Fig. 15.8, and it will be easier to understand with the comments in the code.

Using the tokenize function given above to parse the template $< p >$ Vue $</p >$, we will get three tokens:

```
01 const tokens = tokenize(`<p>Vue</p>`)
02 // [
03 // { type: 'tag', name: 'p' }, // start tag
04 // { type: 'text', content: 'Vue' }, // text node
05 // { type: 'tagEnd', name: 'p' } // end tag
06 // ]
```

Now, you have understood how the finite-state machine works, and how the template compiler cuts the template string into tokens. But for the above example, we don't always need all tokens. For example, in the process of parsing the template, the closing tag Token can be omitted. At this time, we can adjust the code of the tokenize function and selectively ignore the closing tag Token. Of course, sometimes we may need more tokens, depending on the specific needs, and then flexibly adjust the code implementation accordingly.

All in all, with finite automata, we can parse the template into tokens, and then we can use them to build an AST. But before building an AST, we need to think about whether we can simplify the code of the tokenize function. In fact, we can use regular expressions to simplify the code of the tokenize function. The reason why the above did not use regular expressions from the beginning is that regular expressions are essentially finite automata. When you write a regular expression, you are actually writing a finite automaton.

15.3   Constructing AST

In fact, there can be very large differences between compilers for different purposes. The only thing they have in common is that they all convert source code into object code. However, if you dig into the details, you will find that the implementation ideas of different compilers may even be completely different, including the construction method of AST. For general-purpose languages (GPL), such as scripting languages like JavaScript, if you want to construct an AST for it, a more commonly used algorithm is called recursive descent algorithm, which needs to solve many problems encountered at the GPL level, such as the most basic operator precedence problem. However, for a DSL like Vue.js template, the first thing to be sure of is that it does not have operators, so there is no so-called operator precedence problem. The difference between a DSL and a GPL is that the GPL is Turing complete, and we can use the GPL to implement a DSL. A DSL does not require Turing completeness; it just needs to meet a specific purpose in a specific scenario.

Constructing an AST for Vue.js template is a very simple matter. HTML is a markup language with a very fixed format and natural nesting of tag elements, forming a parent–child relationship. Therefore, an AST used to describe HTML will have a tree structure very similar to HTML tags. For example, suppose the following template:

```
01 < div > < p > Vue </p > < p > Template </p > </div >
```

In the above template, the outermost root node is the *div* tag, which has two p tags as sub-nodes. At the same time, both p tags have a text node as a sub-node. We can design the AST corresponding to this template as:

```
01 const ast = {
02 // The logical root node of the AST
03 type: 'Root',
04 children: [
05 // The div root node of the template
06 {
07 type: 'Element',
08 tag: 'div',
09 children: [
10 // The first sub-node of the div node p
11 {
12 type: 'Element',
13 tag: 'p',
14 // text node of p node
15 children: [
16 {
17 type: 'Text',
18 content: 'Vue'
19 }
20 ]
21 },
22 // second sub-node p of div node
23 {
24 type: 'Element',
25 tag: 'p',
26 // text node of p node
27 children: [
28 {
29 type: 'Text',
30 content: 'Template'
31 }
32 ]
33 }
34 ]
35 }
36 ]
37 }
```

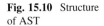

Fig. 15.10 Structure
of AST

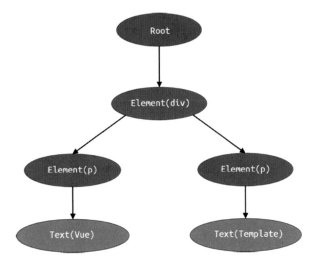

As you can see, AST is structurally "isomorphic" with templates, and they both
have a tree structure, as shown in Fig. 15.10.

With the knowledge about the structure of AST, our next task is to construct such
an AST using the token generated by the program after template parsing. First, we
use the tokenize function explained in the previous section to tokenize the template
given at the beginning of this section.

```
01 const tokens = tokenize ('< div > < p > Vue </p > < p > Template </p >
</div >')
```

Executing the above code, we will get the following tokens:

```
01 const tokens = [
02 {type: "tag", name: "div"}, // div start tag node
03 {type: "tag", name: "p"}, // p start tag node
04 {type: "text", content: "Vue"}, // text node
05 {type: "tagEnd", name: "p"}, // p end tag node
06 {type: "tag", name: "p"}, // p start tag node
07 {type: "text", content: "Template"}, // text node
08 {type: "tagEnd", name: "p"}, // p end tag node
09 {type: "tagEnd", name: "div"} // div end tag node
10 ]
```

The process of constructing the AST from the Token list is actually the process of
scanning the Token list. Starting from the first token, we scan the entire list of tokens
sequentially until all tokens in the list are processed. In this process, we need to
maintain a stack elementStack, which will be used to maintain the parent–child
relationship between elements. Every time a start tag node is encountered, we
construct an AST node of type Element and push it onto the stack. Similarly,
whenever a closing tag node is encountered, we pop the node at the top of the

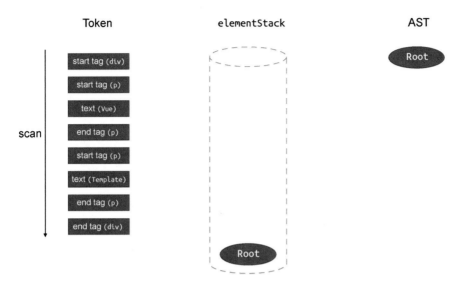

Fig. 15.11 The current state of the token list, parent element stack, and AST

stack. In this way, the node at the top of the stack will always act as the parent node. All nodes encountered during the scanning process will be used as sub-nodes of the current top node of the stack and added to the children attribute of the top node of the stack.

Take the above example again. Figure 15.11 shows the status of the Token list, the parent element stack, and the AST before scanning the Token list.

In Fig. 15.11, the left side is the token list. We will scan the token list from top to bottom. The middle and the right side show the state of the stack elementStack and the state of the AST, respectively. As you can see, they all have only the root node at first.

Next, we scan the token list. First, the first token is scanned, that is, the "start tag (div)," as shown in Fig. 15.12.

Since the currently scanned token is a start tag node, we create an AST node Element (div) of type Element, and then use this node as the sub-node of the top node of the current stack. Since the current top node is the root node, we add the newly created Element (div) node to the AST as a sub-node of the root node, and finally push the newly created Element (div) node into the elementStack stack.

Next, we scan the next token, as shown in Fig. 15.13.

The second token scanned is also a start tag node, so we create another AST node Element (p) of type Element, and then use this node as the sub-node of the current top node of the stack. Since the current top node of the stack is Element (div) node, we add the newly created Element (p) node to the AST as a sub-node of the Element (div) node, and finally, push the newly created Element (p) node into the elementStack stack.

Next, we scan the next token, as shown in Fig. 15.14.

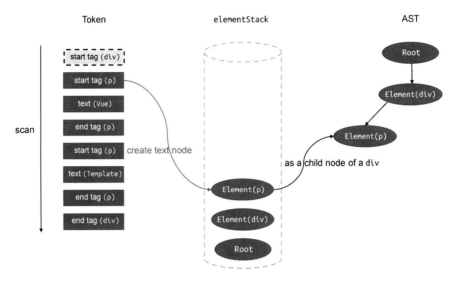

Fig. 15.12 The current state of the token list, parent element stack, and AST

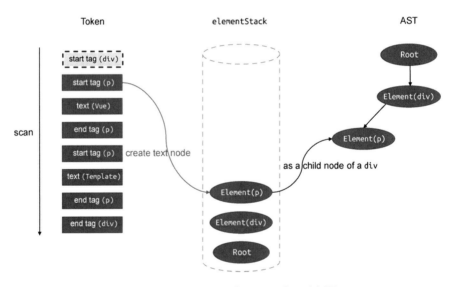

Fig. 15.13 The current state of token list, parent element stack, and AST

The third token scanned is a text node, so we create an AST node Text (Vue) of type Text, and then use this node as the sub-node of the current top node of the stack. Since the current stack top node is an Element (p) node, we add the newly created Text (p) node to the AST as a sub-node of the Element (p) node.

Next, scan the next token, as shown in Fig. 15.15.

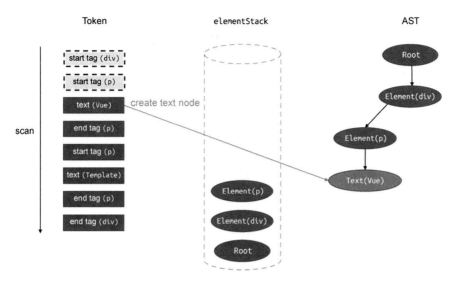

Fig. 15.14 The current state of token list, parent element stack, and AST

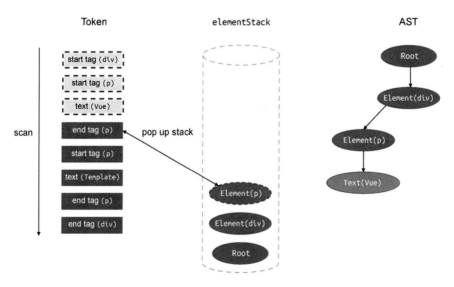

Fig. 15.15 The current state of token list, parent element stack, and AST

At this time, the token reached by the scan is a knot tag, so we need to pop the Element (p) node at the top of the stack from the elementStack stack. Next, scan the next token, as shown in Fig. 15.16.

The scanned token at this time is a start tag. We create a new AST node Element (p) for it and use it as the sub-node of the current top-of-stack node Element (div). Finally, push the Element (p) into the elementStack stack, making it the new top-of-stack node.

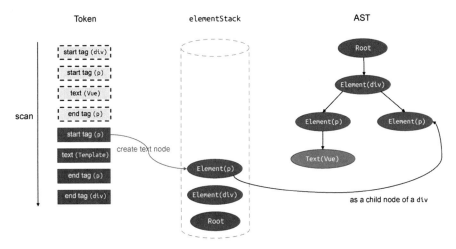

Fig. 15.16 The current state of token list, parent element stack, and AST

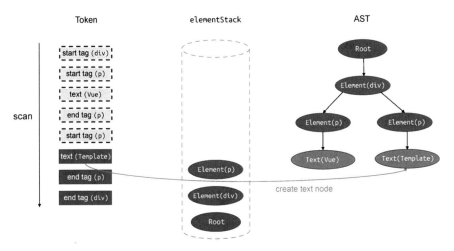

Fig. 15.17 The current state of token list, parent element stack, and AST

Next, scan the next Token, as shown in Fig. 15.17.

At this time, the scanned Token is a text node, so you only need to create a corresponding AST node Text (Template) for it, and then add it to the AST as a sub-node of the current stack top node Element (p).

Next, scan the next Token, as shown in Fig. 15.18.

The token scanned at this time is an end tag, so we pop the current top node Element (p) from the elementStack stack. Next, scan the next token, as shown in Fig. 15.19.

At this point, the last token has been scanned, which is a div end tag, so we need to pop the current top node Element (div) from the elementStack again. At this point,

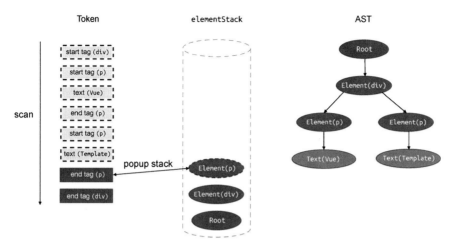

Fig. 15.18   The current state of token list, parent element stack, and AST

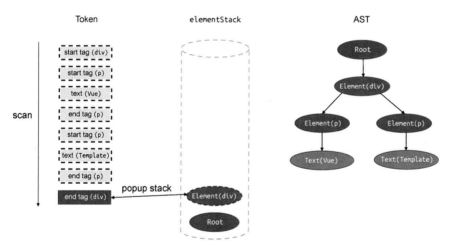

Fig. 15.19   The current state of token list, parent element stack, and AST

all tokens have been scanned and the AST has been built. Figure 15.20 shows the final state.

As shown in Fig. 15.20. After all tokens are scanned, an AST is built.

The specific implementation of scanning the token list and building the AST is as follows:

```
01 // parse function receives the template as a parameter
02 function parse(str) {
03 // First, tokenize the template to get tokens
04 const tokens = tokenize(str)
05 // Create a root node
```

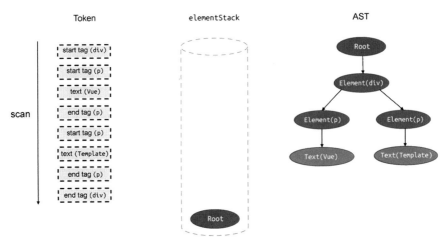

Fig. 15.20 The current state of token list, parent element stack, and AST

```
06 const root = {
07 type: 'Root',
08 children: []
09 }
10 // Create an elementStack stack, initially with only the root root
node
11 const elementStack = [root]
12
13 // Turn on a while loop to scan tokens until all tokens have been
scanned
14 while (tokens.length) {
15 // Get the current top-of-stack node as the parent parent
16 const parent = elementStack[elementStack.length - 1]
17 // The token that is currently scanned
18 const t = tokens[0]
19 switch (t.type) {
20 case 'tag':
21 // If the current Token is the start tag, an AST node of type Element
is created
22 const elementNode = {
23 type: 'Element',
24 tag: t.name,
25 children: []
26 }
27 // Add it to the children of the parent node
28 parent.children.push(elementNode)
29 // Push the current node onto the stack
30 elementStack.push(elementNode)
31 break
32 case 'text':
33 // If the current token is text, an AST node of type Text is created
34 const textNode = {
35 type: 'Text',
```

```
36 content: t.content
37 }
38 // Add it to the children of the parent node
39 parent.children.push(textNode)
40 break
41 case 'tagEnd':
42 // When the end tag is encountered, the top node pops up
43 elementStack.pop()
44 break
45 }
46 // Consume tokens that have already been scanned
47 tokens.shift()
48 }
49
50 // Finally return AST
51 return root
52 }
```

The above code is a good restoration of the idea of building AST introduced above, we can use the following code to test it:

```
01 const ast = parse('< div > < p > Vue </p > < p > Template </p > </div
>')
```

Run this code. We will get consistent with the AST given at the beginning of this section. It is important to note here that the current implementation still has many problems, such as the inability to handle self-closing labels. These problems are discussed in detail in Chap. 16.

15.4 AST Transformation and Plug-In Architecture

In the previous section, we completed the construction of the template AST. In this section, we will discuss the transformation of the AST. The so-called conversion of the AST refers to the process of performing a series of operations on the AST to convert it into a new AST. The new AST can be the original language, or the description of the original DSL, or it can be the description of other languages or other DSLs. For example, we can operate on the template AST to convert it into a JavaScript AST. The converted AST can be used for code generation. This is actually the process of Vue.js template compiler compiling templates into rendering functions, as shown in Fig. 15.21.

Fig. 15.21 The process of template compiler compiling templates into rendering functions

Here the transform function is used to complete the AST transformation work.

15.4.1 Access to Nodes

In order to transform the AST, we need to have access to each node of the AST, so that we have the opportunity to modify, replace, delete, and carry out other operations for specific nodes. Since AST is a tree data structure, we need to write a depth-first traversal algorithm to achieve access to nodes in AST. However, before we start writing the conversion code, it is necessary to write a dump utility function to print the information of the node in the current AST, as shown in the following code:

```
01 function dump(node, indent = 0) {
02 // The type of node
03 const type = node.type
04 // The description of the node; if it is the root node, there is no description
05 // If it is a node of type Element, node.tag is used as the description of the node
06 // If it is a node of type Text, node.content is used as the description of the node
07 const desc = node.type === 'Root'
08 ? ''
09 : node.type === 'Element'
10 ? node.tag
11 : node.content
12
13 // Print the type and description of the node
14 console.log(`${'-'.repeat(indent)}${type}: ${desc}`)
15
16 // Recursively print child nodes
17 if (node.children) {
18 node.children.forEach(n => dump(n, indent + 2))
19 }
20 }
```

Let's follow the example given in the previous section and see what the output looks like using the dump function Result:

```
01 const ast = parse ('<div><p>Vue</p><p>Template</p></div>')
02 console.log (dump (ast))
```

Run the above code and you will get the following output:

```
01 Root:
02 --Element: div
03 ----Element: p
04 ------Text: Vue
```

```
05 ----Element: p
06 ------Text: Template
```

As you can see, the dump function shows the nodes in the AST in a clear format. When writing the conversion code for the AST later, we will use the dump function to show the converted result.

Next, we will work on implementing access to the nodes in the AST. The way to access the node is to start from the AST root node and perform depth-first traversal, as shown in the following code:

```
01 function traverseNode(ast) {
02 // The current node, ast itself is the root node
03 const currentNode = ast
04 // If there are child nodes, the traverseNode function is called
recursively to traverse
05 const children = currentNode.children
06 if (children) {
07 for (let i = 0; i < children.length; i++) {
08 traverseNode(children[i])
09 }
10 }
11 }
```

The traverseNode function is used to traverse the AST in a depth-first manner, and its implementation is almost identical to the dump function. With the traverseNdoe function, we can achieve access to the nodes in the AST. For example, we can implement a transformation function to convert all p tags in the AST to h1 tags, as shown in the following code:

```
01 function traverseNode(ast) {
02 // The current node - ast itself is the root node
03 const currentNode = ast
04
05 // Operate on the current node
06 if (currentNode.type === 'Element' && currentNode.tag === 'p') {
07 // Convert all p tags to h1 tags
08 currentNode.tag = 'h1'
09 }
10
11 // If there are child nodes, the traverseNode function is called
recursively to traverse
12 const children = currentNode.children
13 if (children) {
14 for (let i = 0; i < children.length; i++) {
15 traverseNode(children[i])
16 }
17 }
18 }
```

In the above code, we check the type attribute and tag attribute of the current node to ensure that the node being operated on is a p tag. Next, we modify the tag attribute value of the eligible node to "h1" to realize the conversion from p tag to h1 tag. We can use the dump function to print the converted AST information, as shown in the following code:

```
01 // Encapsulate the transform function, which is used to convert the
AST
02 function transform(ast) {
03 // Call traverseNode to complete the conversion
04 traverseNode(ast)
05 // print AST information
06 console.log(dump(ast))
07 }
08
09 const ast = parse(`<div><p>Vue</p><p>Template</p></div>`)
10 transform(ast)
```

Run the above code and we will get the following output:

```
01 Root:
02 --Element: div
03 ----Element: h1
04 ------Text: Vue
05 ----Element: h1
06 ------Text: Template
```

As you can see, all p tags have become h1 tags.

We can also perform other transformations on the AST. For example, implement a transformation that repeats the contents of a text node twice:

```
01 function traverseNode(ast) {
02 // The current node - ast itself is the root node
03 const currentNode = ast
04
05 // Operate on the current node
06 if (currentNode.type === 'Element' && currentNode.
tag === 'p') {
07 // Convert all p tags to h1 tags
08 currentNode.tag = 'h1'
09 }
10
11 // If the type of the node is Text
12 if (currentNode.type === 'Text') {
13 // Repeat its content twice; here we use the repeat() method of the
string
14 currentNode.content = currentNode.content.repeat(2)
15 }
16
```

```
17 // If there are child nodes, the traverseNode function is called
recursively to traverse
18 const children = currentNode.children
19 if (children) {
20 for (let i = 0; i < children.length; i++) {
21 traverseNode(children[i])
22 }
23 }
24 }
```

As shown in the code above, we added the handling code for the text type node. Once it is checked that the current node is of type Text, the repeat (2) method is called to repeat the contents of the text node twice. Finally, we will get the following output:

```
01 Root:
02 --Element: div
03 ----Element: h1
04 ------Text: VueVue
05 ----Element: h1
06 ------Text: TemplateTemplate
```

As you can see, the contents of the text node are all repeated twice.

However, as the functions continue to increase, the traverseNode function will become more and more "bloated." At this time, our natural thought is whether we can decouple the operation and access of nodes. The answer is "absolutely"; we can use the callback function mechanism to achieve decoupling, as shown in the code of the traverseNode function below:

```
01 // Receive the second parameter, context
02 function traverseNode(ast, context) {
03 const currentNode = ast
04
05 // context.nodeTransforms is an array in which each element is a
function
06 const transforms = context.nodeTransforms
07 for (let i = 0; i < transforms.length; i++) {
08 // Pass both the current node currentNode and context to the
callback function registered in nodeTransforms
09 transforms[i](currentNode, context)
10 }
11
12 const children = currentNode.children
13 if (children) {
14 for (let i = 0; i < children.length; i++) {
15 traverseNode(children[i], context)
16 }
17 }
18 }
```

In the above code, we first add a second parameter context to the traverseNode function. The content of the context is described in detail below. Next, we store the callback function in the transforms array, then iterate through the array and call the callback functions registered in it one by one. Finally, we pass the current node currentNode and the context object as parameters to the callback function, respectively.

With the modified traverseNode function, we can use it as follows:

```
01 function transform(ast) {
02 // Create a context object inside the transform function
03 const context = {
04 // register nodeTransforms array
05 nodeTransforms: [
06 transformElement, // The transformElement function is used to
convert label nodes
07 transformText // The transformText function is used to convert
text nodes
08 ]
09 }
10 // Call traverseNode to complete the conversion
11 traverseNode(ast, context)
12 // print AST information
13 console.log(dump(ast))
14 }
```

The above transformElement and transformText functions are implemented as follows:

```
01 function transformElement(node) {
02 if (node.type === 'Element' && node.tag === 'p') {
03 node.tag = 'h1'
04 }
05 }
06
07 function transformText(node) {
08 if (node.type === 'Text') {
09 node.content = node.content.repeat(2)
10 }
11 }
```

As you can see, after decoupling, node operations are encapsulated in independent functions such as transformElement and transformText. We can even write as many similar conversion functions as we want, just register them in the context. nodeTransforms. This solves the problem of "bloated" traverseNode functions caused by increased functionality.

15.4.2 Conversion and Node Operations

In the above, we registered the conversion function in the array. So, why use a context object? Is it not possible to define an array directly? In order to clarify this problem, we have to mention the knowledge about context. You may have heard more or less about Context. We can think of Context as a "global variable" within a certain scope of the program. In fact, context is not a concrete thing, it depends on the specific usage scenario. Let's give a few examples to get a visual feel.

- When writing React applications, we can use React.createContext functions to create a context object, which allows us to pass data down the component tree layer by layer. No matter how deep the component tree is, as long as the component is within the level of this component tree, it can access the data in the context object.
- When writing Vue.js applications, we can also provide data to an entire component tree through capabilities such as provide/inject. These data can be called context.
- When writing Koa applications, the context parameter received by the middleware function is also a kind of context object, and all middleware can access the same data through context.

From the above three examples, we can realize that a context object is actually a "global variable" in a certain scope of the program. In other words, we can also treat global variables as global contexts.

Going back to the context.nodeTransforms array we explained in this section, the context here can be regarded as the AST transformation function, the context data in the process. All AST transformation functions can share data through context. Context objects usually maintain the current state of the program, such as which node is currently transformed; who is the parent node of the currently transformed node; even what sub-node is the node of the parent node currently, etc. This information is useful for writing complex transformation functions. So, the next thing we have to do is to construct the transformation context information, as shown in the following code:

```
01 function transform(ast) {
02 const context = {
03 // Add currentNode to store the node currently being transformed
04 currentNode: null,
05 // Increase childIndex to store the current node's position index
in the children of the parent node
06 childIndex: 0,
07 // Add parent to store the parent node of the current
transformation node
08 parent: null,
09 nodeTransforms: [
10 transformElement,
11 transformText
12 ]
```

```
13 }
14
15 traverseNode(ast, context)
16 console.log(dump(ast))
17 }
```

In the above code, we have extended some important information for the transformation context object.

- currentNode: used to store the node currently being transformed
- childIndex: used to store the position index of the current node in the children of the parent node
- parent: used to store the parent of the current transformation node

Next, we need to set the data in the transformation context object in the appropriate place, as shown in the following code of the traverseNode function:

```
01 function traverseNode(ast, context) {
02 // Set the node information for the current transformation
context.currentNode
03 context.currentNode = ast
04
05 const transforms = context.nodeTransforms
06 for (let i = 0; i < transforms.length; i++) {
07 transforms[i](context.currentNode, context)
08 }
09
10 const children = context.currentNode.children
11 if (children) {
12 for (let i = 0; i < children.length; i++) {
13 // Recursively call traverseNode to set the current node as the
parent node before transforming the child node
14 context.parent = context.currentNode
15 // Set the location index
16 context.childIndex = i
17 // When called recursively, the context is passed through
18 traverseNode(children[i], context)
19 }
20 }
21 }
```

Observing the above code, we find the key point is that before recursively calling the traverseNode function to perform sub-node conversion, we must set the values of context.parent and context.childIndex, so as to ensure that the information stored in the context object is correct in the next recursion and transformation.

With the context data, we can implement the node replacement function. What is node replacement? When converting the AST, we may want to replace some nodes with other types of nodes. For example, replace all text nodes with one element node. To complete the node replacement, we need to add context.replaceNode function to the context object. The function, which takes the new AST node as an argument and

replaces the currently transitioning node with the new node, is shown in the
following code:

```
01 function transform(ast) {
02 const context = {
03 currentNode: null,
04 parent: null,
05 // A function that replaces a node, receiving a new node as a
parameter
06 replaceNode(node) {
07 // To replace the node, we need to modify the AST
08 // Find the position of the current node in the children of the
parent node: context.childIndex
09 // Then replace it with a new node
10 context.parent.children[context.childIndex] = node
11 // Since the current node has been replaced by the new node, we need
to update the currentNode to the new node
12 context.currentNode = node
13 },
14 nodeTransforms: [
15 transformElement,
16 transformText
17 ]
18 }
19
20 traverseNode(ast, context)
21 console.log(dump(ast))
22 }
```

Observe the replaceNode function in the above code. In this function, we first get
the location index of the current node through the context.childIndex property, then
get the collection where the current node is located through context.parent.children,
and finally use context.childIndex and context.parent.children to complete the node
replacement. In addition, since the current node has been replaced with a new node,
we should update the value of the context.currentNode property with the new node.

Next, we can use the replaceNode function in the transformation function to
replace the nodes in the AST. The transformText function converts a text node to an
element node as shown in the code below:

```
01 // The second argument to the transformText function is the context
object
02 function transformText(node, context) {
03 if (node.type === 'Text') {
04 // If the currently transformed node is a text node, call the
context.replaceNode function to replace it with the element node
05 context.replaceNode({
06 type: 'Element',
07 tag: 'span'
08 })
09 }
10 }
```

As shown in the above code, the second parameter of the transformation function is the context object, so we can use any property or function on this object inside the transformation function. Inside the transformText function, first check whether the currently transformed node is a text node, and if so, call the context.replaceNode function to replace it with a new span tag node. The following example is used to verify the node replacement function:

```
01 const ast = parse ('< div > < p > Vue </p > < p > Template </p > </div >')
02 transform (ast)
```

Run the above code, the results before and after the conversion are as follows:

```
01 // before conversion
02 Root:
03 --Element: div
04 ----Element: p
05 ------Text: VueVue
06 ----Element: p
07 ------Text: TemplateTemplate
08
09 // After conversion
10 Root:
11 --Element: div
12 ----Element: h1
13 ------Element: span
14 ----Element: h1
15 ------Element: span
```

As you can see, all the text nodes in the converted AST become span tag nodes.

In addition to replacing nodes, sometimes we also want to remove the currently visited node. We can do this by implementing context.removeNode function, as shown in the following code:

```
01 function transform(ast) {
02 const context = {
03 currentNode: null,
04 parent: null,
05 replaceNode(node) {
06 context.currentNode = node
07 context.parent.children[context.childIndex] = node
08 },
09 // Used to delete the current node.
10 removeNode() {
11 if (context.parent) {
12 // Call the array's splice method to remove the current node based on its index
13 context.parent.children.splice(context.childIndex, 1)
14 // Leave context.currentNode blank
15 context.currentNode = null
16 }
```

```
17 },
18 nodeTransforms: [
19 transformElement,
20 transformText
21 ]
22 }
23
24 traverseNode(ast, context)
25 console.log(dump(ast))
26 }
```

Removing the currently visited node is also very simple; Just take its position index context.childIndex, and then call the array's splice method to remove it from the children list it belongs to. In addition, when the node is removed, do not forget to leave the value of the empty. One thing to note here is that since the current node is removed, subsequent transformation functions will no longer need to process the node. Therefore, we need to make some adjustments to the traverseNode function, as shown in the following code:

```
01 function traverseNode(ast, context) {
02 context.currentNode = ast
03
04 const transforms = context.nodeTransforms
05 for (let i = 0; i < transforms.length; i++) {
06 transforms[i](context.currentNode, context)
07 // Because any transformation function may remove the current
node, after each transformation function has finished executing,
08 // You should check whether the current node has been removed, and
if it is removed, you can just go back09 if (!context.currentNode) return
10 }
11
12 const children = context.currentNode.children
13 if (children) {
14 for (let i = 0; i < children.length; i++) {
15 context.parent = context.currentNode
16 context.childIndex = i
17 traverseNode(children[i], context)
18 }
19 }
20 }
```

In the modified traverseNode function, we add A line of code to check whether the context.currentNode exists. Since any conversion function may remove the currently visited node, after each conversion function is executed, it should check whether the currently visited node has been removed. If it is removed by a conversion function, the traverseNode returns directly, and no subsequent processing is required.

With the context.removeNode function, we can implement the conversion function to remove the text node, as shown in the following code:

```
01 function transformText(node, context) {
02 if (node.type === 'Text') {
03 // If it is a text node, call the context.removeNode function
directly to remove it
04 context.removeNode()
05 }
06 }
```

With the above transformText conversion function, run the following use case:

```
01 const ast = parse(`<div><p>Vue</p><p>Template</p></div>`)
02 transform(ast)
```

The output before and after transformation is as follows:

```
01 // before conversion
02 Root:
03 --Element: div
04 ----Element: p
05 ------Text: VueVue
06 ----Element: p
07 ------Text: TemplateTemplate
08
09 // after conversion
10 Root:
11 --Element: div
12 ----Element: h1
13 ----Element: h1
```

15.4.3 Entry and Exit

In the process of converting AST nodes, it is often necessary to decide how to convert the current node according to the situation of its sub-nodes. This requires that the transformation operation of the parent node must wait for all its sub-nodes to be converted before executing. However, the transformation workflow we currently design does not support this capability. The transformation workflow described above is a workflow that starts from the root node and executes sequentially, as shown in Fig. 15.22.

As you can see from Fig. 15.22, the root node is the first to be processed. The deeper the node level, the lower the processing will be. The problem with this sequential workflow is that when a node is processed, it means that its parent node has been processed, and we cannot go back and reprocess the parent node.

A more ideal conversion workflow should be shown in Fig. 15.23.

As can be seen from Fig. 15.23, the access to the node is divided into two stages, namely the entry stage and the exit stage. When the transformation function is in the entry stage, it will first enter the parent node and then enter the sub-node. When the

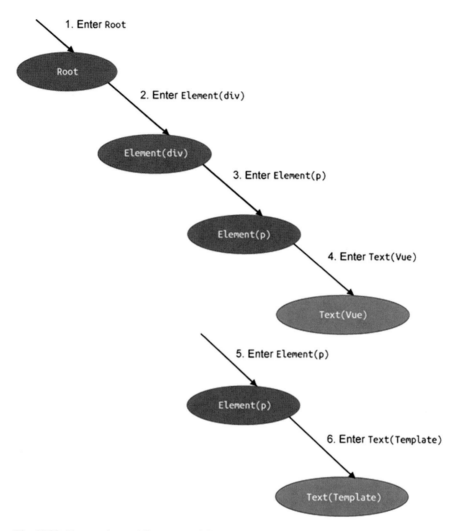

Fig. 15.22 Execute the workflow sequentially

transformation function is in the exit stage, it will exit the child node first and then the parent node. In this way, as long as we process the currently visited node in the exit node phase, we must be able to ensure that all its sub-nodes are processed.

To implement the transformation workflow shown in Fig. 15.23, we need to redesign the ability of the transformation function, as shown in the code of the traverseNode function below:

```
01 function traverseNode(ast, context) {
02 context.currentNode = ast
03 // 1. Increase the array of callback functions for the exit phase
```

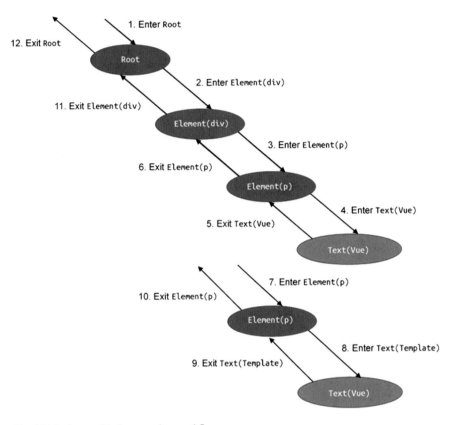

Fig. 15.23 A more ideal conversion workflow

```
04 const exitFns = []
05 const transforms = context.nodeTransforms
06 for (let i = 0; i < transforms.length; i++) {
07 // 2. The conversion function can return another function, which
is the callback function for the exit phase
08 const onExit = transforms[i](context.currentNode, context)
09 if (onExit) {
10 // Add the callback function exit phase to the array of exitFns
11 exitFns.push(onExit)
12 }
13 if (!context.currentNode) return
14 }
15
16 const children = context.currentNode.children
17 if (children) {
18 for (let i = 0; i < children.length; i++) {
19 context.parent = context.currentNode
20 context.childIndex = i
21 traverseNode(children[i], context)
22 }
```

```
23 }
24
25 // Execute callback functions cached into exitFns at the final
stage of node processing
26 // Note that here we want to do it in reverse order
27 let i = exitFns.length
28 while (i--) {
29 exitFns[i]()
30 }
31 }
```

In the above code, we add an array of exitFns to store the callbacks returned by the conversion function. Then, at the end of the traverseNode function, we execute these callbacks cached in the exitFns array. This ensures that when the callback function of the exit phase executes, the sub-node of the currently visited node has all been processed. With these capabilities, when we write the transformation function, we can write the transformation logic in the callback function of the exit phase, so as to ensure that the sub-node must be fully processed before converting the currently visited node, as shown in the following code:

```
01 function transformElement (node, context) {
02 // enter node
03
04 // return a callback function that will be executed when exiting
the node
05 return () => {
06 // Write the logic of the exit node here; When the code is running,
the sub-node of the current conversion node must have finished processing
07 }
08 }
```

Another point to note is that the callback functions in the exit phase are executed in reverse order. This means that if multiple conversion functions are registered, their registration order will determine the execution result of the code. Suppose the two transformation functions we register are transformA and transformB, as shown in the following code:

```
01 function transform(ast) {
02 const context = {
03 // omit some code
04
05 // register the two transformation functions, transformA before
transformB
06 nodeTransforms: [
07 transformA,
08 transformB
09 ]
10 }
11
12 traverseNode(ast, context)
```

```
13 console.log(dump(ast))
14 }
```

In the above code, the transformation function transformA is registered before transformB. This means that when performing the transformation, the "entry phase" of transformA will be executed before the "entry phase" of transformB, and the "exit phase" of transformA will be executed after the "exit phase" of transformB:

```
01 -- transformA   Enter phase execution
02 ---- transformB   Enter phase execution
03 ---- transformB   Exit phase execution
04 -- transformA   Exit phase execution
```

The advantage of this design is that the transformation function transformA will have the opportunity to wait for the transformB to finish executing before deciding how it should work on a case-by-case basis. If the order of transformA and transformB is reversed, the execution order of the transformation functions will also change:

```
01 -- transformB Enter phase execution
02 ---- transformA Enter phase execution
03 ---- transformA Exit phase execution
04 -- transformB Exit phase execution
```

It can be seen that when the transformation logic is written at the exit stage of the transformation function, it can not only ensure that all sub-nodes are processed and completed, but also ensure that all subsequent registered transformation functions are executed.

15.5   Converting Template AST to JavaScript AST

In the previous section, we discussed how to convert AST and implemented a basic plug-in architecture, that is, by registering custom transformation functions to achieve the operation of AST. In this section, we will discuss how to convert template AST to JavaScript AST to pave the way for subsequent code generation.

Why do we convert template AST to JavaScript AST? We have mentioned many times: we need to compile templates into rendering functions. And rendering functions are described by JavaScript code, so we need to convert template AST to JavaScript AST to describe rendering functions.

Now we use the template given in last section as an example.

```
01 < div > < p > Vue </p > < p > Template </p > </div >
```

The rendering function equivalent to this template is as follows:

```
01 function render() {
02 return h('div', [
03 h('p', 'Vue'),
04 h('p', 'Template')
05 ])
06 }
```

The above paragraph The JavaScript AST corresponding to the JavaScript code of the render function is our conversion target. So, what does its corresponding JavaScript AST look like? Just as a template AST is a description of a template, a JavaScript AST is a description of JavaScript code. So, essentially we need to design some data structure to describe the code that renders the function.

First, let's look at the code that renders the function above. It is a function declaration, so we first describe the function declaration statement in JavaScript. A function declaration statement consists of the following parts.

- id: function name, which is an identifier Identifier
- params: parameter of the function, which is an array
- body: The body of the function; since the body of the function can contain multiple statements, it is also an array

To simplify the problem, we do not consider the case of arrow functions, generator functions, async functions, etc. Then, based on the above information, we can design a basic data structure to describe the function declaration statement:

```
01 const FunctionDeclNode = {
02 type: 'FunctionDecl' // represent the node is a function
declaration
03 // The name of the function is an identifier, and the identifier
itself is also a node
04 id: {
05 type: 'Identifier',
06 name: 'render' // name is used to store the name of the identifier,
where it is the name of the rendering function render
07 },
08 params: [], // parameters, the current rendering function does not
need parameters, so here is an empty array
09 // The body of the rendering function has only one statement, that
is, the return statement
10 body: [
11 {
12 type: 'ReturnStatement',
13 return: null // Leave blank temporarily; it will be completed in
the follow-up explanation
14 }
15 ]
16 }
```

As shown in the above code, we use an object to describe a JavaScript AST node. Each node has a type field, which is used to represent the type of the node. For function declaration statements, its type is FunctionDecl. Next, we use the id field to store the name of the function. The name of the function should be a legal identifier, so the id field itself is also a node of type Identifier. Of course, when we design the JavaScript AST, we can adjust it according to the actual situation. For example, we can design the id field as a value of type string. Although this is not complete and conforms to the semantics of JavaScript, it can meet our needs. For the parameters of the function, we use the params array to store. At present, the rendering function we designed does not need parameters, so it is temporarily set to an empty array. Finally, we use the body field to describe the function body of the function. There can be multiple statements in the function body of a function, so we use an array to describe 398 in this chapter. Each element in the array corresponds to a statement. For the rendering function, there is currently only one return statement, so we use a node of type ReturnStatement to describe the return statement.

After introducing the node structure of the function declaration statement, let's take a look at the return value of the rendering function. The rendering function returns a virtual DOM node, which is embodied in the call of the h function. We can use a node of type CallExpression to describe a function call statement, as shown in the following code:

```
01 const CallExp = {
02 type: 'CallExpression',
03 // The name of the called function, which is an identifier
04 callee: {
05 type: 'Identifier',
06 name: 'h'
07 },
08 // Parameters
09 arguments: []
10 }
```

A node of type CallExpression has two properties.

- callee: The name used to describe the called function, which itself is an identifier node.
- arguments: The formal parameters of the called function, and the words of multiple parameters are described as arrays.

We observe the return value of the render function again:

```
01 function render() {
02 // The first parameter of the h function is a string literal
03 // The second parameter of the h function is an array
04 return h('div', [/*...*/])
05 }
```

As you can see, the first argument of the outermost h function is a string literal, which we can describe using a node of type StringLiteral:

```
01 const Str = {
02 type: 'StringLiteral',
03 value: 'div'
04 }
```

The second argument of the outermost h function is an array, which we can describe using a node of type ArrayExpression:

```
01 const Arr = {
02 type: 'ArrayExpression',
03 // Elements in Array
04 elements: []
05 }
```

Use the above CallExpression, StringLiteral, ArrayExpression, and other nodes to populate the return value of the render function; the final result is shown in the following code:

```
01 const FunctionDeclNode = {
02 type: 'FunctionDecl' // Represent that the node is a function declaration
03 // The name of the function is an identifier, and the identifier itself is a node
04 id: {
05 type: 'Identifier',
06 name: 'render' // name is used to store the name of the identifier, in this case the name of the rendering function, render
07 },
08 params: [], // parameters, currently the rendering function does not require parameters, so here is an empty array
09 // The body of the rendered function has only one statement, the return statement
10 body: [
11 {
12 type: 'ReturnStatement',
13 // The outermost h function call
14 return: {
15 type: 'CallExpression',
16 callee: { type: 'Identifier', name: 'h' },
17 arguments: [
18 // The first argument is the string literal 'div'
19 {
20 type: 'StringLiteral',
21 value: 'div'
22 },
23 // The second parameter is an array
24 {
25 type: 'ArrayExpression',
26 elements: [
27 // The first element of the array is the call to the h function
28 {
```

```
29 type: 'CallExpression',
30 callee: { type: 'Identifier', name: 'h' },
31 arguments: [
32 // The first parameter of the h function call is a string literal
33 { type: 'StringLiteral', value: 'p' },
34 // The second parameter is also a string literal
35 { type: 'StringLiteral', value: 'Vue' },
36 ]
37 },
38 // The second element of the array is also a call to the h function
39 {
40 type: 'CallExpression',
41 callee: { type: 'Identifier', name: 'h' },
42 arguments: [
43 // The first parameter of the h function call is a string literal
44 { type: 'StringLiteral', value: 'p' },
45 // The second parameter is also a string literal
46 { type: 'StringLiteral', value: 'Template' },
47 ]
48 }
49 ]
50 }
51 ]
52 }
53 }
54 ]
55 }
```

As shown in the JavaScript AST code above, it is a full description for the rendering function code. Our next task is to write a transformation function that converts the template AST to the aforementioned JavaScript AST. But before we start, we need to write some helper functions for creating the AST node in JavaScript, as shown in the following code:

```
01 // to create the StringLiteral node
02 function createStringLiteral(value) {
03 return {
04 type: 'StringLiteral',
05 value
06 }
07 }
08 // to create the Identifier node
09 function createIdentifier(name) {
10 return {
11 type: 'Identifier',
12 name
13 }
14 }
15 // Used to create ArrayExpression Node
16 function createArrayExpression(elements) {
17 return {
18 type: 'ArrayExpression',
```

```
19 elements
20 }
21 }
22 // Used to create CallExpression Node
23 function createCallExpression(callee, arguments) {
24 return {
25 type: 'CallExpression',
26 callee: createIdentifier(callee),
27 arguments
28 }
29 }
```

With these aids we can write covert code more easily.

To convert the template AST to JavaScript AST, we also need two conversion functions: transformElement and transformText, which are used to handle the label node and the text node, respectively. The implementation is as follows:

```
01 // Transform text nodes
02 function transformText(node) {
03 // If it's not a text node, do nothing
04 if (node.type !== 'Text') {
05 return
06 }
07 // The JavaScript AST node corresponding to the text node is
actually a string literal.
08 // So you only need to use node.content to create a node of type
StringLiteral
09 // Finally, add the JavaScript AST node corresponding to the text
node to the node.jsNode property
10 node.jsNode = createStringLiteral(node.content)
11 }
12
13 // Transform the label node
14 function transformElement(node) {
15 // Write the transformation code in the callback function for the
exit phase.
16 // This ensures that all the child nodes of the label node are
processed
17 return () => {
18 // If the node being transformed is not an element node, nothing is
done
19 if (node.type !== 'Element') {
20 return
21 }
22
23 // 1. Create an h function call statement,
24 // The first argument of the h function call is the label name, so
let's use node.tag to create a string literal node
25 // as the first parameter
26 const callExp = createCallExpression('h', [
27 createStringLiteral(node.tag)
28 ])
```

```
29 // 2. Handle the parameters of the h function call
30 node.children.length === 1
31 // If the current tag node has only one child node, the jsNode of the
child node is used directly as the parameter
32 ? callExp.arguments.push(node.children[0].jsNode)
33 // If the current label node has multiple child nodes, an
ArrayExpression node is created as a parameter
34 : callExp.arguments.push(
35 // Each element of the array is a jsNode of a child node
36 createArrayExpression(node.children.map(c => c.jsNode))
37 )
38 // 3. Add the JavaScript AST corresponding to the current tag node
to the jsNode property
39 node.jsNode = callExp
40 }
41 }
```

As shown in the above code and comments, the overall implementation is not complicated. There are two points to note:

- When converting the label node, we need to write the transformation logic in the callback function in the exit phase, so as to ensure that all its sub-nodes are processed
- Whether it is a text node or a label node, the converted JavaScript AST node is stored under the node.jsNode attribute of the node

Use the above two conversion functions to complete the transformation of label nodes and text nodes, that is, convert the template into a call to the h function. However, the AST obtained after conversion is only used to describe the return value of the render function, so the last step we need to do is to complete the JavaScript AST, that is, attach the function declaration statement node used to describe the render function itself to the JavaScript AST. This requires us to write transformRoot function to achieve the transformation of the root node of the Root:

```
01 // Convert the Root node
02 function transformRoot(node) {
03 // Write the logic in the callback function in the exit phase to
ensure that all child nodes are processed
04 return () => {
05 // If it is not the root node, nothing is done
06 if (node.type !== 'Root') {
07 return
08 }
09 // node is the root node, and the first child node of the root node is
the root node of the template.
10 // Of course, we will not consider the case where the template has
multiple root nodes for the time being
11 const vnodeJSAST = node.children[0].jsNode
12 // Create a declaration statement node for the render function,
using vnodeJSAST as the return statement of the render function body
13 node.jsNode = {
```

```
14 type: 'FunctionDecl',
15 id: { type: 'Identifier', name: 'render' },
16 params: [],
17 body: [
18 {
19 type: 'ReturnStatement',
20 return: vnodeJSAST
21 }
22 ]
23 }
24 }
25 }
```

After this step, the template AST will be converted to the corresponding JavaScript AST and can be by the root node to access the converted JavaScript AST. In the next section, we will discuss how to generate rendering function code based on the converted JavaScript AST.

15.6 Code Generation

In the previous section, we completed the construction of the JavaScript AST. In this section, we will discuss how to generate the code of the rendering function from the JavaScript AST, that is, code generation. Code generation is essentially the art of string stitching. We need to access the nodes in the JavaScript AST to generate matching JavaScript code for each type of node.

In this section, we will implement the generate function to complete the code generation task. Code generation is also the last step of the compiler:

```
01 function compile(template) {
02 // template AST
03 const ast = parse(template)
04 // convert template AST to JavaScript AST
05 transform(ast)
06 // code generation
07 const code = generate(ast.jsNode)
08
09 return code
10 }
```

Like AST transformation, code generation also requires context objects. This context object is used to maintain the running state of the program during code generation, as shown in the following code:

```
01 function generate(node) {
02 const context = {
03 // Store the final generated rendering function code
```

```
04 code: '',
05 // When generating code, complete the splicing of the code by
calling the push function
06 push(code) {
07 context.code += code
08 }
09 }
10
11 // Call the genNode function to complete the code generation work,
12 genNode(node, context)
13
14 // return the rendering function code
15 return context.code
16 }
```

In the above code of the generate function, first we define the context object context, which contains context.code properties to store the final generated rendering function code; we also define the context.push function to complete the code stitching, then call the genNode function to complete the code generation work, and finally return the final generated rendering function code.

Also, we want the resulting code to be readable, so we should consider the format of the generated code, such as indentation and line breaks.

```
01 function generate(node) {
02 const context = {
03 code: '',
04 push(code) {
05 context.code += code
06 },
07 // The current level of indentation, with an initial value of
0, that is, no indentation
08 currentIndent: 0,
09 // This function is used to wrap lines, that is, to append the n
character to the code string.
10 // In addition, indentation should be preserved when wrapping, so
we also need to append currentIndent * 2 space characters
11 newline() {
12 context.code += '\n' + ` `.repeat(context.currentIndent)
13 },
14 // Used for indentation, that is, to make currentIndent call the
newline function after self-increment
15 indent() {
16 context.currentIndent++
17 context.newline()
18 },
19 // Unindent, that is, to make currentIndent call the newline
function self-decrement
20 deIndent() {
21 context.currentIndent--
22 context.newline()
23 }
```

```
24 }
25
26 genNode(node, context)
27
28 return context.code
29 }
```

In the above code, we added context.currentIndent attribute, which represents the level of indentation, the initial value is 0, which represents no indentation; we also added the context.newline () function, which appends a line break\ n after the code string each time it is called. Since the indentation needs to be preserved during line breaks, we also append context.currentIndent * 2 space characters. Here we assume that the indentation is two space characters, which we can design to be configurable later. At the same time, we also added context.indent () function to complete the code indentation. Its principle is very simple, that is, let the indentation level context.currentIndent increase automatically, and then call the context.newline () function. The corresponding context.deIndent () function is used to cancel the indentation, that is, let the indentation level context.currentIndent decrease automatically, and then call the context.newline () function.

With these basic capabilities, we can start writing genNode functions to complete the code generation work. The principle of code generation is actually very simple, just need to match various types of JavaScript AST nodes, and call the corresponding generation function, as shown in the following code:

```
01 function genNode(node, context) {
02 switch (node.type) {
03 case 'FunctionDecl':
04 genFunctionDecl(node, context)
05 break
06 case 'ReturnStatement':
07 genReturnStatement(node, context)
08 break
09 case 'CallExpression':
10 genCallExpression(node, context)
11 break
12 case 'StringLiteral':
13 genStringLiteral(node, context)
14 break
15 case 'ArrayExpression':
16 genArrayExpression(node, context)
17 break
18 }
19 }
```

Inside the genNode function, we use the switch statement to match different types of nodes and call the corresponding generator function.

- For FunctionDecl nodes, use the genFunctionDecl function to generate the corresponding JavaScript code for the code of that type

- For ReturnStatement nodes, use the genReturnStatement function to generate the corresponding JavaScript code for the code of that type
- For CallExpression nodes, use the genCallExpression function to generate the corresponding JavaScript code for the code of that type
- For StringLiteral nodes, use the genStringLiteral function to generate the corresponding JavaScript code for the code of that type
- For ArrayExpression nodes, use the genArrayExpression function to generate the corresponding JavaScript code for the code of that type

Since we are currently only dealing with these five types of JavaScript nodes, the current genNode function is sufficient to complete the above case. Of course, if you need to increase the node type in the future, you only need to add the corresponding processing branch to the genNode function.

Next, we will gradually improve the code generation. First, let's implement the code generation of the function declaration statement, that is, the genFunctionDecl function, as shown in the following code:

```
01 function genFunctionDecl(node, context) {
02 // Remove the tool function from the context object
03 const { push, indent, deIndent } = context
04 // node.id is an identifier that describes the name of the function,
which is node.id.name
05 push(`function ${node.id.name} `)
06 push(`(`)
07 // Call genNodeList to generate code for the function's parameters
08 genNodeList(node.params, context)
09 push(`) `)
10 push(`{`)
11 // retraction
12 indent()
13 // Generate code for the function body, where the genNode function
is called recursively
14 node.body.forEach(n => genNode(n, context))
15 // unindent
16 deIndent()
17 push(`}`)
18 }
```

genFunctionDecl function is used to generate the corresponding JavaScript code for the node of the function declaration type. Take the declaration node of the rendering function as an example, the final generated code will be:

```
01 function render () {
02 ... Function body
03 }
```

We also notice that the genNodeList function is called inside the genFunctionDecl function to generate the corresponding code for the function's parameters. It is implemented as follows:

```
01 function genNodeList(nodes, context) {
02 const { push } = context
03 for (let i = 0; i < nodes.length; i++) {
04 const node = nodes[i]
05 genNode(node, context)
06 if (i < nodes.length - 1) {
07 push(', ')
08 }
09 }
10 }
```

genNodeList function receives an array of nodes as arguments and recursively call the genNode function for each node. The point to note here is that each node is processed, and the comma character (,) needs to be concatenated after the generated code. For example:

```
01 // If the array of nodes is
02 const node = [Node 1, Node 2, Node 3]
03 // then the generated code will be similar to
04 'Node 1, Node 2, Node 3'
05 // If you add parentheses before and after this code, then it will
be available for the parameter declaration of the function
06 ('Node 1, Node 2, Node 3')
07 // If you add square brackets before and after this code , then it
will be an array
08 ['Node 1, Node 2, Node 3']
```

From the above example, the genNodeList function will add comma characters between the node codes. In fact, the genArrayExpression function takes advantage of this feature to realize the code generation of array expressions, as shown in the following code:

```
01 function genArrayExpression(node, context) {
02 const { push } = context
03 // append square brackets
04 push('[')
05 // call genNodeList to generate code for array elements
06 genNodeList(node.elements, context)
07 // complete square brackets
08 push(']')
09 }
```

However, since the current render function does not receive any parameters for the time being, the genNodeList function will not generate any code for it. For the genFunctionDecl function, another thing to note is that since the function body itself is also an array of nodes, we need to traverse it and recursively call the genNode function to generate the code.

For nodes of type ReturnStatement and StringLiteral, generating code for them is simple as follows:

```
01 function genReturnStatement(node, context) {
02 const { push } = context
03 // Append return keyword and space
04 push(`return `)
05 // Call genNode function to recursively generate return value
code
06 genNode(node.return, context)
07 }
08
09 function genStringLiteral(node, context) {
10 const { push } = context
11 // For string literals, just append the string corresponding
to node.value
12 push(`'${node.value}'`)
13 }
```

Finally, only the genCallExpression function is left; its implementation is as follows:

```
01 function genCallExpression(node, context) {
02 const { push } = context
03 // Get the called function name and parameter list
04 const { callee, arguments: args } = node
05 // Generate function call code
06 push(`${callee.name}(`)
07 // Call genNodeList to generate parameter code
08 genNodeList(args, context)
09 // Complete brackets
10 push(`)`)
11 }
```

As you can see, in the genCallExpression function, we also use the genNodeList function to generate the corresponding code for the parameters of the function call. With the implementation of the above generator function, we will get the expected rendering function code. Run the following test case:

```
01 const ast = parse(`<div><p>Vue</p><p>Template</p></div>`)
02 transform(ast)
03 const code = generate(ast.jsNode)
```

The resulting code string is as follows:

```
01 function render () {
02 return h('div', [h('p', 'Vue'), h('p', 'Template')])
03 }
```

15.7 Summary

In this chapter, we first discussed the workflow of the Vue.js template compiler. Vue.js' template compiler is used to compile templates into rendering functions. Its workflow is roughly divided into three steps.

1. Analyze the template and parse it into a template AST
2. Convert the template AST into a JavaScript AST used to describe the rendering function
3. Generate the rendering function code from the JavaScript AST

Next, we discuss the implementation principle of parser and how to build a lexical analyzer with a finite-state automatic mechanism. The process of lexical analysis is the process of migrating the finite-state machine between different states. In this process, the state machine generates tokens to form a list of tokens. We will use this list of tokens to construct an AST that describes the template. Specifically, we scan the token list and maintain a start tag stack. Whenever a start tag node is scanned, it is pushed to the top of the stack. The top node is always the parent of the next scanned node. In this way, when all tokens are scanned, a tree AST can be constructed.

Then, we discussed the transformation and plug-in architecture of the AST. AST is a tree data structure. In order to access the nodes in the AST, we traverse the AST in a depth-first way. During the traversal process, we can perform various operations on the AST nodes to realize the transformation of the AST. In order to decouple the access and operation of nodes, we design a plug-in architecture to encapsulate the operations of nodes into independent transformation functions. These transformation functions can be registered through context.nodeTransforms. Here, the context is called the transformation context. The context object usually maintains the current state of the program, such as the currently visited node, the parent node of the currently visited node, the location index of the currently visited node, etc. With the context object and the important information it contains, we can easily implement the ability to replace and delete nodes. However, sometimes, the transformation work of the currently visited node depends on the transformation result of its sub-node, so in order to complete the transformation of sub-node first, we divide the entire conversion process into "entry stage" and "exit stage." Each transformation function is executed in two stages, which allows for more fine-grained transformation control.

After that, we discussed how to convert the template AST into a JavaScript AST that describes the rendering function. Template AST is used to describe templates; similarly, JavaScript AST is used to describe JavaScript code. Only after converting the template AST to JavaScript AST can we generate the final rendering function code from this.

Finally, we discussed the generation of the rendering function code. Code generation is the last step of the template compiler, and the generated code will be used as the rendering function of the component. The code generation process is the process of string splicing. We need to write corresponding code generation functions for different AST nodes. To make the generated code more readable, we also discussed how to indent and wrap the generated code. We encapsulate the code used for indentation and line wrapping as utility functions and define it in the context object during the code generation process.

Chapter 16
Parsers

In Chap. 15, we first discussed how a parser worked and learned that a parser was essentially a state machine. However, we also mentioned that regular expressions were actually a finite-state machine. Therefore, using regular expressions can save us a lot of code when writing parsers. In this chapter, we will use regular expressions more to implement HTML parsers. In addition, a complete HTML parser is more complicated than expected. We know that browsers parse HTML text, but how does it do it? In fact, there is a specification for parsing HTML text, that is, the WHATWG specification for parsing HTML, which defines the complete error handling and the state transition process of the finite-state machine, and also mentions some special states, such as DATA, CDATA, RCDATA, RAWTEXT, etc. So, what do these states mean? What are the effects on the parser? What is an HTML entity, and how does the Vue.js template parser need to handle HTML entities? These issues will be discussed in this chapter.

16.1 Text Patterns and Their Impact on Parsers

Text mode refers to some special states that the parser enters when working. In different special states, the parser's parsing behavior for text will be different. Specifically, when the parser encounters some special tags, it will switch modes, which will affect its parsing behavior for text. These special tags are:

- $<$ title $>$ tags, $<$ textarea $>$ tags; when the parser encounters these two tags, it will switch to RCDATA mode
- $<$ style $>$, $<$ xmp $>$, $<$ iframe $>$, $<$ noembed $>$, $<$ noframes $>$, $<$ noscript $>$ and other tags; when the parser encounters these tags, it will switch to RAWTEXT mode
- When the parser encounters $<$! [CDATA [string, it will enter CDATA mode

H. Yang, *Vue. JS Framework*, https://doi.org/10.1007/978-981-99-4947-2_16

§ **13.2.5.1 Data state**

Consume the next input character:

↳ **U+0026 AMPERSAND (&)**

Set the *return state* to the data state. Switch to the character reference state.

↳ **U+003C LESS-THAN SIGN (<)**

Switch to the tag open state.

↳ **U+0000 NULL**

This is an unexpected-null-character parse error. Emit the current input character as a character token.

↳ **EOF**

Emit an end-of-file token.

↳ **Anything else**

Emit the current input character as a character token.

Fig. 16.1 The description of the data state in the WHATWG specification

§ **13.2.5.2 RCDATA state**

Consume the next input character:

↳ **U+0026 AMPERSAND (&)**

Set the *return state* to the RCDATA state. Switch to the character reference state.

↳ **U+003C LESS-THAN SIGN (<)**

Switch to the RCDATA less-than sign state.

↳ **U+0000 NULL**

This is an unexpected-null-character parse error. Emit a U+FFFD REPLACEMENT CHARACTER character token.

↳ **EOF**

Emit an end-of-file token.

↳ **Anything else**

Emit the current input character as a character token.

Fig. 16.2 The description of the RCDATA state in the WHATWG specification

The parser's initial mode is DATA mode. For Vue.js template DSLs, < script > tags are not allowed in templates, so Vue.js template parser switches to RAWTEXT mode when it encounters < script > tags.

The behavior of the parser varies depending on the mode of operation. Section 13.2.5.1 of the WHATWG specification shows the workflow of the parser under the initial mode, as shown in Fig. 16.1.

We do some necessary explanation of Fig. 16.1. In the default DATA mode, the parser switches to the tag open state when it encounters the character <. In other words, in this mode, the parser is able to parse the tag element. When the parser encounters the character &, it switches to the character reference state, also known as the HTML character entity state. That is, in DATA mode, the parser can handle HTML character entities.

Let's take a look at how the parser works when it is in the RCDATA state. Figure 16.2 shows Section 13.2.5.2 of the WHATWG specification.

§ **13.2.5.9 RCDATA less-than sign state**

Consume the <u>next input character</u>:

   ↪ **U+002F SOLIDUS (/)**
        Set the *temporary buffer* to the empty string. Switch to the <u>RCDATA end tag open state</u>.

   ↪ **Anything else**
        Emit a U+003C LESS-THAN SIGN character token. <u>Reconsume</u> in the RCDATA state.

Fig. 16.3 WHATWG specification on the description of RCDATA less-than sign state

Figure 16.2 shows that when the parser encounters the character <, it will not switch to the label start state, but will switch to the RCDATA less-than sign state. Figure 16.3 shows how the parser works in the RCDATA less-than sign state.

Seen from Fig. 16.3, in the RCDATA less-than sign state, if the parser encounters the character/, then it will directly switch to the end tag state of RCDATA, that is, RCDATA end tag open state; otherwise, the current character < will be treated as a normal character, and then continue to process the following characters. It can be seen that in the RCDATA state, the parser cannot recognize the tag element. This actually suggests that the character < can be used as normal text in < textarea >, and the parser will not consider the character < to be the beginning of the tag, as shown in the following code:

```
01 < textarea >
02 < div > asdf </div > asdfasdf
03 </textarea >
```

In the above HTML code, there is a < div > tag in the < textarea > tag. However, the parser does not parse < div > as a tag element, but as normal text. However, as can be seen from Fig. 16.2, in RCDATA mode, the parser still supports HTML entities. Because when the parser encounters the character &, it will switch to the character reference state, as shown in the following code:

```
01 <textarea>&copy;</textarea>
```

When the browser renders this HTML code, it will display the character in the text box. The parser works similarly in RAWTEXT mode as it does in RCDATA mode. The only difference is that in RAWTEXT mode, the parser no longer supports HTML entities. Figure 16.4 shows how the finite-state machine works in RAWTEXT mode as defined in Section 13.2.5.3 of the WHATWG specification.

Comparing Figs. 16.4 and 16.2, RAWTEXT mode does not support HTML entities. In this mode, the parser treats HTML entity characters as normal characters. The parser of the Vue.js single-file component enters RAWTEXT mode when it encounters a < script > tag, where it treats all the contents of the < script > tag as normal text.

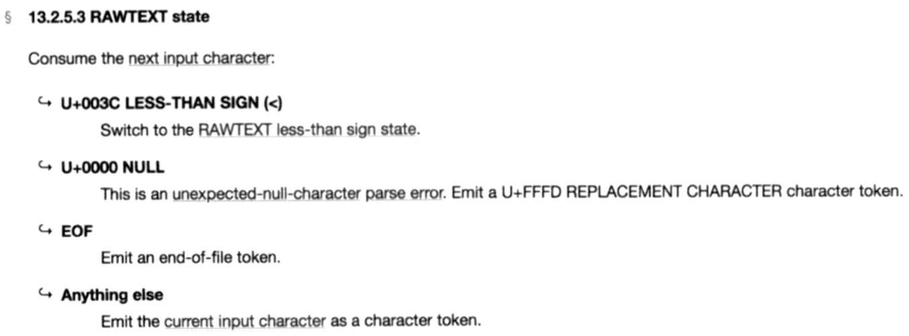

§ **13.2.5.3 RAWTEXT state**

Consume the next input character:

↳ **U+003C LESS-THAN SIGN (<)**
   Switch to the RAWTEXT less-than sign state.

↳ **U+0000 NULL**
   This is an unexpected-null-character parse error. Emit a U+FFFD REPLACEMENT CHARACTER character token.

↳ **EOF**
   Emit an end-of-file token.

↳ **Anything else**
   Emit the current input character as a character token.

Fig. 16.4 Description of the RAWTEXT state in the WHATWG spec

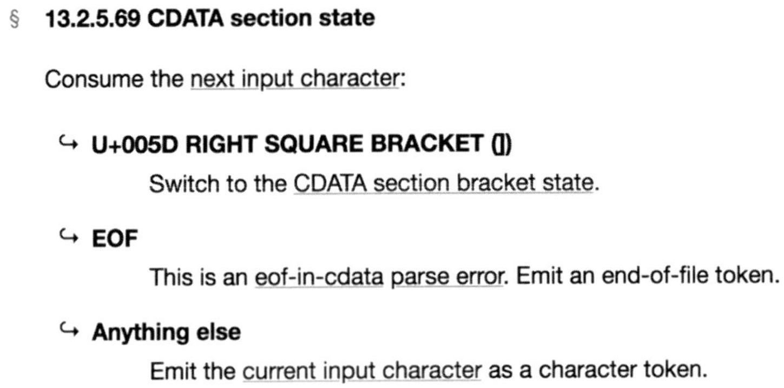

§ **13.2.5.69 CDATA section state**

Consume the next input character:

↳ **U+005D RIGHT SQUARE BRACKET (])**
   Switch to the CDATA section bracket state.

↳ **EOF**
   This is an eof-in-cdata parse error. Emit an end-of-file token.

↳ **Anything else**
   Emit the current input character as a character token.

Fig. 16.5 The CDATA section state in the WHATWG specification

The CDATA mode goes a step further than the RAWTEXT mode. Figure 16.5 shows how the finite-state machine works in CDATA mode, as defined in Section 13.2.5.69 of the WHATWG specification.

In CDATA mode, the parser treats any character as a normal character until it encounters the CDATA end flag.

In fact, the PLAINTEXT mode is also defined in the WHATWG specification, which is similar to the RAWTEXT mode. The difference is that once the parser enters PLAINTEXT mode, it will not exit. In addition, Vue.js template DSL parser does not use PLAINTEXT mode, so we will not go into it too much.

When writing the parser code later, we will define the above mode as a state table, as shown in the following code:

```
01 const TextModes = {
02 DATA: 'DATA',
03 RCDATA: 'RCDATA',
04 RAWTEXT: 'RAWTEXT',
05 CDATA: 'CDATA'
06 }
```

16.2   Recursive Descent Algorithm Construction Template AST

In this section, we will start implementing a more complete template parser. The basic architecture model of the parser is as follows:

```
01 // Define the text schema as a state table
02 const TextModes = {
03 DATA: 'DATA',
04 RCDATA: 'RCDATA',
05 RAWTEXT: 'RAWTEXT',
06 CDATA: 'CDATA'
07 }
08
09 // Parser function, receiving templates as parameters
10 function parse(str) {
11 // define context objects
12 const context = {
13 // source is template content for consumption during parsing
14 source: str,
15 // parser is currently in text mode; initial mode is DATA
16 mode: TextModes.DATA
17 }
18 // Call the parseChildren function to start parsing, and it returns
the child nodes that are parsed
19 // The parseChildren function takes two arguments:
20 // The first argument is the context object context
21 // The second argument is the node stack composed of the parent
node; the stack is empty at the beginning
22 const nodes = parseChildren(context, [])
23
24 // The parser returns the Root node
25 return {
26 type: 'Root',
27 // children using nodes as root
28 children: nodes
29 }
30 }
```

In the above code, we first define a state table, TextModes, which is used to describe predefined text patterns. Then, we define the parse function in which we define the context object, which is used to maintain various states of the program during the execution of the parser. Next, call the parseChildren function for parsing, which returns the parsed sub-nodes and uses these sub-nodes as children to create the root node. Finally, the parse function returns the root node to complete the construction of the template AST.

The idea of this code is different from the construction idea of the template AST we described in Chap. 15. In Chap. 15, we first tokenized the template content to obtain a series of tokens, and then built the template AST based on these tokens. In fact, the process of creating the token and constructing the template AST can be carried out at the same time, because the template and the template AST have isomorphic properties.

In addition, in the above code, the parseChildren function is the core of the entire parser. We will call it recursively and use it to continuously consume the template content. The parseChildren function returns the parsed sub-node. For example, suppose you have the following template:

```
01 < p > 1 </p >
02 < p > 2 </p >
```

The above template has two root nodes, that is, two < p > tags. The parseChildren function parses this template and gets an array of these two < p > nodes:

```
01 [
02 { type: 'Element', tag: 'p', children: [/*...*/] },
03 { type: 'Element', tag: 'p', children: [/*...*/] },
04 ]
```

The array will be the children of the root node of Root.

The parseChildren function takes two arguments.

- The first argument: the context object context
- The second argument: the stack composed of parent nodes, which is used to maintain the parent–child relationship between nodes

The parseChildren function is also essentially a finite-state machine, and how many states the finite-state machine has depends on the number of sub-node types. In a template, the sub-node of an element can be one of the following.

- Label nodes, such as < div >
- Text interpolation nodes, such as {{val}}
- Normal text nodes, such as: text
- Annotation nodes, such as <!---->
- CDATA nodes, such as <! [CDATA [xxx]] >

In standard HTML, there will be more types of nodes, such as DOCTYPE nodes. To reduce complexity, we only consider nodes of the above types.

Figure 16.6 shows the state transition process of the parseChildren function during the parsing of the template.

The state transition process of the parseChildren function during the parsing of the template can be summarized as follows.

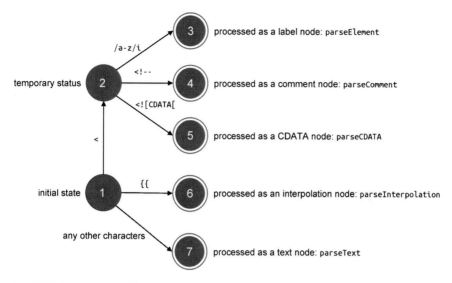

Fig. 16.6 The state transition process of the parseChildren function during the parsing of the template

- When the character $<$ is encountered, the temporary state is entered.
  - If the next character matches the regular/a-z/i, it is considered a label node, so the parseElement function is called to complete the parsing of the label. Note the i in the regular expression /a-z/i, which means case insensitive
  - If the string starts with $<!$ --, it is considered a comment node, so the parseComment function is called to complete the parsing of the comment node
  - If the string starts with $<!$ [CDATA [, it is considered that this is a CDATA node, so the parseCDATA function is called to complete the parsing of the CDATA node
- If the string starts with {{, it is considered to be an interpolation node, so the parseInterpolation function is called to complete the parsing of the interpolation node
- In other cases, as normal text, the parseText function is called to complete the parsing of the text node

  When implementing into the code, we also need to incorporate text patterns, as shown in the following code:

```
01 function parseChildren(context, ancestors) {
02 // Define an array of nodes to store sub-node as the final return
value
03 let nodes = []
04 // Get the current state from context objects, including mode mode
and template content source
05 const { mode, source } = context
06
```

```
07 // Open while loop; as long as the condition is met, string will
always be parsed
08 // isEnd () will be explained in detail later
09 while(!isEnd(context, ancestors)) {
10 let node
11 // Only DATA mode and RCDATA mode support interpolation node
resolution
12 if (mode === TextModes.DATA || mode === TextModes.RCDATA) {
13 // Only DATA mode supports tag node resolution
14 if (mode === TextModes.DATA && source[0] === '<') {
15 if (source[1] === '!') {
16 if (source.startsWith('<!--')) {
17 // comment
18 node = parseComment(context)
19 } else if (source.startsWith('<![CDATA[')) {
20 // CDATA
21 node = parseCDATA(context, ancestors)
22 }
23 } else if (source[1] === '/') {
24 // end tag; you need to throw an error here; the reason will be
explained in detail later
25 } else if (/[a-z]/i.test(source[1])) {
26 // tags
27 node = parseElement(context, ancestors)
28 }
29 } else if (source.startsWith('{{')) {
30 // parse interpolation
31 node = parseInterpolation(context)
32 }
33 }
34
35 // node does not exist, indicating that it is in another mode,
that is, non-DATA mode, non-RCDATA mode
36 // In this case, everything is processed as text
37 if (!node) {
38 // Parse text node
39 node = parseText(context)
40 }
41
42 // Add nodes to the nodes array
43 nodes.push(node)
44 }
45
46 // When the while loop stops, it means that the sub-node has parsed
and returned sub-node
47 return nodes
48 }
```

The above code completely describes the state transition process shown in Fig. 16.6. Here are a few points to note.

Table 16.1 Different modes and their characteristics

Mode	Whether tags can be parsed	Whether to support HTML entity
DATA	Y	Y
RCDATA	N	Y
RAWTEXT	N	N
CDATA	N	N

- The return value of the parseChildren function is an array of child nodes. Each *while* loop will parse one or more nodes. These nodes will be added to the nodes array and returned as the return value of the parseChildren function
- The current text mode needs to be determined during the parsing process. According to Table 16.1, the parser only supports the parsing of interpolated nodes when in DATA mode or RCDATA mode. Moreover, the parser only supports the parsing of label nodes, comment nodes, and CDATA nodes when in DATA mode
- As described in Sect. 16.1, the parser switches modes when a particular label is encountered. Once the parser switches to a mode other than DATA mode and RCDATA mode, all characters will be parsed as text nodes. Of course, even in DATA mode or RCDATA mode, if the label node, comment node, CDATA node, and interpolation node cannot be matched, then they will be parsed as text nodes

In addition to the above three points, you may still have questions about this code. One of them is when the while loop stops. And what is the purpose of the isEnd () function? Here we give a simple explanation. The parseChildren function is used to parse child nodes, so the *while* loop must encounter the end label of the parent node before it stops. This is a normal idea. But there are some problems with this idea, but we will ignore it for the time being and discuss it in detail later.

We can use an example to more intuitively understand the job responsibilities and workflow of the parseChildren function, and other parsing functions when parsing templates. Take the following template as an example:

```
01 const template = `<div>
02 <p>Text1</p>
03 <p>Text2</p>
04 </div>`
```

It should be emphasized here that we cannot ignore whitespace characters when parsing templates. These whitespace characters include newline (\n), carriage return (\r), space ("")、 tab (\t), and page feed (\f). If we use the plus sign (+) for the newline and the minus sign (−) for the space character, then the above template can be expressed as:

```
01 const template = '< div > + -- < p > Text1 </p > + -- < p > Text2 </p > +
</div >'
```

Next, we perform the parsing process with this template as input.

The parser is initially in DATA mode. After parsing, the first character encountered by the parser is <, and the second character can match the /a-z/i regular expression, so the parser will enter the label node state and call the parseElement function to parse.

The parseElement function will do three things: parse the start tag, parse the sub-node, and parse the end tag.

You can use the following pseudocode to express what the parseElement function does:

```
01 function parseElement() {
02 // parse start tag
03 const element = parseTag()
04 // here the parseChildren function is called recursively
to parse < div > tag sub-node
05 element.children = parseChildren()
06 // parse end tag
07 parseEndTag()
08
09 return element
10 }
```

If a tag is not self-closing, it can be considered that a complete tag element is composed of three parts: the start tag, the sub-node, and the end tag. Therefore, within the parseElement function, we call three parsing functions, respectively, to handle these three parts. Take the above template as an example.

- parseTag parses the start tag. The parseTag function is used to parse the start tag, including the attributes and instructions on the start tag. Therefore, after the parseTag parsing function is executed, the content <div> of the string will be consumed and after processing, the template content will become:

```
01 const template = `+--<p>Text1</p>+--<p>Text2</p>+</div>`
```

- Recursively call the parseChildren function to parse the sub-node. The parseElement function produces a label node element when parsing the start tag. After parseElement finishes executing, the remaining template content should be parsed as sub-nodes of the element, i.e., element.children. Therefore, we call the parseChildren function recursively. In this process, the parseChildren function consumes the contents of the string: + -- < p > Text1 </p > + -- < p > Text2 </ p > +. The processed template content will become:

```
01 const template = '</div >'
```

- parseEndTag to process the end tag. You can see that after being processed by the parseChildren function, the template content is only one end tag left. Therefore, you only need to call the parseEndTag parser to consume it

After the above three steps, the template is parsed and finally the template AST is obtained. But it is worth noting here that in order to parse the sub-node of the tag, we recursively call the parseChildren function. This means that a new finite-state machine is running, which we call "finite-state machine 2." The template content processed by "finite-state machine 2" is as follows:

```
01 const template = `+---<p>Text1</p>+---<p>Text2</p>+`
```

Next, we continue to analyze the state transition process of "finite-state machine 2." When "finite-state machine 2" starts running, the first character of the template is a line break (the character + stands for a line break). Therefore, the parser enters the text node state and calls the parseText function to complete the parsing of the text node. The parseText function treats all characters before the next < character as the content of the text node. In other words, the parseText function consumes the template content + -- and produces a text node. In parseText parsing, after the function is executed, the remaining template content is as follows:

```
01 const template = `<p>Text1</p>+---<p>Text2</p>+`
```

Next, the parseChildren function continues to execute. At this time, the first character of the template is <, and the next character can match the regular/a-z/i. So the parser again enters the execution phase of the parseElement parsing function, which consumes the template content < p > Text1 </p >. After this step, the remaining template content is as follows:

```
01 const template = `+---<p>Text2</p>+`
```

You can see that the first character of the template at this time is a newline character, so call the parseText function to consume the template content + --. Now, the rest of the template is as follows:

```
01 const template = `<p>Text2</p>+`
```

The parser will call the parseElement function again to process the label node. After that, the remaining template content is as follows:

```
01 const template = `+`
```

You can see that there is now only one newline left in the template content. The parseChildren function will continue to execute and call the parseText function to consume the remaining content and generate a text node. Eventually, the template is parsed and State Machine 2 stops running.

While the "state machine 2" runs, we called the parseElement function twice more to process the label node. The first call is made to process the content <p > Text1</p>, and the second call is to process the content <p > Text2</p>. We know that the parseElement function recursively calls the parseChildren function to complete the parsing of the child node, which means that the parser opens two new state machines.

From the above example, we can realize that the parseChildren parser function is the core of the entire state machine, and state transition operations are completed within this function. While the parseChildren function runs, in order to process the label node, the parseElement parser function is called, which indirectly calls the parseChildren function and generates a new state machine. As the level of tag nesting increases, new state opportunities are created as the parseChildren function is called recursively, which is what the word "recursive" in "recursive descent" means. The call of the parent parseChildren function is used to construct the parent template AST node, and the lower parseChildren function that is called recursively is used to construct the lower template AST node. Eventually, a template AST of a tree-shaped structure is constructed, which is the meaning of the word "descent" in "recursive descent."

16.3   Start and Stop of Finite-State Machines

In the previous section, we discussed the implications of the recursive descent algorithm. As we know, the parseChildren function is essentially a state machine that starts a while loop that makes the state machine run automatically, as shown in the following code:

```
01 function parseChildren(context, ancestors) {
02 let nodes = []
03
04 const { mode } = context
05 // Run finite-state machine
06 while (!isEnd(context, ancestors)) {
07 // Omit some code
08 }
09
10 return nodes
11 }
```

The question here is, when should the finite-state machine stop? In other words, when should the while loop stop running? This involves the judgment logic of the isEnd () function. To figure this out, we need to simulate the operation of the finite-state machine.

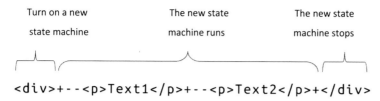

Turn on a new   The new state   The new state
state machine   machine runs   machine stops

`<div>+--<p>Text1</p>+--<p>Text2</p>+</div>`

Fig. 16.7 Enabling a new finite-state machine

We know that when the parseElement function is called to parse a tag node, the parseChildren function is called recursively, thereby opening a new finite-state machine, as shown in Fig. 16.7.

For ease of description, we can refer to the new finite-state machine shown in Fig. 16.7 as "finite-state machine 1." "Finite-state machine 1" starts, runs, and continues to parse the template until the next $< p >$ tag is encountered.

Because the $< p >$ tag is encountered," finite-state machine 1 "will also call the parseElement function to parse. Then repeat the above process, that is, push the currently resolved label node into the parent node stack, and then recursively call the parseChildren function to start a new finite-state machine, namely "finite-state machine 2." As you can see, there are two finite-state machines running at the same time.

At this time, "finite-state machine 2" has the execution right of the program, and it continues to parse the template until it encounters the end tag $</p >$. Because this is an end tag, and there is a label node with the same name as the end tag in the parent node stack, the "finite-state machine 2" stops running and pops up the top node in the parent node stack.

At this point, "finite-state machine 2" has stopped running, but "finite-state machine 1" is still running, so it will continue to parse the template until the next $< p >$ tag is encountered. At this point, "finite-state machine 1" will call the parseElement function again to parse the tag node, so it will perform stack pressing and open a new "finite-state machine 3," as shown in Fig. 16.8.

At this time, "finite-state machine 3" has execution rights of the program, and it will continue to parse the template until it encounters the end tag $< /p >$. Because this is an end tag, and there is a label node with the same name as the end tag in the parent node stack, the "finite-state machine 3" will stop running and pop up the top node in the parent node stack.

When the "finite-state machine 3" stops running, the execution right of the program is returned to "finite-state machine 1." " Finite-state machine 1 "will continue to parse the template until it encounters the last $</div >$ end tag. At this time," finite-state machine 1" finds that there is a tag node with the same name as the end tag in the parent node stack, so it pops the node out of the parent node stack and stops running, as shown in Fig. 16.9.

Then the parent node stack is empty, the finite-state machine all stops running, and the template parsing is completed.

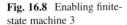

Fig. 16.8 Enabling finite-
state machine 3

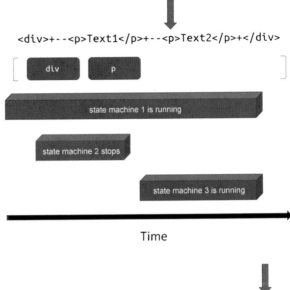

Fig. 16.9 State machine
1 stops

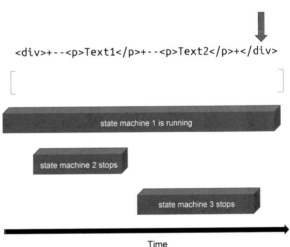

From the above description, we can clearly recognize when the parser will start a
new finite-state machine, and when the state opportunity will stop. The conclusion is
when the parser encounters the start tag, it will push the tag into the parent node stack
and start a new state machine. When the parser encounters the end tag and there is a
start tag node with the same name in the parent node stack, it will stop the currently
running finite-state machine. According to the above rules, we can give the logic of
the isEnd function, as shown in the following code:

```
01 function isEnd(context, ancestors) {
02 // When the template content is parsed, stop
03 if (!context.source) return true
04 // get parent label node
```

Fig. 16.10 The first type of
template interpretation

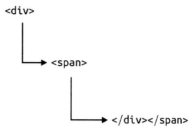

```
05 const parent = ancestors[ancestors.length - 1]
06 // Stop if an end tag is encountered and the tag has the same name as
the parent label node
07 if (parent && context.source.startsWith(`</${parent.tag}`)) {
08 return true
09 }
10 }
```

The code shows the stop time of the finite-state machine, as follows:

- The first stop time is when the template content is parsed
- The second stop time is when the end tag is encountered, then the parser will take
  the node at the top of the parent node stack as the parent node, check whether the
  end tag has the same name as the parent node's label; if the same, then the finite-
  state machine stops running

It should be noted here that in the second stop time, we directly compare the name
of the end tag with the label name of the top node of the stack. This is indeed
possible, but strictly speaking it is flawed. For example, the following template
shows:

```
01 < div > < span > </div > </span >
```

Observing the above template, we can see that it has an obvious problem. Can
you find it? In fact, there are two ways to interpret this template, and Fig. 16.10
shows the first one.

As shown in Fig. 16.10, the flow of this interpretation is as follows.

- "State Machine 1" encounters the <div> start tag and calls the parseElement
  parse function, which opens "State Machine 2" to complete the resolution of the
  child node
- "State machine 2" encounters the < span > start tag and calls the parseElement
  parsing function, which will turn on "State machine 3" to complete the sub-node
  parsing
- "State machine 3" encounters the </div > end tag. Since the node name at the top
  of the parent node stack is span, not div, so "finite-state machine 3" will not stop
  running. At this time, the "finite-state machine 3" encounters an unexpected state,

because the end tag $</\text{div}>$ lacks a corresponding start tag, so the "finite-state machine 3" will throw an error: "Invalid end tag"

The idea of the above process is consistent with our current implementation, and the state opportunity encounters an unexpected state. The following parseChildren function code can reflect this:

```
01 function parseChildren(context, ancestors) {
02 let nodes = []
03
04 const { mode } = context
05
06 while(!isEnd(context, ancestors)) {
07 let node
08
09 if (mode === TextModes.DATA || mode === TextModes.RCDATA) {
10 if (mode === TextModes.DATA && context.source[0] === '<') {
11 if (context.source[1] === '!') {
12 // omit some code
13 } else if (context.source[1] === '/') {
14 // final-state machine encountered a closing tag; it should throw an
error because it is missing the corresponding start tag
15 console.error('invalid end tag')
16 continue
17 } else if (/[a-z]/i.test(context.source[1])) {
18 // omit some code
19 }
20 } else if (context.source.startsWith('{{')) {
21 // omit some code
22 }
23 }
24 // omit some code
25 }
26
27 return nodes
28 }
```

In other words, to parse the template in the above example according to our current method, the final error message is "Invalid end tag." But in fact, there is another better way to parse. Observe the template given in the example above, where there is a complete piece of content, as shown in Fig. 16.11.

As you can see from Fig. 16.11, there is a complete piece of content in the template, and we expect the parser to parse it normally, which is likely to be in line with the user's intent as well. But in reality, either interpretation has little impact on the program. The difference between the two is in error handling. For the first interpretation method, we get the error message: "Invalid end tag." For the second interpretation method, after the "full content" part is parsed, the parser will print the error message: "$<$ span $>$ tag is missing closing tag." Obviously, the second interpretation method is more reasonable.

Fig. 16.11 The second way
of template interpretation

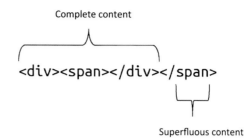

In order to implement the second interpretation method, we need to adjust the logic of the isEnd function. When determining whether the state machine should be stopped, we should not always compare it to the parent node at the top of the stack, but to all nodes in the entire parent stack. As long as there is a node in the parent stack with the same name as the currently encountered end tag, stop the finite-state machine, as shown in the following code:

```
01 function isEnd(context, ancestors) {
02 if (!context.source) return true
03
04 // Compare with all nodes in the parent stack
05 for (let i = ancestors.length - 1; i >= 0; --i) {
06 // Stop the finite-state machine as long as there is a node in the
stack with the same name as the current end tag
07 if (context.source.startsWith(`</${ancestors[i].tag}`)) {
08 return true
09 }
10 }
11 }
```

The following template is parsed again according to the new idea:

```
01 < div > < span > </div > </span >
```

The process is as follows:

* "Finite-state machine 1" encounters the < div > start tag, calls the parseElement parsing function, and turns on "finite-state machine 2" to parse the sub-node
* "finite-state machine 2" encounters the < span > start tag, calls the parseElement parsing function, and turns on "finite-state machine 3" to parse the sub-node
* "Finite-state machine 3" encounters </div > end tag. Due to the existence of a tag node named div in the node stack, "state machine 3" stops

In this process, when the "finite-state machine 2" calls the parseElement parser function, the parseElement function can find that < span > is missing a closing tag, so it will print the error message "< span > tag is missing a closing tag," as shown in the following code:

```
01 function parseElement(context, ancestors) {
02 const element = parseTag(context)
03 if (element.isSelfClosing) return element
04
05 ancestors.push(element)
06 element.children = parseChildren(context, ancestors)
07 ancestors.pop()
08
09 if (context.source.startsWith(`</${element.tag}`)) {
10 parseTag(context, 'end')
11 } else {
12 // missing closing tag
13 console.error(`${element.tag} tag missing closing tag')
14 }
15
16 return element
17 }
```

16.4 Parsing Label Nodes

In the implementation of the parseElement function given in the previous section, we
call the parseTag function whether it is parsing the start tag or the closing tag. At the
same time, we use the parseChildren function to parse the part between the opening
tag and the closing tag, as shown in the following code and comments:

```
01 function parseElement(context, ancestors) {
02 // call the parseTag function to parse the opening tag
03 const element = parseTag(context)
04 if (element.isSelfClosing) return element
05
06 ancestors.push(element)
07 element.children = parseChildren(context, ancestors)
08 ancestors.pop()
09
10 if (context.source.startsWith(`</${element.tag}`)) {
11 // Call the parseTag function again to parse the closing tag,
passing the second parameter: 'end'
12 parseTag(context, 'end')
13 } else {
14 console.error(`${element.tag} tag missing closing tag`)
15 }
16
17 return element
18 }
```

The entire parsing process of the tag node is shown in Fig. 16.12.

It should be noted here that since the format of the start tag and the end tag is very
similar, we use the parseTag function to process it uniformly, and specify the specific

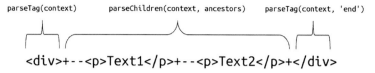

Fig. 16.12 The process of parsing tag nodes

processing type through the second parameter of the function. When the value of the second parameter is string "end," it means that the end tag is parsed. In addition, whether it is dealing with the start tag or the end tag, the parseTag function will consume the corresponding content. In order to achieve the consumption of template content, we need to add two utility functions in the context object, as shown in the following code:

```
01 function parse(str) {
02 // context object
03 const context = {
04 // template content
05 source: str,
06 mode: TextModes.DATA,
07 // advanceBy function is used to consume the specified number of characters; it receives a number as an argument
08 advanceBy(num) {
09 // According to the given number of characters num, intercept the template content after position num and replace the current template content
10 context.source = context.source.slice(num)
11 },
12 // There may be useless whitespace characters for both start and end tags, such as < div >
13 advanceSpaces() {
14 // Match blank characters
15 const match = /^[\t\r\n\f ]+/.exec(context.source)
16 if (match) {
17 // call advanceBy function to consume space characters
18 context.advanceBy(match[0].length)
19 }
20 }
21 }
22
23 const nodes = parseChildren(context, [])
24
25 return {
26 type: 'Root',
27 children: nodes
28 }
29 }
```

In the above code, we add advanceBy function and advanceSpaces function to the context object. The advanceBy function is used to consume the specified number of characters. The implementation principle is very simple, that is, call the slice function of string, intercept the remaining string according to the specified position, and use the intercepted result as the new template content. The advanceSpaces function is used to consume unwanted space characters because there may be space characters in the label, such as the minus sign (−) in the template < div---- > for space characters.

With advanceBy and advanceSpaces functions, we can give the implementation of the parseTag function, as shown in the following code:

```
01 // Since parseTag is used to handle both the start tag and the end
tag, we design the second parameter type,
02 // to represent whether the current processing is the start tag or
the end tag, the default value of type is 'start ', that is, the default is
to process as the start tag
03 function parseTag(context, type = 'start') {
04 // get advanceBy function from context object
05 const { advanceBy, advanceSpaces } = context
06
07 // Regular expressions that handle start and end tags are
different
08 const match = type === 'start'
09 // Match the start label
10 ? /^<([a-z][^\t\r\n\f />]*)/i.exec(context.source)
11 // Match the end label
12 : /^<\/([a-z][^\t\r\n\f />]*)/i.exec(context.source)
13 // After a successful match, the value of the first capture group
of the regular expression is the tag name
14 const tag = match[1]
15 // consume the entire contents of the regex match, such as ' < div '
16 advanceBy(match[0].length)
17 // consume useless space characters in the tag
18 advanceSpaces()
19
20 // After consuming the matched contents, if the string starts
with'/> ', it means that this is a self-closing tag
21 const isSelfClosing = context.source.startsWith('/>')
22 // If it is a self-closing label, consume '/>', otherwise consume
'>'
23 advanceBy(isSelfClosing ? 2 : 1)
24
25 // return tag nodes
26 return {
27 type: 'Element',
28 // tage name
29 tag,
30 // tag attribute temporarily empty
31 props: [],
32 // sub-node empty
33 children: [],
34 // whether self-closing
35 isSelfClosing
36 }
37 }
```

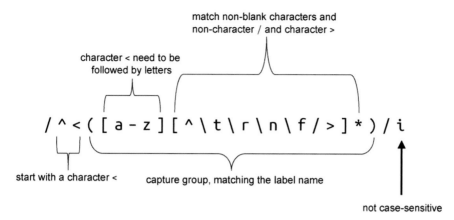

Fig. 16.13 Regular expressions used to match the start tag and the end tag

The above code has two key points.

- Since the parseTag function is used to resolve both the start and end tags, a parameter is required to identify the type of tag currently being processed, that is, type
- For the start and end tags, the regular expressions used to match them are only different: the end tag starts with the string </. Figure 16.13 shows the meaning of the regular expression used to match the start tag

Here are several examples of using the regular shown in Fig. 16.13 to match the start tag.

- For string '< div >', string '< div' is matched; the remainder is '>'
- For string '< div/>', string '< div' is matched; the remainder is '/>'
- For string '< div ---->', where the minus (−) represents space, string ' < div 'is matched; the remainder is '---->'

In addition, the regex shown in Fig. 16.16 has a capture group that captures tag names.

In addition to the regex, several other key points of the parseTag function are as follows.

- After completing the regular matching, we need to call the advanceBy function to consume all the contents matched by the regex
- According to the third regex matching example given above, since there may be useless space characters in the tag, such as < div ---->, we need to call the advanceSpaces function to consume space characters
- After consuming the content matched by the regex, you need to check whether the remaining template content starts with string/>. If so, it means that the current

parsing is a self-closing label. In this case, you need to set the isSelfClosing attribute of the label node to true
- Finally, determine whether the label is self-closing. If so, call the advnaceBy function to consume the content/>, otherwise, just consume the content >

After the above processing, the parseTag function will return a label node. parseElement function needs to complete the text mode switch according to the type of node after getting the label node generated by the parseTag function, as shown in the following code:

```
01 function parseElement(context, ancestors) {
02 const element = parseTag(context)
03 if (element.isSelfClosing) return element
04
05 // Switch to the correct text mode
06 if (element.tag === 'textarea' || element.tag === 'title') {
07 // switch to RCDATA mode if the tag parsed by parseTag is < textarea
> or < title >
08 context.mode = TextModes.RCDATA
09 } else if (/style|xmp|iframe|noembed|noframes|noscript/.test
(element.tag)) {
10 // //if the tag parsed by parseTag is:
11 // <style>、<xmp>、<iframe>、<noembed>、<noframes>、<noscript>
12 // then switch to RAWTEXT mode
13 context.mode = TextModes.RAWTEXT
14 } else {
15 // otherwise switch to DATA mode
16 context.mode = TextModes.DATA
17 }
18
19 ancestors.push(element)
20 element.children = parseChildren(context, ancestors)
21 ancestors.pop()
22
23 if (context.source.startsWith(`</${element.tag}`)) {
24 parseTag(context, 'end')
25 } else {
26 console.error(`${element.tag} tag missing closing tag')
27 }
28
29 return element
30
```

At this point, we have implemented the parsing of the tag node. But the current implementation ignores the attributes and instructions in the node, which will be explained in the next section.

16.5   Parsing Attributes

The parseTag parsing function described in the previous section consumes the entire start tag, which means that the function needs to be able to handle the existence of attributes and instructions in the start tag, for example:

```
01 < div id = "foo" v-show = "display"/>
```

The div tag in the above template has an id attribute and a v-show instruction. To handle attributes and directives, we need to add parseAttributes to the parseTag function, as shown in the following code:

```
01 function parseTag(context, type = 'start') {
02 const { advanceBy, advanceSpaces } = context
03
04 const match = type === 'start'
05 ? /^<([a-z][^\t\r\n\f />]*)/i.exec(context.source)
06 : /^<\/([a-z][^\t\r\n\f />]*)/i.exec(context.source)
07 const tag = match[1]
08
09 advanceBy(match[0].length)
10 advanceSpaces()
11 // call the parseAttributes function to complete the parsing of
attributes and instructions, and get the props array,
12 // The props array is an array composed of instruction nodes and
property nodes
13 const props = parseAttributes(context)
14
15 const isSelfClosing = context.source.startsWith('/>')
16 advanceBy(isSelfClosing ? 2 : 1)
17
18 return {
19 type: 'Element',
20 tag,
21 props, // add the array of props to the tag node
22 children: [],
23 isSelfClosing
24 }
25 }
```

One of the key points of the above code is that we need to consume the " beginning part" of the tag and useless space characters before calling the parseAttribute function. For example, suppose the contents of the tag are as follows:

```
01 < div id = "foo" v-show = "display" >
```

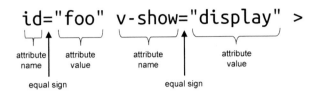

The "beginning part" of the tag refers to the string < div, so when the "beginning part" of the tag is consumed and the useless whitespace characters are used; the remaining content is as follows:

```
01 id = "foo" v-show = "display" >
```

The above paragraph is the content to be processed by the parseAttributes function. Since this function is only used to parse properties and directives, it will continue to consume the content of the above template until it encounters the "end part" of the tag. The closing part refers to the character > or the string />. From this we can give the overall framework of the parseAttributes function, as shown in the following code:

```
01 function parseAttributes (context) {
02 // Used to store the attribute nodes and instruction nodes
generated during the parsing process
03 const props = []
04
05 // Start the while loop and consume the template content
continuously until it encounters the "end part" of the tag
06 while (
07 !context.source.startsWith('>') &&
08 !context.source.startsWith('/>')
09 ) {
10 // parse attribute or instruction
11 }
12 // Return the parsing result
13 return props
14 }
```

In fact, the parseAttributes function consumes the template content, which is the process of constantly parsing attribute names, equals, and attribute values, as shown in Fig. 16.14.

The parseAttributes function continuously consumes strings from left to right. Take Fig. 16.14 as an example, the parsing process of this function is as follows.

- First, parse the name id of the first attribute and consume the string "id." At this time, the remaining template content is as follows:

```
01 = "foo" v-show = "display" >
```

When parsing the attribute name, in addition to consuming the attribute name, it also consumes the space characters that may exist after the attribute name

```
01 id = "foo" v-show = "display" >
```

But in any case, after the attribute name is resolved, the remaining content of the template must start with the equal sign, that is,

```
01 = "foo" v-show = "display" >
```

If after consuming the attribute name, the template content does not start with the equal sign, then the template content is illegal, we can selectively throw an error
• Second, we need to consume the equal sign character. Since there may also be space characters between the equal sign and the attribute value, we also need to consume the corresponding space character. After this step, the rest of the template is as follows:

```
01 "foo" v-show = "display" >
```

• Next, it's time to process the attribute value. There are three cases of attribute values in the template
• The attribute value is wrapped in double quotes: id = "foo"
• The attribute value is wrapped in single quotes: id = "foo"
• The attribute value is not enclosed in quotation marks: id = foo

According to the above example, the content of the template must start with quotation marks ("). So, we can determine whether the attribute value is referenced by checking whether the current template content starts with quotation marks. If the attribute value is referenced by quotation marks, the quotation marks are consumed.

```
01 foo "v-show =" display ">
```

Since the attribute value is quoted in quotation marks, it means that in the remaining template content, the content before the next quotation mark should be resolved as the attribute value. In this example, the content of the attribute value is string foo. So, we consume the attribute value and the quotation marks after it. Of course, if the attribute value is not quoted in quotation marks, then in the remaining template content, all characters before the next whitespace character should be used as the attribute value.

After the attribute value and quotation marks are consumed, since there may be space characters between the attribute value and the next attribute name, we also need to consume the corresponding space characters. After this step is processed, the remaining template content is as follows:

```
01 v-show = "display" >
```

As you can see, after the above operation, the first attribute is processed.

- At this time, there is still one instruction left in the template, we just need to re-execute the above steps to complete the parsing of the v-show instruction. When the v-show instruction is parsed, it will encounter the "end part" of the tag, that is, the character >

At this point, the while loop in the parseAttributes function will stop to complete the parsing of attributes and instructions.

The following parseAttributes function gives a concrete implementation of the above logic:

```
01 function parseAttributes(context) {
02 const { advanceBy, advanceSpaces } = context
03 const props = []
04
05 while (
06 !context.source.startsWith('>') &&
07 !context.source.startsWith('/>')
08 ) {
09 // The regular is used to match attribute names
10 const match = /^[^\t\r\n\f />][^\t\r\n\f />=]*/.exec
(context.source)
11 // Get the property name
12 const name = match[0]
13
14 // The name of the consuming attribute
15 advanceBy(name.length)
16 // A space character between the consumption attribute name and
the equal sign
17 advanceSpaces()
18 // consuming equal signs
19 advanceBy(1)
20 // The space character between the consumption equal sign and
the attribute value
21 advanceSpaces()
22
23 // attribute values
24 let value = ''
25
26 // Get the first character of the current template content
27 const quote = context.source[0]
28 // Determine whether the attribute value is quoted in quotation
marks
29 const isQuoted = quote === '"' || quote === "'"
30
31 if (isQuoted) {
32 // Property values are quoted in quotation marks, consuming
quotation marks
33 advanceBy(1)
```

```
34 // Get the index of the next quote
35 const endQuoteIndex = context.source.indexOf(quote)
36 if (endQuoteIndex > -1) {
37 // Get the content before the next quote as the property value
38 value = context.source.slice(0, endQuoteIndex)
39 // Consumption attribute value
40 advanceBy(value.length)
41 // Consumption quotation marks
42 advanceBy(1)
43 } else {
44 // Missing quotes error
45 console.error(' Missing quotes ')
46 }
47 } else {
48 // The code runs so far that the property value is not
referenced in quotation marks
49 // Everything before the next space character is the attribute
value
50 const match = /^[^\t\r\n\f >]+/.exec(context.source)
51 // Gets the property value
52 value = match[0]
53 // Consumption attribute value
54 advanceBy(value.length)
55 }
56 // The space character after the consumption attribute value
57 advanceSpaces()
58
59 // Create a property node with the property name + property
value to add to the props array
60 props.push({
61 type: 'Attribute',
62 name,
63 value
64 })
65
66 }
67 // return
68 return props
69
```

In the above code, there are two important regular expressions:

- /^[^\t\r\n\f />][^\t\r\n\f />=]*/, used to match the property name
- /^[^\t\r\n\f >]+/, used to match the property value that is not quoted in quotation marks

Let's take a look at how these two regular expressions work separately. Figure 16.15 shows the matching principle of the regular expression used to match the property name.

As shown in Fig. 16.15, we can divide the regular expression into two parts, A and B.

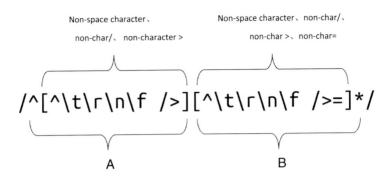

Fig. 16.15 Regular expression used to match the attributes

Fig. 16.16 Matching
principle for the second
regular expression

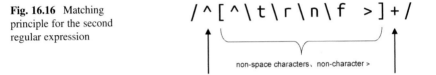

- Part A is used to match a position. This position cannot be a space character, nor the character/or the character >, and the string must start with this position
- Part B is used to match 0 or more positions, which cannot be space characters or characters /、 > 、 =. Note that the equals (=) character is not allowed in these positions, which only matches the content before the equals sign, that is, the attribute name

Figure 16.16 shows the matching principle of the second regular expression.

This expression matches from the beginning of the string and matches one or more non-whitespace characters、 the non-character >. In other words, the regular expression matches the string until it encounters space or the character >, which enables the extraction of attribute values.

With the parseAttributes function, assuming the following template is given:
01 < div id = "foo" v-show = "display" > </div >
Parsing the above template, you will get the following AST:

```
01 const ast = {
02 type: 'Root',
03 children: [
04 {
05 type: 'Element'
06 tag: 'div',
07 props: [
08 // attribute
09 { type: 'Attribute', name: 'id', value: 'foo' },
10 { type: 'Attribute', name: 'v-show', value: 'display' }
11 ]
```

```
12 }
13 ]
14 }
```

As you can see, in the props attribute of the div tag node, there are two nodes of type Attribute, which are the parsing results of the parseAttributes function.

We can add more common properties and directives in the Vue.js to test, as shown in the following template:

```
01 <div :id="dynamicId" @click="handler" v-on:
mousedown="onMouseDown" ></div>
```

After parsing the above template, we get the following AST:

```
01 const ast = {
02 type: 'Root',
03 children: [
04 {
05 type: 'Element'
06 tag: 'div',
07 props: [
08 // attribute
09 { type: 'Attribute', name: ':id', value: 'dynamicId' },
10 { type: 'Attribute', name: '@click', value: 'handler' },
11 { type: 'Attribute', name: 'v-on:mousedown', value:
'onMouseDown' }
12 ]
13 }
14 ]
15 }
```

You can see that in an attribute node of type Attribute, its name field retains the attribute name written in the template intact. We can analyze the attribute name further to get more specific information. For example, if the attribute name starts with the character @, it is considered a v-on instruction binding. We can even treat properties starting with v- as instruction bindings, and thus assign different node types to them, for example:

```
01 // instruction, type Directive
02 { type: 'Directive', name: 'v-on:mousedown', value:
'onMouseDown' }
03 { type: 'Directive', name: '@click', value: 'handler' }
04 // Common Attribute
05 { type: 'Attribute', name: 'id', value: 'foo' }
```

Not only that, in order to get more specific information, we can even further analyze the data of instruction nodes, and we can also design more syntax rules, which all depend on the design of the framework designer at the syntax level and the capabilities given to the framework.

16.6 Parsing Text and Decoding HTML Entities

16.6.1 Parsing Text

In this section, we will discuss the parsing of text nodes. The following template is given:

```
01 const template = '<div>Text</div>'
```

When parsing the above template, the parser will first go through the parseTag function, which will consume the beginning part of the tag "< div >." After processing, the remaining template content is as follows:

```
01 const template = 'Text </div >'
```

Next, the parser will call the parseChildren function to start a new finite-state machine to process this template. Let's review the state transition process of the finite-state machine.

Finite-state machine starts at "state 1." In "state 1," the first character T of the template is read. Since this character is neither the character < nor the interpolation delimiter {{, the state will enter "state 7," that is, the parseText function is called to process the text content. At this time, the parser will look for the position index of the next < character or the interpolation delimiter {{ in the template, denoted as index I. Then, the parser will intercept the content from the head of the template to the position of index I. This intercepted string will be the content of the text node. Take the following example of template content:

```
01 const template = 'Text </div >'
```

The parseText function will try to find the positional index of the first occurrence of the character < in this template content. In this example, the index value of the character < is 4. Then, the parseText function will intercept the content between index [0,4) as the text content. In this example, the text content is the string "Text."

Suppose there is interpolation in the template, as shown in the following template:

```
01const template = 'Text- {{val}} </div >'
```

When processing this template, the parseText function finds the index where the first interpolation delimiter {{appears. In this example, the delimiter's index is

5. Thus, the parseText function intercepts the content between index [0,5) as the text content. In this example, the text content is the string "Text- ."

The following parseText function gives the specific implementation:

```
01 function parseText (context) {
02 // endIndex is the end index of the text content, and the rest of the
template is used as the text content by default
03 let endIndex = context.source.length
04 // find the positional index of the character <
05 const ltIndex = context.source.indexOf ('<')
06 // find the positional index of the delimiter {{
07 const delimiterIndex = context.source.indexOf ('{{')
08
09 // take the smaller of ltIndex and current endIndex as the new
ending index
10 if (ltIndex > -1 && ltIndex < endIndex) {
11 endIndex = ltIndex
12 }
13 // take the smaller of delimiterIndex and current endIndex as the
new ending index
14 if (delimiterIndex > -1 && delimiterIndex < endIndex) {
15 endIndex = delimiterIndex
16 }
17
18 // At this time endIndex is the end index of the final text content,
call the slice function to intercept the text content
19 const content = context.source.slice (0, endIndex)
20 // consume the text content
21 context.advanceBy (content.length)
22
23 // return text node
24 return {
25 // node type
26 type: 'Text',
27 // text content
28 content
29 }
30 }
```

As shown in the above code, since the order of occurrence of the characters < and delimiter {{ is unknown, we need to take the smaller one of the two as the end point for text interception. With the interception end point, you only need to call the slice function of string to intercept the string, and the intercepted content is the text content of the text node. Finally, we create a text node of type Text as the return value of the parseText function.

Parse the following template with the above parseText function:

```
01 const ast = parse ('< div > Text </div >')
```

to get the following AST:

```
01 const ast = {
02 type: 'Root',
03 children: [
04 {
05 type: 'Element',
06 tag: 'div',
07 props: [],
08 isSelfClosing: false,
09 children: [
10 // text node
11 { type: 'Text', content: 'Text' }
12 ]
13 }
14 ]
15 }
```

In this way, we realize the parsing of text nodes. Parsing text nodes itself is not complicated, the complexity is that we need to decode HTML entities after parsing text content. To do this, it is necessary for us to understand what an HTML entity is.

16.6.2   Decode Named Character References

An HTML entity is a piece of text that begins with the character &. Entities are used to describe reserved characters in HTML, some characters that are difficult to enter with a normal keyboard, and some invisible characters. For example, in HTML, the character < has a special meaning, and if you want to display the character < as normal text, you need to express it as an entity:

```
01 <div>A&lt;B</div>
```

where string < is an HTML entity and is used to represent the character <. If we do not use HTML entities, but directly, the character <, then illegal HTML content will be generated:

```
01 <div>A<B</div>
```

This causes browsers to parse results that are not as expected.

HTML entities always start with the character & and end with the character;. In the early days of the Web, the number of HTML entities was small, so the trailing semicolon was allowed to be omitted. However, as the HTML character set became larger and larger, HTML entities appeared to be included. For example, &lt and < &ltcc are both legal entities, and browsers would not be able to distinguish them without a semicolon. Therefore, the WHATWG specification clearly states that if no semicolon is added to the entity, a parsing error will occur. However, for historical reasons (there are a lot of cases of semicolon omission on the Internet), modern browsers are able to parse HTML entities defined in the earlier specification that can omit the semicolon.

There are two types of HTML entities, one is called named character reference, also called named entity, as the name suggests, this type of entity has a specific name, such as < above. The WHATWG specification gives all named character references—there are more than 2000, which can be queried through the named character reference table.

```
01 // 共 2000+
02 {
03 "GT": ">",
04 "gt": ">",
05 "LT": "<",
06 "lt": "<",
07 // Omit some code
08 "awint;": "",
09 "bcong;": "≌",
10 "bdquo;": "„",
11 "bepsi;": "□",
12 "blank;": " ",
13 "blk12;": "▒",
14 "blk14;": "░",
15 "blk34;": "▓",
16 "block;": "█",
17 "boxDL;": "╗",
18 "boxDl;": "╖",
19 "boxdL;": "╕",
20 // Omit some code
21 }
```

In addition to named character references, there is also a class of character references that do not have a specific name and can only be represented by numbers. Such entities are called numeric character references. Unlike named character references, numeric character references start with string & #, which has one more character # than the beginning of named character references, such as <. In fact, < corresponds to <; in other words, < is equivalent to <. Numeric character references can be represented in either decimal or hexadecimal. For example, the hexadecimal value for the decimal number 60 is 3c, so the entity < can also be represented as <. As you can see, when using a hexadecimal number to represent an entity, it needs to start with a string & #x.

After understanding HTML entities, let's discuss why Vue.js template parser decodes HTML entities in text nodes. In order to understand this problem, we need to understand a major premise: in Vue.js template, text nodes contain HTML entities that are not parsed by the browser. This is because the text nodes in the template will eventually be set to the page, and the text content set by the el.textContent will not be decoded by the HTML entity, for example:

```
01 el.textContent = '&lt;'
```

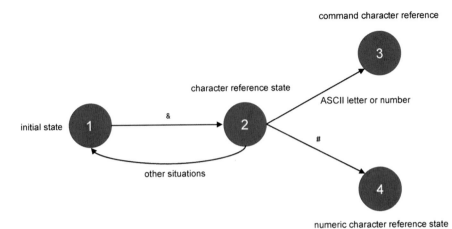

Fig. 16.17   The finite-state machine that parses character references

The final el will be rendered as a string '<' intact, without rendering the character <. This means that if the user writes an HTML entity in the Vue.js template, and the template parser does not decode it, the content of the page will not be rendered as expected by the user. Therefore, we should decode the HTML entity present in the text node during the parsing stage.

The decoding behavior of the template parser should be consistent with the behavior of the browser. Therefore, we should implement the decoding logic according to the WHATWG specification. The specification clearly defines the state transition process of the finite-state machine when decoding HTML entities. Figure 16.17 shows a simplified version of the state transition process, which we will add later.

Assuming that the finite-state machine is currently in initial DATA mode. As you can see from Fig. 16.17, when the parser encounters the character &, it enters the "character reference state," consumes the character &, and then parses the next character. If the next character is an ASCII letter or number (ASCII alphanumeric), it enters the "named character reference state," where the ASCII letter or number refers to the ten from 0 to 9, the number and the character set a–z plus the character set A–Z. Of course, if the next character is #, it enters the "numeric character reference state."

Once the finite-state machine enters the named character reference state, the parser will perform a more complicated matching process. Let's experience this process visually through a few examples. Suppose the text is as follows:

```
01 a&ltb
```

The above text will be parsed as:

```
01 a<b
```

Why do you get such parsing results? Next, we analyze the entire parsing process.

- First, when the parser encounters the character &, it will enter the character reference state. Next, the next character l is parsed, which causes the parser to enter the named character reference state and look for items starting with the character l in the named character reference table (hereinafter referred to as "reference table"). Since there are many items starting with the character l in the reference table, such as lt, lg, le, etc., the parser considers this to be a "match"
- So, it starts parsing the next character t and tries to look for items starting with lt in the reference table. Since there are also multiple items starting with lt in the reference table, such as lt, ltcc;, ltri;, etc., the parser considers it to be a "match" at this time
- So, it starts parsing the next character b, and tries to find the item starting with ltb in the reference table. The result is that there is no eligible item in the reference table, and the match ends at this point

When the match ends, the parser checks the last matching character. If the character is a semicolon (;), a legal match is generated, and the corresponding character is rendered. But in the above example, the last matching character is the character t, not a semicolon (;). Therefore, a parsing error will be generated, but due to historical reasons, the browser is still able to parse it. In this case, the browser's parsing rule is the shortest principle, where "shortest" refers to the shortest name of the named character reference. As an example, suppose the text content is as follows:

```
01 a&ltcc;
```

We know that ⪦ is a legal named character reference, so the above text will be rendered as: a⊲. However, if the semicolon in the above text is removed, that is,

```
01 a&ltcc
```

When the parser processes entities in this text, the last matching character will not be the semicolon, but the character c. According to the "shortest principle," the parser will only render character references with shorter names. In string &ltcc, the name of &lt is shorter than &ltcc, so it will eventually render &lt as a legal character reference, while string cc will render as a normal character. So, the above text will eventually be rendered as:a<cc.

It should be noted that the above parsing process is limited to ordinary text that is not used as attribute values. In other words, the text used as attribute values will have different parsing rules. For example, given the following HTML text:

```
01 <a href="foo.com?a=1&lt=2">foo.com?a=1&lt=2</a>
```

You can see that the href attribute value of the a tag has the same content as its text sub-node, but the results after they are parsed are different, where the &lt in the attribute value will be displayed intact, and the &lt in the text sub-node will be parsed as the character <. This is also expected. It is clear that &lt = 2 will constitute the query parameter in the link, and if the &lt in it is decoded as the character <, it will break the user's URL. In fact, this is also fully defined in the WHATWG specification. For historical reasons, for character references in attribute values, if the last matching character is not a semicolon, and the next character of the matching character is an equal sign, ASCII letter or number, then the match will be parsed as plain text.

Knowing the principle, we set out to implement it. The first question we are facing is how to deal with the omission of semicolons. Regarding semicolons in character references, we can summarize as follows.

- When a semicolon is present: perform a full match
- When a semicolon is omitted: perform a shortest match

To do this, we need to carefully design a named character reference table. Since the number of named character references is very large, here we only take a part of them as the contents of the named character reference table, as shown in the following code:

```
01 const namedCharacterReferences = {
02 "gt": ">",
03 "gt;": ">",
04 "lt": "<",
05 "lt;": "<",
06 "ltcc;": "⪦"
07 }
```

The above table is carefully designed. Observing the namedCharacterReferences object, you can find that there are multiple entities corresponding to the same character, that is, the version with semicolon and the version without semicolon, such as "gt" and "gt;". Other entities have only the version with semicolon because these entities are not allowed to omit the semicolon, such as "ltcc;". We can implement the decoding logic of the entity according to this table. Suppose we have the following text content:

```
01 a&ltccbbb
```

When decoding this text, we first divide the text into two parts based on the character &.

- One part is the normal text: a
- The other part is: &ltccbbb

For the normal text part, since it does not need to be decoded, the index is left intact. And for the part that may be a character reference, the decoding work is performed.

- Step 1: Calculate the maximum length of the entity name in the named character reference table. Since the longest named entity in the namedCharacterReferences object is ltcc;, which has 5 characters, the maximum length is 5
- Step 2: Truncate the string ltccbbb according to the maximum length, that is, "ltccbbb" .slice (0,5), the final result is: "ltccb"
- Step 3: Use the truncated string "ltccb" as the key to name the character reference table corresponding to the value of the query, that is, decoding. Since there is no key value of "ltccb" in the reference table namedCharacterReferences, it does not match
- Step 4: When a mismatch is found, we subtract the maximum length by 1 and re-execute the second step until a match is found. In the above example, the final match will be "lt." Therefore, the above text will eventually be decoded as:

```
01 <ccbbb
```

In this way, we achieve decoding according to the "shortest principle" when the character reference omits the semicolon.

The following decodeHtml function gives the specific implementation:

```
01 // The first parameter is the text content to be decoded
02 // The second parameter is a Boolean value that represents whether the
text content is a property value
03 function decodeHtml(rawText, asAttr = false) {
04 let offset = 0
05 const end = rawText.length
06 // The decoded text is returned as a return value
07 let decodedText = ''
08 // The maximum length of an entity name in a reference table
09 let maxCRNameLength = 0
10
11 // The advance function is used to consume text of a specified length
12 function advance(length) {
13 offset += length
14 rawText = rawText.slice(length)
15 }
16
17 // Consume the string until it has finished processing
18 while (offset < end) {
19 // Used to match the beginning of a character reference; if the match is
successful, then the value of head[0] will have three possibilities:
20 // 1. head[0] === '&', This indicates that the character reference is
a named character reference
21 // 2. head[0] === '&#', This indicates that the character reference is
a numeric character reference in decimal
```

```
22 // 3. head[0] === '&#x', This indicates that the character reference
is a numeric character reference in hexadecimal
23 const head = /&(?:#x?)?/i.exec(rawText)
24 // If there is no match, there is nothing left to decode
25 if (!head) {
26 // Calculate the length of the remaining content
27 const remaining = end - offset
28 // Add the rest to the decodedText
29 decodedText += rawText.slice(0, remaining)
30 // Consume leftovers
31 advance(remaining)
32 break
33 }
34
35 // head.index is the index of the matching character & position in
rawText
36 // The content before the intercept character & is added to the
decodedText
37 decodedText += rawText.slice(0, head.index)
38 // Content before consuming characters &
39 advance(head.index)
40
41 // If the condition is met, the description is a named character
reference, otherwise it is a numeric character reference
42 if (head[0] === '&') {
43 let name = ''
44 let value
45 // The next character of the & character must be an ASCII letter or
number in order to be a legal named character reference
46 if (/[0-9a-z]/i.test(rawText[1])) {
47 // Calculate the maximum length of an entity name based on the
reference table,
48 if (!maxCRNameLength) {
49 maxCRNameLength = Object.keys(namedCharacterReferences).reduce(
50 (max, name) => Math.max(max, name.length),
51 0
52 )
53 }
54 // Intercept the text from the maximum length and try to find the
corresponding item in the reference table
55 for (let length = maxCRNameLength; !value && length > 0; --length) {
56 // Truncate characters between the character & and the maximum length
as the entity name
57 name = rawText.substr(1, length)
58 // Use the entity name to find the value of the corresponding item in the
index table
59 value = (namedCharacterReferences)[name]
60 }
61 // If the value of the corresponding item is found, the decoding is
successful
62 if (value) {
63 // Check that the last matching character of the entity name is a
semicolon
```

```
64 const semi = name.endsWith(';')
65 // If the decoded text is used as an attribute value, the last matching
character is not a semicolon,
66 // and the next character of the last matching character is an equal
sign (=), an ASCII letter, or a number,
67 // For historical reasons, the character & and the entity name name are
used as normal text
68 if (
69 asAttr &&
70 !semi &&
71 /[=a-z0-9]/i.test(rawText[name.length + 1] || '')
72 ) {
73 decodedText += '&' + name
74 advance(1 + name.length)
75 } else {
76 // In other cases, the decoded content is stitched onto decodedText
normally
77 decodedText += value
78 advance(1 + name.length)
79 }
80 } else {
81 // If no corresponding value is found, decoding failed
82 decodedText += '&' + name
83 advance(1 + name.length)
84 }
85 } else {
86 // If the next character of the character & is not an ASCII letter or
number, the character & is treated as normal text
87 decodedText += '&'
88 advance(1)
89 }
90 }
91 }
92 return decodedText
93 }
```

With the decodeHtml function, we can parse the text after Decode text content through it at node:

```
01 function parseText(context) {
02 // omit some code
03
04 return {
05 type: 'Text',
06 content: decodeHtml(content) // call decodeHtml function to decode
content
07 }
08 }
```

16.6.3   Decode Numeric Character References

In the previous section, we used the following regular expression to match the beginning of a character reference in a text:

```
01 const head = /&(?:#x?)?/i.exec(rawText)
```

We can determine the type of character reference based on the matching result of the regular.

- If head[0] === '&', it means that the matching is a named character reference
- If head [0] === '&#', it means that the matching is a numeric character reference in decimal
- If head [0] === '&#x ', it means that the matching is a numeric character reference in hexadecimal

The format of numeric character reference is prefix + Unicode code point. The key to decoding numeric character references is how to extract the Unicode code points in character references. Considering that the prefix of numeric character reference can be expressed in decimal (&#) or hexadecimal (&#x), we use the following code to complete the extraction of code points:

```
01 // Determine whether it is expressed in decimal or hexadecimal
02 const hex = head[0] === '&#x'
03 // Choose different regulars according to different base notation
04 const pattern = hex ? /^&#x([0-9a-f]+);?/i : /^&#([0-9]+);?/
05 // Finally, the value of body [1] is the Unicode code point
06 const body = pattern.exec(rawText)
```

With a Unicode code point, just call the String.fromCodePoint function to decode it to the corresponding character:

```
01 if (body) {
02 // Convert the code point string to a number according to the
corresponding base system
03 const cp = parseInt(body[1], hex ? 16 : 10)
04 // Decode
05 const char = String.fromCodePoint(cp)
06 }
```

However, before actually decoding, the value of the code point needs to be checked for legitimacy. This is also clearly defined in the WHATWG specification.

- If the code point value is 0x00, the decimal number 0, which represents the null character (NULL) in Unicode; this will be a parsing error and the parser will replace the code point value with 0xFFFD

- If the code point value is greater than 0x10FFFF (0x10FFFF is the maximum value in Unicode), this is also a parsing error and the parser will replace the code point value with 0xFFFD
- If the code point value is in the range of the surrogate pair, which is also a parsing error, the parser will replace the code point value with 0xFFFD, where the surrogate pair is the code point reserved for UTF-16, the range is [0xD800, 0xDFFF]
- If the code point value is noncharacter, this is also a parsing error, but nothing needs to be done. The noncharacter here represents the code point permanently reserved in Unicode and is used inside Unicode. Its value range is [0xFDD0, 0xFDEF] and also includes: 0xFFFE, 0x FFFF, 0x1FFFE, 0x1FFFF, 0x2FFFE, 0x2FFFF, 0x3FFFE, 0x3FFFF, 0x4FFFE、0x4FFFF、0x5FFFE、0x5FFFF、0x6FFFE、0x6FFFF、0x7FFFE、0x7FFFF、0x8FFFE、0x8FFFF、0x9FFFE、0x9FFFF、0xAFFFE、0xAFFFF、0xBFFFE、0xBFFFF、0xCFFFE、0xCFFFF、0xDFFFE、0xDFFFF、0xEFFFE、0xEFFFF、0xFFFFE、0xFFFFF、0x10FFFE、0x10FFFF
- A parsing error occurs if the code point value corresponds to a carriage return character (0x0D), or if the code point value is a non-ASCII space in the control character set. At this time, you need to use the code point as an index to find the corresponding replacement code point in the following table:

```
01 const CCR_REPLACEMENTS = {
02 0x80: 0x20ac,
03 0x82: 0x201a,
04 0x83: 0x0192,
05 0x84: 0x201e,
06 0x85: 0x2026,
07 0x86: 0x2020,
08 0x87: 0x2021,
09 0x88: 0x02c6,
10 0x89: 0x2030,
11 0x8a: 0x0160,
12 0x8b: 0x2039,
13 0x8c: 0x0152,
14 0x8e: 0x017d,
15 0x91: 0x2018,
16 0x92: 0x2019,
17 0x93: 0x201c,
18 0x94: 0x201d,
19 0x95: 0x2022,
20 0x96: 0x2013,
21 0x97: 0x2014,
22 0x98: 0x02dc,
23 0x99: 0x2122,
24 0x9a: 0x0161,
25 0x9b: 0x203a,
26 0x9c: 0x0153,
27 0x9e: 0x017e,
28 x9f: 0x0178
29 }
```

If there is a corresponding replacement code point, the character corresponding to the replacement code point is rendered, otherwise the character corresponding to the original code point is directly rendered Character.

The above implementation of the code point legitimacy check is as follows:

```
01 if (body) {
02 // Convert the code point string to a number according to the
corresponding base system
03 const cp = parseInt (body[1] , hex ? 16 : 10)
04 // Check the legitimacy of the code point
05 if (cp === 0) {
06 // If the code point value is 0x00, replace it with 0xfffd
07 cp = 0xfffd
08 } else if (cp > 0x10ffff) {
09 // If the code point value exceeds the maximum value for Unicode,
replace it with 0xfffd
10 cp = 0xfffd
11 } else if (cp >= 0xd800 && cp <= 0xdfff) {
12 // If the code point value is in the surrogate pair range, replace it
with 0xfffd
13 cp = 0xfffd
14 } else if ((cp >= 0xfdd0 && cp <= 0xfdef) || (cp & 0xfffe) ===
0xfffe) {
15 // If the code point value is in the noncharacter range, do nothing
and leave it to the platform
16 // noop
17 } else if (
18 // The range of the control character set is: [0x01, 0x1f] plus
[0x7f, 0x9f]
19 // remove ASICC space characters: 0x09 (TAB) 、 0x0A (LF) 、 0x0C (FF)
20 // 0x0D (CR) is also an ASICC blank character, but it needs to be
included
21 (cp >= 0x01 && cp <= 0x08) ||
22 cp === 0x0b ||
23 (cp >= 0x0d && cp <= 0x1f) ||
24 (cp >= 0x7f && cp <= 0x9f)
25 ) {
26 // Look for replacement code points in the CCR_REPLACEMENTS table,
and if they cannot find them, use the source code points
27 cp = CCR_REPLACEMENTS [cp] || cp
28 }
29 // Finally, decode it
30 const char = String.fromCodePoint (cp)
31 }
```

In the above code, we completely restore the code point legitimacy check logic, which has the following key points.

• The code point range of control character set is [0x01, 0x1f] and [0x7f, 0x9f]. This, the code point range contains ASCII white characters: 0x09 (TAB), 0x0A

(LF), 0x0C (FF), and 0x0D (CR), but the WHATWG specification requires 0x0D (CR)

- The code point 0xfffd corresponds to the symbol. You must have seen this character in the case of "messy code," which is a substitution character in Unicode, usually indicating that there was an "error" in the decoding process, such as using the wrong decoding method

Finally, we integrate the above code into the decodeHtml function, so as to achieve a perfect HTML text decoding function:

```
01 function decodeHtml(rawText, asAttr = false) {
02 // omit some code
03
04 // Consume the string until it has finished processing
05 while (offset < end) {
06 // omit some code
07
08 // If the condition is met, the description is a named character
reference, otherwise it is a numeric character reference
09 if (head[0] === '&') {
10 // omit some code
11 } else {
12 // Determine whether it is a decimal representation or a
hexadecimal representation
13 const hex = head[0] === '&#x'
14 // Depending on the base-based notation, different regulars are
chosen
15 const pattern = hex ? /^&#x([0-9a-f]+);?/i : /^&#([0-9]+);?/
16 // Ultimately, the value of body[1] is the Unicode code point
17 const body = pattern.exec(rawText)
18
19 // If the match is successful, the String.fromCodePoint function
is called to decode
20 if (body) {
21 // Convert the code point string to a number according to the
corresponding base system
22 const cp = Number.parseInt(body[1], hex ? 16 : 10)
23 // Legality check of code points
24 if (cp === 0) {
25 // If the code point value is 0x00, replace it with 0xfffd
26 cp = 0xfffd
27 } else if (cp > 0x10ffff) {
28 // If the code point value exceeds the maximum value for Unicode,
replace it with 0xfffd
29 cp = 0xfffd
30 } else if (cp >= 0xd800 && cp <= 0xdfff) {
31 // If the code point value is in the surrogate pair range, replace it
with 0xfffd
32 cp = 0xfffd
33 } else if ((cp >= 0xfdd0 && cp <= 0xfdef) || (cp & 0xfffe) ===
0xfffe) {
34 // If the code point value is in the noncharacter range, do nothing
```

```
and leave it to the platform
35 // noop
36 } else if (
37 // The range of the control character set is: [0x01, 0x1f] plus
[0x7f, 0x9f]
38 // Remove ASICC blanks: 0x09 (TAB), 0x0A (LF), 0x0C (FF)
39 // 0x0D(CR) is also an ASICC blank character, but it needs to be
included
40 (cp >= 0x01 && cp <= 0x08) ||
41 cp === 0x0b ||
42 (cp >= 0x0d && cp <= 0x1f) ||
43 (cp >= 0x7f && cp <= 0x9f)
44 ) {
45 // Look for replacement code points in the CCR_REPLACEMENTS table,
and if they cannot find them, use the source code points
46 cp = CCR_REPLACEMENTS[cp] || cp
47 }
48 // Decoded and appended to decodedText
49 decodedText += String.fromCodePoint(cp)
50 // Consume the entire content referenced by numeric characters
51 advance(body[0].length)
52 } else {
53 // If there is no match, no decoding operation is performed, just
head[0] is appended to the decodedText and consumed
54 decodedText += head[0]
55 advance(head[0].length)
56 }
57 }
58 }
59 return decodedText
60 }
```

16.7   Analytic Interpolation and Annotation

Textual interpolation is a common method used to render dynamic data in Vue.js templates:

```
01 {{count}}
```

By default, interpolation starts with string {{and ends with string}}. We usually refer to these two special strings as delimiters. The middle of the delimiter can be any valid JavaScript expression, for example:

```
01 {{obj.foo}}
or 01 {{obj.fn () }}
```

The parser enters the text "interpolation state 6" when it encounters the starting delimiter ({{) for text interpolation and calls the parseInterpolation function to parse the interpolation content.

The parser parsing interpolation only needs to extract the content between the start delimiter and the end delimiter of text interpolation, as a JavaScript expression can be; the specific implementation is as follows:

```
01 function parseInterpolation(context) {
02 // Consumption start delimiter
03 context.advanceBy('{{'.length)
04 // The index of the position where the end delimiter is found
05 closeIndex = context.source.indexOf('}}')
06 if (closeIndex < 0) {
07 console.error(' Interpolation is missing an end delimiter ')
08 }
09 // Intercept the content between the opening and ending delimiters
as an interpolation expression
10 const content = context.source.slice(0, closeIndex)
11 // The content of the consumption expression
12 context.advanceBy(content.length)
13 // End of consumption delimiter
14 context.advanceBy('}}'.length)
15
16 // A node with a return type of Interpolation, representing an
interpolation node
17 return {
18 type: 'Interpolation',
19 // The content of an interpolation node is an expression node of
type Expression
20 content: {
21 type: 'Expression',
22 // The content of the expression node is an interpolated expression
that has been decoded by HTML
23 content: decodeHtml(content)
24 }
25 }
26 }
```

With the above parseInterpolation function, the following template content is parsed:

```
01 const ast = parse(`<div>foo {{ bar }} baz</div>`)
```

will end up with the following AST:

```
01 const ast = {
02 type: 'Root',
03 children: [
04 {
05 type: 'Element',
```

```
06 tag: 'div',
07 isSelfClosing: false,
08 props: [],
09 children: [
10 { type: 'Text', content: 'foo ' },
11 // Interpolate nodes
12 {
13 type: 'Interpolation',
14 content: [
15 type: 'Expression',
16 content: ' bar '
17 ]
18 },
19 { type: 'Text', content: ' baz' }
20 ]
21 }
22 ]
23 }
```

The idea of parsing comments is very similar to that of parsing interpolation, as shown in the following parseComment function:

```
01 function parseComment(context) {
02 // The beginning of the consumption note
03 context.advanceBy('<!--'.length)
04 // Find the location index of the end section of the comment
05 closeIndex = context.source.indexOf('-->')
06 // Intercept the contents of an annotation node
07 const content = context.source.slice(0, closeIndex)
08 // Consume content
09 context.advanceBy(content.length)
10 // The end of the consumption note
11 context.advanceBy('-->'.length)
12 // Return a node of type Comment
13 return {
14 type: 'Comment',
15 content
16 }
17 }
```

With the parseComment function, parse the following template content:

```
01 const ast = parse(`<div><!-- comments --></div>`)
```

end up with the following AST:

```
01 const ast = {
02 type: 'Root',
03 children: [
04 {
05 type: 'Element',
```

```
06 tag: 'div',
07 isSelfClosing: false,
08 props: [],
09 children: [
10 { type: 'Comment', content: ' comments ' }
11 ]
12 }
13 ]
14 }
```

16.8 Summary

In this chapter, we first discussed the parser's text mode and its impact on the parser. Text mode refers to some special states that the parser enters during operation, such as RCDATA mode, CDATA mode, RAWTEXT mode, and the initial DATA mode. In different modes, the parser's parsing behavior of text will be different.

Next, we discussed how to use the recursive descent algorithm to construct the template AST. During the operation of the parseChildren function, in order to process the tag nodes, the parseElement parser function is called, which indirectly calls the parseChildren function, and generates a new finite-state machine. As the level of tag nesting increases, new finite-state machines are also created as the parseChildren function is called recursively, which is the meaning of the word "recursion" in "recursive descent." The upper-level parseChildren function is called to construct the AST node of the upper-level template, and the lower-level parseChildren function that is called recursively is used to construct the lower-level template AST node. Finally, a tree-structured template AST will be constructed, which is the meaning of the word "descent" in "recursive descent."

In the process of analyzing the template to build the AST, the parseChildren function is the core. Every time the parseChildren function is called, it means that a new finite-state machine is turned on. The finite-state machine has two end times.

- The first end time is when the template content is parsed.
- The second end time is when the end tag is encountered. At this time, the parser will take the node at the top of the parent node stack as the parent node. Check whether the end tag has the same name as the parent node's tag. If it is the same, the finite-state machine stops running.

We also discussed the parsing of text nodes. Parsing text nodes is not complicated by itself. The complexity is that we need to decode the HTML entity of the parsed text content. The WHATWG specification also defines the state transition process in the process of decoding HTML entities. There are two types of HTML entities, named character references and numeric character references. The decoding scheme of named characters and references can be summarized into two types.

- When a semicolon is present: perform a full match
- When a semicolon is omitted: perform a shortest match

For numeric character references, it needs to be implemented step by step according to the rules defined in the WHATWG specification.

Chapter 17
Compilation Optimization

Compilation optimization refers to the process of extracting as much key information as possible in the process of compiling templates into rendering functions by the compiler, and using this to guide the process of generating the optimal code. The strategy and specific implementation of compilation optimization are determined by the design ideas of the framework. Different frameworks have different design ideas, so the compilation optimization strategy is not the same. However, the direction of optimization is basically the same, that is, distinguish dynamic content from static content as much as possible, and adopt different optimization strategies for different content.

17.1 Dynamic Node Collection and Patch Flags

17.1.1 Problems of Traditional Diff Algorithms

In Part III, we introduced three kinds of Diff algorithms about traditional virtual DOM when we explained the renderer. But no matter what, when a Diff algorithm is comparing the old and new virtual DOM trees, it always traverses the virtual DOM hierarchy "layer by layer." For example, suppose we have the following template:

```
01 < div id = "foo" >
02 < p class = "bar" > {{text}} </p >
03 </div >
```

In the above template, the only possible change is the content of the text sub-node of the p tag. That is, when the value of the data text changes in response, the most efficient way to update is to directly set the text content of the p tag. However, the traditional Diff algorithm can obviously not be so efficient. When the responsive data text changes, a new virtual DOM tree will be generated. The process of

---

H. Yang, *Vue. JS Framework*, https://doi.org/10.1007/978-981-99-4947-2_17

comparing the old and new virtual DOM trees with the traditional Diff algorithm is as follows.

- Compare the div node, and the attributes and child nodes of this node.
- Compare the p node, and the attributes and child nodes of this node.
- Compare the text sub-node of the p node. If the content of the text sub-node has changed, update it; otherwise do nothing.

It can be seen that compared with directly updating the text content of the p tag, the traditional Diff algorithm has many meaningless comparison operations. If you can skip these meaningless operations, the performance will be greatly improved. And this is the source of the idea of Vue.js 3 compilation optimization.

In fact, the structure of the template is very stable. Through compilation methods, we can analyze a lot of key information, such as which nodes are static and which nodes are dynamic. Combined with this key information, the compiler can directly generate the code for native DOM operations, which can even throw away the virtual DOM, thus avoiding the performance overhead caused by the virtual DOM. However, considering the flexibility of the rendering function and the compatibility issues of Vue.js 2, Vue.js 3 finally chose to keep the virtual DOM. As a result, it is bound to face the additional performance overhead it brings.

So, why does the virtual DOM incur additional performance overhead? The root cause is that the renderer does not get enough information at runtime. The traditional Diff algorithm cannot use any key information extracted at compile time, which makes it impossible for the renderer to do relevant optimizations at runtime. The Vue.js 3 compiler will "attach" the key information obtained at compile time to the virtual DOM it generates, and this information will be passed to the renderer through the virtual DOM. Eventually, the renderer will execute a "shortcut path" based on these key information, thereby improving the runtime performance.

17.1.2   Block and PatchFlags

Why we say that the traditional Diff algorithm cannot avoid useless comparison operations between old and new virtual DOM trees is because it does not have enough critical information at runtime to distinguish between dynamic content and static content. In other words, as long as the runtime can distinguish between dynamic, content and static content, it can achieve the ultimate optimization strategy. Suppose we have the following template:

```
01 < div >
02 < div > foo </div >
03 < p > {{bar}} </p >
04 </div >
```

In the above template, only {{bar}} is dynamic content. Therefore, ideally, when the value of the reactive data bar changes, we only need to update the text node of the p tag. To achieve this, we need to provide more information to the runtime, which requires us to start with the structure of the virtual DOM. Let's take a look at how the traditional virtual DOM describes the template above:

```
01 const vnode = {
02 tag: 'div',
03 children: [
04 { tag: 'div', children: 'foo' },
05 { tag: 'p', children: ctx.bar },
06 ]
07 }
```

There are no flags in the traditional virtual DOM that can reflect the dynamics of nodes. But after compilation and optimization, the compiler will "attach" the key information it extracts to the virtual DOM node, as shown in the following code:

```
01 const vnode = {
02 tag: 'div',
03 children: [
04 { tag: 'div', children: 'foo' },
05 { tag: 'p', children: ctx.bar, patchFlag: 1 }, // this is the
dynamic node
06 ]
07 }
```

As can be seen, the virtual node used to describe the p tag has an additional attribute, patchFlag, which is a number. As long as the virtual node has this attribute, we consider it to be a dynamic node. The patchFlag attribute here is the so-called patch flag.

We can understand the patch flag as a series of numeric tokens and assign it different meanings depending on the numeric values, examples are as follows.

- Number 1: Represent the node with dynamic textContent (such as the p tag in the template above).
- Number 2: Represent the element with dynamic class binding.
- Number 3: Represent the element with dynamic style binding.
- Number 4: Other. . . .

Usually, we will define the mapping of patch flags in the runtime code, for example:

```
01 const PatchFlags = {
02 TEXT: 1, // representative node has dynamic textContent
03 CLASS: 2, // representative element has dynamic class binding
04 STYLE: 3
05 // other...
06 }
```

With this information, we can extract its dynamic sub-node at the virtual node creation stage and store it in the array in the dynamic children of the virtual node:

```
01 const vnode = {
02 tag: 'div',
03 children: [
04 { tag: 'div', children: 'foo' },
05 { tag: 'p', children: ctx.bar, patchFlag: PatchFlags.TEXT } //
This is the dynamic node
06 ],
07 // Extract the dynamic nodes in children into the dynamicChildren
array
08 dynamicChildren: [
09 // The p tag has a patchFlag attribute, so it is a dynamic node
10 { tag: 'p', children: ctx.bar, patchFlag: PatchFlags.TEXT }
11 ]
12 }
```

We will discuss how to extract dynamic nodes in the next section. Looking at the vnode object above, we can see that it has an extra dynamicChildren property compared with ordinary virtual nodes. We call virtual nodes with this property "blocks," that is, Blocks. Therefore, a Block is essentially a virtual DOM node, but it has one more dynamicChildren property than ordinary virtual nodes to store dynamic sub-nodes. It should be noted here that a Block can not only collect its direct dynamic sub-nodes, but also all dynamic child nodes. For example, suppose we have the following template:

```
01 <div>
02 <div>
03 <p>{{ bar }}</p>
04 </div>
05 </div>
```

In this template, the p tag is not the direct sub-node of the outermost div tag, but its descendant node. Therefore, the block corresponding to the outermost div tag can collect the p tag into its dynamicChildren array, as shown in the following code:

```
01 const vnode = {
02 tag: 'div',
03 children: [
04 {
05 tag: 'div',
06 children: [
07 { tag: 'p', children: ctx.bar, patchFlag: PatchFlags.TEXT } //
this is the dynamic node
08 ]
09 },
10 ],
11 dynamicChildren: [
```

```
12 // Block can collect all dynamic child nodes
13 { tag: 'p', children: ctx.bar, patchFlag: PatchFlags.TEXT }
14 ]
15 }
```

With the concept of Block, the renderer's update operation will be based on Block. That is to say, when the renderer updates a Block, it will ignore the children array of the virtual node, but directly find the dynamic Children array of the virtual node, and only update the dynamic nodes in the array. In this way, the static content is skipped and only the dynamic content is updated when updating. At the same time, due to the corresponding patch flag in the dynamic node, when updating the dynamic node, it can also achieve targeted update. For example, when a dynamic node's patchFlag value is 1, we know that it only has dynamic text nodes, so we only need to update its text content.

Since Block has so many benefits, under what circumstances do we need to turn an ordinary virtual node into a Block node? In fact, when we write template code, the root node of all templates will be a Block node, as shown in the following code:

```
01 <template>
02 <!-- this div tag is a Block -->
03 <div>
04 <!-- -- this p tag is not a Block because it is not the root node -->
05 <p>{{ bar }}</p>
06 </div>
07 <!-- The h1 tag is a Block -->
08 <h1>
09 <!-- This span tag is not a Block because it is not the root node -->
10 <span :id="dynamicId"></span>
11 </h1>
12 </template>
```

In fact, except for the root node in the template that needs to be the Block role, any node with instructions such as v-for, v-if/v-else-if/v-else need to be used as Block nodes, which we will discuss in detail in subsequent chapters.

17.1.3 Collecting Dynamic Nodes

The rendering function code generated by the compiler does not directly contain the data structure used to describe the virtual node, but contains the helper function used to create the virtual DOM node, as shown in the following code:

```
01 render() {
02 return createVNode('div', { id: 'foo' }, [
03 createVNode('p', null, 'text')
04 ])
05 }
```

where the createVNode function is used to create the virtual DOM node helper function; its basic implementation is similar to:

```
01 function createVNode(tag, props, children) {
02 const key = props && props.key
03 props && delete props.key
04
05 return {
06 tag,
07 props,
08 children,
09 key
10 }
11 }
```

As you can see, the return value of the createVNode function is a virtual DOM node. Inside the createVNode function, some additional processing is usually done for props and children.

The key information extracted by the compiler during the optimization phase will affect the final generated code, which is embodied in the helper functions used to create virtual DOM nodes. Suppose we have the following template:

```
01 <div id="foo">
02 <p class="bar">{{ text }}</p>
03 </div>
```

After compiling and optimizing this template, the compiler will generate a render function with a patch flag, as shown in the following code:

```
01 render() {
02 return createVNode('div', { id: 'foo' }, [
03 createVNode('p', { class: 'bar' }, text, PatchFlags.TEXT) //
PatchFlags.TEXT is the patch flag
04 ])
05 }
```

In the above code, the createVNode function call used to create the p tag has a fourth argument, which is PatchFlags. TEXT. This parameter is the so-called patch flag, which means that the current virtual DOM node is a dynamic node, and the dynamic element is sub-node with dynamic text. This implements the marking of dynamic nodes.

The next step we have to think about is how to turn the root node into a Block, and how to collect dynamic child nodes into the dynamicChildren array of the Block. An important fact here is that within the render function, the call to the createVNode function is a layer-by-layer nested structure, and the execution order of the function is "inner layer executes first, outer layer executes later," as shown in Fig. 17.1.

```
render() {                          The outer layer executes later
  return createVNode('div', {}, [
    createVNode('div', {}, [
      createVNode('div', {}, [
        createVNode('div', {}, [
          createVNode('div', {}, [
            // ...                   The inner layer executes first
          ])
        ])
      ])
    ])
  ])
}
```

Fig. 17.1 Inside-out execution

When the outer createVNode function executes, the inner createVNode function has already finished executing. Therefore, in order for the outer block node to collect the inner dynamic node, a stack structure of data is required to temporarily store the inner dynamic node, as shown in the following code:

```
01 // dynamic node stack
02 const dynamicChildrenStack = []
03 // current dynamic node set
04 let currentDynamicChildren = null
05 // openBlock is used to create a new dynamic node set and push the
set into the stack
06 function openBlock() {
07 dynamicChildrenStack.push((currentDynamicChildren = []))
08 }
09 // closeBlock is used to pop the set of dynamic nodes created by
openBlock from the stack
10 function closeBlock() {
11 currentDynamicChildren = dynamicChildrenStack.pop()
12 }
```

Next, we also need to adjust the createVNode function, as shown in the following code:

```
01 function createVNode(tag, props, children, flags) {
02 const key = props && props.key
03 props && delete props.key
04
05 const vnode = {
06 tag,
07 props,
08 children,
09 key,
10 patchFlags: flags
11 }
12
```

```
13 if (typeof flags !== 'undefined' && currentDynamicChildren) {
14 // Dynamic node - add it to the current dynamic node collection
15 currentDynamicChildren.push(vnode)
16 }
17
18 return vnode
19 }
```

Inside the createVNode function, check if the node has a patch flag. If it does, it means that the node is a dynamic node, so it is added to the current dynamic node collection currentDynamicChildren.

Finally, we need to redesign the execution of the render function as shown in the following code:

```
01 render() {
02 // 1. Use createBlock instead of createVNode to create block
03 // 2. Each time before calling createBlock, call openBlock
04 return (openBlock(), createBlock('div', null, [
05 createVNode('p', { class: 'foo' }, null, 1 /* patch flag */),
06 createVNode('p', { class: 'bar' }, null),
07 ]))
08 }
09
10 function createBlock(tag, props, children) {
11 // block is essentially a vnode
12 const block = createVNode(tag, props, children)
13 // set the current dynamic node set as block.dynamicChildren
14 block.dynamicChildren = currentDynamicChildren
15
16 // close block
17 closeBlock()
18 // return
19 return block
20 }
```

Looking at the code inside the render function, we use the nature of the comma operator to ensure that the return value of the render function is still a VNode object. The key point here is the createBlock function; any virtual node that should be a Block role should use this function to complete the creation of the virtual node. Since the createVNode and createBlock functions are executed from the inside out, when createBlock executes, all createVNode functions in the inner layer have already been executed. At this time, all dynamic child nodes belonging to the current Block are stored in the currentDynamicChildren array. Therefore, we only need to use the currentDynamicChildren array as the value of the block.dynamicChildren property. In this way, we have completed the collection of dynamic nodes.

17.1.4   Runtime Support for Renderers

Now, we have the vnode.dynamicChildren of the dynamic node collection, and the patch flag attached to it. Based on these two points, targeted updates can be implemented in the renderer.

Recall the traditional way of updating nodes, as shown in the patchElement function below, which is taken from the renderer explained in Part III:

```
01 function patchElement(n1, n2) {
02 const el = n2.el = n1.el
03 const oldProps = n1.props
04 const newProps = n2.props
05
06 for (const key in newProps) {
07 if (newProps[key] !== oldProps[key]) {
08 patchProps(el, key, oldProps[key], newProps[key])
09 }
10 }
11 for (const key in oldProps) {
12 if (!(key in newProps)) {
13 patchProps(el, key, oldProps[key], null)
14 }
15 }
16
17 // When dealing with children, call the patchChildren function
18 patchChildren(n1, n2, el)
19 }
```

From the above code, the renderer uses the patchChildren function to update the child nodes of the label when updating the label node. But this function will use the Diff algorithm of the traditional virtual DOM to update, which is relatively inefficient. With dynamicChildren, we can directly compare dynamic nodes, as shown in the following code:

```
01 function patchElement(n1, n2) {
02 const el = n2.el = n1.el
03 const oldProps = n1.props
04 const newProps = n2.props
05
06 // omit some code
07
08 if (n2.dynamicChildren) {
09 // Call the patchBlockChildren function, which will only update
the dynamic node
10 patchBlockChildren(n1, n2)
11 } else {
12 patchChildren(n1, n2, el)
13 }
14 }
15
```

```
16 function patchBlockChildren(n1, n2) {
17 // Update only dynamic nodes
18 for (let i = 0; i < n2.dynamicChildren.length; i++) {
19 patchElement(n1.dynamicChildren[i], n2.dynamicChildren[i])
20 }
21 }
```

After modification, in the function patchElement, we preferentially detect whether there is a dynamic node collection in the virtual DOM, that is, a dynamicChildren array. If present, the patchBlockChildren function is called directly to complete the update. In this way, the renderer will only update dynamic nodes and skip all static nodes.

Dynamic node sets enable the renderer to skip static nodes when performing updates, but for individual dynamic node updates, we can do targeted updates because of the corresponding patch flags, as shown in the following code:

```
01 function patchElement(n1, n2) {
02 const el = n2.el = n1.el
03 const oldProps = n1.props
04 const newProps = n2.props
05
06 if (n2.patchFlags) {
07 // Targeted update
08 if (n2.patchFlags === 1) {
09 // only need to update class
10 } else if (n2.patchFlags === 2) {
11 // only need to update style
12 } else if (...) {
13 // ...
14 }
15 } else {
16 // full update
17 for (const key in newProps) {
18 if (newProps[key] !== oldProps[key]) {
19 patchProps(el, key, oldProps[key], newProps[key])
20 }
21 }
22 for (const key in oldProps) {
23 if (!(key in newProps)) {
24 patchProps(el, key, oldProps[key], null)
25 }
26 }
27 }
28
29 // When dealing with children, calling the patchChildren function
30 patchChildren(n1, n2, el)
31 }
```

You can see that in the patchElement function, we achieve targeted updates of props by detecting patch flags. This avoids full props updates and maximizes performance.

17.2   Block Trees

In the previous section, we agreed that the root node of the component template must be the Block role. In this way, starting from the root node, all dynamic child nodes will be collected into the dynamicChildren array of the root node. However, if only the root node is the Block role, the Block tree will not be formed. Since the Block tree will be formed, it means that in addition to the root node, there will be other special nodes acting as Block roles. In fact, nodes with structured instructions, such as those with v-if and v-for instructions, should all play the Block role. Next, we will discuss why in detail.

17.2.1   Nodes with V-if Instructions

First, let's look at the following template:

```
01 <div>
02 <section v-if="foo">
03 <p>{{ a }}</p>
04 </section>
05 <div v-else>
06 <p>{{ a }}</p>
07 </div>
08 </div>
```

Assume that only the outermost div tag will play the Block role. Then, when the value of foo is true, the dynamic node collected by block is as follows:

```
01 cosnt block = {
02 tag: 'div',
03 dynamicChildren: [
04 { tag: 'p', children: ctx.a, patchFlags: 1 }
05 ]
06 // ...
07 }
```

When the value of the variable foo is false, the dynamic nodes collected by the block are as follows:

```
01 cosnt block = {
02 tag: 'div',
03 dynamicChildren: [
04 { tag: 'p', children: ctx.a, patchFlags: 1 }
05 ]
06 // ...
07 }
```

It can be found that whether the value of the variable foo is true or false, the dynamic nodes collected by the block are unchanged. This means that no updates will be made during the Diff phase. But we also saw that in the above template, the < section > tag with the v-if directive and the < div > tag with the v-else directive. Obviously, the labels before and after the update are different, and if not done, any update will cause serious bugs. Not only that, but the following template will have the same problem:

```
01 <div>
02 <section v-if="foo">
03 <p>{{ a }}</p>
04 </section>
05 <section v-else> <!-- even if this is section -->
06 <div> <!-- this div tag is ignored during Diff -->
07 <p>{{ a }}</p>
08 </div>
09 </section >
10 </div>
```

In the above template, even if the tag with the v-if instruction and the tag with the v-else instruction are both < section > tags, the update will still fail due to the different structure of the virtual DOM tree of the two branches.

In fact, the root cause of the above problem is that the dynamic nodes collected in the dynamicChildren array ignore the virtual DOM tree hierarchy. In other words, structured instructions will cause the structure of the template to change before and after the update, that is, the template structure is unstable. So, how to make the structure of the virtual DOM tree stable? In fact, it is very simple, just let the node with v-if/v-else-if/v-else and so on, and the node of the structured instruction also acts as a Block.

Take the following template as an example:

```
01 <div>
02 <section v-if="foo">
03 <p>{{ a }}</p>
04 </section>
05 <section v-else> <!-- even if this is section -->
06 <div> <!-- this div tag is ignored during Diff -->
07 <p>{{ a }}</p>
08 </div>
09 </section >
10 </div>
```

If both < section > tags in the above template are Block characters, then a Block tree will be formed:

```
01 Block(Div)
02 - Block(Section v-if)
03 - Block(Section v-else)
```

The parent Block will collect child Blocks in addition to dynamic child nodes. Therefore, the two child Block (section) will be collected as the dynamic nodes of the parent Block (div) into the dynamicChildren array of the parent Block (div), as shown in the code below:

```
01 cosnt block = {
02 tag: 'div',
03 dynamicChildren: [
04 /* Block(Section v-if) or Block(Section v-else) */
05 { tag: 'section', { key: 0 /* The key value will vary depending on
the block */ }, dynamicChildren: [...] },
06 ]
07 }
```

In this way, when the v-if condition is true, the dynamicChildren array of the parent block will contain Block (section v-if); when the v-if condition is false, the dynamicChildren array of the parent block will contain Block (section v-else). During the Diff process, the renderer can distinguish the two blocks before and after the update according to the key value of the block, and replace the old block with the new block. This solves the update problem caused by unstable DOM structure.

17.2.2 Nodes with V-for Instructions

Not only nodes with v-if instructions will make the structure of the virtual DOM tree unstable, but nodes with v-for instructions will also make the virtual DOM tree unstable, and the latter situation will be slightly more complicated.

Consider the following template:

```
01 <div>
02 <p v-for="item in list">{{ item }}</p>
03 <i>{{ foo }}</i>
04 <i>{{ bar }}</i>
05 </div>
```

Assuming the list is an array, the value of the list array changes from [1,2] to [1] during the update process. According to the previous idea, that is, only the root node will play the role of Block, then in the above template, only the outermost <

div > tag will be used as Block. Therefore, the block tree corresponding to this template before and after the update is as follows:

```
01 // before update
02 const prevBlock = {
03 tag: 'div',
04 dynamicChildren: [
05 { tag: 'p', children: 1, 1 /* TEXT */ },
06 { tag: 'p', children: 2, 1 /* TEXT */ },
07 { tag: 'i', children: ctx.foo, 1 /* TEXT */ },
08 { tag: 'i', children: ctx.bar, 1 /* TEXT */ },
09 ]
10 }
11
12 // after update
13 const nextBlock = {
14 tag: 'div',
15 dynamicChildren: [
16 { tag: 'p', children: item, 1 /* TEXT */ },
17 { tag: 'i', children: ctx.foo, 1 /* TEXT */ },
18 { tag: 'i', children: ctx.bar, 1 /* TEXT */ },
19 ]
20 }
```

Observe the above code, there are four dynamic nodes in the block tree (prevBlock) before the update, and only three dynamic nodes in the updated block tree (nextBlock). How to perform Diff operation at this time? Some people might argue that a traditional Diff using the nodes in the two dynamicChildren arrays before and after the update would be fine. This is obviously wrong, because a very important precondition of traditional Diff is that the node performing Diff operation must be a node of the same level. But the nodes in the dynamicChildren array are not necessarily at the same level, which we mentioned in the previous chapter.

In fact, the solution is very simple. We just need to make the tag with the v-for directive also play the Block role. This ensures that the virtual DOM tree has a stable structure, that is, no matter how v-for changes at runtime, the Block tree looks the same, as shown in the following code:

```
01 const block = {
02 tag: 'div',
03 dynamicChildren: [
04 // This is a Block, which has dynamicChildren
05 { tag: Fragment, dynamicChildren: [/* node for v-for */] }
06 { tag: 'i', children: ctx.foo, 1 /* TEXT */ },
07 { tag: 'i', children: ctx.bar, 1 /* TEXT */ },
08 ]
09 }
```

Since the v-for instruction renders a fragment, we need to use a node of type Fragment to express the rendering result of the v-for instruction and act as a Block.

17.2.3   Fragment Stability

In the previous section, we used a Fragment to express the virtual node generated by
the v-for loop and let it act as a Block to solve the problem of unstable virtual DOM
tree structure caused by the v-for instruction. However, we need to take a closer look
at the Fragment node itself. Given the following template:

```
01 <p v-for="item in list">{{ item }}</p>
```

When the list array is changed from [1, 2] to [1], the corresponding contents of the
Fragment node before and after the update are as follows:

```
01 // before update
02 const prevBlock = {
03 tag: Fragment,
04 dynamicChildren: [
05 { tag: 'p', children: item, 1 /* TEXT */ },
06 { tag: 'p', children: item, 2 /* TEXT */ }
07 ]
08 }
09
10 // after update
11 const prevBlock = {
12 tag: Fragment,
13 dynamicChildren: [
14 { tag: 'p', children: item, 1 /* TEXT */ }
15 ]
16 }
```

We found that the collected dynamic nodes of Fragment itself still face structural
instability. The so-called structural instability refers to the inconsistency in the
number or order of dynamic nodes collected in the dynamicChildren array of a
block before and after the update. This inconsistency will prevent us from directly
performing targeted updates, what should I do? In fact, for this situation, there is no
better solution; we can only give up the idea of targeted update according to the
dynamic nodes in the dynamicChildren array, and fall back to the traditional virtual
DOM Diff method, that is, directly use the children of Fragment instead of
dynamicChildren to perform Diff operation.

But it should be noted that the sub-node (children) of a fragment can still be an
array of blocks, for example:

```
01 const block = {
02 tag: Fragment,
03 children: [
04 { tag: 'p', children: item, dynamicChildren: [/*...*/], 1 /* TEXT
*/ },
05 { tag: 'p', children: item, dynamicChildren: [/*...*/], 1 /* TEXT
*/ }
06 ]
07 }
```

In this way, when the sub-node of the fragment is updated, the optimization mode can be restored.

Since there are unstable Fragments, there are stable Fragments. So, what kind of Fragment is stable? Yes, in the following cases.

• The expressions of the v-for directive are constants:

```
01 <p v-for="n in 10"></p>
02 <!-- or -->
03 <p v-for="s in 'abc'"></p>
```

Since the expressions 10 and "abc" are constants, the above two Fragments will not change no matter how they are updated. So these two Fragments are stable. For stable fragments, we do not need to fall back to traditional Diff operations, which will have certain performance advantages.
• There are multiple root nodes in the template. Vue.js 3 no longer restricts the template of the component to have only one root node. When there are multiple root nodes in the template, we need to use Fragment to describe it. For example:

```
01 <template>
02 <div></div>
03 <p></p>
04 <i></i>
05 </template>
```

At the same time, the fragment used to describe templates with multiple root nodes is also stable.

17.3 Static Lifting

After understanding the Block tree, let's look at other optimizations, one of which is static improvement. It can reduce the performance overhead and memory usage of creating a virtual DOM when updating.

Suppose we have the following template:

```
01 <div>
02 <p>static text</p>
03 <p>{{ title }}</p>
04 </div>
```

In the absence of static promotion, its corresponding rendering function is as follows:

```
01 function render() {
02 return (openBlock(), createBlock('div', null, [
```

```
03 createVNode('p', null, 'static text'),
04 createVNode('p', null, ctx.title, 1 /* TEXT */)
05 ]))
06 }
```

As you can see, there are two p-tags in this description of the virtual DOM, one is pure static, and the other has dynamic text. When the value of the reactive data title changes, the entire render function will be re-executed and a new virtual DOM tree will be generated. There is an obvious problem with this process, that is, the pure static virtual nodes will also be recreated once when updating. Obviously, this is not necessary, so we need to find a way to avoid the performance overhead caused by this. The solution is the so-called static hoisting, that is, to promote purely static nodes outside the rendering function, as shown in the following code:

```
01 // hoist static nodes outside the rendering function
02 const hoist1 = createVNode('p', null, 'text')
03
04 function render() {
05 return (openBlock(), createBlock('div', null, [
06 hoist1, // static node reference
07 createVNode('p', null, ctx.title, 1 /* TEXT */)
08 ]))
09 }
```

As can be seen, when a purely static node is promoted outside the render function, only references to the static node will be held in the render function. When the responsive data changes and the render function is re-executed, the static virtual node will not be recreated, thus avoiding additional performance overhead.

It should be emphasized that static promotion is in tree units. Take the following template as an example:

```
01 <div>
02 <section>
03 <p>
04 <span>abc</span>
05 </p>
06 </section >
07 </div>
```

In the above template, the entire < section > element and its descendants will be promoted, except for the root node's div tag, which will be the Block role and cannot be promoted. If we replace the static string abc in the above template with the dynamically bound {{abc}}, the entire tree will not be promoted.

Although a node that contains dynamic bindings will not itself be promoted, there may still be purely static properties on the dynamic node, as shown in the following template:

```
01 <div>
02 <p foo="bar" a=b>{{ text }}</p>
03 </div>
```

In the above template, the p tag has dynamically bound text content, so the entire node will not be statically promoted. However, all props of this node are static, so when we finally generate the render function, we can promote the pure static props outside the render function, as shown in the following code:

```
01 // Statically promoted props object
02 const hoistProp = { foo: 'bar', a: 'b' }
03
04 function render(ctx) {
05 return (openBlock(), createBlock('div', null, [
06 createVNode('p', hoistProp, ctx.text)
07 ]))
08 }
```

This also reduces the overhead and memory footprint of creating a virtual DOM.

17.4   Pre-stringing

Based on static promotion, we can further use the optimization of pre-stringing method. The optimization of pre-stringing is an optimization strategy based on static promotion. The statically promoted virtual node or virtual node tree itself is static, so can it be pre-stringed? As shown in the template below:

```
01 <div>
02 <p></p>
03 <p></p>
04 // ... 20 p tags
05 <p></p>
06 </div>
```

Assuming that the above template contains a large number of continuous pure static tag nodes, when using the static promotion optimization strategy, the compiled code is as follows:

```
01 cosnt hoist1 = createVNode('p', null, null, PatchFlags.HOISTED)
02 cosnt hoist2 = createVNode('p', null, null, PatchFlags.HOISTED)
03 // ... 20 hoistx variables
04 cosnt hoist20 = createVNode('p', null, null, PatchFlags.HOISTED)
05
06 render() {
07 return (openBlock(), createBlock('div', null, [
08 hoist1, hoist2, /* ...20 variables */, hoist20
09 ]))
10 }
```

Pre-stringing can serialize these static nodes into strings and generate a VNode of type Static:

```
01 const hoistStatic = createStaticVNode
('<p></p><p></p><p></p>...20↑...<p></p>')
02
03 render() {
04 return (openBlock(), createBlock('div', null, [
05 hoistStatic
06 ]))
07 }
```

There are several distinct advantages to doing this.

- Large chunks of static content can be set through innerHTML, which has certain performance advantages.
- Reduce the performance overhead of creating virtual nodes.
- Reduce memory usage.

17.5   Caching Inline Event Handlers

When it comes to optimization, you have to mention the cache of internal connection event handlers. Caching internal connection event handlers avoids unnecessary updates. Suppose the template content is as follows:

```
01 <Comp @change="a + b" />
```

The above template shows a component bound to the change event, and the event handler bound to the change event, the program is an internal connection statement. For such templates, the compiler creates an internal connection event handler, as shown in the following code:

```
01 function render(ctx) {
02 return h(Comp, {
03 // internal connection event handler
04 onChange: () => (ctx.a + ctx.b)
05 })
06 }
```

Obviously, each time the render is re-rendered (that is, when the render function re-executes), a completely new props object is created for the Comp component. At the same time, the value of the onChange property in the props object will also be a brand-new function. This will cause the renderer to update the Comp component, causing additional performance overhead. To avoid this kind of useless update, we need to cache the internal connection event handler, as shown in the following code:

```
01 function render(ctx, cache) {
02 return h(Comp, {
03 // Cache the internal connection event handler into the
cache array
04 onChange: cache[0] || (cache[0] = ($event) => (ctx.a + ctx.b))
05 })
06 }
```

Rendering the second parameter of the function is an array cache, which comes from the component instance. We can add the internal connection event handling function to the cache array. In this way, when the render function re-executes and creates a new virtual DOM tree, the event handler in the cache will be read first. In this way, no matter how many times the render function is executed, the value of the onChange property in the props object remains unchanged, so the Comp component update will not be triggered.

17.6   V-once

Vue.js 3 not only caches the internal connection event handler, but also caches the virtual DOM with v-once. Vue.js 2 also supports v-once instructions. When the compiler encounters a v-once instruction, it will use the cache array we introduced in the previous section to cache and render all or part of the execution result of the function, as shown in the following template:

```
01 <section>
02 <div v-once>{{ foo }}</div>
03 </section>
```

In the above template, the div tag has dynamically bound text content. But it is marked with the v-once instruction, so this template will be compiled as:

```
01 function render(ctx, cache) {
02 return (openBlock(), createBlock('div', null, [
03 cache[1] || (cache[1] = createVNode("div", null, ctx.foo, 1 /*
TEXT */))
04 ]))
05 }
```

As you can see from the compilation result, the virtual node corresponding to the div tag is Cached in the cache array. Since the virtual node has been cached, when the render function is re-executed in a subsequent update, it will preferentially read the cached content instead of recreating the virtual node. At the same time, because the virtual node is cached, it means that the virtual nodes before and after the update will not change, so there is no need for these cached virtual nodes to participate in the

Diff operation. Therefore, the following content often appears in the actual compiled code:

```
01 render(ctx, cache) {
02 return (openBlock(), createBlock('div', null, [
03 cache[1] || (
04 setBlockTracking(-1), // prevent this VNode from being collected
by Block
05 cache[1] = h("div", null, ctx.foo, 1 /* TEXT */),
06 setBlockTracking(1), // Restore
07 cache[1] // The value of the entire expression
08 )
09 ]))
10 }
```

Note the setBlockTracking (-1) function call in the above code, which is used to suspend the collection of dynamic nodes. In other words, dynamic nodes wrapped with v-once will not be collected by the parent Block. Therefore, dynamic nodes wrapped by v-once naturally do not participate in Diff operations when components are updated.

The v-once directive is often used in dynamic bindings that do not change, such as binding a constant:

```
01 <div>{{ SOME_CONSTANT }}</div>
```

To improve performance, we can mark this content with a v-once:

```
01 <div v-once>{{ SOME_CONSTANT }}</div>
```

This way, the update of this content will be skipped when the component is updated, thereby improving update performance.

In fact, the v-once directive can improve performance in two ways.

- Avoid the performance overhead of recreating the virtual DOM when the component is updated. Because the virtual DOM is cached, there is no need to recreate it when updating.
- Avoid useless Diff overhead. This is because the virtual DOM tree marked by v-once is not collected by the parent Block node.

17.7 Summary

In this chapter, we mainly discussed Vue.js 3's efforts in compilation optimization. Compilation optimization refers to the process of extracting key information through compiled means and using this to guide the process of generating optimal code. Specifically, Vue.js 3 compiler fully analyzes templates, extracts key information, and attaches it to the corresponding virtual nodes. During the runtime phase, the renderer executes "shortcut paths" through these key information to improve performance.

The core of compilation optimization is to distinguish dynamic nodes from static nodes. Vue.js 3 will mark dynamic nodes with a patch flag, that is, patchFlag. At the same time, Vue.js 3 also proposed the concept of Block. A Block is essentially a virtual node, but compared with ordinary virtual nodes, there will be an extra dynamicChildren array. This array is used to collect all dynamic child nodes, which takes advantage of the characteristics of the nested calls of the createVNode function and the createBlock function, that is, executed in an "inside-out" manner. Coupled with a node stack used to temporarily store dynamic nodes, the collection of dynamic child nodes can be completed.

Since Block collects all dynamic descendant nodes, the comparison operation of dynamic nodes ignores the DOM hierarchy. This will bring additional problems, that is, structured instructions such as v-if, v-for, etc. will affect the DOM hierarchy and make it unstable. This will indirectly cause the alignment algorithm based on Block tree to fail. The solution is very simple, just make the node with v-if, v-for and other instructions also play the role of Block.

In addition to block trees and patch flags, Vue.js 3 has made other efforts in compilation optimization, as follows.

- Static promotion: Can reduce the performance overhead and memory consumption caused by creating a virtual DOM when updating.
- Pre-stringed: On the basis of static promotion, static nodes are stringed. Doing so can reduce the performance overhead and memory consumption caused by creating virtual nodes.
- Cache internal connection event handlers: Avoid unnecessary component updates.
- V-once directive: Caching all or part of virtual nodes avoids the performance overhead of recreating the virtual DOM when the component is updated, and also avoids useless Diff operations.

Part VI
Server-Side Rendering

Chapter 18
Isomorphic Rendering

Vue.js can be used to build client-side applications, where the component's code runs in the browser and outputs DOM elements. At the same time, Vue.js can also be run in a Node.js environment, where it can render the same component as a string and send it to the browser. This actually describes two ways of rendering, namely client-side rendering (CSR) and server-side rendering (SSR). In addition, as a modern front-end framework, Vue.js can not only perform CSR or SSR independently, but also combine the two to form so-called isomorphic rendering. In this chapter, we will discuss the similarities and differences between CSR, SSR, and isomorphic rendering, as well as the implementation mechanism of Vue.js isomorphic rendering.

18.1 CSR, SSR, and Isomorphic Rendering

When designing software for CSR, SSR, and isomorphic rendering, we often encounter the question: "Should I use server-side rendering?" There is no answer to this question. The exact answer depends on the needs and scenarios of the software. To choose the appropriate architectural strategy for the software, we need to be aware of different rendering strategies and their respective advantages and disadvantages. Server-side rendering is not a new technology, nor is it a new concept. Before Web 2.0, websites were mainly responsible for providing a variety of content, usually some news sites, personal blogs, novel sites, etc. These sites mainly emphasized the content itself, not the high-intensity interaction with the user. At that time, the traditional server-side rendering technology was basically used to implement the site. For example, the more popular PHP/JSP and other technologies. Figure 18.1 shows the workflow of server-side rendering.

1. The user requests the site through the browser.
2. The server requests the API to obtain data.

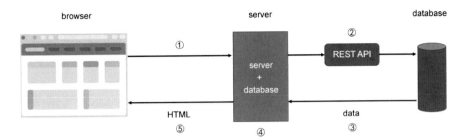

Fig. 18.1 The workflow of server-side rendering

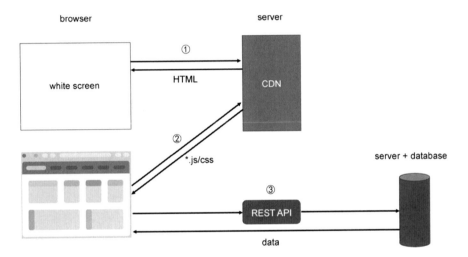

Fig. 18.2 The workflow of CSR

3. The interface returns data to the server.
4. The server splices the final HTML string according to the template and the obtained data.
5. The server sends the HTML string to the browser, which parses the HTML content and renders it.

When the user makes a page jump through hyperlink again, the above five steps will be repeated. It can be seen that the user experience of traditional server-side rendering is very poor, and any small operation may cause the page to refresh.

Later, AJAX was the representative, giving birth to Web 2.0. At this stage, a large number of SPA (single-page application) was born, which is the CSR technology we will introduce next. Unlike SSR, which completes the fusion of templates and data at the server level, CSR completes the fusion of templates and data in the browser and renders the final HTML page. Figure 18.2 shows the detailed workflow of CSR.

• The client side sends a request to the server or CDN to obtain a static HTML page. Note that the HTML page fetched at this point is usually an empty page. In the

HTML page, tags such as $<$ style $>$, $<$ link $>$, and $<$ script $>$ will be included. For example:

```
01 <!DOCTYPE html>
02 <html lang="zh">
03 <head>
04 <meta charset="UTF-8">
05 <meta name="viewport" content="width=device-width, initial-
scale=1.0">
06 <title>My App</title>
07 <link rel="stylesheet" href="/dist/app.css">
08 </head>
09 <body>
10 <div id="app"></div>
11
12 <script src="/dist/app.js"></script>
13 </body>
14 </html>
```

This is an empty HTML page with $<$ rel link $=$ "stylesheet" $>$ and $<$ script $>$ tags. After the browser gets the page, it will not render any content, so from the user's point of view, the page is in the "white screen" stage.

- Although the HTML page is empty, the browser will still parse the HTML content. Since the HTML page has tags such as $<$ link rel $=$ "stylesheet" $>$ and $<$ script $>$, the browser will load the resources referenced in the HTML, such as app.css and app.js. Then, the server or CDN will return the corresponding resources to the browser, and the browser will interpret and execute the CSS and JavaScript code. Because the rendering task of the page is done by JavaScript, when the JavaScript is interpreted and executed, the page content will be rendered, that is, the "white screen" ends. But the initial rendered content is usually a "skeleton," because the API has not been requested to obtain data.
- The client side then requests the API to obtain data through AJAX technology. Once the interface returns the data, the client side will complete the dynamic rendering of the content and render the complete page.

When the user clicks "jump" to another page again, the browser will not really perform the jump action, that is, it will not refresh, but dynamically render the page through front-end routing, which will be very friendly to the user's interactive experience. However, it is clear that CSR produces a so-called white screen problem compared to SSR. In fact, CSR does not only produce white screen problems, but it is also not SEO (Search Engine Optimization) friendly.

SSR and CSR have their own advantages and disadvantages. SSR is more SEO friendly, while CSR is less SEO friendly. Because the content of SSR arrives faster, it does not produce white screen problems. In contrast, CSR will have white screen problems. In addition, because SSR completes page rendering at the server level, it needs to consume more server level resources. CSR can reduce the consumption of

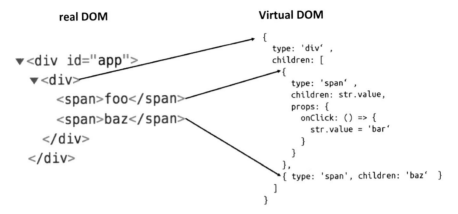

Fig. 18.3 The relationship between the real DOM and the virtual DOM

server level resources. For user experience, because CSR does not need to make real "jump," users will feel "smoother," so CSR has a better user experience than SSR. From these perspectives, neither SSR nor CSR can be used as a "silver bullet." We need to decide which one to use based on the actual needs of the project. For example, if your project needs SEO very much, then SSR should be used.

So, can we combine the advantages of SSR and CSR? The answer is "yes," which is the isomorphic rendering we will discuss next. Isomorphic rendering is divided into first rendering (that is, first visit or refresh the page) and non-first rendering. Figure 18.3 shows the workflow of the first rendering of isomorphic rendering.

In fact, the first rendering in isomorphic rendering is consistent with the workflow of SSR. That is, when the page is first accessed or refreshed, the entire content of the page is rendered at the server level, and the browser ends up with the rendered HTML page. However, the page is purely static, which means that the user cannot have any interaction with the page, because the script of the entire application has not been loaded and executed. In addition, the static HTML page will also contain tags such as < link > and < script >. In addition, the HTML page produced by isomorphic rendering is one of the biggest differences from the HTML page generated by SSR, that is, the former will contain the initialization data required for the current page. To put it bluntly, the data requested by the server through the API is serialized as a string, concatenated into a static HTML string, and finally sent to the browser. This is actually done for subsequent activation operations, which will be explained in detail later.

Assuming the browser has received the static HTML page rendered for the first time, the browser will parse and render the page next. During the parsing process, the browser will find < link > and < script > tags in the HTML code, so it will get the corresponding resources from the CDN or server, which is consistent with CSR. When the JavaScript resources are loaded, an activation operation will be performed. The activation here is what we often call "hydration" in Vue.js. Activation consists of two parts of work.

- Vue.js establishes a connection between the currently rendered DOM elements of the page and the virtual DOM rendered by Vue.js components.
- Vue.js extracts the data sent by the server level serialization from the HTML page to initialize the entire Vue.js application.

After activation, the entire application has been completely taken over by the Vue.js as a CSR application. Subsequent operations will follow the process of CSR applications. Of course, if the page is refreshed, server-side rendering will still be performed, and then activation will be performed, and so on.

It can be seen that except for the fact that homogeneous rendering also requires some server-side resources, other aspects of performance are very good. Since isomorphic rendering still requires server level rendering work during the first rendering and browser refresh, it also requires some server level resources. However, compared with all page jumps that require the server to complete the rendering, homogeneous rendering occupies relatively less server-side resources.

In addition, the most common misconception about isomorphic rendering is that it can improve the interactive time (TTI). The truth is that isomorphic rendering still needs to wait, like CSR, for JavaScript resources to load and client-side activation to complete before responding to user actions. Therefore, isomorphic rendering theoretically cannot improve interaction time.

The term "isomorphic" of isomorphic rendering means that the same set of code can run both on the server level and on the client side. For example, let's use Vue.js to write a component that can run either on the server level and be rendered as an HTML string or on the client side, just like a normal CSR application. We'll discuss how Vue.js component is rendered as an HTML string at the server level in Sect. 18.2.

18.2 Rendering Virtual DOM as HTML Strings

Since "isomorphic" means that the same code can be run at both the server level and the client side, in this section we discuss how to render virtual DOM as HTML string at the server level.

Given the following virtual node object, which is used to describe a normal div tag:

```
01 const ElementVNode = {
02 type: 'div',
03 props: {
04 id: 'foo'
05 },
06 children: [
07 { type: 'p', children: 'hello' }
08 ]
09 }
```

To render the virtual node ElementVNode as a string, we need to implement the renderElementVNode function. The function receives the virtual node used to describe the common tag as an argument and returns the rendered HTML string:

```
01 function renderElementVNode(vnode) {
02 // Return the rendered result, which is HTML string
03 }
```

Without considering any boundary conditions is very simple, as shown in the following code:

```
01 function renderElementVNode(vnode) {
02 // Take out the tag name tag and tag attribute props, and the
sub-node of tags
03 const { type: tag, props, children } = vnode
04 // start tag header
05 let ret = `<${tag}`
06 // handle tag attribute
07 if (props) {
08 for (const k in props) {
09 // Concatenate strings in the form key="value"
10 ret += ` ${k}="${props[k]}"`
11 }
12 }
13 // Closure of start tag
14 ret += `>`
15
16 // deal with sub-nodes
17 // If the type of the child node is a string, it is text content, and
it is directly concatenated
18 if (typeof children === 'string') {
19 ret += children
20 } else if (Array.isArray(children)) {
21 // If sub-node type is array, recursively call renderElementVNode
to finish rendering
22 children.forEach(child => {
23 ret += renderElementVNode(child)
24 })
25 }
26
27 // end tag
28 ret += `</${tag}>`
29
30 // return spliced HTML strings
31 return ret
32 }
```

Next, we can call renderElementVNode to finish rendering ElementVNode:

```
01 console.log(renderElementVNode(ElementVNode)) // <div
id="foo"><p>hello</p></div>
```

As you can see, the output is the expected HTML string. In effect, rendering a virtual node of normal tag type as an HTML string is essentially a concatenation of strings. However, the implementation of renderElementVNode function given above is only used to demonstrate the core principle of rendering virtual DOM as HTML string and does not meet the production requirements, because it has the following drawbacks.

- When renderElementVNode function renders a virtual node of tag type, it also needs to consider whether the node is a self-closing tag.
- The processing of attributes (props) will be more complicated, and it is necessary to consider whether the attribute name is valid and implement HTML escaping for the attribute value.
- There are various types of sub-nodes, which may be any type of virtual node, such as Fragment, component, functional component, text, etc., which need to be handled.
- The text of the tag sub-node also needs to be HTML escaped.

The above problems are all boundary conditions, and we will deal with them one by one. The self-closing tag is dealt with first, its term is called void element, and its full list is as follows:

```
01 const VOID_TAGS = 'area,base,br,col,embed,hr,img,input,link,
meta,param,source,track,wbr'
```

You can see the full void element in the WHATWG specification.

For void element, since it does not need a closing tag, when generating an HTML string for such a tag, it does not need to generate the corresponding closing tag, as shown in the following code:

```
01 const VOID_TAGS = 'area,base,br,col,embed,hr,img,input,link,
meta,param,source,track,wbr'.split(',')
02
03 function renderElementVNode2(vnode) {
04 const { type: tag, props, children } = vnode
05 // decide whether it is void element
06 const isVoidElement = VOID_TAGS.includes(tag)
07
08 let ret = `<${tag}`
09
10 if (props) {
11 for (const k in props) {
12 ret += ` ${k}="${props[k]}"`
13 }
```

```
14 }
15
16 // if it is void element, self-closing
17 ret += isVoidElement ? `/>` : `>`
18 // If it is a void element, return the result directly, without
dealing with children, because void element has no children
19 if (isVoidElement) return ret
20
21 if (typeof children === 'string') {
22 ret += children
23 } else {
24 children.forEach(child => {
25 ret += renderElementVNode2(child)
26 })
27 }
28
29 ret += `</${tag}>`
30
31 return ret
32 }
```

In the code above, we added handling of void elements. One thing to note is that since self-closing tags do not have sub-nodes, the processing of children can be skipped.

Next, we need to deal with HTML attributes more strictly. Handling attributes requires consideration of many aspects; the first is the handling of boolean attributes. The so-called Boolean attribute does not mean that the value of such attributes is a Boolean type, but means that if such an instruction exists, it represents true, otherwise it represents false. For example, the checked and disabled attributes of the < input/> tag:

```
01 <!-- checke checkbox -->
02 <input type="checkbox" checked />
03 <!-- unchecked checkbox -->
04 <input type="checkbox" />
```

As you can see from the HTML code example above, when rendering a Boolean attribute, it is usually not necessary to render its attribute value.

Another thing to consider about attributes is security. The composition of attribute names is clearly defined in Section 13.1.2.3 of the WHATWG specification.

Attribute names must consist of one or more characters other than the following.

- The code point ranges for control characters are [0x01, 0x1f] and [0x7f, 0x9f].
- U + 0020 (SPACE), U + 0022 ("), U + 0027 ('), U + 003E (>), U + 002F (/), and U + 003D (=).
- noncharacters, where noncharacters represent the code points that are permanently reserved in Unicode. These code points are used within Unicode. Its value range is [[0xFDD0, 0xFDEF] and also includes 0xFFFE, 0xFFFF, 0x1FFFE, 0x1FFFF, 0x2FFFE, 0x2FFFF, 0x3FFFE, 0x3FFFF, 0x4FFFE, 0x4FFFF,

0x5FFFE, 0x5FFFF, 0x6FFFE, 0x6FFFF, 0x7FFFE, 0x7FFFF, 0x8FFFE,
0x8FFFF, 0x9FFFE, 0x9FFFF, 0xAFFFE, 0xAFFFF, 0xBFFFE, 0xBFFFF,
0xCFFFE, 0xCFFFF, 0xDFFFE, 0xDFFFF, 0xEFFFE, 0xEFFFF, 0xFFFFE,
0xFFFFF, 0x10FFFE, 0x10FFFF.

Considering that Vue.js template compiler already handles noncharacters and
control character sets during compilation, we only need to deal with it in a small
scope. Any attribute name that does not meet the above conditions is unsafe and
illegal.

In addition, props objects in virtual nodes usually contain relevant attributes that
are only used for component runtime logic. For example, the key attribute is only
used for the Diff algorithm of the virtual DOM, and the ref. attribute is only used to
implement the functions of template ref. These attributes should be ignored when
performing server-side rendering. In addition, server-side rendering does not need to
consider event binding. Therefore, event handlers in props objects should also be
ignored.

A more rigorous attribute handling scheme is as follows:

```
01 function renderElementVNode(vnode) {
02 const { type: tag, props, children } = vnode
03 const isVoidElement = VOID_TAGS.includes(tag)
04
05 let ret = `<${tag}`
06
07 if (props) {
08 // Call renderAttrs function for rigorous processing
09 ret += renderAttrs(props)
10 }
11
12 ret += isVoidElement ? `/>` : `>`
13
14 if (isVoidElement) return ret
15
16 if (typeof children === 'string') {
17 ret += children
18 } else {
19 children.forEach(child => {
20 ret += renderElementVNode(child)
21 })
22 }
23
24 ret += `</${tag}>`
25
26 return ret
27 }
```

As you can see, inside the renderElementVNode function, we call the renderAttrs
function to implement the processing of props. The specific implementation of the
renderAttrs function is as follows:

```
01 // Properties that should be ignored
02 const shouldIgnoreProp = ['key', 'ref']
03
04 function renderAttrs(props) {
05 let ret = ''
06 for (const key in props) {
07 if (
08 // detect the property name; if it is an event or an attribute that
should be ignored, ignore it
09 shouldIgnoreProp.includes(key) ||
10 /^on[^a-z]/.test(key)
11 ) {
12 continue
13 }
14 const value = props[key]
15 // Call renderDynamicAttr to complete the rendering of the
attribute
16 ret += renderDynamicAttr(key, value)
17 }
18 return ret
19 }
```

The implementation of the renderDynamicAttr function is as follows:

```
01 // Used to determine whether the attribute is a boolean attribute
02 const isBooleanAttr = (key) =>
03 (`itemscope,allowfullscreen,formnovalidate,ismap,nomodule,
novalidate,readonly` +
04 `,async,autofocus,autoplay,controls,default,defer,disabled,
hidden,` +
05 `loop,open,required,reversed,scoped,seamless,` +
06 `checked,muted,multiple,selected`).split(',').includes(key)
07
08 // Used to determine whether the attribute name is legal and safe
09 const isSSRSafeAttrName = (key) => !/[>/="'\u0009\u000a\u000c
\u0020]/.test(key)
10
11 function renderDynamicAttr(key, value) {
12 if (isBooleanAttr(key)) {
13 // for the boolean attribute, if the value is false, then nothing
needs to be rendered, otherwise only key needs rendering
14 return value === false ? `` : ` ${key}`
15 } else if (isSSRSafeAttrName(key)) {
16 // For other safe properties, perform full rendering,
17 // Note: For the property value, we need to perform an HTML escape
operation on it
18 return value === '' ? ` ${key}` : ` ${key}="${escapeHtml
(value)}"`
19 } else {
20 // Skip unsafe attributes and print warning
21 console.warn(
22 `[@vue/server-renderer] Skipped rendering unsafe
attribute name: ${key}`
```

```
23 )
24 return ``
25 }
26 }
```

This allows rendering of virtual nodes of normal element types. In fact, in Vue.js, since the two properties of class and style can be represented by a variety of legal data structures. For example, the value of class can be string, object, and array, so in theory we need to consider these situations. However, the principles are the same. For classes or styles represented by different data structures, we only need to serialize different types of data structures into string representations.

In addition, observing the implementation of the renderDynamicAttr function in the above code, we can see that when processing attribute values, we call escapeHtml to escape them, which is crucial for defending against XSS attacks. HTML escape refers to the conversion of special characters into corresponding HTML entities. The conversion rules are simple.

- If the string is concatenated as normal content, the following characters should be escaped.

  - Escape the character & as an entity &
  - Escape the character < as an entity <
  - Escape the character > as entity >

- If the string is concatenated as an attribute value, the following two characters should be escaped in addition to the above three characters.

  - Escape the character as entity "
  - Escape the character as entity '

The implementation is as follows:

```
01 const escapeRE = /["'&<>]/
02 function escapeHtml(string) {
03 const str = '' + string
04 const match = escapeRE.exec(str)
05
06 if (!match) {
07 return str
08 }
09
10 let html = ''
11 let escaped
12 let index
13 let lastIndex = 0
14 for (index = match.index; index < str.length; index++) {
15 switch (str.charCodeAt(index)) {
16 case 34: // "
17 escaped = '&quot;'
18 break
19 case 38: // &
```

```
20 escaped = '&amp'
21 break
22 case 39: // '
23 escaped = '&#39;'
24 break
25 case 60: // <
26 escaped = '&lt;'
27 break
28 case 62: // >
29 escaped = '&gt;'
30 break
31 default:
32 continue
33 }
34
35 if (lastIndex !== index) {
36 html += str.substring(lastIndex, index)
37 }
38
39 lastIndex = index + 1
40 html += escaped
41 }
42
43 return lastIndex !== index ? html + str.substring(lastIndex,
index) : html
44 }
```

The principle is simple; just find the character to escape in the given string and replace it with the corresponding HTML entity.

18.3   Rendering Components as HTML Strings

In Sect. 18.2, we discussed how to render virtual nodes of normal tag types as HTML strings. In this section, we will build on this and discuss how to render virtual nodes of component types as HTML strings.

Suppose we have the following component and a virtual node to describe the component:

```
01 // component
02 const MyComponent = {
03 setup() {
04 return () => {
05 // this component renders a div tag
06 return {
07 type: 'div',
08 children: 'hello'
09 }
10 }
```

```
11 }
12 }
13
14 // VNode object used to describe the component
15 const CompVNode = {
16 type: MyComponent,
17 }
```

We will implement the renderComponentVNode function and use it to render the virtual node of the component type as an HTML string:

```
01 const html = renderComponentVNode(CompVNode)
02 console.log(html) // output: <div>hello</div>
```

In fact, rendering the component as an HTML string is not essential to rendering the normal tag node as an HTML string difference. We know that the component's render function is used to describe the content to be rendered by the component, and its return value is the virtual DOM. Therefore, we only need to execute the component's render function to obtain the corresponding virtual DOM, and then render the virtual DOM as an HTML string as the return value of the renderComponentVNode function. The most basic implementation is as follows:

```
01 function renderComponentVNode(vnode) {
02 // Get setup component options
03 let { type: { setup } } = vnode
04 // Execute setup function to get render function render
05 const render = setup()
06 // Execute render function to get subTree, that is, the content to
be rendered by the component
07 const subTree = render()
08 // Call renderElementVNode to complete rendering and return its
result
09 return renderElementVNode(subTree)
10 }
```

The logic of the above code is very simple; it only shows the most basic principle of rendering components, and there are still many problems.

- The subTree itself may be a virtual node of any type, including component types. Therefore, we cannot directly use renderElementVNode to render it.
- When executing the setup function, you should also provide a setupContext object. When executing the render function render, you should also point its *this* to the renderContext object. In fact, in terms of component initialization and rendering, the complete process is consistent with the client-side rendering process explained in Chap. 13. For example, you also need to initialize data, you also need to get the execution result of the setup function, and check whether the return value of the setup function is a function or setupState.

For the first problem, we can solve it by encapsulating a generic function, as shown in the following code for the renderVNode function:

```
01 function renderVNode(vnode) {
02 const type = typeof vnode.type
03 if (type === 'string') {
04 return renderElementVNode(vnode)
05 } else if (type === 'object' || type === 'function') {
06 return renderComponentVNode(vnode)
07 } else if (vnode.type === Text) {
08 // Processing text...
09 } else if (vnode.type === Fragment) {
10 // Processing fragments...
11 } else {
12 // Other VNode types
13 }
14 }
```

With renderVNode, we can use it to render subTrees in renderComponentVNode:

```
01 function renderComponentVNode(vnode) {
02 let { type: { setup } } = vnode
03 const render = setup()
04 const subTree = render()
05 // Render subTree with renderVNode
06 return renderVNode(subTree)
07 }
```

The second question concerns the initialization process of the component. Let's first review the overall process of the component during client-side rendering, as shown in Fig. 18.4.

During server-side rendering, the initialization process of the component is basically the same as the initialization process of the component during client-side rendering, but there are two important differences.

- Server-side rendering is the current snapshot of the application, and it does not have to be re-rendered after data changes. Therefore, all data does not need to be responsive at the server level. Using this, we can reduce the overhead of creating responsive data objects during server-side rendering.
- Server-side rendering only needs to obtain the subTree to be rendered by the component, and does not need to call the renderer to complete the real DOM creation. Therefore, the step of "setting the render effect to complete the rendering" can be ignored during server-side rendering.

Figure 18.5 shows the flow of initializing the component during server-side rendering.

Fig. 18.4 The initialization
process of a component
during client-side rendering

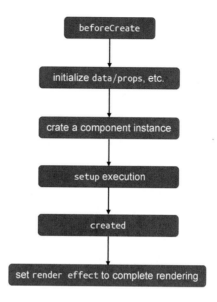

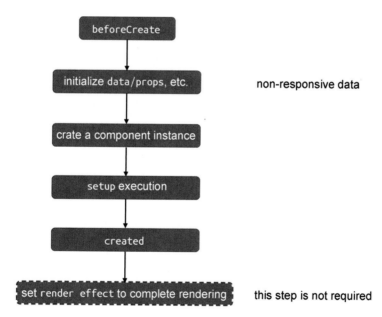

Fig. 18.5 The initialization process of the component during server-side rendering

As can be seen, you only need to slightly adjust the logic of the client side to initialize the component to realize the rendering of the component on the server side. In addition, since the component does not need to render real DOM elements during server-side rendering, there is no need to create and execute the render effect. This means that the component's beforeMount and mounted hooks will not be triggered. Also, since server-side rendering does not have the logic to re-render after data changes, the beforeUpdate and updated hooks are not executed at the server level. The full implementation is as follows:

```
01 function renderComponentVNode(vnode) {
02 const isFunctional = typeof vnode.type === 'function'
03 let componentOptions = vnode.type
04 if (isFunctional) {
05 componentOptions = {
06 render: vnode.type,
07 props: vnode.type.props
08 }
09 }
10 let { render, data, setup, beforeCreate, created, props:
propsOption } = componentOptions
11
12 beforeCreate && beforeCreate()
13
14 // You do not need to use reactive() to create a reactive version of
data
15 const state = data ? data() : null
16 const [props, attrs] = resolveProps(propsOption, vnode.props)
17
18 const slots = vnode.children || {}
19
20 const instance = {
21 state,
22 props, // props does not need shallowReactive
23 isMounted: false,
24 subTree: null,
25 slots,
26 mounted: [],
27 keepAliveCtx: null
28 }
29
30 function emit(event, ...payload) {
31 const eventName = `on${event[0].toUpperCase() + event.slice(1)}`

32 const handler = instance.props[eventName]
33 if (handler) {
34 handler(...payload)
35 } else {
36 console.error('the event does not exist')
37 }
38 }
39
40 // setup
41 let setupState = null
42 if (setup) {
43 const setupContext = { attrs, emit, slots }
44 const prevInstance = setCurrentInstance(instance)
```

```
45 const setupResult = setup(shallowReadonly(instance.props),
setupContext)
46 setCurrentInstance(prevInstance)
47 if (typeof setupResult === 'function') {
48 if (render) console.error('setup function returns the rendering
function; render option will be ignored')
49 render = setupResult
50 } else {
51 setupState = setupContext
52 }
53 }
54
55 vnode.component = instance
56
57 const renderContext = new Proxy(instance, {
58 get(t, k, r) {
59 const { state, props, slots } = t
60
61 if (k === '$slots') return slots
62
63 if (state && k in state) {
64 return state[k]
65 } else if (k in props) {
66 return props[k]
67 } else if (setupState && k in setupState) {
68 return setupState[k]
69 } else {
70 console.error('not existing')
71 }
72 },
73 set (t, k, v, r) {
74 const { state, props } = t
75 if (state && k in state) {
76 state[k] = v
77 } else if (k in props) {
78 props[k] = v
79 } else if (setupState && k in setupState) {
80 setupState[k] = v
81 } else {
82 console.error('not existing')
83 }
84 }
85 })
86
87 created && created.call(renderContext)
88
89 const subTree = render.call(renderContext, renderContext)
90
91 return renderVNode(subTree)
92 }
```

Looking at the above code, this implementation is basically consistent with the
logic of client-side rendering. This code is also very similar to the code for

component rendering given in Chap. 13; the only difference is that in server-side rendering, there is no need to use the reactive function to create a responsive version of the data *data*, and the *props* data does not need to be shallow responsive.

18.4   Principles of Client-Side Activation

After discussing how to render components as HTML strings, let's discuss the implementation principle of client-side activation. What is client-side activation? We know that for isomorphic rendering, the component's code will be executed once on the server level and the client side, respectively. At the server level, the component will be rendered as a static HTML string, and then sent to the browser, which will render this pure static HTML. This means that the corresponding DOM element already exists in the page at this time. At the same time, the component will also be packaged into a JavaScript file, which will be downloaded to the browser on the client side for interpretation and execution. At this time, the question arises: when the component's code is executed on the client side, will the DOM element be created again? The answer is "no." After the browser renders the HTML string sent by the server, the corresponding DOM element already exists in the page, so the component code does not need to create the corresponding DOM element again when running on the client side. However, when the component code is running on the client side, it still needs to do two important things:

- Establish a connection between the DOM element in the page and the virtual node object
- Add event bindings for the DOM elements in the page

We know that after a virtual node is mounted, in order to ensure the correct operation of the updater, it is necessary to store a reference to the real DOM object through the vnode.el property of the virtual node. The same is true for isomorphic rendering. In order for the application to run correctly during subsequent updates, we need to establish the correct connection between the existing DOM object and the virtual node object in the page. In addition, in the process of server-side rendering, the props related to events in the virtual node will be ignored. So, when the component code is running on the client side, we need to bind these events to the element correctly. In fact, these two steps reflect the meaning of client-side activation.

After understanding the meaning of client-side activation, let's take a look at its specific implementation. When the component performs pure client-side rendering, we use the renderer's renderer.render function to complete the rendering, for example:

```
01 renderer.render(vnode, container)
```

For homogeneous applications, we will use a separate renderer.hydrate function to complete the activation:

```
01 renderer.hydrate(vnode, container)
```

In fact, we can use code to simulate the entire process from server-side rendering to client-side activation, as follows:

```
01 // html represents a string rendered by the server
02 const html = renderComponentVNode(compVNode)
03
04 // Suppose the client has obtained the string rendered by the
server
05 // Get the mount point
06 const container = document.querySelector('#app')
07 // Set the innerHTML of the mount point to simulate the content
rendered by the server-side
08 container.innerHTML = html
09
10 // Then call the hydrate function to complete the activation
11 renderer.hydrate(compVNode, container)
```

where the code of CompVNode is as follows:

```
01 const MyComponent = {
02 name: 'App',
03 setup() {
04 const str = ref('foo')
05
06 return () => {
07 return {
08 type: 'div',
09 children: [
10 {
11 type: 'span',
12 children: str.value,
13 props: {
14 onClick: () => {
15 str.value = 'bar'
16 }
17 }
18 },
19 { type: 'span', children: 'baz' }
20 ]
21 }
22 }
23 }
24 }
25
26 const CompVNode = {
```

real DOM   virtual DOM

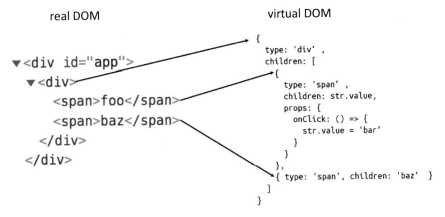

Fig. 18.6 Relationship between the real DOM and the virtual DOM

```
27 type: MyComponent,
28 }
```

Next, we proceed to implement renderer.hydrate function. Like the renderer.render function, the renderer.hydrate function is also part of the renderer, so it will also be returned by the createRenderer function, as shown in the following code:

```
01 function createRenderer(options) {
02 function hydrate(node, vnode) {
03 // ...
04 }
05
06 return {
07 render,
08 // as the return value of the createRenderer function
09 hydrate
10 }
11 }
```

This way, we can implement the activation at server side through the renderer.hydrate function. Before implementing it, let's take a look at the relationship between the real DOM elements that already exist in the page and the virtual DOM objects. Figure 18.6 shows the relationship between the real DOM rendered by the MyComponent component in the code above and the virtual DOM object it renders.

As can be seen from Fig. 18.6, real DOM elements and virtual DOM objects are both tree structures, and there is a one-to-one correspondence between nodes. Therefore, we can consider them to be "isomorphic." The principle of activation is based on this fact: recursively establish a relationship between the real DOM element and the virtual DOM node. In addition, there is no node corresponding to the container element (or mount point) in the virtual DOM. Therefore, when activated, it should start from the first sub-node of the container element, as shown in the following code:

```
01 function hydrate(vnode, container) {
02 // start from the first sub-node of the container element
03 hydrateNode(container.firstChild, vnode)
04 }
```

where the hydrateNode function takes two parameters, namely the real DOM element and the virtual DOM element. The specific implementation of the hydrateNode function is as follows:

```
01 function hydrateNode(node, vnode) {
02 const { type } = vnode
03 // 1. let vnode.eL reference real DOM
04 vnode.el = node
05
06 // 2. Check the type of virtual DOM; if it is a component, call
mountComponent function to complete activation
07 if (typeof type === 'object') {
08 mountComponent(vnode, container, null)
09 } else if (typeof type === 'string') {
10 // 3. Check if the type of the real DOM matches the type of the
virtual DOM
11 if (node.nodeType !== 1) {
12 console.error('mismatch')
13 console.error('server-side rendering real DOM node is:', node)
14 console.error('client-side rendering virtual DOM node is:',
vnode)
15 } else {
16 // 4. If it is a normal element, call hydrateElement to complete the
activation
17 hydrateElement(node, vnode)
18 }
19 }
20
21 // 5. Important: The hydrateNode function needs to return the next
sibling node of the current node in order to continue the subsequent
activation operation
22 return node.nextSibling
23 }
```

There are many key points of the hydrateNode function. First, it is necessary to establish a connection between the real DOM element and the virtual DOM element, that is vnode.el = node. This will ensure that subsequent update operations can proceed normally. Secondly, we need to detect the type of the virtual DOM and decide what activation operation should be performed accordingly. In the above code, we show the handling of virtual nodes of components and ordinary elements and types. You can see that when activating a node of ordinary element type, we check whether the type of the real DOM element is the same as the type of the virtual DOM. If it is different, we need to print a mismatch error, that is, the node of client-side rendering does not match the node of server-side rendering. At the same time, in order to allow users to quickly locate the problem node and ensure the development experience, we'd better print both the virtual node of client-side rendering and the real DOM node of server-side rendering for users' reference. For components, the activation operation of type nodes can be directly completed through the mountComponent function. For the activation operation of ordinary elements, it can be completed through the hydrateElement function. Finally, the hydrateNode function needs to return the next sibling of the current active node for subsequent activations. The return value of the hydrateNode function is very important, and its use is reflected in the hydrateElement function, as shown in the following code:

```
01 // used to activate the node of the normal element type
02 function hydrateElement(el, vnode) {
03 // 1. Add event for DOM element
04 if (vnode.props) {
05 for (const key in vnode.props) {
06 // Only event type props need handling
07 if (/^on/.test(key)) {
08 patchProps(el, key, null, vnode.props[key])
09 }
10 }
11 }
12 // recursively activate sub-nodes
13 if (Array.isArray(vnode.children)) {
14 // From the first sub-node
15 let nextNode = el.firstChild
16 const len = vnode.children.length
17 for (let i = 0; i < len; i++) {
18 // Activate sub-node; note that whenever a sub-node is activated,
the hydrateNode function will return the next sibling node of the current
sub-node,
19 // So subsequent activations can be made
20 nextNode = hydrateNode(nextNode, vnode.children[i])
21 }
22 }
23 }
```

The hydrateElement function has two key points.

- Because server-side rendering ignores events, the browser just renders static HTML; one of the actions to activate a DOM element is to add an event handler to it.
- Activate the current element's sub-node recursively, starting from the first sub-node el.firstChild, recursively calling the hydrateNode function to complete the activation. Note the trick here: the hydrateNode function will return the next sibling node of the current node, and use this feature to complete all sub-node processing.

For component activation, we also need to deal with the mountComponent function specifically. Since the server-side rendering page already has real DOM elements, when the mountComponent function is called to mount the component, there is no need to create the real DOM element again. Based on this, we need to make some adjustments to the mountComponent function, as shown in the following code:

```
01 function mountComponent(vnode, container, anchor) {
02 // omit some code
03
04 instance.update = effect((() => {
05 const subTree = render.call(renderContext, renderContext)
06 if (!instance.isMounted) {
07 beforeMount && beforeMount.call(renderContext)
08 // If vnode.el exists, it means to perform activation
09 if (vnode.el) {
10 // Directly call hydrateNode to complete activation
11 hydrateNode(vnode.el, subTree)
12 } else {
13 // Normal mount
14 patch(null, subTree, container, anchor)
15 }
16 instance.isMounted = true
17 mounted && mounted.call(renderContext)
18 instance.mounted && instance.mounted.forEach(hook => hook.call
(renderContext))
19 } else {
20 beforeUpdate && beforeUpdate.call(renderContext)
21 patch(instance.subTree, subTree, container, anchor)
22 updated && updated.call(renderContext)
23 }
24 instance.subTree = subTree
25 }, {
26 scheduler: queueJob
27 })
28 }
```

As you can see, the only thing that needs to be adjusted is the component's rendering side effects, the render effect. Remember what the first thing the hydrateNode function does? It creates a connection between the real DOM and the virtual DOM, i.e., vnode.el = node. Therefore, when the rendering side effect performs the mount operation, we first check whether the vnode.el property of the virtual node already exists. If it exists, it means that there is no need for a brand-new mount; only an activation operation is required; otherwise it still follows the previous logic and performs a brand-new mount. The last key point is that the activation operation of the component needs to be performed between the real DOM and the subTree.

18.5   Writing Isomorphic Code

As we introduced in Sect. 18.1, the term "isomorphic" refers to a piece of code that runs both at the server level and on the client side. Therefore, when writing component code, extra attention should be paid to the differences caused by different code running environments.

18.5.1   Component Lifetime

We know that when the component's code is run at the server level, since the component will not be truly mounted, that is, the virtual DOM will not be rendered as a real DOM element, so the component's beforeMount and mounted hook functions will not be executed. And because server-side rendering is a snapshot of the application, there is no re-rendering after data changes, so the component's beforeUpdate and updated hook functions will not be executed. In addition, during server-side rendering, the component will not be uninstalled, so the component's beforeUnmount and unmounted hook functions will not be executed. In fact, only the beforeCreate and created hook functions will be executed at the server level, so you need to pay extra attention when writing component code.

```
01 <script>
02 export default {
03 created() {
04 this.timer = setInterval(() => {
05 // Do something
06 }, 1000)
07 },
08 beforeUnmount() {
09 // Clear timer
10 clearInterval(this.timer)
11 }
12 }
13 </script>
```

Observe the above component code. A timer is set in the created hook function and attempts to clear the component before it is unmounted, i.e., when the beforeUnmount hook function executes. If you run this code on the client side, it won't cause any problems; but if you run it at the server level, it will cause a memory leak. Because the beforeUnmount hook function does not run at the server level, this timer will never be cleared.

In fact, setting a timer in the created hook function makes no sense for server-side rendering. This is because the server level renders a snapshot of the application. The so-called snapshot refers to the content that the page should render in the current data state. So, before the timer expires and the data state is modified, the snapshot of the application has been rendered. So we say that the code inside the timer has no meaning when server-side rendering. When encountering this kind of problem, we usually have two solutions:

- Option 1: Move the code that creates the timer to the mounted hook, that is, only execute the timer on the client side
- Option 2: Wrap this code with environment variables so that it does not run at the server level

Option 1 should be well understood, while Option 2 depends on the environment variables of the project. For example, in homogeneous projects built by tools such as webpack or Vite, such environment variables are usually included. Taking Vite as an example, we can use import.meta.env.SSR to determine the running environment of the current code:

```
01 <script>
02 export default {
03 created() {
04 // Only execute when non-server-side rendering, that is, only
execute at client side
05 if (!import.meta.env.SSR) {
06 this.timer = setInterval(() => {
07 // do something
08 }, 1000)
09 }
10 },
11 beforeUnmount() {
12 clearInterval(this.timer)
13 }
14 }
15 </script>
```

As you can see, we use import.meta.env.SSR to make the code run only in a specific environment. In fact, the build tool will output two separate packages for the client side and server level, respectively. When the build tool packages the resource for the client side, it will exclude the code wrapped by import.meta.env. SSR from the resource. In other words, the code above wrapped by! import.meta.env. SSR will only exist in the client-side package.

18.5.2 Using Cross-Platform APIs

Another key point of writing isomorphic code using cross-platform APIs is to use cross-platform APIs. Since the component code runs on both the browser and the server, avoid using platform-specific APIs when writing code. For example, objects such as window, document, etc. exist only in the browser environment. However, sometimes you have to use these platform-specific APIs. In this case, you can use environment variables such as import.meta.env.SSR for code guards:

```
01 <script>
02 if (!import.meta.env.SSR) {
03 // Use browser platform-specific APIs
04 window.xxx
05 }
06
07 export default {
08 // ...
09 }
10 </script>
```

Similarly, Node.js-specific APIs do not work in the browser. Therefore, to ease the mental burden of development, we can choose a cross-platform third-party library. For example, use Axios as the network request library.

18.5.3 Introducing Modules Only at One End

Usually, the code of the component we write is controllable. In this case, we can use cross-platform API to ensure that the code is "isomorphic." However, the code of third-party modules is very uncontrollable. Suppose we have the following component:

```
01 <script>
02 import storage from './storage.js'
03 export default {
04 // ...
05 }
06 </script>
```

The above component code itself has no problem, but it depends on the./storage.js module. If there is non-homogeneous code in this module, errors will still occur. Suppose the./storage.js module code is as follows:

```
01 // storage.js
02 export const storage = window.localStorage
```

You can see that the./storage.js module depends on the browser environment specific API, namely window.localStorage. Therefore, an error occurs when performing server-side rendering. There are two solutions to this problem. One is to use import.meta.env.SSR as code guard:

```
01 // storage.js
02 export const storage = !import.meta.env.SSR ? window.
localStorage : {}
```

Although this can solve the problem, in most cases we cannot modify the code of third-party modules. Therefore, more often, we will use the second solution introduced next to solve the problem, that is, conditional introduction:

```
01 <script>
02 let storage
03 // Only introduce the./storage.js module under non-SSR
04 if (!import.meta.env.SSR) {
05 storage = import('./storage.js')
06 }
07 export default {
08 // ...
09 }
10 </script>
```

The above code is the modified component code. As you can see, we have done code guarding through import.meta.env. SSR to achieve module loading in a specific environment. However, only loading a template in a specific environment means that the function of the template is only effective in this environment. For example, in the above code, the code of./storage.js template will only take effect on the client side. That is, the server level will miss the function of this module. In order to make up for this defect, we usually need to implement another module with the same function and can run on the server side according to the actual situation, as shown in the following code:

```
01 <script>
02 let storage
03 if (!import.meta.env.SSR) {
04 // for client side
05 storage = import('./storage.js')
06 } else {
07 // for server level
08 storage = import('./storage-server.js')
09 }
10 export default {
11 // ...
12 }
13 </script>
```

As you can see, we introduce different module implementations depending on the environment.

18.5.4   Avoiding State Contamination Caused by Cross Requests

When writing isomorphic code, additional attention should be paid to avoid state pollution caused by cross requests. In server-side rendering, we create a brand-new application instance for each request, for example:

```
01 import { createSSRApp } from 'vue'
02 import { renderToString } from '@vue/server-renderer'
03 import App from 'App.vue'
04
05 // Each time request comes, the render function is executed once
06 async function render(url, manifest) {
07 // Create an application instance for the current request
08 const app = createSSRApp(App)
09
10 const ctx = {}
11 const html = await renderToString(app, ctx)
12
13 return html
14 }
```

As you can see, every time the render function is called for server-side rendering, the createSSRApp function will be called for the current request to create a new application instance. This is to avoid state pollution caused by different requests sharing the same application instance.

In addition to creating separate application instances for each request, state pollution can also occur in the code of individual components, as follows:

```
01 <script>
02 // module-level global variables
03 let count = 0
04
05 export default {
06 create() {
07 count++
08 }
09 }
10 </script>
```

If the code of the above component is run in the browser, it will not cause any problems, because the browser and the user are in a pair relationship, each browser is independent. But if this code is running in the server, the situation will be different, because the server and the user are in a one-to-many relationship. When user A sends a request to the server, the server will execute the code of the above component, that is, execute count ++. Then, user B also sends a request to the server, and the server executes the above component's code again. At this time, the count has been incremented once due to user A's request. Therefore, for user B, user A's request will affect him, thus causing cross-contamination between requests. Therefore, when writing component code, pay extra attention to the global variables that appear in the component.

18.5.5 < ClientOnly > Components

Finally, let's introduce a component that is very helpful for writing isomorphic code, namely < ClientOnly > components. In daily development, we often use third-party modules. And they are not necessarily SSR friendly, for example:

```
01 <template>
02 <SsrIncompatibleComp />
03 </template>
```

Suppose <SsrIncompatibleComp /> is an SSR-incompatible third-party component, we have no way to modify its source code; what should we do then? At this time, we will think, since this component is not compatible with SSR, can we only render the component on the client side? In fact, it is possible, we can implement a < ClientOnly > component by ourselves, which can make part of the content of the template only rendered in the client side, as shown in the following template:

```
01 <template>
02 <ClientOnly>
03 <SsrIncompatibleComp />
04 </ClientOnly>
05 </template>
```

As you can see, we wrapped the SSR-incompatible <SsrIncompatibleComp/> component with the < ClientOnly > component. In this way, the component is ignored during server-side rendering and only rendered on the client side. So how does the < ClientOnly > component do this? This is actually taking advantage of the difference between CSR and SSR. The following is the implementation of the < ClientOnly > component:

```
01 import { ref, onMounted, defineComponent } from 'vue'
02
03 export const ClientOnly = defineComponent({
04 setup(_, { slots }) {
05 // markup variable, true only when client-side rendering
06 const show = ref(false)
07 // onMounted hook will only execute on client side
08 onMounted(() => {
09 show.value = true
10 })
11 // Nothing is rendered at the server level, but the < ClientOnly >
```

```
component's slot content is rendered on the client side
    12 return () => (show.value && slots.default ? slots.default() :
null)
    13 }
    14 })
```

As you can see, the overall implementation is very simple. The principle is to take advantage of the fact that the onMounted hook will only execute on the client side. We created a tag variable *show* with an initial value of *false* and set it to *true* only during client-side rendering. This means that the < ClientOnly > component's slot content will not be rendered when server-side rendering. In client-side rendering, the < ClientOnly > component's slot content will not be rendered until the mounted hook is triggered. This achieves that the content wrapped by the < ClientOnly > component will only be rendered on the client side.

In addition, the < ClientOnly > component does not cause the client-side activation to fail. Because the mounted hook has not been triggered when the client side is activated, the server level is the same as the content of client-side rendering, that is, nothing is rendered. After activation is complete and the mounted hook is triggered to execute, the slot content of the < ClientOnly > component will be rendered on the client side.

18.6   Summary

In this chapter, we first discussed how CSR, SSR, and isomorphic rendering work, and their respective advantages and disadvantages.

When we choose a rendering architecture for an application, we need to choose a suitable rendering scheme according to the software requirements and scenarios.

Next, we discussed how Vue.js rendered virtual nodes as strings. Take a normal label node as an example. When rendering it as a string, the following should be considered.

- Handling of self-closing labels. For self-closing labels, there is no need to render the closing label part for it, nor to deal with its children, nodes.
- The legitimacy of attribute names, and the escape of attribute values.
- Escape of text sub-nodes.

The specific escape rules are as follows.

- For normal content, the following characters in the text should be escaped.

  - Escape the character & as an entity &
  - Escape the character < as an entity <
  - Escape the character > as entity >

- For attribute values, the following two characters should be escaped in addition to the above three characters.

- Escape the character as entity "
- Escape the character as entity '

Then, we discussed how to render the component as an HTML string. Rendering the component on the server side is not fundamentally different from rendering normal tags. We only need to execute the component's render function to get the subTree rendered by the component and render it as an HTML string. In addition, when rendering the component, we need to consider the following points.

- There is no re-rendering after data changes in server-side rendering, so there is no need to call the reactive function to wrap data and other data, and there is no need to use the shallowReactive function to wrap the props data. Because of this, we also do not need to call the beforeUpdate and updated hooks.
- In server-side rendering, there is no need to call the component's beforeMount and mounted hooks since no real DOM elements need to be rendered.

We discussed the principle of client-side activation. During the isomorphic rendering process, the component's code is executed once at the server level and in the browser, respectively. At the server level, the component is rendered as a static HTML string and sent to the browser. The browser will render the static HTML content returned by the server level and download the component code packaged in the static resource. When the download is complete, the browser will interpret and execute the component code. When the component code is executed on the client side, since there is already a corresponding DOM element in the page, the renderer will not perform the logic to create the DOM element, but will perform the activation operation. The activation operation can be summarized into two steps.

- Establish a connection between the virtual node and the real DOM element, that is, vnode.el = el. This ensures that subsequent updates run correctly.
- Add event bindings for DOM elements.

Finally, we discussed how to write homogeneous component code. Since component code runs on both the server level and the client, we should pay extra attention when writing component code. The details can be summarized as the following points.

- Pay attention to the life cycle of the component. Lifecycle hook functions such as beforeUpdate, updated, beforeMount, mounted, beforeUnmount, unmounted, etc. will not be executed at the server level.
- Use cross-platform API. Since the component's code runs in both the browser and the server, extra attention should be paid to the cross-platform nature of the code when writing component code. Usually when we choose a third-party library, we will choose a library that supports cross-platform, such as using Axios as the network request library.
- End-specific implementation. Whether on the client side or at the server level, the function should be consistent. For example, the component needs to read cookie information. On the client side, we can read document.cookie; on the server side,

we need to read according to the request header. Therefore, many functional modules need to be implemented separately for the client side and server level.

- Avoid state pollution caused by cross-request. State pollution can be both application-level and module-level. For applications, we should create an independent application instance for each request. For modules, we should avoid using module-level global variables. This is because multiple requests will share module-level global variables without special handling, resulting in cross-contamination between requests.
- Only part of the content in the client-side rendering component. This requires us to encapsulate the < ClientOnly > component by ourselves. The content wrapped by this component will only be rendered on the client side.

Printed in the United States
by Baker & Taylor Publisher Services